D0323722
WITHDRAWN

Contractual Marketing Systems

Contractual Marketing Systems

Donald N. Thompson
Harvard University

With an Introduction by
E. T. Grether

Heath Lexington Books
D.C. Heath and Company
Lexington, Massachusetts

Published simultaneously in Canada.

Printed in the United States of America.

Library of Congress Catalog Card Number: 72-152510

Table of Contents

	Preface	vii
	The Papers and Authors	ix
	Introduction: Contractual Marketing Systems—Some Observations, *E. T. Grether*	xv
Part One	**The Theory of Franchising and Other Contractual Marketing Systems**	1
Chapter 1	Contractual Marketing Systems: An Overview, *Donald N. Thompson*	3
Chapter 2	The Economic Base of Franchising, *Louis P. Bucklin*	33
Chapter 3	Optimal Franchising in Theory, *Michael C. Lovell*	63
Part Two	**Minority-Group Capitalism through Franchised Business**	79
Chapter 4	The Feasibility of Minority-Group Capitalism Through Franchising, *E. Patrick McGuire*	81
Chapter 5	Franchising and the Inner-City, *Roger Dickinson*	97
Part Three	**Conflict and Conflict Resolution in Contractual Marketing Systems**	109
Chapter 6	Potential Conflict Management Mechanisms in Distribution Channels: An Interorganizational Analysis, *Louis W. Stern*	111
Chapter 7	The Development of Conflict in Contractual Marketing Systems: A Case Study, *Larry J. Rosenberg*	147
Chapter 8	Conflict and Its Resolution in a Franchise System, *Jerry S. Cohen*	175
Part Four	**The Development of Contractual Marketing Systems Outside of the United States**	185
Chapter 9	The Internationalization of Contractual Marketing Systems, *Stanley Hollander*	187
Chapter 10	Contractual Interdependence in Marketing Processes of Developing Latin American Communities, *Charles C. Slater*	211

Chapter 11 Contractual Marketing Systems in Canada: The Anticombines Response, *Joel Bell* 245

Chapter 12 The Evolution of Various Forms of Contractual Marketing Systems in Japan, *Masanori Tamura* 271

Chapter 13 The Development of Contractual Marketing Systems in the Textile Industry in Japan, *Takemasa Ishihara* 293

Part Five **Contractual Systems in the Public Sector** 313

Chapter 14 Contractual Marketing in the Government Industry Procurement Administration Process, *Samuel Hassen* 315

Preface

In August 1970, forty-five scholars from marketing, economics, and related disciplines met to consider the status, problems, and prospects for contractual marketing systems. The workshop, sponsored by the American Marketing Association and held at the C.W. Post campus of Long Island University, was designed to foster the exchange of information and research findings among those involved in teaching or research in contractual marketing. Fourteen papers were commissioned and funded by the workshop. Most of the authors received additional financial support from other sources; acknowledgement of such support is found in the individual papers. The fourteen papers are published here for the first time. Each has been edited and shortened, but appears essentially as presented.

The papers examine the theory of contractual systems, the implications of this form of marketing arrangement for minority-group capitalism, issues of conflict and its resolution in contractual systems, the forces creating and shaping contractual systems outside the United States, and contractual systems in military/space program procurement. Implicit in each of the papers is a feeling of the sudden and still growing importance of this form of marketing organization, and a recognition of the relative paucity of literature in the field to date.

The range of approaches in the papers is extreme; from the highly personalized, subjective, and descriptive to the highly mathematical and abstract. The conclusions reported range from confidence that contractual marketing systems will aid in combatting economic concentration and as a spur to minority-group entrepreneurship, to the hypothesis that there is a continuing and destructive conflict built into the relationship between franchisor and franchisee which is inherent in the existing form of franchise systems.

For the success of the workshop and the publication of this volume, I am indebted for the contributions, assistance, and moral support of a large number of people—more than can possibly be acknowledged. Deserving of first mention is Dr. Ira O. Scott, Jr., former Dean of the Roth School of Business at Long Island University, who assisted in the conception, planning, and financing of the workshop, and who offered the use of the beautiful LIU campus in Brookville for it.

The workshop owes its beginning to the financial generosity of Mr. Carleton H. Palmer of Center Island, New York, former Chairman of the Board of E.R. Squibb & Sons. Other financial support came from the National Science Foundation and from Long Island University, the latter through the assistance of Dr. Edward Cook.

A personal obligation must be recognized to Dr. E. T. Grether, University of California at Berkeley, who has contributed so much to the thinking on vertical and contractual marketing relationships, and who introduced me and many others to the area. Professor Grether suggested some of the format of the workshop, as well as contributing the Introduction.

Not to be overlooked are the efforts of Mrs. Irene Krohn, an able secretary; Mrs. Roseann Naurocki, who provided flawless typing; Pat Pearson, Gretchen Bell, and Robert Krohn, who made the workshop chairman look good by working long hours behind the scenes to put out fires and meet deadlines; Dr. John Davis of Long Island University, who provided much encouragement and assistance at critical times; and Dr. Hirofumi Matsusaki of Université Laval in Quebec City, who assisted in preparing the collected papers for publication.

My wife Ardeen put in a large number of hours as a hostess, chauffeur, and problem solver of last resort at the workshop, as well as helping to assemble and edit the papers. Without her assistance, half the workshop attendees might still be stranded at Kennedy airport, and this volume would have appeared sometime in mid-1982.

One caveat is in order. The two papers on contractual marketing in Japan have undergone moderate editing; any errors or misinterpretations which might have crept in were inadvertent, but are strictly my responsibility, not that of the writers. Apologies are hereby extended, with the hope that they are unneeded.

Donald N. Thompson

Cambridge, Massachusetts
November 1970

The Papers and Authors

Introduction

E. T. Grether's "Contractual Marketing Systems: Some Observations" offers historical background and some personal observations on the evolution of contractual systems, and of teaching and research on them, in this country since 1920. Professor Grether provides an overview of the implications and findings of some of the papers in this volume and their relationship to one another, and introduces the concept of synergistic mutuality (mutually reinforcing effects) as a way of viewing the strengths of franchise and similar systems.

Mr. Grether is Flood Professor of Economics and Emeritus Dean, Schools of Business Administration, the University of California, Berkeley, His research interests are in the area of marketing and public policy. Professor Grether is a prolific contributor to the literature of his profession; his books include: *Resale Price Maintenance in Great Britain* (1935); *Essays in Social Economics* (1935); *Price Control Under Fair Trade Legislation* (1939); *The Steel and Steel Using Industries of California* (1946); *Marketing in the American Economy* (1952); and *Marketing and Public Policy* (1966).

Part One The Theory of Franchising and Other Contractual Marketing Systems

Donald N. Thompson's "Contractual Marketing Systems: An Overview" discusses the four forms of vertical market organization within marketing channels; the role of contracts and contracting; contractually constrained decision making and the minority entrepreneur; the growth and significance of franchising; controls in contractual systems; conflict in contractual systems; and, the literature on contractual systems.

Mr. Thompson is Fellow in Law and Business Administration, Harvard University, and Associate Professor, the University of Alberta. Professor Thompson is author of *Franchise Systems and Antitrust* (1971) and of a number of articles and papers on marketing and public policy. He was chairman of the American Marketing Association workshop on Contractual Marketing Systems, at which the papers in this collection were presented.

Louis P. Bucklin's "The Economic Base of Franchising" discusses the nature of the advantages of franchising and similar contractual systems and evaluates the short-run and long-run consequences of such advantages. He undertakes a conceptual derivation of these advantages, develops a series of models to illustrate and define them, and reports on an empirical econometric analysis using one of the models.

Mr. Bucklin is Associate Professor and Chairman of the Marketing Group, Schools of Business Administration, University of California, Berkeley. His major research interests have been in the area of distributive trades and distributive systems. Professor Bucklin is the author of a number of research studies on these topics published in professional journals and monographs. A broader treatment of the topics in his article is found in *Managerial Analysis in Marketing* (1970), a text for which Professor Bucklin was a coauthor.

Michael C. Lovell's "Optimal Franchising In Theory" considers how various provisions of the franchise contract affect the behavior of an optimizing franchisor and the overall profitability of a franchise system. Under one assumption of customer density, Lovell determines the optimal franchise size, optimal franchisee price and sales volume, and optimal franchise royalty and licensing fees.

Mr. Lovell is Professor of Economics at Wesleyan University in Connecticut. His research on optimal franchising stems from earlier work on product differentiation and market structure published in the *Western Economic Journal* (June, 1970); he is currently engaged in research comparing franchise operations with the effects of fair trade laws. Professor Lovell has published papers in a wide variety of areas of economics and econometrics. He is a coauthor of *Sales Anticipations and Inventory Behavior* (1969).

Part Two Minority Group Capitalism Through Franchised Business

E. Patrick McGuire's "The Feasibility of Minority-Group Capitalism through Franchising" examines the obstacles to and the feasibility of the franchising approach to black capitalism. McGuire discusses in detail some of the impediments to black franchising: financing initial franchise fees, recruiting motivated franchisees, training the black entrepreneur, and locating and maintaining the ghetto-based franchisor. He reaches some interesting conclusions about the potential quantitative contribution of franchising to minority capitalism.

Mr. McGuire is Senior Specialist in Marketing Management Research at The Conference Board in New York City, and is a Lecturer in the Marketing Department, Graduate School of Business, Rutgers University. He is the author of twelve books on marketing and management, and of a number of Conference Board reports in these and other areas.

Roger Dickinson's "Franchising and the Inner-City" presents a personalized, subjective view of the challenge of inner-city economic development, the failure of contractual marketing arrangements in the inner-city, the environment there, and a discussion of existing and proposed economic intermediary institutions and their applications to the problem.

Mr. Dickinson is Professor of Marketing at the Graduate School of Business, Rutgers University, and Book Note Editor of the *Journal of Retailing*. Professor Dickinson's major research interests have been in the area of retail distribution, and in minority business enterprise. He is the author of a number of research monographs and articles in each area.

Part Three Conflict and Conflict Resolution in Contractual Marketing Systems

Louis S. Stern's "Potential Conflict Management Mechanisms in Distribution Channels: An Interorganizational Analysis" draws on the literature of political science, international relations, sociology, organizational behavior, and industrial relations for insights into potential mechanisms for managing, reducing, or resolving conflict in distribution channels. He discusses four main categories of conflict management mechanisms: supraorganizational, interpenetration, boundary, and bargaining and negotiation. He points out the problem of transferring findings from one discipline or context to another, but argues that insights generated by a selective adaptation of the behavioral sciences to channel analysis can increase the efficiency of distribution.

Mr. Stern is Professor of Marketing, The Ohio State University. His research interests are in the areas of distribution channel analysis and public policy, particularly antitrust policy. Professor Stern has published on a wide variety of marketing topics in such periodicals as the *Journal of Business* and the *Harvard Business Review*; he is author of *Distribution Channels: Behavioral Dimensions* (1969), and coauthor of *Managerial Analysis in Marketing* (1970) and *Competition in the Marketplace* (1970).

Larry J. Rosenberg's "The Development of Conflict in Contractual Marketing Systems: A Case Study" discusses the evolution of conflict from underlying causes to overt behavior in a vertical marketing system. The research methodology attempts to measure conflict in the attitudes and acts of channel members toward one another, and to link issues and incidents to demonstrate the development of conflict. Rosenberg describes his concepts and model, and research instruments and design in sufficient detail to permit the reader to evaluate the transferability or generalizability of methodology and/or findings.

Mr. Rosenberg is Assistant Professor of Marketing, Schools of Business, New York University. His research interests are in the behavioral dimensions of distribution channels; he has published several papers in this area, and was a contributor to *Distribution Channels: Behavioral Dimensions* (1969).

Jerry S. Cohen's "Conflict and Its Resolution in a Franchise System" raises the hypothesis that there is a continuing and destructive conflict built into the relationship between franchisor and franchisee which is inherent in the system itself. A number of bases of such conflict are discussed, with each having the common characteristic that a franchisor can force the franchisee to make decisions which maximize franchisor profits while simultaneously reducing franchisee profits (or producing franchisee losses). Mr. Cohen discusses two remedies: the greater use of present laws and the passage of new laws to relax the control exercised by the franchisor and remove some of the basic causes of conflict.

Mr. Cohen is in charge of the Washington office of Harold E. Kohn, P.A., Attorneys at Law. He is a former Chief Counsel and Staff Director for the Senate Antitrust and Monopoly Subcommittee, and former Assistant Attorney

General for the State of Michigan in Charge of the Criminal Division. Mr. Cohen has authored articles in *Trial*, the magazine of the American Trial Lawyers Association, and in the *George Washington Law Review*, and contributed to the text *Legal and Criminal Psychology* (1968).

Part Four The Development of Contractual Marketing Systems Outside of the United States

Stanley C. Hollander's "The Internationalization of Contractual Marketing Systems" evaluates factors in international marketing which are conducive to the use of contractual rather than ownership ties. He discusses some important clusters of internationalized systems, including travel-serving systems, designer and luxury boutiques, general merchandise retailing through gasoline service stations, and a number of voluntary arrangements including private branding, agency stores, voluntary chains, and cooperative chains. He introduces the problem of why contractual relationships are so much more effective at middleman-supplier levels than at the customer-dealer level.

Mr. Hollander is Professor of Marketing at the Graduate School of Business Administration, Michigan State University, and a member of the editorial boards of the *Journal of Marketing, Journal of Retailing,* and *MSU Business Topics.* He has a primary interest in domestic and international aspects of retailing; marketing history; and marketing theory. Professor Hollander has contributed extensively to the literature of his profession. He was guest editor of the Special International Issue of the *Journal of Retailing* (1968); his books include *Markets and Marketing in Developing Economies* (1968), *Multinational Retailing* (1970), and coeditorship of a forthcoming symposium on government-retailing relationships in selected countries.

Charles C. Slater's "Contractual Interdependence in Marketing Processes of Developing Latin American Communities" demonstrates the role of marketing in economic development, specifically the influence of market coordination on producer decisions to change the effectiveness with which they utilize capital and other resources. Slater introduces several cases indicating producer responses to vertical market coordination, and discusses the necessary preconditions for retailing organization to provide backward vertical market coordination through contractual supply arrangements. He details the economies of operating a large-scale retail outlet in La Paz, Bolivia, and the social and economic impact of the actual introduction of such an outlet.

Mr. Slater is a Professor in the Graduate School of Business Administration, University of Colorado. He has written extensively on the topics of Marketing as a social process in developing and developed societies, the conduct and performance of consumer marketing institutions, and on economic development. He is the coauthor of three books which are relevant to his paper here: *Market Processes of Recife, Brazil* (1969); *Market Processes of La Paz, Bolivia* (1969); and *Food Marketing Processes of San Juan,* Puerto Rico (1970).

Joel Bell's "Contractual Marketing Systems in Canada: The Anticombines Response" considers the combines approach to contractual marketing arrangements in Canada, a topic of particular interest as the Canadian government has recently undertaken a comprehensive review of competition policy. The author discusses current attitudes in Canada toward competition policy, existing Canadian legislation, the recommendations of the Economic Council of Canada on contractual and other restrictions, and considers at length a number of specific contractual restrictions and their economic implications. He concludes with some policy recommendations directed at the behavior patterns involved in contractual arrangements.

Mr. Bell is Special Policy Advisor to the Minister of Consumer and Corporate Affairs, Government of Canada. His research interests are in the economic and legal aspects of anticombines, and in the economic and social implications of foreign investment. He has authored a number of Canadian government staff publications in each area, has written for professional publications such as the *McGill Law Journal,* and is a contributor to publications of the Private Planning Association of the Canadian-American Committee.

Masanori Tamura's "The Evolution of Various Forms of Contractual Marketing Systems in Japan" discusses the emergence and development of contractual marketing systems in Japan, and environmental factors influencing the evolution of such systems—specifically the Japanese distribution revolution and the influence of rapid economic growth. Case histories are presented of the development of contractual systems in the home electric appliance industry, the automobile industry, the supermarket industry, and in voluntary chains.

Mr. Tamura is Assistant Professor of Marketing in the School of Business Administration, Kobe University, Japan. His research interests include the development of conceptual models of marketing behavior and the quantitative analysis of consumer behavior patterns. Professor Tamura has published a number of journal articles on marketing theory, marketing strategy, and consumer behavior, writing both in Japanese and in English.

Takemasa Ishihara's "The Development of Contractual Marketing Systems in the Textile Industry in Japan" discusses the introduction of synthetic fibers to the Japanese textile industry, an event accompanied by the development of contractual marketing systems by large manufacturers in the industry, and the interaction with other evolving marketing institutions such as supermarkets (which play an unusual role in Japanese domestic textile marketing). He outlines the evolving distribution structure for cotton and synthetic textiles during the prewar period, the period of wartime controls, and the postwar boom, including the evolving roles of merchant wholesalers, spinners, and manufacturers in the marketing structure.

Mr. Ishihara is Assistant Professor in the School of Business Administration, Osaka City University, Japan. His research interests are in the areas of marketing channels and marketing structures, especially the dynamics of interaction between micro channel systems and macro distribution systems. Professor Ishihara has published a number of articles in Japan on these subjects, writing both in Japanese and in English.

Part Five Contractual Systems in the Public Sector

Samuel Hassen's "Contractual Marketing in the Government Industry Procurement Administration Process" discusses the experience of, and problems encountered by, the Defense Contract Administration Service, a component of the Defense Supply Agency which manages defense contracts for the Army, Navy, Air Force, NASA, and other government agencies. He describes the classes of contractual procurement and types of contracts used, typical contract clauses, and the problems associated with each. Dr. Hassen also covers the role of the government Contracting Officer in administering the contract and in settling disputes and problems found in the government-industry sector.

Mr. Hassen is Deputy Director, Contract Administration Directorate of the Defense Administration Services Region, New York, and Adjunct Associate Professor, C.W. Post campus of Long Island University. Formerly a practicing attorney, he has lectured on Contract Administration at Contracting Officers School, Air Materiel Command in New York, Boston, and Chicago and at the Air Force Institute of Technology School for Contracting Officers, Ohio State University. Dr. Hassen has published several papers through the Office of the Secretary of Defense on the legal aspects of contracting.

Introduction: Contractual Marketing Systems—Some Observations

E. T. Grether*

In the booming 1920s before a class in Marketing at the University of California, Berkeley, I suggested a new idea for organizing production and marketing under which small local and regional enterprises might be able to compete more equally with large national or regional companies. My scheme involved a contractual system under which locally owned independent firms would agree to standardize their operations under central office supervision so that it would be possible to advertise regionally and nationally. I noted how such a set of arrangements could maintain all the advantages of independent local ownership—including local loyalty and pride and high incentives—along with the benefits of national or regional promotion, recognition, and reputation. My thinking was influenced by the success at the time of cooperative merchandising groups, especially in the grocery trade. Apparently, my enthusiasm for this approach was contagious for a member of the class, a mature man of some business experience and with some connections in the financial world, succeeded in interesting a group of local capitalists to underwrite this system. And then the collapse of 1929 and the Great Depression dried up the sources of capital. Otherwise, I might have served on the Board of Directors of one of the early pioneering variants of what is now called franchising.

The Short Run and Long Run

This episode and its timing is an appropriate take-off point for some observations provoked by reading this interesting collection of papers on *Contractual Marketing Systems.* There is no equal to a sharp economic depression or a stock market decline to make us face up to the underlying verities. (I trust that the present Administration in Washington, D.C., does not misinterpret this observation.) It is clearly evident *now* that much of the so-called franchise boom, like that of the conglomerates, was based upon short-run promotional and manipulative incentives and factors, and excessive speculation—not upon soundly conceived, careful, long-range planning and execution. Unfortunately, the essays in this volume could not face up adequately to the analytical requirements of segregating and distinguishing the short run and long run, especially under recent stock market adjustments. Hopefully, out of these discussions and further work that they

* University of California.

should help engender, the short-run chaff will be separated from the solid, more durable kernels.

But this outcome will not come easily or quickly in a field so broad, diverse, and varied, as depicted by Thompson's classifications and quantitative data. The papers in this volume set the stage for much more careful, precise empirical case studies and for normative model building related to specific private and public interests and policies.

It is well to recall, to begin with, the Marshallian warning against sharp classifications and definitions when there are no identifiable counterparts in nature. Contractual marketing systems presumably lie in the broad bands of the spectrum between so-called complete integration and free, independent marketing (disintegration). Unfortunately, the boundary bands themselves are not clearly determinate since there is no such thing as complete integration and the so-called free market is under innumerable constraints, including explicit and implicit contractual constraints. Hollander notes the host of auxiliary functional flows outside any given ownership or contractual system. All ownership integration is only partial and all so-called free marketing is only partially free. The free market system is undergirded by the law of contracts. So-called contractual systems merely formalize and add a longer-term dimension to some sectors of free market relations, without, however, outright ownership. And, as is noted in the papers, there are always uneasy processes of adjustment within contractual systems towards outright ownership. These adjustments, however, may stem not merely from strength—that is, the desire of strong franchisors to enhance their own internal equities; but from weaknesses—that is, the necessity of buying up weak franchisees (or dealers) in order to maintain distribution, or the system. The latter is particularly true in manufacturer-dealer systems.

Control: The Basic Criterion

But the test of both the validity of the concept of a system and the understanding of how a system functions are found not in the relative overlappings or in the balance of ownership and of contractual and free relations but in the amount and character of the controls exercised over the participants in relation to common goals. It is important to reemphasize that only a small portion of the economic and marketing universe is or can be brought within any given system, whether ownership or contractual. Furthermore, the systems concept is equally applicable to many sectors of the economy in the so-called free sectors because of group behavior arising out of relatively spontaneous forces of market leadership and of strong consciousness of kind, and out of the recognition of oligopolistic interdependencies. Finally, any system, franchised or contractual, horizontal or vertical, is a subsystem of the general market system and, hence, subject to its regulatory discipline. The degree of insulation from such discipline is a key aspect of antitrust concerns.

Ownership systems from a control viewpoint may be decentralized and even free swinging; contractual systems vary enormously in the loci and character of controls and leadership. It is likely that there was more central control during the earlier historical period of low economic and market concentration than is recognized. It was exercised by powerful wholesale houses, through long term credits, close working relationships, subrosa partial ownership, and so on, instead of overtly. It was a very healthy shock to my academic book knowledge early in my teaching career to discover that a lot of apparent independent merchants in my area were really tied houses, in whole or in part.

1930 and Now

Suppose that the Great Depression had not intervened and I had convened a similar workshop and series of discussions as of 1930 to consider my then proposed contractual system. In what ways does this collection of papers 40 years later differ from what might have been presented then? The present papers are both much more multidisciplinary and multinational in their approaches and content and, of course, reflect current problems and moods. In 1930, the discussions would have been limited to the United States or at best would have included Great Britain and the participants would have been economists and legal scholars. My university did not even have a department of sociology in 1930. Scholarship increasingly is multinational and multidisciplinary. It is amazing and heartening that Thompson on relatively short notice was able to assemble scholars from countries as distant as Japan (Ishihara and Tamura) or with high research competence in other parts of the world (Slater, Hollander, Bell). Ultimately, the consequences of such interactions should not only serve to strengthen research and analysis but also to underwrite international and interdisciplinary working relationships, including political relationships. But this outcome will arise out of a continuing process of becoming—with full fruition always on the horizon. These essays portray the difficulties of international comparisons and understandings while suggesting the high importance of recognizing basic uniformities and similarities. The essays also illustrate sharply the difficulties of transferring the tools, conceptualizations, and generalizations from one discipline into new areas of application. There is no escape from the hard facts of reality in private and public policies and decision making.

Conflict and Its Resolution

No doubt, the recent and current social and political context explains the most prominent issue in the discussions—viz., conflict and its resolution (especially Stern, Cohen, and Rosenberg). But the applications of the borrowings from research and analysis and experience in sociology, political science, and industrial relations seem to dangle over the broad terrain in search of landing places, and seem able to land in only very narrow places, as say, fast food franchising.

In a horizontal or multilevel contractual system, *market* forces, including competition, to some extent are replaced by formal *internal* understandings and relationships. Market competition, a form of conflict, when internalized and canalized, can and often does become personalized, bitter conflict. (My investigations of resale price maintenance in the 1930s emphasized this conclusion to me.)

As noted in the papers, the internal conflicts to some extent are not unlike those in the trade union field and its focus upon the division of the proceeds, working conditions, and so on. But it can be highly misleading to apply the trade union approach too directly because franchisor-franchisee or manufacturer-dealer relations and mutual interdependencies are much more *entrepreneurial* than those of employer and worker (even allowing for some amount of codetermination in the labor field, as in Germany). The variety and ranking of conflict issues between manufacturers and dealers, and distributors and dealers, clearly demonstrate this basic difference (Rosenberg). The basis of the entrepreneurial mutuality should be the development of synergistic effects. Unless the franchisor-franchisee reinforce each other's efforts, then the employer-employee relationship should be preferred. When franchisees *de facto* but not *de jure* are really employees, the franchisor with high economic power is merely shifting some legal responsibility to the franchisees in the guise of their alleged independent status. Powerful corporations or franchisors with high market power can use the franchise contracts as unilateral control devices, especially when there is always a waiting line of applicants. Admittedly, too, franchisors with little to offer could survive out of the results of the efforts of family-type franchisees who exert themselves longer and harder than they would as employees (Bucklin's reverse Russian roulette base). In such instances, synergism is absent or the interacting effects are depressant as is a mixture of alcohol and barbiturates in human consumption.

Harmony through Synergistic Mutuality

From the standpoint of conjoined private and public policy, there is a great need for analysis in terms of the synergistic or mutually reinforcing effects in franchise systems, over long enough time periods so that the more mature results can be interpreted. Clearly there is high mutual interdependence between new franchisors and their franchisees—so much so that the latter must be given strong inducements. There is a simple generalization that in successful mature systems the franchisor no longer needs or even recognizes this mutuality. This may be true in any single instance since the franchisor presumably is not dependent upon any single franchisee and there should be a waiting line of potential entrants in a successful system. Yet, in general it should not be true unless local entrepreneurship and administration are meaningless in the franchise system. Theoretically, the optimum return for the franchisor is based upon equivalent suboptimization in the case of each franchisee. The termination of unsuccessful franchisees and their replacement out of a waiting list does not necessarily reflect the absence of mutual interdependence and reinforcement, but merely personal failure in a given instance. Of course, the relative contribution in the processes of mutual reinforcement will be expected to vary depending upon the types of factors discussed in the papers (especially Bucklin, Lovell, and Rosenberg). Hence, there will be and should be differences in the tests of success and failure and in the division of the proceeds. But agreement upon an equitable sharing should involve much less conflict if there is a basic understanding of the nature of the harmony and reinforcement of interests together with some measures of relative contributions. Such understanding should make it possible to avoid the labyrinth of regulations so characteristic of federal contractual relations (Hassen).

Chain store history is replete with evidences to support the above observation that may also suggest a solution to the failure thus far in the minority-group field. One of the presumed original advantages of the multiples or chains was the possibility for employment in the stores of persons of lower level ability and hence of lower income requirements than in independent operation. It was presumed that a store built and stocked and administered out of a central office could be run by persons of lower level ability and income than if they were independent. Increasingly, however, experience has demonstrated the high dependence upon local management even under the above conditions. Obviously, this lesson has even greater relevance for franchisor-franchisee relations in which the local ownership and incentives are stressed as prime assets.

But all of this is meaningless if the hypothesis is correct that destructive conflict is inherent and endemic in franchise systems (Cohen). In sharp contrast is the hypothesis or generalization that harmonious interests usually are greater (Thompson). Allegedly, the first generalization aids in explaining the abject failure of franchising in minority-group capitalism (McGuire, Dickinson). From my point of view, the analysis of mutual-synergistic relationships suggests the pathway to success, assuming that destructive conflict is not endemic. Incidentally, it is interesting to speculate upon the similarities of internal destructive conflict and external traditional, so-called ruinous, competition. It is likely that both conceptions point towards conclusions and public policies unnecessarily drastic or even nonsensical, or to the proliferation of new legislation instead of using existing statutes and agencies.

The failures in the minority community may not be so much because of inherent conflicts but because of undue haste in an atmosphere of urgency. Given time, proper recruitment and training, and above all the demonstration of potential synergistic benefits and the appropriate sharing of the proceeds, there should be an increasing number and proportion of successes. Equivalent or better results should be obtainable in franchise systems (under proper conditions and with careful planning) than under ownership systems. Ideally, such systems ultimately should spring out of the minority groups themselves and preferably should eventually resemble the well-established, cooperative voluntary chains set up by retail dealers. Most likely, however, the lessons of hard experience for a considerable time period must be learned from systems with strong top leadership, perhaps, comparable to the voluntary chains under the aegis of wholesalers.

Aggressive Competition and Public Policies

The current mood, including the financial-stock market disfavor, could obscure long-run forces and trends and lead to inappropriate, perhaps unsound public policies. During the years of the Great Depression, marketing came under a series of governmental interventions intended to weaken or even subvert competitive forces. The active competitor was dubbed a chiseler and became the villain in the market drama. The Supreme Court of the United States in the Schecter decision saved us from the overt abrogation of our national policy of competition through the NRA code procedures. But state legislatures and Congress enacted a variety of statutes intended to subvert *aggressive* competitive pressures. This effort was checkmated, however, through an unexpected and little understood set of forces which I labelled at the time as "intertype competition" (for lack of better verbiage), or competition between diverse types of enterprises overlapping each other in our markets.[1] In 1955, Palamountain used the same concept and verbiage, "intertype competition," as evidence of the Schumpeterian process of "Creative Destruction."[2]

I mention this for two reasons. First, there is current revival of interest in Palamountain's analysis of competition and especially of conflict, evidenced in the essays of this volume. Second, it is likely that an equivalent type of competitive manifestation has developed in the post-World War II period. So-called intertype competition prior to World War I expressed itself primarily in the distributive sectors and through multiline, overlapping enterprises. The marketing landscape today, however, would be scarcely recognizable to a Rip Van Winkle of 1930. Since World War II, the processes of diversification have not only continued in wholesaling and retailing but increasingly have entered manufacturing and other sectors. The most dramatic evidence has been through the so-called conglomerates, the great stock market favorites until recently. The current stock market disfavor of the conglomerates, like that of many franchisors, should not be allowed to obscure the broad underlying drift towards diversification. Too frequently potential synergetic diversification gave way to short-run financial and stock market maniplation. But there will be continuing processes of concentric overlapping between enterprises through diversification instead of simple, commodity-type competition. Contractual marketing arrangements, especially franchising, can be deployed effectively either in specialized areas of high standardization (Bucklin) or more broadly. They will continue to be flexible means of filling in overlooked niches or for widening assortments. Their variety and form will be vitally influenced by our evolving national national economic policy in the area of diversification and conglomeration. Undoubtedly, contractual systems would move into the gaps, if diversification through ownership is constrained under public policies.

One must be impressed by the amazing resiliencies and capacities for adjustment of our competitive production and marketing systems. Contractual marketing systems lie at the sensitive margins of the continuing processes of adjustment. To state this is to suggest reasons for optimism concerning future developments to offset the pessimism of much of current evaluation.

Notes

1. E. T. Grether, *Price Control Under Fair Trade Legislation,* New York: Oxford University Press (1939), 12 and 204.

2. J. C. Palamountain, *The Politics of Distribution,* Cambridge, Mass: Harvard University Press (1955), 38–48.

Part One
The Theory of Franchising and Other Contractual Marketing Systems

Contractual Marketing Systems: An Overview

Donald N. Thompson*

There are found four forms of vertical organization within marketing channels: free and open bargaining, without restrictions; ownership integration; administered marketing channels; and contractual integration. Conventional marketing systems of the free and open variety have been rapidly replaced by vertically organized marketing systems of the last three types; this is probably the most significant development in marketing organization in the past decade. Market competition increasingly involves rivalry between these types of systems, as well as between the units that comprise each system. This has been most notable since 1960 when vertical systems began to penetrate the core markets of conventional channels, with the result that whole networks of individual firms were threatened. This paper is concerned to some extent with all forms of vertical market organization and behavior, but focuses on the emergence, growth, and influence of contractual systems.

Definitions of marketing terms are a necessary part of a paper that attempts to tie together material which has received such a fragmented, diversified treatment in the past. *Free and open (or conventional) channels* may be defined as those in which there is no ownership or contractual relation between the parties and the market supplier merely sells the product to the buyer. Marketing textbooks claim that goods and services in the American economy have historically been distributed through such loosely aligned systems, in which relatively autonomous manufacturers, wholesalers, and retailers bargain aggressively with each other, do business on an individual transaction basis, and alter business relationships with impunity.[a] Each of these characteristics is actually or potentially a source of diseconomies. The autonomy of small operating units under free and open bargaining may result in duplication of effort, inefficiency in scheduling of material flows and human efforts, high selling costs, and the sacrifice of economies of scale. McCammon has argued that the functional rigidity characteristic of most conventional channels may almost guarantee the ignoring of economies possible through realigning activities within the channel.[1] Thus, conventional channels are and have been highly vulnerable distribution mechanisms.

---

* Harvard University. Financial assistance from the National Science Foundation is gratefully acknowledged.

[a] There is little evidence that any significant number or importance of firms have operated with these characteristics (especially the individual transaction basis) in the past decade.

In contrast, vertical marketing systems consist of centrally programmed networks of establishments which are managed (usually by professionals) *as a system*. These networks are designed to achieve managerial, technological, and/or promotional economies through the integration, coordination, and synchronization of marketing flows from producer to ultimate user. Vertically coordinated systems can achieve efficiencies in activity and material flow scheduling, because the requirements of their member organizations can be more accurately forecast. Thus, activities such as transportation and storage can be planned to minimize costs to the system as a whole. Scheduling economies have two components: one resulting from the increased stability of operations; another from increased certainty of material supply at a predeterminable price.

Vertically coordinated systems also achieve economies through eliminating and simplifying activities such as outside selling, and through the programming of ordering, billing, and financing. Functions such as inventory holding and data processing may be repositioned forward or backward in the channel to achieve economies of scale. For example in retail cooperative or wholesaler-sponsored groups, the price-marking of merchandise may be moved backward to the wholesaling or manufacturing levels, because units in the channel can perform this function at a lower unit cost than can retailers.[2]

With *ownership integration,* one organization has combined successive stages of production and distribution under a single ownership. Ownership integration maximizes control, and thus the opportunity to achieve operating economies through corporate directives enforced by status sanctions. While ownership integrated corporations have existed for a long period, it is claimed that their growth has been particularly rapid in recent years, with firms operating 11 or more stores having a stable 20 percent of total retail sales between 1929 and 1958, and increasing their share to 30 percent by 1968.[3]

With an *administered system,* a channel member influences or controls the behavior of vertically adjacent firms by exerting leadership or economic muscle within the channel. The objective is to achieve transportation, storage, and other economies, or to control the pricing and merchandising of the product at other levels of distribution. Administered systems pertain to a line of classification of merchandise, rather than to a complete store operation. The greater the administrative expertise of one channel member (or economic dependence by another member), the less the need for ownership or contractual integration and the greater the likelihood of reliance on an administered channel.[4] Manufacturing organizations have historically relied on administrative expertise to coordinate reseller marketing efforts. There has been a recent expansion of such relationships through vendor-developed comprehensive programs for distribution through the entire channel. Davidson cites as examples the retail merchandising arrangements of O.M. Scott and Sons in lawn products, of Villager in women's apparel, of Magnavox in home entertainment, and of Kraftco Corporation in supermarkets.[5]

Finally, vertical coordination of marketing activities can be achieved through the use of *contractual agreements*. Independent firms at different distributive levels can integrate their programs on a contractual basis to obtain systemic economies and an increased market impact. Such contractual systems have expanded more rapidly in recent years than their corporate or administered counterparts (with the expansion being most apparent in the service sector), yet have received considerably less publicity.

Contractual integration occurs where the various stages of production and distribution are independently owned, but the relationships between vertically adjacent firms are covered in a contractual arrangement such as those found in franchise, voluntary, and cooperative forms of organization. Such traditional areas of contractual marketing are by no means the extent of such systems. Retailers belonging to programmed merchandising groups, stockless purchasing agreements, nonprofit shipping associations, or taking part in programs sponsored by resident buying offices account for a significant fraction of total retail volume. Negotiated contractual acquisition procedures in the governmental and military sectors account for more than 14 billion dollars a year in purchases, and contractual marketing systems in the agribusiness sector are becoming more common.[6] In addition, contractual systems in and between countries outside the United States are increasing rapidly in importance and complexity.

Specific institutional types characteristic of corporate, administered, or contractual systems may be viewed, like products, as having life cycles consisting of sequential stages: inception, growth, maturity, and decline. The time required to reach a mature stage in each institutional type is declining. Conventional department stores reached life cycle maturity in about 70 years, specialized variety stores in 50 years, and supermarkets in 25 years. Franchising organizations in the service sector have achieved maturity over a period of less than 15 years.

The implications of the accelerated replacement of the *ad hoc* linkages associated with conventional channels, with the more stable, programmed linkages in vertically coordinated channels are considerable. Davidson has projected:

> Further acceleration of institutional life cycles is to be expected. There will be an attendant massive impact upon existing institutional forms. The reasons include a variety of total vertical marketing systems models, a growing number of entrepreneurs and managers with interorganizational administrative skills, and a stock market that will instantly fund on a large scale any promising new concept.[7]

The Role of Contracts and Contracting

The role of the contract in the exchange/planning process is one on which little has been written. Under nineteenth century law, the private contract was the most common control device under which business enterprises operated. The courts did not alter or void such contracts so long as they were entered into voluntarily, and generally refused to consider questions of inequality of bargaining power or fairness in the contract. The exalted position occupied by the law of contract was summarized by Sir George Jessel in 1875:

> If there is one thing more than any other which public policy requires, it is that men of full age and competent understanding shall have the utmost liberty of contracting, and that contracts when entered into freely and voluntarily, shall be held good and shall be enforced by courts of justice.[8]

The first basic change was the development and widespread adoption of standardized or form contracting by business after 1920. The firm had a set of terms for buying and/or selling printed on the business documents used in these exchanges. Typically these terms and provisions were lengthy and printed in small type (on the back of the forms) but legally a part of the transaction. Such clauses were strictly enforced by the courts, without considerations of their fairness. The traditional strict enforcement-of-contract utilized by most courts is illustrated in the 1933 *Kirkmyer* case, where the court stated:

> While there is a natural impulse to be impatient with a form of contract which places the comparatively helpless dealer at the mercy of the manufacturer, *we cannot make contracts for parties or protect them from the provisions of contracts which they have made for them.* . . . [Dealers] cannot, when they get into trouble, expect the courts to place in the contract the protection which they themselves have failed to insert.[9]

Since 1950, the trend of case law and statutes has been away from the strict contractualism that characterized judicial reasoning in *Kirkmyer*. The writings of legal scholars like Kessler contributed much to changing judicial attitudes towards contracts, particularly form contracts.[10] Consider the court's decision in the 1966 *Madsen* case which the dealer won, and which was concerned with a Chrysler franchisee's repeated failure to fulfill his "minimum sales responsibility."

> [The "minimum sales responsibility"] . . . *is an arbitrary, coercive, and unfair provision* since it would enable Chrysler to terminate roughly one-third to one-half of all dealerships at any time. . . . to permit Chrysler to base termination of the franchise on the dealer's failure to achieve minimum sales responsibility

would be *particularly unfair here,* since the dealer has, at the urging of some Chrysler official, invested substantial funds in new sales and service facilities.[11]

The Uniform Commercial Code[b] takes several additional steps toward further court supervision of sales contracts. It imposes the requirement of good faith on every contract subject to the Code. It further provides that "obligations of good faith, diligence, reasonableness, and care" may not be disclaimed by contract;[c] this serves to eliminate oppression or unfair surprise through the use of form contracts drawn by one of the parties.[12]

The trend toward strictness in interpreting product liability and full disclosure is marked, and disclaimer of liability clauses in form sales contracts have been found contrary to public policy, or void in some states.[13] This trend in favor of consumerism is notable in the interpretation of implied warranty. Hertz was held liable for a breach of implied warranty for leasing a defective automobile;[14] a subdivision builder was found to have implicitly warranted the habitability of a home he sold.[15] The dysfunctional nature of implied warranty disclaimers, and of contracts involving disproportionate bargaining power, suggests that considerably more tinkering with these legal concepts will take place before a new balance is reached.[d]

Recent cases indicate that the private right of action under the Clayton Act is a powerful weapon for members of contractual systems who feel they have been wronged by overly restrictive agreements, or by contract provisions in restraint of trade. At least six class actions involving contractual systems have been filed in the past several years; the amendment in July 1966, to Rule 23[e] of the Federal Rules of Civil Procedure, gov-

[b] The Code has been adopted in 49 States (the exception being Louisiana), the District of Columbia, the Virgin Islands, and will shortly become law in Puerto Rico.

[c] There exists disagreement in the literature as to whether a franchise agreement is in fact a contract. Some franchise agreements (automobiles, carbonated beverages) have been held not to be valid contracts in various cases. Many franchises are not meant to be valid legal contracts, and are deliberately drawn so as to be unenforceable as contracts. The franchise agreement also is not an ordinary business contract in that the terms of the agreement are not a result of independent bargaining by two parties. The alternatives open to the franchisee may be to accept the terms offered him by the franchisor, or to choose some other business. The source of the franchisor's power lies in the economics of the situation and the termination provisions in the franchise agreement.

[d] The lawmakers may get there first. On July 2, 1970, the Senate passed a bill under which the use of *any kind* of warranty clause to deny an implied warranty of fitness would be prohibited. The ban was aimed mainly at standard disclaimers in new car warranties of the type that read: "This warranty is expressly in lieu of any other express or implied warranty, condition, or guarantee . . . including any implied warranty of merchantability or fitness . . ." The federal standards would be enforced by cease and desist orders of the Federal Trade Commission and by injunctions obtained in federal courts by the Attorney General. Consumers could sue for monetary damages in federal court if implied warranties were not satisfactorily honored.

[e] Under Rule 23, one or more members of a class may sue or be sued as representative parties on behalf of all class members if three criteria are met; (1) if the class

erning class actions, has raised the likelihood that many more private contract actions will be instituted as class actions.[16]

A legal contract may fail to exist across a broad spectrum of what are normally considered as contractual relationships. Thus, a purchasing agent may order using his company's form purchase contract, which contains several dozen paragraphs of small print favoring the buyer. The seller may fail to read the small print, and accept the buyer's order on the seller's own acknowledgement-of-order form. This form has several dozen paragraphs favoring the seller which are inconsistent with the buyer's provisions. The seller's acknowledgement form is checked by the buyer's clerk, who notes only the specification and quantity of goods and the price, without checking the form contract terms against the purchase order. The buyer and seller have planned an exchange; but there is no agreement, and in no way do they have a contract. This scenario is acted out frequently in governmental and DOD purchasing, as well as in voluntary chains, franchise arrangements, and other contractual systems.

Businessmen are often unconcerned about planning their contractual transactions so their contracts *are* legally valid. In at least 18 states, long-term requirements contracts (to supply some percentage of a firm's needs for a good or service rather than a definite quantity), are probably not legally enforceable where their effect is to unduly restrain competition. Yet seven of ten franchise agreements randomly chosen and examined by the writer contained such requirements clauses for use in all states. In every state without enabling legislation, resale price maintenance (and distribution controls imposed with the purpose of facilitating resale price maintenance) is *per se* illegal.[17] Four of the ten franchise agreements checked contained resale price maintenance provisions applicable in every state where the franchisor does business. Moreover, five house counsel contacted from the ten franchisors represented were aware of the legal inconsistencies involved, but did not feel that the lack of valid legal sanction made any difference. There were thought to be too many nonlegal sanctions available, in particular internal sanctions within the defaulting firm or the termination of further business relationships, to worry about the invalidity of contract terms.

It might be hypothesized that only where a large bargaining power differential exists between contractual partners is it likely that their transactions will be legally valid. It is likely that firms which contract with General Motors do business as GM specifies, sign the contracts that GM tenders

---

is so numerous that joinder of all members is not practical; (2) if there are common questions of law or fact; and (3) if the representative parties will fairly and accurately protect the interests of the class. The court determines whether a class action may be maintained; if so, the court orders that each member of the class be notified that the judgment, whether favorable or not, will include all members who do not request exclusion from the class by a specified date.

without alteration, or agree to operate without a contract if GM prefers not to be so bound.

The exception to this is the case where an organization with less power is capable of pooling its resources with other similar organizations to challenge legally the power of the dominant party.[18] A good example is the formation by franchised auto dealers of the National Automobile Dealers Association. The Association has succeeded in several states and federally in bringing about new legislation, and in supporting individual dealers against the imposition of unilateral contracts by automobile manufacturers and against the arbitrary cancellation of their franchises. A more recent example is the formation in Washington, D.C. of the National Association of Franchised Businessmen by 1,700 individual franchisees, most of them owners of one or two franchised units who lack the economic muscle of multiple franchise holders in dealing with their franchisors.

Contractually Constrained Decision-Making and the Minority Entrepreneur

A consideration of some importance in our society is the opportunity which contractually constrained decision making may hold for members of minority groups seeking to establish themselves in business. The scope of the problem is easy to document. Nonwhites have failed to maintain a proportionate status in the census category of "managers, officials, and proprietors." The figures as of March 1967 show that 14.2 percent of employed white males were "managers, officials, and proprietors," while only 3.5 percent of employed nonwhite males are in this category.[19] The nonwhite percentage has actually *dropped* since 1964. (Between 1950 and 1960, the number of black-owned businesses in the United States declined by 20 percent.) Of the 3,182 senior officers and directors of the *Fortune* 50 largest companies (as listed in *Poor's Register*), 3 are black, and 3,179 are white. Less than 3 percent of the nearly five million businesses in the United States are owned by persons from the 30 million black, Spanish-surname, and native Indian citizens who together make up almost 15 percent of the population. Approximately a quarter of those businesses are limited-income beauty parlors and barber shops.[20] As of January 1970, blacks held only 41 of the 36,200 franchised automobile dealerships, and operated 24 of the 13,822 commercial banks with 0.24 percent of the industry's assets. Of the 6,000 radio stations in the United States (of which 112 are beamed directly at the black community), only 11 have black owners. In predominantly black communities, about 80 percent of the dollar volume of business is controlled by whites, the majority of them absentee owners.

The picture in the major population centers is similar. New York City, with a black population of about 1,100, 000, has exactly 12 black-owned *or* managed enterprises employing ten persons or more. Newark, New Jersey, has a population of 400,000 of which more than half are black. Of 12,172 licensed businesses in Newark, only 10 percent have black owners. In Los Angeles, there are 600,000 blacks; less than 5 percent of 131,039 licensed businesses are owned by blacks. In Washington, D.C., where blacks comprise 63 percent of 810,000 people, less than 13 percent of the businesses are owned by blacks.[21] The nonwhite-owned businesses that do exist are generally of the small, service type and marginal-product retailing establishments with little to offer the ambitious individual. As one result, those nonwhites with entrepreneurial capability work instead in white-owned businesses, or go into teaching or government service.

James Farmer has stated the qualitative aspect as follows:

> In practical terms, what the rebels are revolting against is their lack of control over their own lives. They feel purchased, possessed, and exploited. The houses, stores and institutions are owned by others. They lack the economic and political leverages to effect change. They lack self-determination. They see their community as being akin to a colony. Theirs is a colonial revolt. It is a revolt against economic, cultural and social imperialism. Hence the slogan black power becomes all the more meaningful, as an aspiration and a goal.[22]

There is general agreement among economists that inability to obtain proper financing and training are two of the most important reasons for the lack of nonwhites in the entrepreneurial class. The advantages of contractually constrained decision making, managerial assistance, lower financial requirements, and consumer acceptance of the trademarked product or service have the potential to substantially reduce this imbalance. To date, this has most emphatically not happened. Of 138 franchise operations with 27,155 outlets surveyed by the Department of Commerce, only 354 were minority owned. This is 1.3 percent, *less than half the national average* of minority businesses.[23] There are only eight nonwhite-controlled franchisors in the United States; among them Jet Food, Rib Cage International, and Village Maid Services. The most substantial company in the group is All-Pro Chicken, which has seven area directorships, seven company-owned units in operation, and eight franchise units of which six are minority owned. The President of All-Pro Chicken is former professional football player Brady Keys, Jr., who has been successful in securing financing for All-Pro from the First National City Capital Corporation, Aetna, Connecticut Mutual, Travelers, and the Ford Foundation.

Federal Reserve Board member Dr. Andrew Brimmer is among those who would argue that contractually constrained businesses (or indeed any form of minority-group capitalism) are not a viable solution to nonwhite deprivation. Brimmer claims that the urban minority-group family, with its generally low income, high unemployment, large debts, and few assets, is one of the worst possible sources of business talent. Moreover, Brimmer maintains that self-employment offers a poor economic future for nonwhites; as a rule, they can make more money working for someone else.[24]

In spite of the criticisms offered and the visible lack of success,[f] the United States Department of Commerce and the Small Business Administration have inaugurated a program to exploit the advantages of constrained decision making by identifying franchisors which award franchises on a nondiscriminatory basis, and by circulating their names to minority-group citizens.[26] (About 85,000 copies of this material had been distributed as of June 1970.) When and if funds are available, the SBA supplements these efforts with managerial and financial assistance (including loans under Title IV of the Economic Opportunity Act of 1964) to persons obtaining franchises under the program. In the period from March 1967, to December 1969, the SBA made a total of 2,611 franchise loans, involving 650 different franchise companies; 403 of these loans, or 15.4 percent, were to minority-group persons. The franchise loans represented 6.9 percent of all SBA's loans during the period. The average dollar amount for all franchise loans was approximately $48,000; for minority franchise loans, approximately $25,000. The SBA and the Office of Minority Business Enterprise jointly sponsor a program named "25 X 2," which provides no funds but asks franchisors to provide twenty-five franchise opportunities to minority persons over a two-year period. As of July 1970, 95 franchisors had agreed to participate, including Arby's International, Lums, Mopar, Pizza Hut, Rayco, and Ziebert Process Corporation; none had as of that date produced a profitable franchisee under the plan.

Of somewhat more interest is the role that purely private enterprise has played in opening up entrepreneurial opportunities for minorities through constrained decision-making schemes. International Industries have a program designated "Two Plus You," under which a prospective minority entrepreneur may obtain a franchise (typically with International House of Pancakes), with a down payment of $1,000 or less, as compared with the $25,000 required under the standard franchise contract. The minority franchisee is given ten years to complete payments to the franchisor at no interest, rather than the usual 4½ year payback at 7½ percent simple interest. The Two Plus You training course is more extensive than the course provided for standard franchise applicants, and the trainee is paid a salary while he is in training. As of February 1970, there had been six graduates of "Two Plus You," with four others in training.

---

[f] There are some success stories. In 1966 the first replacement of a nonblack by a black Oldsmobile franchisee took place in south-side Chicago. The black business community responded to this black-owned dealership, sales and profits increased appreciably, and the success was followed by the transfer of additional automobile franchises to black ownership. However there were still only seven nonwhite franchisees of a total of 13,000 General Motors dealerships in April 1970.[25]

Such programs illustrate a number of steps that must be taken if contractually constrained decision making is to be extended to minority groups. Financial requirements, particularly front-end arrangements, must be decreased or altered; standard training periods must be extended and training content revised; and it must be recognized that a huge communication problem exists between white franchisor and minority franchisee. Most minority-group persons lack *any* entrepreneurial background, heritage, or training. There is also an implicit credibility gap between franchisor and franchisee, and care must be taken not to widen that gap by unrealistic success or earnings projections, or unreasonable demands on the franchisee.

The Growth and Significance of Franchising

The growth in franchising represents only one segment of the growth of contractual systems during the last decade; it is the segment which has been by far the most visible, and received the greatest coverage in the popular press.

Although it has become common to apply the term franchising to a whole range of different economic and legal relationships, the contractual bond of interest is one in which an organization, the franchisor, which has developed a pattern or formula for the manufacture and/or sale of a product or service, extends to other firms, the franchisees, the right to carry on the business, *subject to* a number of restrictions and controls. In almost all cases of significance, the franchisee operates using the franchisor's name as a trade name.

There are two quite distinct classes of franchise systems, one involving a product or service, the other revolving around trademark licensing arrangements. These two break down further into six identifiable types, designated by kinds of market supplier and franchisee. Thus, a franchise agreement may exist between manufacturer and retailers in the case of Chevrolet or Mary Carter Paints; between manufacturer and wholesalers in the case of Coca Cola or Falstaff beer; between wholesaler and retailers in the case of Western Auto or Ben Franklin Stores. A trademark owner-franchisor may contract with manufacturers in the case of Fruit of the Loom fabricated textiles; with wholesalers or retailers in the cases of Hertz or Kelly Girl; or with franchisees on the same level of distribution as the franchisor in the case of Sealy Mattresses or Quality Chekd Dairy Products.

Table 1-1 projects the 1969 total for franchised business at $124.4 billion, and for total franchised business excluding passenger car dealers, gasoline service stations, and bottlers of carbonated beverages, at $37.6 billion. There are over 500,000 franchised businesses in the United States, about one business enterprise in nine in the nonfarm sector.[27] It must be

Table 1-1
Total Dollar Sales and Number of Franchisees by Component Areas of Franchised Business for 1969

	Franchised Establishments (number)	Sales ($000's)
I. Product and Service Franchise Systems		
1. Manufacturer-retailer systems		
passenger car dealers, franchised	36,200	56,610,000
gasoline service stations	287,600	27,200,000
hearing aids, swimming pools, etc.	7,400	487,000
2. Manufacturer-wholesaler systems		
carbonated beverage bottlers	4,000	3,000,000
3. Wholesaler-retailer systems		
cooperative and voluntary programs in food, drug, hardware, home and auto, variety store, and automobile aftermarket sectors	89,750	25,930,000
II. Trademark Licensing Franchise Systems		
4. Trademark Licensor-Manufacturer systems		
fabricated textiles	N.A.	725,000
5. Trademark licensor association-association member systems		
bread, milk, mattress industries	1,381	1,814,600
6. Trademark licensor-retailer systems		
food, beverage, and soft ice cream; temporary help services; hotels and motels; auto, truck, and trailer rentals; tool and equipment rental; coin-operated and regular laundry and dry cleaning services; etc.	109,598	8,649,000
Total, Representative Franchised Businesses	535,929	124,424,600
Total, Exclusive of Passenger Car Dealers, Gasoline Service Stations, and Bottlers of Carbonated Beverages	208,129	37,614,600

Source: *U.S. Census of Business, Retail Trade Summary Statistics; U.S. Census of Business, Wholesale Trade Summary Statistics; U.S. Census of Business, Selected Service Summary Statistics; Moody's Industrials*; trade publications; private estimates by industry officials; government studies on specific industries. The disaggregated figures are shown in Donald N. Thompson, "Submission. . . ." Figures available only to the years 1967–68 have been projected as growing no more quickly than total sales at retail for the relevant period to produce 1969 estimates.

emphasized that these are conservative estimates. The latest *Franchise Annual,* or the Department of Commerce' listing of franchised business, records literally hundreds of businesses in dozens of categories that are not included here: travel agencies, art galleries, youth nightclubs, nursing homes, beauty salons, shoplifting controls, diet programs, and social introductions being only a few. I would estimate that the figures given do represent in excess of 90 percent of the dollar volume of franchised business today. The total for all franchised businesses represents 34.5 percent of total retail sales for 1969, and the total exclusive of traditional franchised business represents 10.4 percent, although a comparison of franchised sales with total retail sector sales is somewhat misleading, as a substantial segment of franchised sales represents wholesale transactions.

This 10.4 percent represents the dynamic, newer areas of the industry which have been referred to by Harry Kursh as the "franchise boom."[28] My own limited investigations, based on a randomly drawn sample of franchisors listed in the 1964 and subsequent issues of the Department of Commerce' *Franchise Company Data for Equal Opportunity in Business,* plus some primary data, indicate that the nontraditional areas of franchising are expanding at a rate of 7.5+ percent per year. If the growth rate from this sample is applied to the number of nontraditional franchisees, one arrives at an estimate that a minimum of 13,100 new franchised outlets are being created (net) each year. The figure may be fairly accurate, because an analysis of 1967 data similar to that for 1969 shows that the number of new franchised outlets over that period was 24,700, a growth of 12,350 per year.

The impact of this kind of growth is better appreciated if one considers the history of only one franchisor, Kentucky Fried Chicken Corporation. Starting from close to zero in 1963, Kentucky Fried Chicken is now the United States' largest commercial food service organization, outranked only by the Army, the Navy, and the Department of Agriculture's school lunch program. KFC franchise and company-owned stores grossed $430 million in 1969 from sales through 2,955 outlets in the U.S., Canada, and 19 other countries.

There are indications that members of franchise systems have substantially lower failure rates than do comparable independent businessmen. The overall business closing rate is currently about 7 percent per year, the birth rate about 8.5 percent, with 54 percent of new retail businesses no longer in operation at the end of their first four years. Various studies have shown franchisee failure rates as low as 10 percent, with franchisor failures of about 28 percent of new franchisors, and 5 to 6 percent of total franchisors, per year.[29]

Results from the survey or questionnaire type of studies of franchise operations must be evaluated with great care. Franchisors, being highly dependent on favorable performance statistics for use in attracting new franchisees, are often unwilling to admit to unfavorable results. Also, performance statistics on franchising are frequently not comparable with those from other types of business operation. Many franchisors with large, highly visible outlets will not permit a location failure in the short run after an outlet has opened. The franchisor will simply take over the ailing outlet as a company operation—and thus be able to claim correctly that the location has not failed. Other established franchisors will not permit a franchisee failure, although they are willing to abandon an unsuccessful location and relocate the franchisee. Figures on franchisee turnover are also misleading. The most successful franchisees might be the ones most motivated to sell their operations to realize capital gains. Similarly, franchises (and nonfranchised businesses) requiring low investment and those utilizing mobile operations typically show much higher turnover rates than do higher-investment, fixed-location outlets.

Even considering the questionable nature of available statistics, it is likely that membership in a franchise system does reduce the risk of small business failure. In the more mature franchise operations, the franchisee is required to use tested operating procedures and internal controls to mitigate the effects of his inexperience and ineptitude. He is provided with an established brand name, enforced quality maintenance through quality control, locational analysis on setting up operations, initial training, and continued field supervision. In some cases the franchisor takes responsibility for advertising and merchandising. By virtue of these advantages and of the other attributes of franchising, franchisees can reasonably be expected to show more stability and longer life than their independent counterparts. A study by J. F. Atkinson of failure rates of members of the International Franchise Association indicated that the odds favoring success of franchised small business versus all other retail were eight to one, or higher. This is probably the most accurate estimate available currently.[g]

One of the qualitative contributions frequently cited in the literature is the role of the franchise form in broadening the distributive base of the economy through encouragement of small business. Most franchisees meet the practical tests for a small business: serving only a limited market, governed by the size of his capital and cash reserves, his geographic access to customers, the structure of freight rates, and other business factors. The social values implicit in the independent ownership of one's own business as opposed to being an employee of an integrated firm are cited in the oft-quoted statement of Judge Dawson in *Susser* v. *Carvel*:

> The franchise method of operation has the advantage, from the standpoint of our American system of competitive economy, of enabling numerous groups of individuals with small capital to become entrepreneurs. . . If our economy had not developed . . . [franchising], these individuals would have turned out to be merely employees. The franchise system creates a class of independent businessmen; it provides the public with an opportunity to get a uniform product at numerous points of sale from small independent contractors, rather than employees of a vast chain.[31]

It cannot be inferred, however, that franchisors remain small, or independent. A recent wave of acquisitions and mergers involving franchise

[g] Atkinson defined a failure to include: bankruptcies for any reason, any closings at a loss to the franchisee, and a 30 percent investment loss, even with 'turnover' involved.[30]

systems has greatly altered the size distribution of parent franchisor firms.[h] In recent years Consolidated Foods acquired Chicken Delight; Servomation Corporation bought Red Barn System; United Fruit took over J. Hungerford Smith (parent company of the A & W Root Beer chain and the Baskin Robbins ice cream specialty stores); National Broadcasting Company, a subsidiary of RCA, bought Arnold Palmer Enterprises; Great Western United purchased Shakey's Pizza; General Foods purchased Burger Chef; Pillsbury purchased Burger King; and Household Finance purchased both the Ben Franklin system and the White Stores. In merger and stock exchange transactions RCA merged with Hertz Corporation; Famous Artists Schools exchanged common stock for Evelyn Wood Reading Dynamics Institute; Pet, Inc. gained control of Stuckey's; and Union Tank Car took over the Lindsay chain.

There is strong support for a hypothesis that the larger and more financially sound the franchisor, the more probable the eventual conversion of the franchise system to an ownership-integrated one through purchase or nonrenewal of franchise agreements. The suggestion that franchising as a distribution and financing technique is transitional rather than permanent is reinforced by the fact that the most successful franchisors earn a majority of their revenues not from royalties on franchised operations, but from wholly-owned units run by salaried managers. McDonald's, the largest hamburger chain, makes almost 70 percent of its gross revenue from wholly-owned units; Kentucky Fried Chicken, 74 percent; and Manpower, Inc., the largest of the franchised temporary help agencies, almost 96 percent.[33]

The chief impediment to franchisor take over of the most successful franchisee operations is the problem that stimulated franchising in the first place: a shortage of capital by franchisors. Howard Johnson at present owns two-thirds of its highway restaurants, is opening wholly-owned units at a ratio of 3:1 over new franchised units, and continues to buy out existing and successful franchisees when possible. However, the majority of Howard Johnson's new chain of motor lodges are franchised to investor groups, because the parent company cannot generate from its own cash flow the $1 million average per restaurant/motor lodge required for expansion. Even some of the major automobile franchisors—notably Cadillac—have been buying back franchisees on a limited basis, although the continuation of the franchise system in automobile distribution is quasi-guaranteed by the immense amount of capital that would be required for a complete buy-back. Based on a per-dealer investment of $300,000 and 36,200 franchised dealers, auto franchisees have about $10.2 billion in-

---

[h] This occurs at a time when concentration ratios are increasing in many lines of retail trade. In 1967, the twenty leading chains in their respective categories accounted for 18.1 percent of total drug store sales, 30.4 percent of total grocery store sales, 44.1 percent of total discount department store sales, and 47.6 percent of total conventional department store sales.[32]

vested in land, buildings, equipment, and inventory. Even if the major automobile franchisors could raise this sum in today's capital markets, the rate of return might be less than if the money had been invested in other manufacturing opportunities.

Contractual Controls and Antitrust

A current problem facing contractual systems is the status under the antitrust laws of the controls utilized in those systems.[i] This section will discuss antitrust legislation and judicial or administrative agency interpretation relating to the principal marketing restrictions found in contractual arrangements. The restrictions discussed relate to exclusive distribution (exclusive franchising, exclusive dealing, and tying); to franchisee freedom to choose a territory to serve; to reciprocal buying; and to some minor restrictions such as the format of advertising and promotion.[j]

Although the various controls can be separated for academic consideration, they are rarely found singly in practice. Thus, exclusive franchising and exclusive dealing often appear as the consideration for one another. Quality control provisions often include a limited tying arrangement. Few of the antitrust cases to reach the courts have been limited to a single restriction; sometimes consideration of controls has been clouded by other issues, in particular the question of the relative dominance of the market supplier in the markets he serves.

Exclusive franchising is an agreement, by a market supplier with a dealer, that he will not sell his product to any other dealer within the first dealer's territory, and (usually) that he will not sell there directly himself. Exclusive franchising implies only a system of highly selective distribution. It does not *require* the existence of a reciprocal exclusive dealing arrangement, nor the granting of exclusive territorial rights to the dealer.

It is usually necessary for the market supplier to grant exclusive franchises where the product or service requires substantial dealer investment (in showroom or servicing facilities, inventory, personnel training), or a commitment to substantial advertising or sales promotion activities. This is particularly true where the dealer is required to erect a building according to detailed blueprints furnished by the market supplier, and where the possibility of selling the building or converting it economically to other uses is low.

---

[i] Legal challenges face contractual marketing systems in areas other than antitrust. More than a dozen states are currently considering franchise legislation on a nonpartisan basis, with support coming from the conservative Governor of California, the liberal Attorney General of New York, and a collection of senators including Hart of Michigan, Brooke of Massachusetts, Williams of New Jersey, and Bible of Nevada.

[j] The controls may or may not be included in the formal contract, but are frequently enforced in contractual systems. Their legal status remains the same whether or not they are formally stated in the contract.

There is no question that exclusivity has some anticompetitive effect, in that intraband competition may be effectively foreclosed. Nevertheless, the courts have held that exclusive franchises are *per se* legal, and that a supplier may grant rights to use his trade name to whomever he wishes, given only that he does not engage in an unfair act or an unreasonable restraint of trade, or seek to monopolize the relevant market.[34] Even the Auto Dealer's Day in Court legislation has not been found to abrogate these rights of the market supplier.

When exclusive franchising is used to enforce other controls, the situation may change. For example, when a supplier threatens to refuse to deal with a franchisee who will not maintain resale prices, the court may find that there exists tacit agreements between the supplier and his other franchisees pursuant to which they have sold at maintained prices. The issue is then not whether the supplier has the right to unilaterally refuse to deal with individual franchisees, but whether he and his dealers may combine to restrain competition through resale price agreements.

Exclusive dealing (which is normally found reciprocally with exclusive franchising) is an agreement by the dealer to purchase, sell, or otherwise deal only in products supplied or approved by a market supplier. One type involves a supplier prohibiting his dealers from selling products which, although not competitive with those trademarked products sold, involve issues of quality maintenance and dilution of dealer sales efforts. A service station franchisee may wish to take on an automobile trailer rental franchise to be operated from the service station. Usually the oil company franchisor does not like to have the station cluttered up with trailers from stock, and may forbid the taking on of the second franchise on the grounds of potential damage to the first.

A second type of exclusive dealing involves a supplier who requires his dealers not to sell trademarked products competitive with those of the supplier. Essentially all of the case law involving exclusive dealing has dealt with this second type.

Once a large or dominant supplier obtains for his exclusive use a large share of available outlets on a lower level of distribution, he has imposed prohibitive cost disadvantages on existing or potential rivals, since they are likely to have to create new outlets in order to enter the market. The same is true if a group of suppliers collectively (if not collusively) obtain exclusive obligations from dealers, producing an aggregate foreclosure. Nevertheless, exclusive dealing requirements have traditionally not been considered to be *per se* illegal except when accompanied by an attempt to monopolize or fix prices. In the *Standard Stations* case, the Court ruled that exclusive dealing would violate Section 3 of the Clayton Act whenever it "foreclosed competition in a substantial share of the line of commerce affected," since such foreclosure created the likelihood of economic harm.[35]

Tying arrangements constitute another method by which a market supplier may restrict the source of products purchased by his dealers. A tying arrangement is an agreement by one party to sell a [tying] product, but only on the condition that the buyer also purchases a different [tied] product. When the leverage power of the tying product is used to force the buyer to purchase the seller's whole line of goods, the arrangement is known as full-line forcing.

In cases where the buyer is licensed to use a trademark or trade name, as in a franchise system, a related issue is whether the trademark can be the tying product. In *Susser* v. *Carvel,* a private antitrust action, the franchise agreement between Carvel and its franchisees required the latter to purchase from Carvel, or from approved sources, all ingredients which formed part of the final ice cream product. The court ruled that the agreement constituted a tying arrangement, with the Carvel trademark the "tying good."[36]

It is usually argued that tying agreements are necessary to the supplier to protect the goodwill or integrity of the tying product. The argument is that the tying product will operate properly only when used in conjunction with the tied product, and that if the user of the tying product is not required to use the tied product he may substitute an inferior good. This argument is weakened, perhaps fatally, if the market supplier exploits the tied market for collateral profits, either by acting as a wholesaler of essential supplies or by extracting kickbacks or commissions from other designated suppliers.[37]

A variation of tying is found in the case of a supplier who offers special services and loans of money and equipment as inducement for a buyer to concentrate on his lines. The Brown Shoe Company, the second largest shoe manufacturer in the country by dollar volume, had for years entered into franchise agreements with independent shoe retailers. In exchange for free signs, business forms, and low-interest loans, each franchisee agreed to concentrate purchases of shoes in the grades and price lines manufactured by Brown, and to refrain from stocking or selling competitive shoes of equal grades and prices. Retailers who did not comply were denied these benefits.

The F.T.C. charged, under Section 5 of the F.T.C. Act, that Brown's plan constituted an illegal tying arrangement, with special benefits offered by Brown to franchised dealers as the tying product. It was found that the leverage of these special benefits was used to secure exclusive patronage for Brown to the detriment of competition in the shoe manufacturing industry.[38] Of interest is the amount of competitive foreclosure necessary to invalidate an exclusionary program. Brown had tied up only 1 percent of total retail shoe outlets, and approximately 4 percent of the choice outlets for which the program was designed. The F.T.C. argued successfully that this degree of competitive foreclosure, in the context of the shoe industry, was sufficient indication of probable competitive injury to warrant issuance of an order against Brown.

Territorial restrictions exist where a market supplier places geographic restriction on resale by the buyer of the trademarked goods or services. In an exclusive territorial division, the buyer agrees to concentrate his business solicitation within the territory. He may normally sell to anyone who comes into his territory unsolicited. In the closed territorial division, the buyer is forbidden to resell to anyone who does not maintain a place of business (or residence) in his territory. In each case there is a tacit understanding that all buyers will be similarly bound, and that territories will not overlap.

Given the sanction of dealer termination, territorial restrictions either limit or eliminate intrabrand competition in the areas affected. With a lesser sanction than termination, the barrier to intrabrand competition is no greater than the required pass-over payment. To the extent that the pass-over reimburses a servicing expense incurred by the invaded dealer, but included in the purchase price of the selling dealer, it merely prevents unjustified profit-taking and has no effect in deterring intrabrand competition.

In the *Schwinn* case,[39] the question was the degree to which a manufacturer can allocate territories for resale, and restrict dealers from selling to other retailers for resale. Schwinn was the second largest United States bicycle manufacturer, with 13 percent of the market. Schwinn's franchised wholesalers were instructed to distribute only to franchised Schwinn retailers in their respective territories. The retailer was authorized to purchase only from or through the distributor to whom his area was assigned, to sell only at one designated location and only to ultimate users, not to nonfranchised retailers, particularly discount houses. Schwinn did not restrict either wholesalers or retailers from carrying other makes of bicycles as long as they gave Schwinn products at least equal prominence with other brands in display and promotion.

The Court found that "where a manufacturer sells products to its distributor subject to territorial restrictions upon resale, a *per se* violation of the Sherman Act results. The same *per se* illegality applied "to restrictions of outlets with which distributors may deal and to restraints upon retailers to whom the goods are sold."

In the case of Schwinn's agency or consignment sales, where title and risk of loss remain with the franchisor, the Court found territorial restrictions to be not *per se* but subject to test under the rule of reasonableness. This requires that there be adequate interbrand competition, that dealers be free to handle competing products, and that there be no element of price fixing involved. These requirements limit or exclude contractual marketing systems of many larger companies.

It is notable that the Court rejected a defense argument by Schwinn that it had adopted territorial controls to enable it and its small, independent franchisees to compete more effectively with ownership integrated giants like Montgomery Ward and Sears, Roebuck.

The Court in *Schwinn* indicated that it would treat other postsale controls on product use in exactly the same way. Thus, the ruling applies in principle to any contractual restrictions on a buyer, however nominal, if they curtail the freedom of that buyer to do as he wishes with the product. Whether this ruling will be applied as firmly against smaller firms as against larger ones with market dominance is uncertain; historical patterns of antitrust enforcement suggest it will not.

The courts have not as yet ruled on whether the Schwinn precedent applies to all six types of franchising, in particular to the situation where a trademark franchisor contracts with wholesalers or retailers—Avis, or McDonald's hamburgers, for example. In these situations, the franchisor does not sell a product, but rather licenses only the use of his name and the method of doing business. There are some considerations unique to such trademark franchising; the franchisor-licensor has an obligation to protect the identity of origin, uniformity, quality, and public image of his trademarked product or service, or risk the diminution or loss of the trademark itself. In trademark franchisor cases, the validity of the controls imposed may continue to rest on whether those controls are necessary to protect the trademark; and trademark franchising, perhaps the most dynamic segment of contractual systems, may be exempted from the most binding of the Court's pronouncements.

Reciprocity, or reciprocal buying, is the action by a firm in a dominant position relative to suppliers of goods or services to it, bringing pressure on these suppliers to purchase from it. The F.T.C. has issued cease and desist orders in situations where coercive reciprocity arrangements appeared to exist, and the Department of Justice has requested divestiture of corporate divisions where it appeared that reciprocity was a calculated part of a merger. The Department of Justice seems to have established the principle that any systemic program of securing reciprocal trade agreements from suppliers, whether contractual in nature or not, violates the antitrust laws even though no coercion is involved.

There are a number of less significant controls which commonly appear in contractual agreements. A market supplier may seek to impose on his buyers restrictions on quality controls to be maintained; quantity, quality, and format of advertising and promotion; facilitating services such as credit, delivery, and business hours offered; standardized architecture and site landscaping; or employee training programs. Each control does represent a restraint on trade, the legitimacy of which is judged on a rule of reason standard. If the control is intended to serve a legitimate business purpose, and does not have the primary purpose of stifling competitors and creating a monopoly, then the courts will generally uphold any resulting (and incidental) restraint of trade.[40]

The decisions all point to the fact that a much higher standard of proof is to be required of market suppliers of the reasonableness of their contractual controls, and of the absence of less restrictive means to achieve the same ends. The Supreme Court in *Schwinn* said that it *may not even be sufficient* to demonstrate sound business reason and intent on the part of a supplier who would impose controls. Assuming nonpredatory motives and business purposes, it may also be necessary to demonstrate that the impact of the control in the marketplace is *procompetitive*.

The issue of whether or not antitrust enforcement encourages a shift from contractual to ownership interpreted marketing systems is not clear. Manufacturers frequently contend that unless they are permitted to establish restrictions on distributors, they will be compelled to take over the distribution function themselves. The major oil companies have maintained their franchise systems in spite of such dire predictions following the *Standard Stations* case in 1949. On the other hand, Schwinn's reaction to the Court ruling was to announce to its dealers in August 1967, that it planned to distribute its products nationally through company-owned sales subsidiaries. Thus, the end of jobber franchising and the substitution of vertical ownership integration was Schwinn's permanent answer to the Court's ruling on territorial restrictions.

Conflict in Contractual Systems

Between members in each type of contractual system, and indeed in every vertical channel, there exists a dynamic field of conflicting and cooperating objectives. Palamountain states that conflict is a prevailing characteristic of interaction within all systems of institutions. Vertical relationships are differentiated from horizontal and intertype systems primarily because they are based on power as a form of conflict resolution.[41] Stern and Heskett hypothesized from their research that: "Power (in the form of inter-organizational control) gravitates to one organization within a system of inter-related organizations.[k] The emergence of a leader within such a system is not only likely, but inevitable."[43] Conflict may remain covert, in which case the frustrated organization does nothing to alter its behavior. It is often overt, in which case the organization exhibits some behavior change in its own goals or operations, or by attempting to influence the behavior of others upon which it is dependent.

Contractual system members usually have more harmonious interests than conflicting ones. All members of the system have a mutual interest in the promotion of the good or service involved. Only in the division of total system profits, and sometimes in the location of system/channel leadership, are they really in conflict. Nevertheless, an emphasis on cooperat-

[k] An appropriate definition of power is that by John Schopler, who defines *O*'s power over *P* as the net increase in the probability of *P* enacting a behavior after *O* has made an intervention, compared to the probability of *P*'s enacting the behavior in the absence of *O*'s intervention. Thus, an application of power by *O* need not result in an overt action on the part of *P*, but may only increase the probability of the desired action.[42]

ing rather than conflicting objectives of contractual system members has been one basis of the misleading concept of a contractual system as simply an extension of the market supplier's own internal organization.

The degree of conflict or cooperation in the contractual channel varies with the stage of life cycle of the system. For example, initially most franchisees are anxious to cooperate with the franchisor, particularly when they accept the value of his services and of the franchise package. As the franchisee grows and matures this may change, particularly if the services provided are intangible. If the franchisee obtains only an initial expertise accompanied by the use of a trademark, he may begrudge the franchisor his continuing financial returns, and may distrust franchisor attempts to exercise control. The situation is most common in trademark licensor-retailer systems.

A franchisor with a new product or untested idea may find it necessary to offer franchisees highly protective arrangements as to territories, customers, or price maintenance. In a mature franchise system, the reverse may occur. The franchisor's profit maximization alternatives may require less protection for individual franchisees, but in the meantime franchisees may have become organized and may insist upon the maintenance of exclusionary arrangements. Where traditional members can band together either formally or informally, a bargaining relationship—ultimately a collective bargaining relationship—may arise. Witness the behavior of automobile franchisees and petroleum franchisees in relation to their franchisors.

One of the root causes of conflict is role incongruency within the contractual system. This may be directly related to the lack of carefully spelled-out provisions in initial contract negotiations. Conflicting role expectations and domain definitions governing interorganization relations may produce conflicting policies relative to inventory levels, sales-quota setting, pricing policies, and the like—as well as provoke an instability throughout the contractual system.[44]

The new franchisee, because of his limited financial resources and organizational status, may find himself in a very subordinate position vis-à-vis the established franchisor. The franchisor tries to control the franchise channel through the building of trademark acceptance with advertising, sales promotion, and packaging of his goods. Many franchisors concentrate on group pressure and persuasion to achieve dominance over their franchisees. Negative methods such as termination of the franchise, refusal to fill the orders of uncooperative franchisees, or refusal to extend trade credit have been used in the past, but are of declining importance today. In a mature franchise system, the market supplier's influence may be based on expert power, with the strength of such power varying directly with the special knowledge which the franchisee perceives the market supplier to possess.

The experience of automobile manufacturers provides a case history of what happened in one industry where a supplier was accused of using coercion, intimidation, and arbitrary franchise cancellation to evoke franchisee compliance with his demands. After extensive hearings in 1956, Congress enacted the so-called Auto Dealer Day In Court Act.[45] The Act permits automobile franchisees to sue in Federal Courts for damages caused by failure of the franchisor to ". . . act in good faith in performing or complying with any of the terms or provisions of the franchise, or in terminating, cancelling, or in reviewing the franchise of said dealer." A comprehensive review by Stewart Macaulay of the first ten years of the Act suggests that the legislation has forced an improvement in relationships between automobile franchisors and their franchisees.[46] Discontent is sufficiently widespread in nonautomobile franchise systems to have caused the franchisee group-initiated introduction, in the last four Congresses, of eight bills to extend coverage of the Act to all franchisees.[47]

Mallen has suggested that a marketing system can adjust to its conflicting-cooperating environment in three different ways. The market supplier may force dealers to cooperate in an autocratic relationship. The supplier may persuade dealers to cooperate in a benevolent relationship, or may offer no strong leadership with a resulting anarchistic relationship.[48] Where anarchy exists, as in the case of some of the newer, relatively unorganized trademark licensor-retailer franchise systems, the conflicting dynamics may destroy the system. If autocracy exists, as in the case in most of the older, established manufacturer-retailer systems, there is less probability of this happening. Autocracy does often produce narrow, self-oriented goal definitions resulting in diminished performance by the channel as a whole.

Also, situations of very low conflict in a mature contractual system may lead to passivity, complacency, and the lack of system innovation. Boulding hypothesizes that there is a level of conflict within any interorganization system below which conflict processes are healthy for the system. He suggests a need to identify the level of hostility above which conflict processes will be malign (where all system members are worse off), and below which they will be benign.[49] Above Boulding's "level of hostility," conflict becomes dysfunctional, and results in reduced system efficiency and performance.

The Literature on Contractual Systems

Microeconomic theory has been the basis for much of the theoretical work undertaken in the area of vertical marketing systems, including contractual systems. Stigler, Baumol, Chamberlain, and the many others who have worked within the area have written in the context of formal maximization or optimization models.[50] Writers like Margolis have developed nonmaximization models with an applicability to contractual systems, but their numbers have been few.[51] Writers like Alderson have given a prominent place to the marketing transaction. Alderson emphasized the tendency of the parties in a transaction to routinize their behavior as a means of conserving resources.[52] Bucklin has combined Alderson's work on postponement with Knight's principle of speculation for a new formulation potentially useful in the analysis of contractual systems.[53] Each has assumed that channel relationships are established by rational, profit-maximizing entrepreneurs who are not influenced by political or personal considerations. The analysis thus becomes a useful, but largely mechanistic explanation of channel phenomena.

The limited usefulness of micro theory for contractual systems occurs because a vertical channel is a political and social complex in a number of senses. These include the achieving of solidarity and bargaining collectively with other systems, the use of bargaining strategem and bluff within the channel, and the attempting to achieve noneconomic control by one or more channel participants.[54] Writers such as Mallen, building on the work of Grether, Palamountain, and Galbraith, have recognized and commented on these aspects.[55] Mallen concluded that voluntary vertical systems result in lower total distribution costs than do either controlled cooperation or anarchy systems. Mallen has also analyzed the nature of cooperative arrangements which are likely to occur in bargaining systems under bilateral monopoly, bilateral oligopoly, and perfect competition.[56] Baligh and Richartz have illustrated alternative states of conflict and cooperation in vertical channels, using economic models in a context in which political and social factors may be introduced.[57] These latter works and their extensions promise to be of somewhat more usefulness in the study of contractual systems.

A highly promising source of material on contractual systems is the extensive literature on economic integration and efficiency. This discusses vertical marketing systems in terms of their components, the flows and other relationships among components, the level of activities, the division of activities into the processes of decision and execution, the degree of integration, and integration as a state of the system. Much of the literature is found in languages other than English, or has been published in English but is generally inaccessible to North American readers.[58] The Swedish economist Lars-Gunnar Mattsson in a study inspired by changes in the organization and structure of the distributive trades in Sweden has discussed three types of integration, their interrelations, and their relations to efficiency in the systems analyzed.[59] Mattsson's conclusions can be reformulated into a series of hypotheses eminently suitable for testing by people working in the contractual systems area.

Sociologists and organization theorists have in general concentrated on explaining behavior and conflict within organizations rather than *between* organizations. Herbert Simon has claimed that the phenomena of intragroup conflict differ little from those of intergroup conflict. However, sociologists like Sherif and Evan would strongly disagree, and the empirical data that exists would seem to support them.[60] There are some exceptions to the intragroup approach; the work of Philip Selznick for example, but its applications to contractual systems are at best peripheral.[61] The writing of people like Merton, Goulder, Blau, Cyert and March, and Thompson, is well known to students of marketing.[62] There are other sociologists who have made great contributions to understanding the nature and process of conflict, particularly in the context of labor-management relations but in a form which may be transferrable to a vertical marketing context. The contributions of Robert Dubin, O. Kahn-Freund, and Ralf Dahrendorf are less known to students of marketing than they deserve.[63] (One might include some of the classical sociologists: Max Weber for his cross-institutional research, George Simmel in conflict and group behavior, and Emile Durkheim in the division of responsibility in a societal context.)

It is likely that the contributions from sociology will be much more substantive in the near future, as the field continues its shift away from microanalyses of individual behavior, toward macro issues. As sociologists move further away from Parsonian Functionalism, which takes the social system (with its existing power arrangements, property relationships, and institutions) as a given, and equilibrium (order, stability) as an ideal, they will have more in common with economists and political scientists than with psychologists and anthropologists, and their work will have more application to marketing channels.[l]

McCammon argues that the literature of systems engineering, game theory, management science, and simulation have much to offer students of vertical systems.[65] Systems engineers use a variety of mathematical techniques such as queuing theory, and linear and dynamic programming, to program marketing-network performance.[66] Game theorists focus on the bargaining and negotiation process, developing bargaining strategies under different assumptions of rationality, cooperation between players, and information availability.[67] Management science deals with problems such as optimizing the efficiency with which inventory is utilized throughout a marketing network, using techniques such as heuristic programming.[68] Simulation techniques may be useful in showing the performance of dynamic systems over time, or in exploring the outcomes of decision alternatives in experimental situations. A model developed by Arnold Amstutz includes as variables changes in government policies, changes in consumer demand, and changes in competitive response patterns.[69]

Finally, notice should be taken of the growing body of literature on specialized topics such as contractual negotiation. Much of this is found in the literature of law, although increasingly it appears in the fields of political science, social psychology, and business administration.[70] Each of these areas, and the ones mentioned above, are developing rapidly, and show promise of making notable contributions to the literature applicable to contractual systems in the near future.

---

[l] Witness the reestablishment at Harvard, after 24 years, of an independent department of sociology, replacing the interdisciplinary efforts of sociologists, psychologists, and anthropologists under the social relations umbrella.[64]

Notes

1. Bert C. McCammon, Jr., *Perspectives for Distribution Programming,* a paper presented at the Vertical Marketing Systems Workshop, Northwestern University (November, 1968). So much of the work in the area of vertical systems has been done in recent years by McCammon that it is hard to footnote the extent of the debt to him. See "The Emergence and Growth of Contractually Integrated Channels in the American Economy" in Peter D. Bennett, ed., *Marketing and Economic Development,* Chicago: American Marketing Association (1965), 496–515; "Alternative Explanations of Institutional Change and Channel Evolution" in Steven Greyser, ed., *Toward Scientific Marketing,* Chicago: American Marketing Association (1963), 477–490; "Marketing Channels: Analytical Systems and Approaches" (with Robert W. Little) in George Schwartz, ed., *Science in Marketing,* New York: John Wiley and Sons, Inc. (1965), 321–368; *Alternative Models for Programming Vertical Marketing Networks* (with Albert D. Bates and Joseph P. Guiltinan), a paper presented during the professional dialogue session on marketing channels, 1968 Fall Conference of the American Marketing Association, Denver, Colorado (August 30, 1968).

2. For an attempt at evaluating some of these factors, see Frederick D. Sturdivant, "Determinants of Vertical Integration in Channel Systems," in Raymond Haas, ed., *Science, Technology, and Marketing,* Chicago: American Marketing Association (1966), 472–479.

3. William R. Davidson, "Changes in Distributive Institutions," *Journal of Marketing* 34 (January, 1970), 7.

4. The earliest comprehensive discussion of administered channels, and the most cited, is Valentine F. Ridgeway, "Administration of Manufacturer-Dealer Systems," *Administrative Science Quarterly* (March, 1957), 464–467.

5. William R. Davidson, *Changes,* 8.

6. The principal types of contractual systems involving forward and backward integration are listed in Bert C. McCammon, Jr., "The Emergence and Growth . . . ," 499.

7. William R. Davidson, *Changes,* 8.

8. *Printing and Numerical Registering Co.* v. *Sampson,* 19 L.R. Equity 462 (1875) at 465.

9. *Ford Motor Co.* v. *Kirkmyer Motor Co.,* 65 F.2d 1001 (4th Cir. 1933) at 1004. Emphasis added.

10. Friedrick Kessler, "Contracts of Adhesion—Some Economic and Legal Thoughts About Freedom of Contract," *Columbia Law Review* 43 (1943), 629.

11. *Clarence Madsen* v. *Chrysler,* 261 F. Supp. (N.D. Ill., 1966) at 488. Emphasis added.

12. U.C.C., Sec. 1–102(3). See E. Allan Farnsworth, "Good Faith and Commercial Reasonableness Under the Uniform Commercial Code," *University of Chicago Law Review* 30 (1963), 666.

13. The definitive article is William L. Prosser, "The Fall of the Citadel," *Minnesota Law Review* 50 (1966), 791.

14. *Cintrone* v. *Hertz Truck Leasing,* 212 A.2d 769 (Sup. Ct. N.J. 1965).

15. *Bethlahmy* v. *Bechtel,* 415 P.2d 698 (Sup. Ct. Idaho, 1966).

16. *Siegal* v. *Chicken Delight,* 311 F. Supp. 847 (N.D. Cal. 1970); *Edwards* v. *H. & R. Block, Inc.* filed, 1970 *Trade Cases; Hoffman* v. *Socony Mobil Oil,* filed, 1970 *Trade Cases; Klinzing* v. *Shakey's, Inc.* 49 Fed. Rules Decisions 32 (E.D. Wisc. 1970); *Woddleton* v. *Credit Clearing Corp.,* filed, 1970 *Trade Cases; Halverson* v. *Convenient Food Mart, Inc.,* filed, 1970 *Trade Cases.*

17. See Donald N. Thompson, "Franchise Operations and Antitrust Law," *Journal of Retailing* 44 (Winter, 1969), 39–53.

18. William M. Evan, *Comment on Noncontractual Relations in Business,* a paper presented to the annual meeting, American Sociological Association (August, 1962), 2.

19. Quoted in Philip F. Zeidman, "The Growth and Importance of Franchising," *Remarks* at the 1967 Federal Bar Association Convention, San Francisco, California (July 28, 1967), and Small Business Administration statistics.

20. Figures from Office of Minority Business Enterprise, United States Department of Commerce.

21. Figures based principally on a survey by the Interracial Council for Business Opportunity, cited in U.S. Congress, Senate, Subcommittee on Urban and Rural Economic Development, Select Committee on Small Business, *The Impact of Franchising on Small Business,* 91st Congress, 2nd Session (1970), 155.

22. Cited in Ross B. Baxter, *Address* before annual meeting of the Center for the Study of Franchise Distribution and Smaller Business, Boston College (April 4, 1970).

23. Ibid. "Minority" includes blacks, Mexican-American, Puerto Rican, American Indian, Eskimo, and Aleut.

24. Some negative aspects of "working for someone else" are discussed in John V. Petrof, "Black Men's Views Of Advancement Opportunities In American Industry" in Philip R. McDonald, *Marketing Involvement In Society And The Economy,* Chicago: American Marketing Association (1969), 34–39.

25. Source: Fred C. Allvine, "Black Business Development," *Journal of Marketing* 34 (April, 1970), 4.

26. U.S. Department of Commerce, *Franchise Company Data for Equal Opportunity in Business,* Washington, D.C.: Department of Commerce (published approximately annually).

27. These and subsequent statistics on the franchise industry are developed in Chapter III of Donald N. Thompson, *Franchise Operations and Antitrust,* Lexington, Mass.: Health Lexington Books, D.C. Heath and Company (1971). Much of the material is reproduced from Donald N. Thompson, "Submission on the Impact of Franchising," *The Impact of Franchising on Small Business: Part II,* Washington, D.C.: Select Committee on Small Business, United States Senate (1970).

28. Harry Kursh, *The Franchise Boom* (rev. ed.), Englewood Cliffs, N.J.: Prentice Hall, Inc. (1968).

29. J. F. Atkinson, *Remarks* to Sixth Annual International Management Conference on Franchising, Boston College (April 3, 1970), and E. Patrick McGuire, "The Feasibility of Minority Group Capitalism Through Franchising," *infra.*

30. Source: J. F. Atkinson, *Remarks.*

31. *Susser* v. *Carvel Corp.,* 206 F. Supp. 636 (S.D.N.Y. 1962), at 640; *aff'd.* 332 F.2d 505 (2d Cir. 1964).

32. Sources: Bert C. McCammon, *Perspectives.*

33. The hypothesis is developed in Alfred R. Oxenfeldt and Anthony O. Kelly, "Will Successful Franchise Systems Ultimately Become Wholly-Owned Chains?," *Journal of Retailing* 44 (Winter, 1969), 69.

34. The monopolization aspect is found in *Lorain Journal Co.* v. *United States,* 342 U.S. 143 (1951).

35. *Standard Oil Co.* v. *United States,* 337 U.S. 293 (1949); see also *Tampa Electric Co.* v. *Nashville Coal Co.,* 365 U.S. 320 (1960), at 335, which may have weakened the severity of the mechanical market foreclosure rule in *Standard Stations.*

36. *Susser* v. *Carvel, op. cit.* The F.T.C. in a proceeding against Carvel under Section 5 of the F.T.C. Act on the same franchise agreement clause indicated that a trademark *alone* might not be a tying good. *Carvel Corp.,* F.T.C. Dkt. 8574 (July 19, 1965).

37. *Engbrecht* v. *Dairy Queen,* 203 F. Supp. 714 (D. Kan. 1962); *Goodyear Tire & Rubber Co.* v. *F.T.C.,* 331 F.2d 394 (7th Cir. 1964); *Atlantic Refining Co.* v. *F.T.C.,* 381 U.S. 357 (1965).

38. *Brown Shoe Co.* v. *F.T.C.,* 339 F.2d 45 (6th Cir. 1964); *reversed* 384 U.S. 316 (1966).

39. *United States* v. *Arnold, Schwinn & Co.,* 388 U.S. 350 (1967).

40. *Dehydrating Process Co.* v. *Smith,* 292 F.2d 753 (1961).

41. Joseph C. Palamountain, Jr., *The Politics of Distribution,* Cambridge, Mass.: Harvard University Press (1955), 52–56.

42. See J. L. Heskett, Louis W. Stern and Frederic J. Beier, *Bases and Uses of Power in Interorganization Relations,* a paper presented at the Vertical Marketing Systems Workshop, Northwestern University (November 6–8, 1968).

43. Louis W. Stern, "Channel Control and Inter-Organization Management," in Peter D. Bennett, ed., *Marketing and Economic Development,* Chicago: American Marketing Association (1965), 664.

44. An excellent discussion is Donald Granbois and Ronald Willett, "Patterns of Conflicting Perceptions Among Channel Members," in L. George Smith (ed.), *Reflections on Progress In Marketing,* Chicago: American Marketing Association (1965), 86–100.

45. 15 U.S.C.A. 1221 *et seq.* (1958).

46. Stewart Macaulay, "Law and Society—Changing a Continuing Relationship Between a Large Corporation and Those Who Deal With It: Auto-

mobile Manufacturers, Their Dealers, and the Legal System," *Wisconsin Law Review,* Part I (Summer, 1965), 483; Part II (Fall, 1965), 740.

47. For example, H. R. 2818, 90th Congress, 2d Sess.

48. Bruce Mallen, "Conflict and Cooperation In Marketing Channels," in L. George Smith (ed.), *Reflections On Progress In Marketing,* Chicago: American Marketing Association (1965), 83–85.

49. Kenneth E. Boulding, "The Economics of Human Conflict," in Elton B. McNeil (ed.), *The Nature of Human Conflict,* Englewood Cliffs, New Jersey: Prentice-Hall, Inc. (1965), 174–178.

50. George J. Stigler, "The Division of Labor is Limited by the Extent of the Market," *The Journal of Political Economy* LIX (June, 1951), 185; William J. Baumol, *Business Behavior, Value, and Growth,* New York: The Macmillan Company (1959); Neil Chamberlain, *A General Theory of Economic Process,* New York: Harper and Row (1955). See also Louis P. Bucklin, *A Theory of Distribution Channel Structure,* Berkeley: Institute of Business and Economic Research, University of California (1966); Bob R. Holdren, *The Structure of A Retail Market and the Market Behavior of Retail Units,* Englewood Cliffs, N.J., Prentice Hall, Inc. (1960); and similar materials.

51. Julius Margolis, "The Analysis of the Firm: Rationalism, Conventionalism, and Behaviorism," *The Journal of Business* XXXI (July, 1958), 187–199, and some of his subsequent work with Herbert A. Simon.

52. Wroe Alderson, *Marketing Behavior and Executive Action,* Homewood, Illinois: Richard D. Irwin, Inc. (1957).

53. Louis P. Bucklin, "Postponement, Speculation, and the Structure of Distribution Channels," *Journal of Marketing Research* II (February, 1965), 26–31. See also Bucklin's paper *The Economic Analysis of Channel Structure,* presented at the Vertical Marketing Systems Workshop, Northwestern University (November 6–8, 1968).

54. Joseph Palamountain, Jr., *The Politics of Distribution,* Cambridge: Harvard University Press (1955); Fritz Machlup and Martha Taber, "Bilateral Monopoly, Successive Monopoly and Vertical Integration," *Economica* (May, 1960), 101–120; E. T. Grether, "Solidarity in the Distribution Trades," *Law and Contemporary Problems* (June, 1937), 376–391.

55. E. T. Grether, *Price Control Under Fair Trade Legislation,* New York: Oxford University Press (1939); Bruce Mallen, "Conflict and Cooperation in Marketing Channels," in George Smith (ed.), *Reflections on Progress in Marketing,* Chicago: American Marketing Association (1964), 65–86; Joseph Palamountain, Jr., *op. cit.;* John Kenneth Galbraith, *American Capitalism: The Concept of Countervailing Power,* Boston: Houghton Mifflin Company (1958).

56. Bruce Mallen, "Introducing the Marketing Channel to Price Theory," *Journal of Marketing* (July, 1965), 29–33.

57. Helmy Baligh and Leon Richartz, *Vertical Market Structures,* Boston: Allyn and Bacon, Inc. (1967). See also Leon Richartz, *A Game Theoretic Formulation of Vertical Market Structures,* a paper presented to the Vertical Marketing Systems Workshop, Northwestern University (November 6–8, 1968).

58. For example U. af Trolle, *Distributionsekonomi 1,* Malmo, Sweden (1963); J. Valdelin and K. Ostrom, "On The Concept of Function Transfer," *The Swedish Journal of Economics* 68, 24–46. In English, see for example James L. Wiek, *An Analysis of The Attitudes and Behavior of Members of Channels of Distribution,* Ann Arbor, Michigan: University Microfilms (1969).

59. Lars-Gunnar Mattsson, *Integration and Efficiency in Marketing Systems,* Stockholm, Sweden: EFI (1969).

60. James G. March and Herbert A. Simon, *Organizations,* New York: John Wiley & Sons, Inc. (1958), 131; Mazafer Sherif, et al., *Intergroup Conflict and Cooperation,* Newman, Oklahoma: The University of Oklahoma Press (1961); William M. Evan, "The Organization Set: Toward a Theory of Interorganizational Relations," in James D. Thompson (ed.), *Approaches to Organizational Design,* Pittsburgh, Pa.: University of Pittsburgh Press (1966).

61. For example Philip Selznick, *Leadership in Administration,* Evanston, Illinois: Row, Peterson & Co. (1967).

62. Robert K. Merton, *Social Theory and Social Structure,* New York: The Free Press (1957); A. W. Gouldner, *Patterns of Industrial Bureaucracy,* Glencoe, Illinois: The Free Press (1957); Peter Blau, *The Dynamics of Bureaucracy,* Chicago: University of Chicago Press (1955); Richard M. Cyert and James G. March, *A Behavioral Theory of the Firm,* Englewood Cliffs, New Jersey: Prentice Hall (1963); James D. Thompson, *Organizations in Action,* New York: McGraw Hill Book Co. (1967).

63. Robert Dubin, "Industrial Conflict and Social Welfare," *Journal of Conflict Resolution* 1 (1957), 179; O. Kahn-Freund, "Intergroup Conflicts and Their Settlement," *British Journal of Sociology* 5 (1954), 193; Ralf Dahrendorf, *Class and Class Conflict in Industrial Society,* Stanford, California: Stanford University Press (1959).

64. See Alvin Gouldner, *The Coming Crisis of Western Sociology,* New York: Basic Books (1970).

65. Bert C. McCammon, Jr., *Alternative Models,* 15–22.

66. Thomas L. Berg, "Designing the Distribution System," in William Stevens (ed.), *The Social Responsibilities of Marketing,* Chicago: American Marketing Association (1967), 481–490.

67. Sidney Siegal and Lawrence E. Fouraker, *Bargaining and Group Decision Making,* New York: McGraw Hill Book Company (1960).

68. Joseph Buchan and Ernest Koenigsberg, *Scientific Inventory Management,* Englewood Cliffs, New Jersey: Prentice-Hall, Inc. (1963).

69. Arnold E. Amstutz, *Computer Simulation of Competitive Market Response,* Cambridge: MIT Press (1967).

70. See John Kennedy, "Practice and Theory in Negotiation: A Conceptual Model for Negotiation," in Frederick E. Webster, Jr. (ed.), *New Directions in Marketing,* Chicago: American Marketing Association (1965), S85–S103.

The Economic Base of Franchising

Louis P. Bucklin*

Of the many dimensions that form the relationship between agencies on different levels of a distribution channel, perhaps the most important is the extent of the role of day-to-day market pressure. Day-to-day market forces comprise the panoply of shifting prices, deals, allowances, promotions, and minor competitive crises that constitute the most visible strains of a marketing agency's work. Their presence in the interfirm relationship is manifested by detailed negotiations for each contract for the sale of goods to provide continuous adjustment to these forces. They disappear when goods are transferred as part of long-range plans where the issue is not optimal profit on each sale, but the means of better exploiting the market for the mutual advantage of both parties.

If the importance of day-to-day forces is defined as a continuum ranging from one pole, where each transaction is negotiated separately in the light of current market conditions, to the other, where the movement of goods is an automatic element part of a long-range marketing plan, then franchising as a *mode* of distribution may be said to occupy the middle ground. At the planned end of the continuum is the integrated system; at the day-to-day pole is the independent system. The demarcation between the three competing systems along the continuum is neither sharp nor clear as the operating characteristics of each system shade into the others. Nevertheless, it will be helpful to think of franchising as occupying the middle ground, with policies sensitive both to the elements of long-range planning and to the daily vicissitudes of the market.

In this article, the nature of any advantages of this middle ground will be explored and their long- and short-run consequences evaluated. There are three parts to this paper. In the first, a conceptual derivation of these advantages is undertaken. In the second, a series of models is developed as a means to exemplify further the nature of these advantages and to illustrate how firms might seek empirically to define them. The third part reports upon an empirical analysis using one of the models.

Economic Base Characteristics

From this perspective of the middle ground in market organization, five different elements of the economic base for franchising may be distin-

* University of California. The author would like to express his appreciation to Stanley F. Stasch for his comments on this essay; to the Institute of Business and Economic Research, University of California, for research support; and to Mrs. Ellen McGibbon for editorial help and typing.

guished. In terms of the long-run viability of this mode of distribution, the most important of these may be characterized as market funnel adjustment. The second, and perhaps the most interesting due to the importance of growth to the economy, is market opportunity recognition. The third is capital mobilization, the fourth is an inverse form of Russian roulette, and the last is market control.

The Market Funnel Adjustment Base

The concept of a market funnel[1] is fundamental to the understanding of why complex vertical marketing systems of any mode develop. The funnel expresses the notion that there are differential economies of scale among the various activities to be performed in the processing and distribution of products. That is to say, there are some activities which are most advantageously performed by smaller units, others which are better undertaken by larger ones. When dealing with the ultimate consumer, for example, marketing activities are usually performed better by relatively small firms or establishments. This is also apt to be true for many institutional markets, where supplies are bought in small quantities, and for the sale of such products as agricultural commodities from farms with low levels of output.

Contrarily, costs for transport, handling, inventory, and exchange may often be reduced to trifling levels when large lots are sold. The result is that when goods are to be moved any significant distance, it is generally advantageous to concentrate the flow at some point in the channnel. At this juncture, the number of organizations that perform the functional acts is reduced, permitting the remaining agencies to operate at high volumes.

The effect of these savings is that unless consumers and/or producers are either extremely large or highly concentrated in a tiny area, most channels will require functional acts to be dispersed at some *levels* and concentrated in others. The funnel describes the physical flow pattern, either as goods are concentrated from many supply sources or distributed from a central point to many local markets for further sale. Depending upon the character of the final buyer, the producer, and the distances between them, the patterns may take the form of an upright, inverted, or double funnel.

While this description of the process is exceedingly brief and simplified, it serves to establish the basis behind the division of marketing responsibilities among firms and agencies in the channel—an issue which lies at the heart of franchising. The rationale is set forth more specifically in Figure 2-1, where two sets of marketing activities, labeled F_1 and S, are employed in the channel for some product. The F_1 set represents those performed first in the sequence; agencies undertaking these will be referred to as first-level firms. The S set is performed next in the flow by second-level firms.

From Figure 2-1 we note that the optimal scale, as measured in sales of product units, for the S set is smaller than for F_1 set. Also, because of

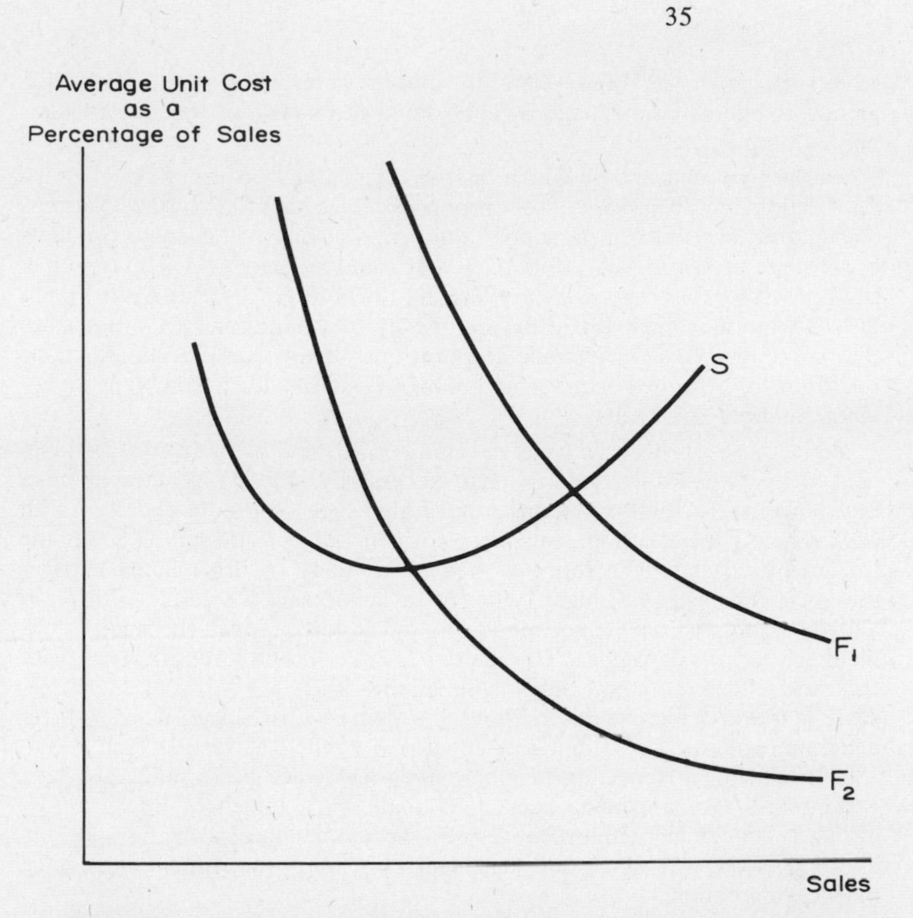

Figure 2–1. Differences in Scale Economies Between First- (F_1, F_2) and Second- (S) Level Activities in a Channel System.

the diseconomies of operating S activities at larger volumes, a combination of S and F_1 into a single agency would result in higher costs than are necessary. Under competitive conditions, we would expect different firms to emerge to specialize in each set. The picture of the inverse funnel appears from the necessary result that fewer firms will operate F_1 activities than S. In this sense, there is an outward spreading of goods from F_1 to S.

Unfortunately, all of the savings from this split cannot be passed on to the consumer. Some are used up in the operation of the market that joins the two sets of agencies in the channel. To judge by the fact that a large proportion of the innovations in large-scale trade institutions have been concerned with the improvement of this market mechanism, all too great a proportion of the savings were lost here. The department store, the chain store, the mail order house were all, among other things, agencies which gained competitive advantage by controlling the nature of this key transfer point in the funnel.

The principal means by which this was accomplished was through standardization of the product flow through both levels. Standardization was wrought in terms of central supply, uniform stocking of the same products at all units at both levels, resources, and time and mode of delivery. The savings were enormous, as exemplified by the shift from F_1 to F_2 in Figure 2-1. The term coined by Little, multilevel merchandiser, aptly describes the nature of today's large trade corporations.[2] It involves the simultaneous operation of a limited number of number *F* units with a commensurately larger number of *S* units.

While there has been, in general, a long-term trend away from traditional central markets, which has, in turn, necessarily shifted agencies in most independent distributive systems toward this type of accommodation with each other,[3] these developments have not generally progressed as far as the integrated systems. The result is that while many of these internal paramarket mechanisms are highly efficient in connecting wholesale with retail activities, there is some concomitant loss in rapport between the retail establishment and the consumer. The standardization at one level interferes with the most effective market adjustment at the other. As some of the large-scale, multilevel merchandisers grew, the pain in this lack of flexibility became more sharp. The debilitating effect was wryly described by one A & P executive who, in reflecting his company's lackluster performance of late, commented "We are being pecked to death by a bunch of ducks."[4] The author is acquainted with executives of a western chain of women's specialty clothing shops, who agree that their central buying procedures inhibit local market adaptation.

The nature of this duck syndrome is given further exemplification in Figure 2-2. System costs are portrayed on the vertical axis; the degree of standardization in wholesale and retail activities is on the right. With increasing standardization, the cost of handling goods at wholesale declines dramatically. At the same time, the inflexibility at retail increases as individual units are less and less able to adjust to the heterogeneous needs of the retail community. One might hypothesize that the larger the multilevel merchandising firm, the higher this entire *S* curve would be.

The sum of the S_1 and *F* curves represent the total costs of distribution for the product and provides a means of assessing the funnel adjustment base for the franchise system. Specifically, the degree of standardization obtainable through independent, franchise, and integrated channel systems may be arranged on a continuum that conceptually parallels that of the degree of day-to-day market influence. The absence of long-term planning makes the independent freer to tap supplies from a number of different

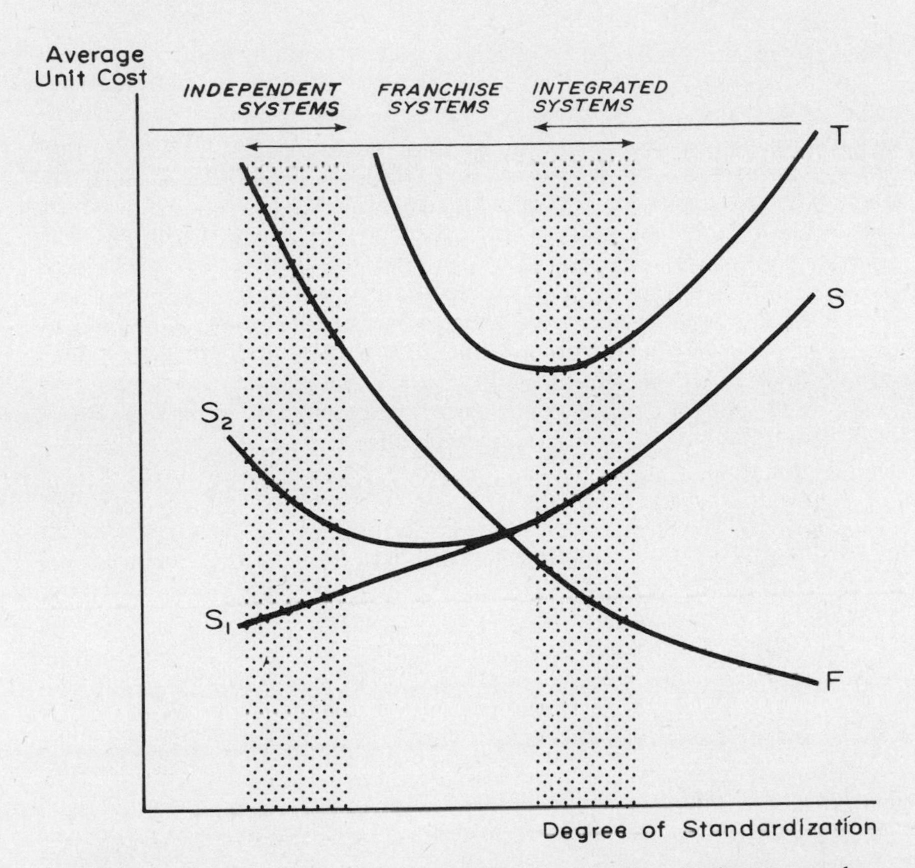

Figure 2-2. The Economic Trade-Off between Standardization and Market Adjustment in Competing Modes of Distribution for First- (*F*) and Second- (*S*) Level Activity Costs.

funnels to adapt to his market. The individual chain store manager is the most circumscribed, while the franchise operator is in the middle. Of course, overlaps exist.

More specifically to the point, the primary long-term economic base of franchising is derived from an opportunity, through a moderate degree of organization, to tap the economies of standardization that exist within activities at the wholesale level. Through independent ownership, however, this system also has the capacity to adjust to local market conditions. The solidity of this base will depend, of course, directly upon the degree of market heterogeneity faced by individual retail units and by the extent of the success integrated merchants come to enjoy in developing decentralized plans of administration.

Market Opportunity Recognition Base

In contrast to franchise channel systems developed early in this century which were not spawned from any sharpness of market vision, much of the recent surge is based precisely upon that kind of recognition and foresight. The take-home market for cooked, ready-to-eat food was snatched brazenly away from a somnolent grocery trade that, despite the increasing sales of ready-to-cook frozen dinners, did not perceive itself to be in the restaurant business. The hardware store only sold tools; it never rented them. Until recently, automobile dealers were afflicted by the same view. The pleas of these same agencies that automobile manufacturers stop direct sales to car-renting firms, which walked off with a trade that the dealers might have readily held, show the typical ironies provided by changes in distribution.

In short, the franchise business has become a field where freshly perceived new market needs can be quickly served, with the hallmarks of success awarded to the most innovative agencies. One key has been to find, in the array of services provided in a larger business, some single element that has been partially or wholly neglected. This element, then, becomes the heart of the new specialized business especially dedicated to it. Another has been to standardize the level of performance of some existing business at some public level never uniformly reached by independents (in this sense a new economic base may be formed vis-à-vis independents as shown in curve S_2 in Figure 2-2). Public response to these new standards clearly shows that for many products (and services, in particular) when the alternatives are between uncertainty in buying and not buying at all, the consumer's choice is all too frequently the latter.

Hence, growth is an economic base for franchising. It thrives upon resistance to change endemic to most mature forms of distribution. Barriers to entry to new fields that would defy the independent have been systematically battered down. In this mode, it represents an innovation in distribution as important as the chain store. In the future, when we may expect barriers to entry at retail to rise, franchising will represent a much-needed competitive force.

Capital Mobilization Base

Historically, middlemen served as the first point for the accumulation of risk capital. For those with little capital to aid in the sale of the goods they made—and few producers did not fall into this category—the merchant wholesaler provided the major avenue of commerce because of his ability to finance. In a more highly developed economy, capital resources are available from a variety of sources (many, ironically, founded by merchant wholesalers longing for a less arduous life). This effect has been one, albeit one among many, which has diminished the importance of the wholesaler in the field of distribution.

Hence, while in the normal course of trade growth the procurement of caiptal does not ordinarily loom as a major barrier, this is not invariably true for those fields where demand increases at a rate significantly above average. When the void is filled by franchising activities, this mode of distribution may be seen in a new light. Franchising is an extraordinarily effective means of mobilizing and organizing new sources of capital. Without doubt, it represents a means of financing that is fully as important as the major stock and bond markets. It is unfortunate that this facet of the business has been recognized only belatedly and brought (all too slowly and painfully, at that) under the same type of public regulation.

Inverse Russian Roulette Base

To devotees of the sport of gambling, Russian roulette is the supreme game in which one places a single cartridge in a revolver, spins the bullet chamber, places the gun to his head, and squeezes the trigger. Franchising may be just this kind of game, except that five of the bullet chambers are loaded instead of just one. Fortunately, the cartridges are packed only with such niceties as seventy-hour work weeks and a minimum-wage-busting pay scale, rather than with gunpowder. The empty chamber consists of that long-awaited pile of riches at the end of the rainbow.

The many stories that emerge from the publicity agents and the trade press of the profits earned by franchisees (how many are apocryphal?) are undoubtedly atypical. Moreover, it is not clear that these profits represent an accurate accounting of the extensive overtime contributed by the franchisee and other members of his family. It is an old truism that people will work for themselves at half the price they will for someone else (a rather uncomfortable thought to any author in the midst of writing an article!). The chance to strike it rich, as clearly evidenced by some of the franchisees who have emerged with integrated chains of their own, is a powerful incentive.[5] For most, however, it seems probable that their extra hours are repaid more in dreams of glory than in real riches.

To the extent that the true expected value of the returns from a potential franchisee's labor and capital is actually the same as his perceptions of it (or what the newspaper advertisements say it is), it would be difficult to condemn this distribution mode. Nevertheless, it is probably true that the system provides a relatively low-cost distributive mechanism. In viewing the differences in labor cost between chain store supermarkets and those of franchisees, a decided advantage may be seen for the latter.[6] Lower wages appear throughout his various scales. Beyond the extra energy provided by the franchisee and his family, the explanation behind this is not clear. It may reflect barriers to unionism in entrepreneur-operated establishments, better exploitation of local labor markets, or the employment of less capable help. Whatever the reason, one of the elements of the economic base of franchising is the lower labor costs obtained. Where the retail units are particularly small, this wage advantage can be a dominant factor.

Market Control Base

Whether this final condition that makes franchising a going mode of distribution can be called part of its economic base is arguable. Perhaps it is better defined as a kind of negative force which prevents the evolution of other marketing modes. It emanates from the power of market control that franchisors in some industries have obtained over the final customer. This power relegates the role of the second-level firm in the system to one which, while important in the process, is nevertheless not fundamentally secure. The second-level firm, one could say, is replaceable.

This replaceability may stem from a number of sources. It may come through distinctive product differentiation of highly technical machines controlled by the first-level firm. It may derive from the force of large-scale advertising campaigns which are of major significance in affecting consumer product choice. Lastly, it may appear where the franchisee has relatively few good alternatives. His capital is sunk, his organization is tuned to the development of someone else's product, and, perhaps most important of all, there may be no opportunities to secure a comparable franchise from another source. Presumably these had been allocated some time ago because of highly selective or exclusive distribution policies practiced by franchisors and, often, the successful first-level firms—for example, automobile manufacturers.

Under conditions such as these, the franchisor not only is able to control most aspects of the franchisee's business, but he has the peace of mind that comes from knowing his best customers are tied to him by powerful bonds that only he can loosen. While this undoubtedly overstates the case in the minds of many franchisors, it is nevertheless apparent that where fear of loss of these intermediary customers exists, forward integration is a likely result. The lines that tie a gasoline jobber to his branded supplier are not always strong. Refiners respond through forward integration.[7] The cords that held ready-mix concrete producers to their cement suppliers were fraying. Forward integration was the result to the extent not subsequently blocked by Federal Trade Commission action.[8]

In sum, the advantages that franchising possesses in many industries, as enumerated earlier, may be sufficient to permit this mode of distribution to exist as long as the risk of loss to other first-level firms of existing franchisees is not high. Where this risk appears to be strong, the possible loss of franchise system economies (due to greater inefficiencies in forward integration) pales in the light of the damage that the loss of volume would wreak.

Models of the Channel System

Ideally, it would be desirable to develop macro-type models of channel systems to evaluate these economic base hypotheses. Unfortunately, both the paucity of data and the great variety to be found in all three modes of distribution make this a difficult, if not impossible, task. Alternatively, we turn to the development of some micro-oriented models of channel systems which offer more promise of empirical testing.

The Basic Marketing Management Model

A basic marketing management model for the operation of the firm with profit maximization as its goal may be taken as a starting point.[9] The sales function for the first-level firm is determined by price and the extent of use of various marketing activities that affect customer patronage. Specifically:

$$q = \phi_1(p,v) \tag{1}$$

$$R = qp = p\phi_1(p,v), \tag{2}$$

where q is the quantity of goods sold, p is their price, v is the vector of marketing activities, and R is sales volume.

Costs of operating the firm stem from the production, or procurement of the product, and the expenses incurred from the level of operation maintained for the various marketing activities:

$$C = \phi_2(q) + \phi_3(v) \qquad or$$

$$C = \phi_2(\phi_1(p,v)) + \phi_3(v). \tag{3}$$

Profits represent the difference between sales and costs:

$$\Pi = R - C = p\phi_1(p,v) - \phi_2(\phi_1(p,v)) - \phi_3(v). \tag{4}$$

The firm maximizes its profits by adjusting price and its set of marketing activities in such a way as to allocate dollars into each input so that the marginal return is equal to the marginal cost. Mathematically, this point is determined in the model by taking the partial derivatives of Π with respect to price and to the n marketing-mix elements of the vector, v. The resulting $n + 1$ equations are set equal to zero, and solutions are derived for the optimal levels for p and the vector, v.

Recursive Models of the Vertical Marketing System

Within the context of this basic marketing model (4), the role of other agencies in the firm's distributive system is implicit but not visible. To bring (4) into the domain of channel analysis, we may make explicit consideration of the impact of the behavior of these other agencies through a recursive model of the system. For the sake of simplicity, only two adjoining levels of a system will be examined, for example, manufacturer-wholesaler, manufacturer-retailer, or wholesaler-retailer. Separate models will be developed for independent, franchise, and integrated systems.

The Independent Systems. In this system, the institutions of the channel may develop long-term relationships with each other. None of these ties, however, are regarded as representing contractual relationships beyond those necessary for each individual transaction. The perspective is from the first-level firm.

To model this, the activities that constitute the vector, v, of (1) are divided into two parts, u and w. The first group, comprising the vector u, are functions designed to influence the second-level institutions within the system. The second, w, consists of activities to affect the final buyer or third level of the system.

In the recursive model, the decisions of the firm are disaggregated and ordered so as to show how the results of one provide the necessary input to another. We start with the recruiting of second-level agencies for the firm's channel. This is expressed as the function:

$$D = \phi_1(g,P,u,w), \tag{5}$$

where D is the number of such agencies, P is the retail price, g the firm's discount to these agencies, u its effort to recruit them, and w the effort the firm makes to convince third-level buyers to use its products. Equation (5) is, in effect, the inducement the first-level firm uses to gain distribution for its product.

A subsequent decision concerns the degree of promotional effort the second-level agencies will provide. This is, in part, a function of the number of such agencies and, again, the inducements the first-level firm makes to encourage such promotion, *viz.:*

$$V = \phi_2(D,g,P,u,w), \tag{6}$$

where V is the level of promotional effort by second-level firms. To the extent that this might be further disaggregated into a number of different types of promotional effort, a set of functions similar to (6) would be necessary.

The quantity sold (q) by the first-level firm may now be set forth as follows:

$$q = \phi_3(P,V,D,w). \tag{7}$$

Decisions made previously with respect to gaining second-level support determine q as well as the retail price and the amount of promotion to third-level buyers.

The complete model for the first level firm's revenues is:

$$R = (1 - g)Pq. \tag{8}$$

The Franchise System. The modeling of the exchange of commitments that characterizes a traditional franchise system involves little change in the basic nature of the recursive framework established for the independent system. Indeed, in large measure, the distinction is a matter of the first-level firm reallocating its expenditures for the various services provided from those of a short-term nature to long term. The abandonment of the salesman and the adoption of consultant and advisory services are characteristic of this shift. However, this is nothing more than a shift of resources among the various elements of the u vector in (5) and (6).

In addition to this shift, the commitment on the part of the first-level firm may involve an altered g. Under the independent system, there may be significant limitations on the extent to which the first-level firm can employ changes in gross margin as a tactic. Competitive retaliation is apt to be swift and the initial advantage is soon lost. Franchising opens up the opportunity for this type of price competition because of the long-term patronage commitments received in exchange from the franchisees. Concomitant price reductions made by other first-level firms will be effectively constrained in their impact, particularly over the short term.

The impact of these commitments appears in the improved functional relationship between changes in D, the number of second-level firms, and R, the franchisor's sales volume. They have the effect of concentrating the franchisee's purchases at a single source. To the extent that they can extend the franchisee's competitive capabilities in the local market, perhaps because of the aggregate benefits of adopting the franchisor's program and standardized marketing mix, sales per second-level unit are further increased.

The franchise operation may also have impact upon long-range cost curves of firms in both levels. Because of the relatively greater assurance of patronage, the franchisor may be more willing to expand his operation along his long-run cost curve, providing him with significant economies of scale. Similarly, franchisees may be more willing to invest in activities such as brand-name advertising and the construction of larger and more modern retail facilities when they are more confident of their source of supply. Commitment to long-term relationships is, of course, a relative term. The commitment could bind the parties for no more than a month beyond the willingness of one to break the relationship. Or, like the Coca Cola contracts, they could bind the institutions for their entire corporate life.

A somewhat different model, however, requires development for the franchising systems of the 1960s. Here, revenues may be a function not only of a percentage, r, of a franchisee's sales volume, but the earnings derived from a franchise fee. The revenues from these sources are characterized in (9):

$$R = rP\Omega_1(P,V,D,w) + iD(l - \Omega_2(u)). \qquad (9)$$

Here, the first term on the right-hand side measures revenues from the sales charge, r, price, P, and the quantity function, Ω_1. Income from franchise fees is determined by the excess of the franchise fee, l, over costs of establishing the franchise unit, $\Omega_2(u)$, times the interest rate, i, times number of franchisees, D.

The interesting element of this model would be the partial derivative, $\partial D/\partial l$, measuring the response of second-level firms to changes in the franchise fee. If this were strongly negative, then, to the extent that the franchisor was seriously concerned with the long-run aspects of his business, nominal franchise fees might be in order. Even if it were only mildly negative, one may wonder whether anything more than a nominal fee would be justified. A four percent sales charge on a franchisee's sales volume of from $100,000 to $200,000 per annum would be significantly larger than the return from any reasonable franchise fee for a business of this size.

The Integrated System. The integrated system is distinguished by the presence of owned second-level units. The ability of these units to attract customers and the operating costs of these units are the major elements of concern. If h may be regarded as the gross margin percentage necessary to operate these units and cover opportunity capital costs, then a model parallel to that of the traditional franchise system may be employed:

$$R = (1 - h)p\psi_1(P,V,D,w). \qquad (10)$$

If $(h + f) > g$, where $f = (l - \Omega_2(u))$, or franchise fee per outlet, then the franchisor will turn to the operation of his own units whenever

$$q_i/q_f > (1 - g)/(1 - h + f),$$

where q_i and q_f represent optimal quantities sold for the integrated and franchise system, respectively.

Some other factors, of course, may come into play in the integrated system. Costs of providing services to owned second-level units may prove to be less than in other systems, and greater efficiencies may be obtained in the operation of logistic support. To the extent that the operation of the entire system reduces risk at both levels, then, again, larger capital investments may be forthcoming. These might reduce the level of h as well as support services.

In comparison with other modes of distribution, a more complex issue emerges where the price, P, to the third-stage buyer cannot be wholly controlled by those first-stage firms. Recent legal decisions, for example, have weakened the ability of the franchisor to dictate price. The result is that where there is some territorial overlap among franchisees, a tendency for price instability at the local level occurs. This, in turn, may restrict the ability of the franchisor to locate as many franchisees in a given territory as he would like.

The problem is comparable to the fair trade policy issue where producers trade higher margins for larger numbers of retail outlets. Given relatively low propensities for consumers to shop, the first-level firm finds this trade-off advantageous. Similarly, in the present situation an inability to control competition effectively among second-level units of a franchise system through fair trade laws or other mechanisms may favor the integrated system which is not subject to this problem.

Combined Franchised and Integrated Systems

Combined franchised and integrated systems may be generated from this system of models by introducing a capital constraint. Second-level units, then, are of two types, with

$$D = D_f + D_i.$$

Total capital, M is available to the firm for use in either franchising new units or owning them at a rate of kP_f and jP_i or, more specifically,

$$M = kD_f + jD_i. \qquad (11)$$

Where $k < j$, and $g \simeq h + f$, then capital-shy firms will clearly tend toward the operation of franchise as opposed to integrated systems. The precise extent may be derived by employing (11) as a constraint on (10).

In some circumstances, g and h may not be equal, but specific market segments exist where one is superior to the other. Such circumstances may frequently appear in smaller markets where the necessarily smaller second-level unit may be more effectively operated as a franchised unit. In larger markets, the distinction between g and h may not be as great, or may favor h. The result is that the distribution of franchised and owned units is a function of the frequency distribution of market sizes which the first-level firm has entered. In this instance, different parameters for (10) would be developed for each market size.

Models of Interdependent Systems

One possible weakness in the recursive model of independent and franchise modes of distribution is the absence of any recognition of interdependencies in the system. By these we mean reactions internal to the system of one agency to another. The problem is equivalent to that encountered in the construction of models of pricing by oligopolists. Price reductions by one firm may elicit actions by others. In this manner the individual oligopolist loses some of his ability to adjust to his market. The analogy carries over to the channel system. Here the first-level firm may lose some of its ability to control its system closely.

For example, second-level firms may react to changes in the sales volume of the first-level firm. Such changes will be reflected not only in the state of operations of second-level firms, but will act as a measure of their confidence in the leadership of the first-level operator. Second-level firms may react by altering their willingness to maintain their membership in the system. They may, concurrently, change the level of support provided the first-level firm. The reaction takes the form of a kind of bandwagon effect.

This type of interaction in the system may be modeled through a set of simultaneous equations. One such set is:

$$R = \theta_1(P,D,V,w) \qquad (12)$$

$$D = \theta_2(P,V,R,u) \qquad (13)$$

$$V = \theta_3(P,D,R,u), \qquad (14)$$

where the notation carries over from the previous section. Given the idiosyncracies of different product and service fields, all three of these equations may be unnecessary. Much depends upon the purchasing patterns of buyers in the third level. For example, in the fast-food restaurant business, the level of promotion, V, may be relatively unimportant (or indistinguishable from) the number of outlets available. In this situation, it might be possible to model adequately the circumstances with only (12) and (13). However, in the case of the distribution of steel and aluminum products through wholesalers, the buying habits of metal users permit a single second-level firm to reach logistically all such third-level buyers, even in a very large metropolitan trading area. The important factor, then, is the sales promotion provided by these wholesalers. The size of the second-level firm sales force becomes the critical factor. Given fluctuations in this coverage, (12) and (14) might sufficiently model the system.

To exemplify this type of interaction further, let us examine Figure 2-3, where a system consisting of (12), labeled *D*, and (13), labeled *R*, is depicted. Both functions have positive slopes. Declining returns to additional second-level units are shown for (12), with other revenue-affecting factors being held constant. In (13), second-level firms are shown to respond linearly to changes in sales of the first-level operator. Again, other factors such as u are being held constant. The intersection of the two equations defines the equilibrium for the system, given u. Revenues and the number of second-level units are determined simultaneously at R_e and D_e.

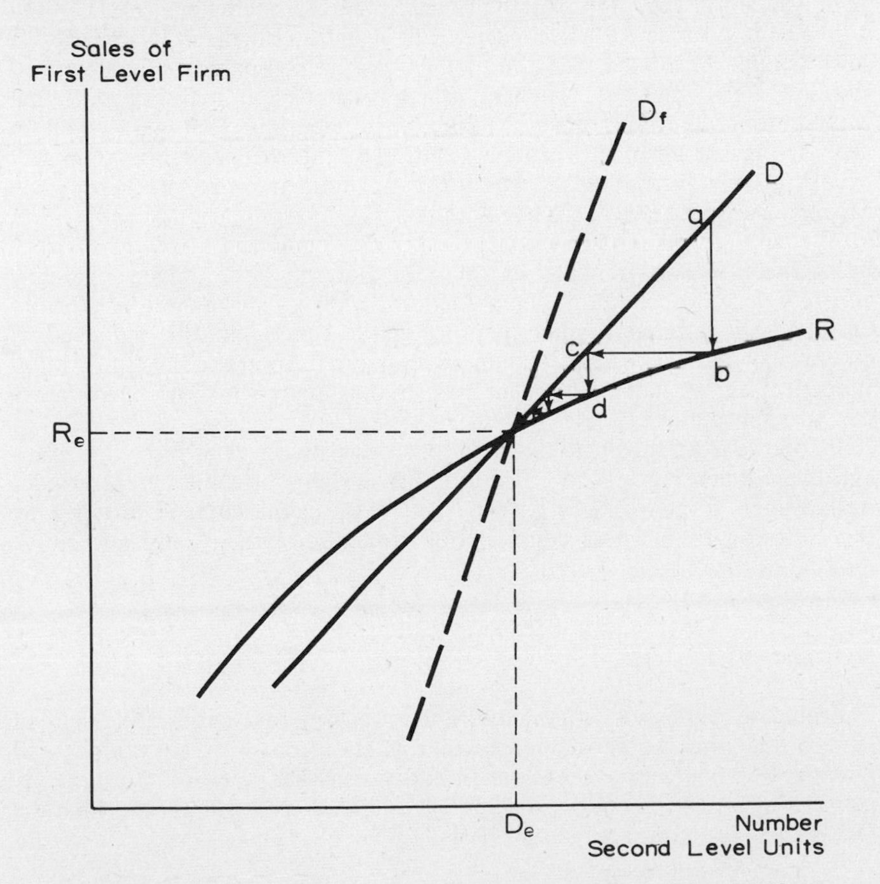

Figure 2-3. The Equilibrium between First-Level Firm Sales and Number of Second-Level Units in an Interdependent Distributive System.

Equilibrium is reached, to look ahead to the next topic for a moment, in the following manner. If, by some means, the first-level operator had signed up a distributors for its product, sales would be determined by the R function at b. However, we see from function D that this, in turn, would only support c second-level units. With the fallout from a to c in distributors, sales again shrink to d. The process is repeated until the equilibrium is reached. In this connection, it is worth noting that if the slope of D were less than that of R, the process of adjustment just developed results in an unstable system with the potential of exploding or collapsing.

In using this model to distinguish between independent and franchised distributive modes, the differences are more likely to appear in the parameters of the model rather than as a need to change its structure. Specifically, it is hypothesized that the response rate of second-level firms to sales, the slope of (13), will be steeper for franchise than for independent systems. This is noted in Figure 2-3 by the function, D_f. A steep slope implies both a greater reluctance for a second-level firm to be influenced by changes in sales volume in his decision to enter or exit as compared to independent systems. Entry into the franchise system will usually require additional capital resources committed to a long-term program. Exit may result in loss of some or all of this capital. Contrarily, the independent system will usually not involve capital changes of the magnitude required by franchising. Movement in and out is easier and less risky.

The implication of this distinction for the operating characteristics of independent versus franchise systems is that the latter, given relatively constant demand conditions, should exhibit a far greater degree of stability of distribution network than the former. Reactions in the independent sector may be like greased lightning compared to those in franchising. Indeed, exit from the latter system may involve many which are involuntary due to bankruptcy.

It follows from this logic that relationships between franchisee and franchisor are much more likely to be at either extreme of some love-hate continuum than in independent systems. Bitterness in the latter is curtailed by the cessation of business contact. For franchisees, their only alternative may be to turn to the courts.

Dynamic Models

From this discussion of stability, it is apparent that another element of system that must be considered further is the process of adjustment and growth. For this purpose, we will initially examine some of the dynamic properties implied by our static model and then proceed to consider the factor of time upon more direct basis.

The Static Channel Multiplier. The dynamic element of the comparative static model of Figure 2-3 may be illustrated through the concept of a channel multiplier. To do this, let us simplify the terms of our model somewhat by defining three basic parameters, the coefficients α, β, and γ. Alpha, as shown below, represents the rate of response of first-level firm sales to the number of second-level units. Beta measures the system membership sensitivity of second-level units to revenues. (The dependent variable here could just as well have been second-level unit promotion.) Gamma reflects the power of the first-level firm to affect second-level unit behavior directly through exercise of various control mechanisms, u.

$$R = \alpha D$$

$$D = \beta R + \gamma u$$

Solving this system for R results in:

$$R = \gamma u / (1 - \alpha\beta), \qquad (15)$$

where $(1 - \alpha\beta)$ is the channel multiplier. Where sales are measured in dollars, α should be a rather large number and β a very small one. Their product should be greater than zero, but less than one. The multiplier reflects the change in first-level firm revenues that a change in the extent of its efforts, u, would have.

The economic base of the system, then, is defined by these three parameters. The higher α and β are (that is, the closer their product approaches to one), the greater the long-run impact that any changes in u will have upon the first-level firms' revenues. The larger γ is, the better the firm is able to control its system with expenditure of a relatively low level of resources. In general, one would expect diminishing returns to occur for γu and that this term would be nonlinear.

Usually, we may hypothesize that α and γ are higher for franchise systems than for the independent. β should be lower. However, until more statistical data are available on how current marketing plan systems behave when sales slide, one might regard this as an unproved contention. Nevertheless, for the older, more traditionally oriented franchise systems, it does not seem unreasonable to regard β as lower.

The Dynamic Channel Multiplier. Though the static multiplier provides some insight into opportunities for expansion or contraction, the path the adjustment takes is not specified. Adjustment, in terms of that model, takes place instantaneously. Adjustment actually derives from lags within the system as one component accommodates the other. In terms of the two equations used for the static multiplier, a number of possible lags might be incorporated. Of these, perhaps the most significant is the translation of intentions to construct new outlets into going entities. This perspective may be expressed in period analysis as follows, with t as a given length of time:

$$R_t = \alpha D_t \tag{16}$$

$$D_t = \beta R_{t-1} + \gamma u_t. \tag{17}$$

The substitution of (16) into (15) results in a first-order difference equation:

$$R_t = \alpha\beta R_{t-1} + \gamma u. \qquad 1 > \alpha\beta > 0$$

The solution to this new equation is:[10]

$$R_t = [R_0 - \gamma u_t/(1 - \alpha\beta)](\alpha\beta)^t + \gamma u_t/(1 - \alpha\beta). \tag{18}$$

R_0 represents some arbitrary starting point, and $(1 - \alpha\beta)$ the static channel multiplier.

In the long run, (18) produces the same results as (14) insofar as $\alpha\beta$ is between one and zero. As t approaches infinity, the first expression disappears. If we accept t as years, the equation specifies the annual adjustment process through which the system may be expected to pass to reach equilibrium. The first expression also reveals the extent of the adjustment, if any, that must be made. The greater the difference between the arbitrary starting point, R_0, and the ultimate equilibrium point, $\gamma u_t/(1 - \alpha\beta)$, then the larger is the nature of the adjustment to be made. If $R_0 = \gamma u_t/(1 - \alpha\beta)$, then clearly no adjustment is necessary as the first term of the expression is again zero.

The opportunity to specify t as equal to any time period ranging from, say, one month to a year, provides another parameter of the model for purposes of distinguishing between the independent and franchise systems. While much would depend upon the type of product being sold, the general trend in modern franchise systems to construct new second-level unit facilities may cause t to be extended. However, where independents must also make new investment, the planning and standardized procedures of franchised systems may make t relatively shorter in these circumstances.

In addition to the added advantage of the time perspective, we may reintroduce the integrated system through this model. Since (17) is based upon a bandwagon-type effect, whereby entrepreneurs outside of the system clamor to be inside (or vice versa), the relationship would presumably be inappropriate for the chain organization. However, with the emphasis on time, the equation may be restructured to be capital constraints on the growth of the chain.

More precisely, one may conceive of β being equal to some rate of cash flow (derived from sales) divided by the capital requirements for a second-level unit. The greater this capital flow, or the lower the capital requirements per unit, the higher the coefficient β and the faster the response of the integrated firm to new market opportunities. As a consequence, unless the firm has access to a large pool of its own resources, or is willing to dilute its equity to construct new units, then this capital constraint will hold and provide a real restriction on growth. In all likelihood, this capital flow coefficient, β, is likely to be significantly smaller than the bandwagon coefficient, β, for the franchise firm. This, then, provides the growth role of the franchise system.

Long-Term Growth. A final consideration in the construction of models for the vertical marketing system regards long-term growth. To this point, growth has been limited to the extent of the promotional effort, u_1, of the first-level firm. Market potential has not been explicitly considered.

To accommodate this factor, the revenue equation for the system may be rewritten as a function of both the number of outlets and the buying power of third-level purchasers. The new system of equations is:

$$R_t = \alpha D_t + \delta Y_0(1 + g) \qquad (19)$$

$$D_t = \beta R_{t-1}, \qquad (20)$$

where δY_0 is the proportion of available income that third-level buyers allocated to this product in time period t_0. The rate of growth of demand from this point in time is g.

Substituting (20) into (19) creates, again, a first-order difference equation whose solution is:

$$R_t = \left[R_0 - \frac{\delta Y_0(1 + g)^t}{1 - \alpha\beta} \right] (\alpha\beta)^t + \frac{\delta Y_0(1 + g)^t}{1 - \alpha\beta},$$

where the channel multiplier again appears as $(1 - \alpha\beta)$ and S_0 is the starting point for the system, together with L_0. As in the previous model, the first expression damps out over time as t approaches a large number $(\alpha\beta < 1)$. The long-run rate of growth parallels that of the market and equals

$$\frac{\delta Y_0(1 + g)^t}{1 - \alpha\beta}.$$

If R_0 is less than this expression at $t = 0$, then the rate of growth of the system will be somewhat higher than g as previously unclaimed opportunities and new potential are realized. In essence, this equation modifies R in Figure 2-3 so that R is annually shifted upward due to regular gains in income.

The growth of any channel system, as a consequence, may be seen as being composed of two parts. One involves the regular growth rate of the customers for its products. The second is representative of an initial exploitation of that opportunity. The first flush of excitement must inevitably give way to a slower pace, an aspect of distribution in this country which has been shown in the development of many new market agencies.

To the extent that the market potential term should be reduced by growth from competing systems—franchise, independent, or chain—then the response rate of the first-level firm's own channel is crucial. Given similar rates of attraction, as measured by the parameter α in the model, the difference is in β and t. The system that can halve its response rate gains an important market advantage and one that will be difficult to dislodge. For this reason, the integrated system may well give way to the franchise if the capital requirements for the latter generate too slow a response to growth opportunities.

Empirical Analysis

Review of a small econometric study conducted by the author may be of some value in providing some empirical perspective of the nature of the systems just discussed. A manufacturer of men's wearing apparel with national distribution volunteered to make available data on its distributive system. In the continuum of relationships between manufacturer and retailer, it could not be said that formal franchise contracts were signed with outlets. Yet, relationships tended to be long term and extended to many consultative arrangements and loyalty on the part of all members.

Unit of Analysis

In this type of study, the unit of analysis is characterized by the nature of the basic observations which are statistically treated. Units might be persons, transactions, firms—among an infinite number of possibilities. In the present instance, the choice lay between some temporal base, such as a year, or a cross-sectional base, such as some geographical unit. The latter was selected, partly because it was the most accessible. More importantly, it was felt that this unit was crucial to the effective analysis of channel systems.

This conclusion is drawn from the nature of the alpha coefficient of the revenue response to second-level units, as, for example, (19). Use of the first-level firm's annual sales data would encompass results from all geographical regions. This would, for most systems, make it apparent that alpha would be a linear coefficient throughout much of the firm's expansion. Any number of new second-level units could be added, and each would contribute new volume.

Yet, few firms are in such a position to expand nationwide in this fashion. Most expand outward from a given base of operation. This provides logistic, promotional, and managerial advantages. As a consequence, the important relationship between sales and outlets is not the one that is generated by the national data, but the one that emanates from each major trading area that the firm invades. Here, a firm may find its sales response from an expansion in number of outlets to be far from linear.

Much depends upon the nature of the product, the convenience or shopping orientation of consumers, the density of distribution of competing products, and the nature of the attitudes of the retailers whose help is enlisted. From Figure 2-4, three different patterns may be seen. In brief, the linear relationship characterized by function *A* is more likely to be found where consumers are highly convenience oriented, the distribution of competitive products is relatively dense, and retailers either handle many different types of products or are relatively small. Function *C*, on the other hand, is characterized by products for which consumer preference is relatively strong, competitive distribution is relatively limited, and retail image or promotion requirements are relatively high. The pattern displayed by function *B* represents a blend of the elements of the other two.

Under these conditions, it may be seen that each major market for the firm is a separate entity calling for special treatment and concern. For purposes of the study of distributive systems, the use of market cross-sections appears particularly necessary. The aggregate data would obscure the conditions producing good relationships between the levels with those creating the bad.

The issue of analytical unit provides one further thorn in terms of the definition of major market. The appropriate size was not clear. Too small a space would create territories where the proportion of apparel, either imported or exported, was high relative to internal consumption and purchases within the boundaries. This would yield misleading sales' data. On the other hand, an unduly large unit would enhance the risk of uneven patterns of distribution within the territory. The problem of the national market would, as a consequence, simply be recreated on a small scale and the data would again be too gross.

Early in the study it had been hoped that counties could serve as the basic unit. However, initial attempts to work with the data at this level revealed counties to be far from self-sufficient in retail sales. Hence, Standard Metropolitan Statistical Areas (SMSAs) were adopted as the only reasonable alternative. Seventy-five were randomly selected from three categories distinguished by population size, the dividing points being 200,000 and 500,000 people.

The Endogenous Variables

The data were made available by the company on magnetic tape and included the sales volume for the year 1965 for each retail customer. From

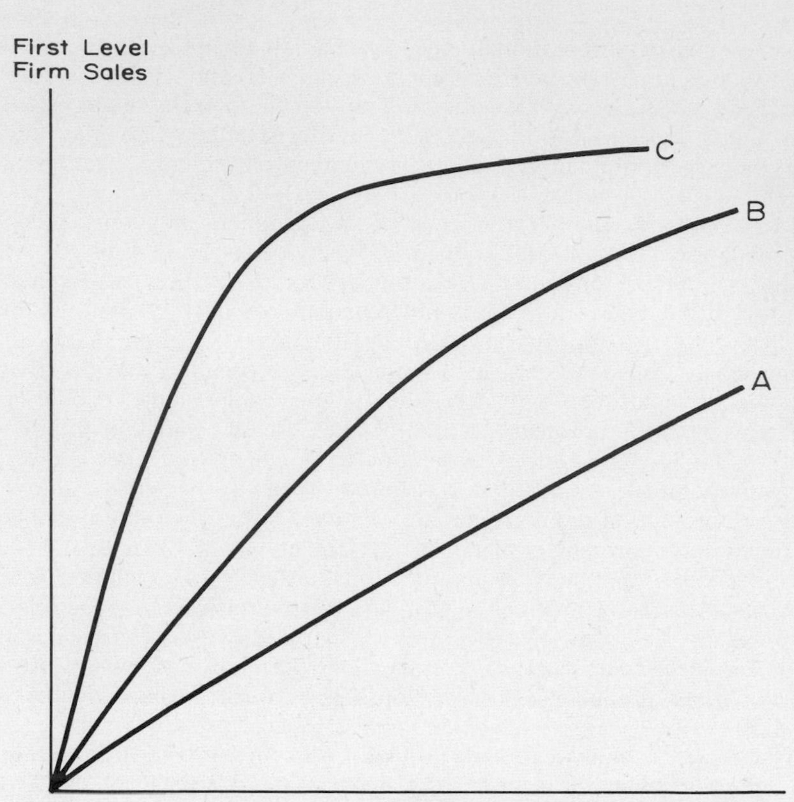

Figure 2-4. Alternative Response Rates of First-Level Firm Sales to Changes in the Number of Second-Level Firms Within a Trading Area.

this base, it was possible to obtain measures of the number of customers and total company sales within each of the seventy-five sample areas. Unfortunately, company records on the volume of retail promotion did not exist. Because of colinearities, the absence of this variable could possibly bias upward the α coefficient derived from the use of the two-equation model. The extent of such bias is impossible to ascertain.

Derivation of the company data for the two-equation model, however, proved to be only the first of a number of problems. Observation of the data showed wide differences in terms of sales volume and the number of retailers—obviously not attributable to variations in penetration or success. This meant that a relatively weak penetration into a large territory might still be productive of a higher sales volume than a relatively greater penetration into a weaker territory. Some means of adjusting the endogenous variables for market size and the number of men's clothing retailers was required.

The problem posed by this difference in size of the units of analysis was by-passed by transforming company sales in each territory into a new variable—percentage market share. Because industry sales by territory were not available, this number was estimated separately from the 1960–1961 *Survey of Consumer Expenditures* of the Bureau of Labor Statistics and the 1966 *Survey of Buying Power* developed by *Sales Management* magazine. The consumer expenditure survey, based upon 14,000 families, included a detailed breakdown of household purchases by product class as well as by related demographics. Certain of the latter variables, for which current information was available by small geographic units in the *Survey of Buying Power,* were selected as tentative predictors of household purchases of men's outerwear. This category, though considerably broader than the line sold by the company, was the closest approximation to sales that could be secured.

The four independent variables used were family size, family income, total retail expenditures, and total apparel expenditures. Possible regional differences in outerwear purchases due to climatic conditions were investigated by computing four different regressions for major components of the nation. Because differences proved to be only minor in all but a few cases, a single equation was employed to predict market potential for each of the seventy-five SMSAs in the sample.

The second endogenous variable in the system, the number of distributors carrying the company products in each of the markets required a parallel form of adjustment. To do this, a distributor density ratio, or the number of company outlets relative to the total number of available outlets carrying men's clothing was computed for each selected SMSA. Data on the number of retailers selling men's clothing were derived from the *Census of Business.*

The Exogenous Variables

In reviewing available data for use in constructing possible exogenous variables for identifying the two equations of the system, three possibilities were secured. These were: (1) the duration of company exposure in the SMSA by years; (2) the size of the SMSA in square miles; and (3) the number of salesmen in the trading area. Upon analysis, the second of these showed little relationship with either endogenous variable and was discarded. The duration of company exposure was found to be related strongly to company sales volume and was used to identify the sales response function. The number of salesmen in each territory was uncorrelated to the endogenous variables in its raw form, but when adjusted by the number of retailers in each area—creating a salesmen-per-store ratio—a significant relationship with distributor density was observed. It was consequently used to identify the distributor response function. The resulting system of equations was:

$$MS = \S_1(DD,T) \tag{21}$$

$$DD = \S_2(MS,SS), \tag{22}$$

where MS represents market share, T is time in area, DD is distributor density, and SS is salesmen per store.

These two exogenous variables also provide necessary additional information about the system to permit identification of each question. It would be useless, of course, to regress market share against retail penetration to obtain the α coefficient and then regress retail penetration against market share to obtain the β coefficient. One would be the inverse of the other and the result may or may not be representative of even one of the equations. Specification of a unique exogenous variable for each question, one that is hypothesized to shift the relation between the endogenous variables, provides a basis for identification.[11]

Fitting the Equations

Because of the possibility that several different functional relationships exist between market share and retail penetration in (21), several functional forms were tested to determine which of the family shown in Figure 2-4 was the most appropriate. A linear relationship was hypothesized to be suitable for (22). Empirical estimates for all of these, as well as a quadratic, for (21) are shown below. The quadratic was included on the speculation that company sales might actually decline if the number of retailers in a territory became too large. Because it was hypothesized that diminishing returns would appear in both of the exogenous variables, each was transformed by the square-root function prior to the regression.

To fit the parameters of the equations, and to evaluate those most representative of the system, the two-stage, least-squares regression methcds produces biased results because of the correlation between the endogenous variables in a simultaneous system and the error terms.[12] All the functions below are such second-stage results, except for the quadratic (26). Here, two-stage estimates proved impossible to secure because of excessively high multicolinearity between the independent variables generated through the first stage. However, the first-stage estimate that is shown provides sufficient evidence to evaluate this equation as a measure of the sales response function.

Inspection of the multiple regression coefficient for the sales response equations reveals that the reciprocal model is the simplest to eliminate from contention. While the R^2 in the two-stage, least-squares method does not have the same statistical meaning as in the first stage, it does not provide an indication of the goodness of fit. In the reciprocal model, this is clearly poor.

Alternative First-Level Firm Sales Response Functions

$$\underset{(.0003)}{MS} = -\underset{(.024)}{.075} + \underset{(.029)}{.101}DD + \underset{(.007)}{.020}T^{1/2} \qquad R^2 = .731 \qquad (23)$$

$$\underset{(.0003)}{MS} = -\underset{(.021)}{.098} + \underset{(.034)}{.116}DD^{1/2} + \underset{(.008)}{.018}T^{1/2} \qquad R^2 = .722 \qquad (24)$$

$$\underset{(.0007)}{MS} = -\underset{(.021)}{.047} - \underset{(.003)}{.006}/DD + \underset{(.012)}{.016}T^{1/2} \qquad R^2 = .375 \qquad (25)$$

$$\underset{(.0003)}{MS} = -\underset{(.018)}{.065} + \underset{(.044)}{.144}DD - \underset{(.045)}{.033}DD^2 + \underset{(.005)}{.016}T^{1/2} \qquad R^2 = .737 \qquad (26)$$

Second-Level Firm Response Function

$$\underset{(.010)}{DD} = -\underset{(.033)}{.017} + \underset{(.540)}{4.80}MS + \underset{(.339)}{.961}SS^{1/2} \qquad R^2 = .725 \qquad (27)$$

The quadratic model, (26), also reveals poor fit despite the high R^2 value. Examination of the standard error of the squared term reveals this to be higher than the coefficient itself. This term, consequently, makes little contribution to the explanatory power of the equation. Hence, the data at least do not suggest any reticence on the part of the retailers to back the product with promotion as the system is expanded.

The choice of equation comes down to either the linear model, (23), or the fractional power equation, (24). Though there is little difference in the statistical measures of goodness of fit between them, those distinctions that do occur favor the linear model. One would be inclined to choose this equation as a result. However, the real answer is that within the range of the data developed from the company records, the predictive power of both equations is about the same. This should be taken as a warning not to extrapolate any policies derived from this analysis too far beyond this range.

Beyond this caveat, either equation will serve optimization needs just about equally well. Because of the slightly better fit, and the ease of further mathematical manipulation, the linear model will be regarded as the best representation of the sales response function.

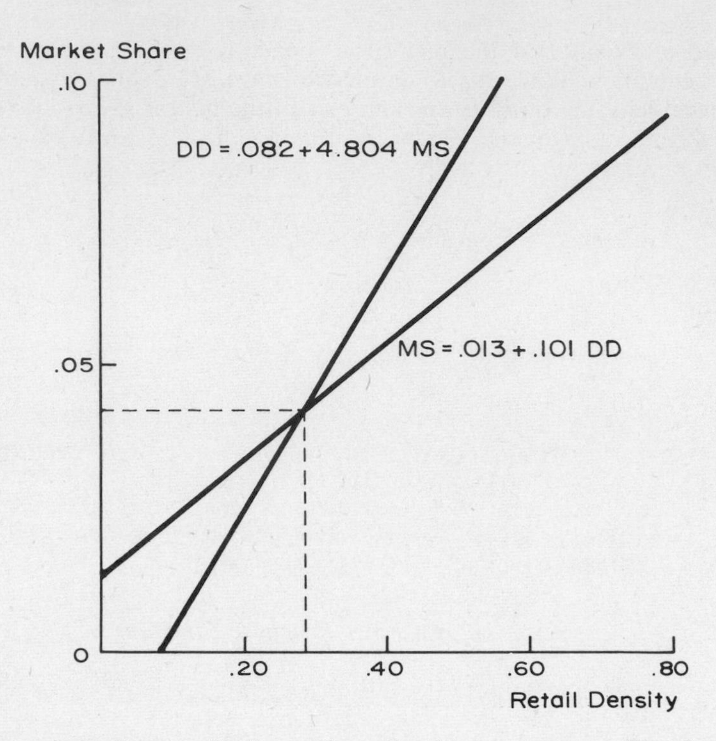

Figure 2-5. Empirically Determined Equilibrium between First-Level Firm Market Share and Second-Level Retail Density for a Menswear Manufacturer in a Typical SMSA.

The Empirical Multiplier

The two equations, linear in the endogenous variables, are plotted on Figure 2-5, with the exogenous variables held equal to their means. It is of interest to note that the retail response equation has a higher slope than the sales function, reflecting the existence of a stable equilibrium in the system.[a] The channel multiplier in this instance of $(1\text{-}\alpha\beta)$ is equal to $(1–4.8 \times .11)$ or .478. The operation of the system, then, serves to about double the impact of changes in the number of salesmen employed in a territory or company time in a territory.

By making a few arbitrary assumptions about the profits obtainable from each territory and the cost of operating a sales force, it is possible to make some managerial estimates from this model as to optimal penetration into each territory. For example, it is assumed, based upon poten-

[a] To define the slope of Equation (27) on the axis of Figure 2-5, one must first solve the equation for MS by dividing through by 4.8. The result is $MS = -.0035 + 208DD + .244SS^{1/2}$.

tial sales and company production and distribution costs, that the average SMSA could produce \$4 million in profits, net of all costs except salesmen's salaries. It is further assumed that to provide one salesman for each retailer in the territory would cost the company \$3 million.[b] Then, profits, Π, for the firm (assuming linearities) are determined by:

$$\Pi = 4{,}000{,}000\, MS - 3{,}000{,}000\, SS \qquad (28)$$

Using (23) and (27) to solve for MS results in:

$$MS = .022 + .189SS^{1/2}.$$

Derivation of the optimal-profit position for the first-level firm is obtained through a model of constrained profit maximization. The profits of the firm, as obtainable from any given SMSA, are constrained by the interactions of its sales with the interests of the retailers. This constraint defines the basic economic position of the firm vis-à-vis the other members of the channel:

$$\Pi = 4{,}000{,}000\ \ MS - 3{,}000{,}000\ \ SS - \lambda(MS - .022 - .18955^{1/2}).$$

Solution of this equation requires the taking of partial derivatives of Π with respect to MS, SS, and λ, the Lagrangian multiplier of the constraint, and setting these equal to zero.

$$\partial \mathrm{MS}/\partial\pi = 4{,}000{,}000 - \lambda = 0$$

$$\partial \mathrm{SS}/\partial\pi = 3{,}000{,}000 - .094\, SS^{-1/2} = 0$$

$$\partial\gamma/\partial\pi = MS - .023 - .189\, SS^{1/2} = 0$$

Solving the system recursively, starting with λ, results in:

$$\lambda = 4{,}000{,}000$$

$$SS = .3545$$

$$MS = .0457$$

[b] This somewhat strange result is a consequence of the definition of SS as the proportion of company salesmen to the number of retail establishments carrying men's clothing in an SMSA. If SS were to take the value of 1.00, then the company would be providing one salesman for each outlet. Given the average number of such outlets per SMSA and an estimate of salesmen's costs, the result of \$3 million per territory was derived.

Solving for retail penetration, *DD*, from (27) shows that the company will maintain distribution in 32 percent of the stores selling menswear in the territory. This new equilibrium position reflects a higher level of sales-force input than was being applied. It represents a shift to the right of Equation (27) in Figure 2-5. This new solution, of course, is for the typical SMSA. To determine the firm's optimal position in each SMSA would require the adjustment of the parameters in (28) to fit the particular case.

Conclusions

Ideally, it would be desirable to model the comparative economic base of franchising in macro terms. The paucity of data and the substantial differences within the different adaptations of each mode of distribution contrive to make this a discouraging task. However, some opportunity does exist for defining strengths or weaknesses of the individual system. Hence, we may draw conclusions by restating our initial concepts on economic base in terms of the parameters of the marketing-management model of the channel.

The major parameters of the model, (15), were singled out as α, β, and γ. The magnitude of each may be interpreted to show direct relevance to one or two of the elements of economic base. The α parameter measures the attractiveness of the channel's marketing package to third-level system buyers. In here is the degree of funnel adjustment built into the program for second-level units to use to adjust to varying local market conditions. If there are economies in labor or system standardization that permit price savings to be passed on to the buyer, then the impact of these factors as well is to be found in this coefficient. All these affect the incremental volume of sales that additional second-level units may contribute to sales. In this sense, α is a measure of the viability of the channel's program in the market place.

The β coefficient may be regarded as the growth element of the equation. It governs the response of second-level firms to the sales success of the system. In effect, growth requires the attraction of capital. In independent and franchise systems, β measures the willingness of outside entrepreneurs to provide this capital. In the integrated system it measures the ability of the firm to generate capital for its own growth. In independent systems a high coefficient suggests some degree of instability of operation. That is, while capital may be attracted to the system readily, it may disappear just as easily. In franchise and integrated systems the barriers to the exit of capital imply greater stability in the fact of a temporary downward trend. Should the trend fail to be temporary, it may signify a slowness in a reduction of units in the short run, coupled with significant capital losses in the long run.

The γ coefficient denotes the role of control within the system, the ability of the first-level firm to direct the activities of those on the second level. More specifically, it may represent either (or both) the ability of the first-level firm to control the horizontal scale of its distribution or the extent of promotion provided by the second level. The higher this coefficient, the greater the power of the first-level firm and the fewer the resources that it has to expend to manage its distributors. A decline in this coefficient in a franchise system suggests either acquiescence in the development of a more independent type of channel or pressure for the first-level firm to integrate forward.

One might hypothesize that, over time, this coefficient would weaken for those franchise systems where the franchisor is not operating on the wholesale supply line but is providing a basic marketing program. One response would be for such franchisors to integrate horizontally into the supply of a greater range of goods to franchisees in order to regain their power.

To close this discussion of alternative modes of distribution, it may be restated that derivation of economic base is feasible only with micro systems. The basic models developed here offer a means for the channel management to assess its position at any point in time. Repeated cross-section studies should provide the firm with a vivid means of charting its progress by observing the changes in the parameters over time.

Notes

1. David A. Revzan, *Wholesaling in Marketing Organization* (New York: John Wiley & Sons, Inc., 1961), 14–16.
2. Robert W. Little, "The Marketing Channel: Who Should Lead This Extra-corporate Organization?" *Journal of Marketing,* 34 (January 1970), 33.
3. Norman R. Collins and John A. Jamison, "Mass Merchandising and the Agricultural Producer," *Journal of Marketing,* 22 (April 1958), 362–363.
4. "Ailing A & P," *The Wall Street Journal* (April 21, 1964), 1.
5. "Franchising: Too Much, Too Soon," *Business Week* (June 27, 1970), 58.
6. National Commission on Food Marketing, *Organization and Competition in Food Retailing,* Technical Study No. 7 (Washington, D.C.: U.S. Government Printing Office, 1966), 330.
7. National Oil Jobbers Council, "The Jobbers' Role in Petroleum Distribution," *The National Oil Jobber* (May 1969).
8. Federal Trade Commission, "Enforcement Policy with Respect to Vertical Mergers in the Cement Industry" (January 1967), mimeo.
9. Henry J. Claycamp and William F. Massy, "Theory of Market Segmentation," *Journal of Marketing Research* (November 1968), 389.
10. Samuel Goldberg, *Introduction to Difference Equations* (New York: John Wiley & Sons, Inc., 1958), 63–64.

11. Lawrence R. Klein, *An Introduction to Econometrics* (Englewood Cliffs, N.J.: Prentice-Hall, Inc., 1962), 10–17.

12. J. Johnston, *Econometric Methods* (New York: McGraw-Hill Book Co., Inc. 1963), 230–233.

3 Optimal Franchising in Theory

Michael C. Lovell*

How various provisions of the franchise contract affect the behavior of an optimizing franchisee and the overall profitability of the franchise operation is the central issue considered in this paper. In return for licensing and royalty fees, the franchise agreement may guarantee its holder a certain market territory. The contract can specify the precise location of the store and the price, but it may be less restrictive. After all, there are certain advantages to be reaped through a decentralization of the decision-making task. The franchisee may be particularly well versed on local conditions; further, a degree of decision-making autonomy, by providing scope for initiative and improving morale, may contribute to higher managerial productivity. Even when certain decision-making responsibilities are decentralized, the subordinate's decision may be subject to manipulation. For example, the price that a franchisee will want to charge may be influenced by adjusting license and royalty fees. But what contract provisions will induce the franchisee to behave in a way that will maximize the profits of franchise headquarters?

In analyzing the characteristics of an optimal franchise contract I will draw primarily upon certain fundamental concepts of microeconomics.[a] In particular, it proves convenient in modeling our problem to suppose that the franchisee is an optimizing economic man striving to maximize his profits subject to the constraints of his contract. Although economic man may be a hackneyed and maligned concept, it is recommended in part because it yields behavioral propositions. For example, an increase in the size of the franchise area, even though it serves to enlarge the sphere of market power, will under most circumstances encourage the profit maximizing franchisee to lower his price. The concept of an optimizing franchisee is also of use in that it will enable us to determine what contract provisions (royalties, licensing fees, etc.) are optimal from the point of view of the franchisor, given that each franchisee behaves so as to maximize his personal profit. The concept of the optimizing franchisee is relevant with regard to certain issues of conflict resolution. Conflict can

* Wesleyan University, Middletown, Connecticut.

[a] The model of franchising developed here draws heavily on the literature of location theory, the theory of teams, and the literature on conflict resolution.[1]

arise from a variety of sources: it may be the result of alternative conceptions of current market conditions; it may be the consequence of a poorly drawn franchise contract; it may result from a genuine conflict of interest. How conflict should be dealt with obviously depends upon its source. The concept of an optimizing franchisee discussed in the first section helps us to identify the various sources of conflict.

The second part of this paper analyzes the behavior of an optimizing franchisee. The third part examines some characteristics of an optimal franchise contract. The fourth specifies the details of such an optimal contract under somewhat more restrictive conditions than are imposed in other sections of the paper. A nontechnical summary of the entire argument is presented in the concluding section.

The Optimizing Franchisee

Suppose, as illustrated in Figure 3-1, that the customers are located on a road, that the store is located at point S on the road, and that the franchise contract gives a franchisee the exclusive right to service all customers located between addresses a_1 and a_2 on the road. What price should the franchisee charge in order to maximize his profits? What is the best location (S) for his store?

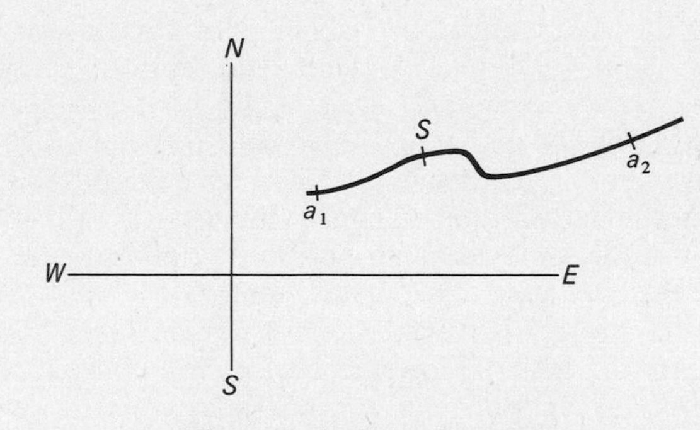

Figure 3–1. Store Location.

As a first step toward modeling this problem, suppose that the franchisee perceives that all customers are basically the same, and that the quantity (q) the representative consumer will purchase declines linearly with delivered price (p_d):[b]

$$q = \alpha - \beta p_d. \tag{2.1}$$

It may not be unreasonable for the franchisee to presume that demand is a linear function of price; certainly, it facilitates the estimation of determining what mode of behavior will maximize profits. It shall also be supposed that demand drops off in proportion to the distance the customer resides from the store. Thus, we suppose that delivery costs are strictly proportional to the distance shipped, and

$$p_d = p + \sigma d \tag{2.2}$$

where d is the distance separating the customer from the store, σ is shipping cost per mile, and p is the price charged at the store. In Figure 3-2 the price funnel illustrates how delivered price increases with distance.

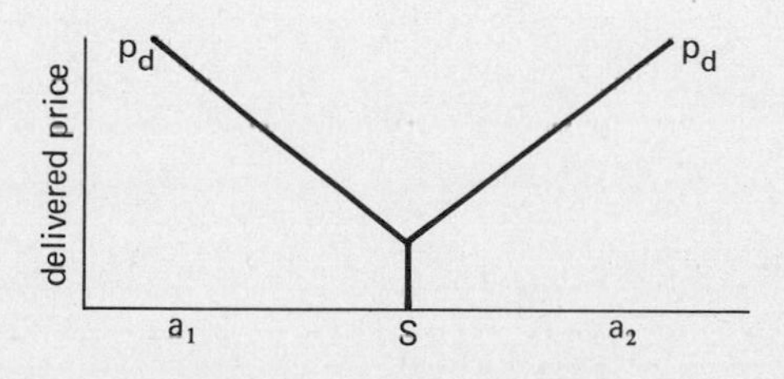

Figure 3-2. Delivered Price.

Here we have artificially straightened the road in forming the horizontal axis, with height representing price.

This model stems from the pioneering contributions of Harold Hotelling[3] and others to location theory. The approach has been used in the study of differences in color and quality as well as location. It has also been employed in analyzing the platforms of political parties. A recent study by Lovell[4] considers how the free play of market forces, zoning restrictions,

[b] More precisely, we should write, $q = \max[0, \alpha - \beta p_d]$. Throughout we shall ease the notational burden by presuming that the indicated solutions satisfy the obvious sign constraints.[2]

and various types of market structure influence price and store location.

How is the best store location and the price charged by an optimizing franchisee influenced by the geographical density of his customers? As a first step in exploring this issue, denote by the function $c(a)$ the number of customers located at address a. We have plotted hypothetical $c(a)$ density curves on Figures 3-3a, 3-3b, and 3-3c. Figure 3-3a indicates a uniform distribution of customers; Figure 3-3b is symmetric; and Figure 3-3c is asymetric and bimodal (a town and a city). The total number of customers residing in the franchise area is given by

$$C = \int_{a_1}^{a_2} c(a)da,$$

and is visualized graphically by the area under the $c(a)$ curve. The $c(a)$ function might be estimated from census data, but it is preferably adjusted to net out the effects of related products upon the demand for the franchised commodity.[c] On Figure 3-3c we have indicated the *mode,* the *median,* and the arithmetic *mean* of the distribution. More customers are located at the mode than anywhere else. Half the customers are to the left and half are to the right of the median. The arithmetic mean or average, is simply the center of gravity of the distribution. Will our franchisee locate his store at the mode (city)? Will he divide the market evenly by locating at the median? Or will he settle on the mean location in order to cater to the average customer?

Total sales of the franchisee depend on the boundaries of the franchise (a_1 and a_2), on the location of the store (S), and on the price p. The art of integration reveals that total sales are:

$$\begin{aligned} q(a_1, a_2, S,p) &= \int_{a_1}^{a_2} q(p_d)c(a)da = \int_{a_1}^{a_2} \alpha - \beta p - \beta\sigma \mid a - S \mid da \\ &= (\alpha - \beta p)C - \beta\sigma \int_{a_1}^{S} (S - a)c(a)da + \int_{S}^{a_2} (a - S)c(a)da \\ &= (\alpha - \beta p)C - \beta\sigma M(S) \qquad (2.3) \end{aligned}$$

where the function

$$M(S) = \int_{a_1}^{S} (S - a)c(a)da + \int_{S}^{a_2} (a - S)c(a)da \qquad (2.4)$$

represents the total distance that would be traveled if all customers were to make one trip to the store. Of course, we may also solve to find the

[c] We neglect for the time being the effects of oligopolistic interactions; that is, the franchise protection will be assumed for the time being to be so complete that the reactions of producers of rival commodities may be neglected. The analysis is further simplified by assuming that the retailer handles a single product.[5]

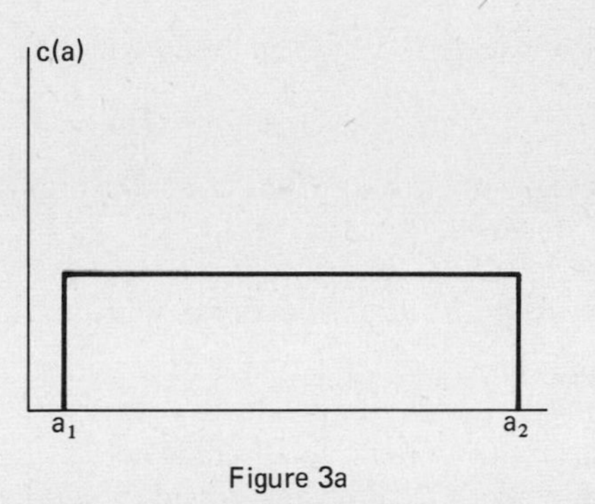

Figure 3a

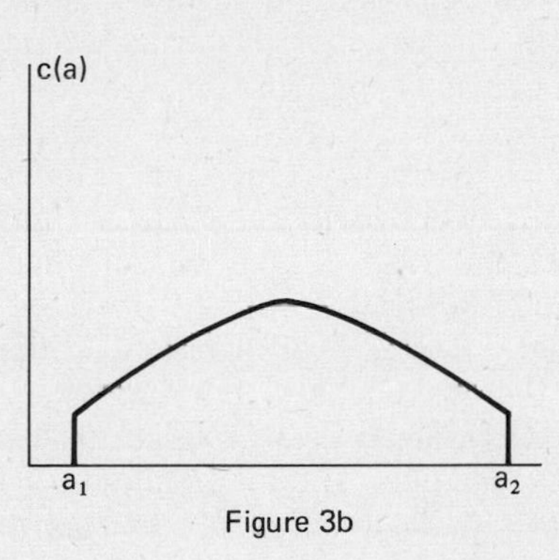

Figure 3b

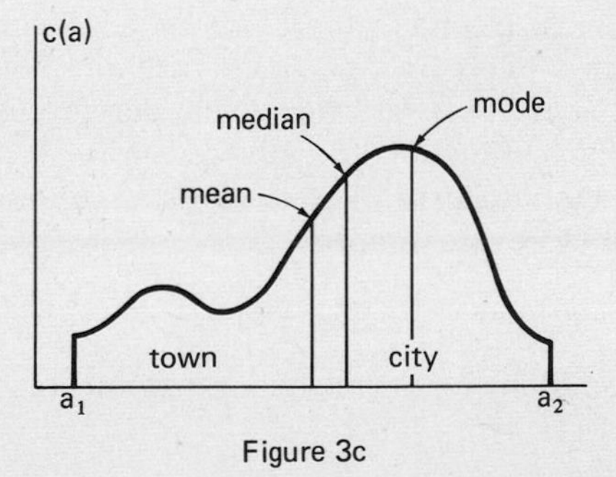

Figure 3c

Figure 3-3. Alternative Customer Distributions.

pricing policy that will yield a specified sales volume:

$$p = \alpha/\beta - q/\beta C - \sigma M(S)/C \tag{2.5}$$

Note that q/C represents average per customer sales while $M(S)/C$ is average customer distance from the store.

Costs must be specified before optimal behavioral patterns can be determined. Let us suppose that total expenditures are linear in output:

$$E = \gamma + \delta q \tag{2.6}$$

Here γ denotes the retail outlet's fixed cost, and δ the unit cost. Included in γ are the retail outlet's rental cost together with the carrying cost of minimum display inventory, licensing fees, overhead personnel, and other such costs that may be regarded, at least as a first approximation, as independent of volume. Incremental cost δ includes the wholesale cost of the product, the cost of packaging, franchise royalty fees, and so on.

A *median rule of franchise location* follows from equation (2.3), plus an obvious truism. It is obviously true that, whatever price p the store ends up charging, it will want to locate so as to maximize the quantity it can sell at that price. But from (2.3) we see that everything separates nicely, and the maximizing location for any specified p involves picking S so as to minimize $M(S)$. But as a proposition of elementary statistics, we know that this means that we must pick the *median* of the distribution. That is, $M(S)/\min$ is obtained when S is the median of $c(a)$. Let M denote this total deviation from the median. The mathematics of the problem says that the store should locate at the median of the distribution rather than at either the city or the town, on Figure 3-3c, and it should locate at the precise point—regardless of whether it is free to set its own price or required to charge a set price as a provision of the franchise contract. Of course, a wise franchisee may worry about the reactions of competing brands if the franchise offers only partial protection. And at best the median rule is only a first approximation, for it was derived under the assumption that demand is a linear function of delivered price.

What quantity should be marketed in order to maximize profit? The total profits of the store are simply

$$\pi = pq - E = (p - \delta)q - \gamma. \tag{2.7}$$

As a first order condition for profit maximization we have

$$\begin{aligned}\frac{\partial \pi}{\partial q} &= (p - \delta) - \frac{\partial p}{\partial q} \\ &= \alpha/\beta - \sigma M(S)/C - 2q/\beta C - \delta = 0.\end{aligned}$$

Hence, the optimal quantity to market is

$$q^{\circ}(S) = [C(\alpha - \beta\delta) - \beta\sigma M(S)]/2. \tag{2.8}$$

When this expression for the optimal quantity is substituted into demand equation (2.5) we find that the profit maximizing price is

$$p^\circ(S) = \alpha/2\beta + \delta/2 - \sigma M(S)/2C. \tag{2.9}$$

Substituting into (2.7) reveals that the optimizing franchisee reaps profits of

$$\pi^\circ = q^{\circ 2}/\beta C - \gamma, \tag{2.10}$$

for

$$p^\circ(S) - \delta = q^\circ/\beta C.$$

The effects on price and sales volume of inappropriate store location are easily discerned from (2.8) and (2.9). It may not be feasible, at least in the short run, to locate the store at the median point serving to minimize $M(S)$. Time is required for existing building leases to expire. Further, if the store sells a variety of different product lines, its owner may not be interested in relocating at the point that is optimal for a particular item. When the store is not optimally located, equation (2.8) reveals, the quantity sold will be reduced. Furthermore, we see from (2.9) that the franchisee will want to charge a lower price.

How will the terms of the franchise contract influence the behavior of the franchisee? From equations (2.8) and (2.9), it is clear that if the franchisee is charged a royalty on each item sold, so that δ is inflated, precisely one-half of the royalty will be passed along to the customer in the form of higher price. As a result, sales will drop by $-\beta C/2$. In contrast, neither a franchise fee of a specified amount per month nor the amortization costs arising from purchasing the franchise in the first place will influence either sales volume or price (at least as long as the burden is not so great as to drive the franchisee out of business), for γ does not appear in either equation. This means that a skillfully drawn franchise contract may induce the franchisee to charge any price thought to be appropriate by the franchisor. Subsequent adjustments in fixed costs γ can then serve to grant the franchisee the appropriate rate of return on his investment. That the profit maximizing price is likely to fall when the size of the exclusive franchise area is increased is suggested by (2.9), for the average distance traveled by the store's customers, $M(S)/C$, normally increases when the franchise area is enlarged.[d]

---

[d] This necessarily happens when the distribution of customers is uniform, or indeed any other symmetrical distribution (Figure 3-3a or 3-3b). However, it is possible to conceive of an asymmetric distribution in which an increase in the franchise area lowers the average distance of customers from the store and causes a price rise. Suppose that initially there is one customer located right at the store, five one mile to the west of the store, and five ten miles to the east; if two new customers two miles to the west are acquired as a result of enlarging the franchise area, the ratio M/C will fall from 5.5 to 59/13, provided the store does not move; in the long run, it will pay the store to move one mile west, M/C will fall to 58/13, and the optimal price will increase further.

Some Characteristics of an Optimal Franchise Contract

Now consider the problem from the point of view of a franchisor, Colonel Sanders himself. Suppose, as illustrated in Figure 3-4, that the road indicated by the wavy line is partitioned into *n* distinct markets. What provisions in the contract will serve to maximize the profits of the franchisor? We shall enumerate a number of characteristics of an optimal franchise contract. It must be conceded at once that, whatever these characteristics

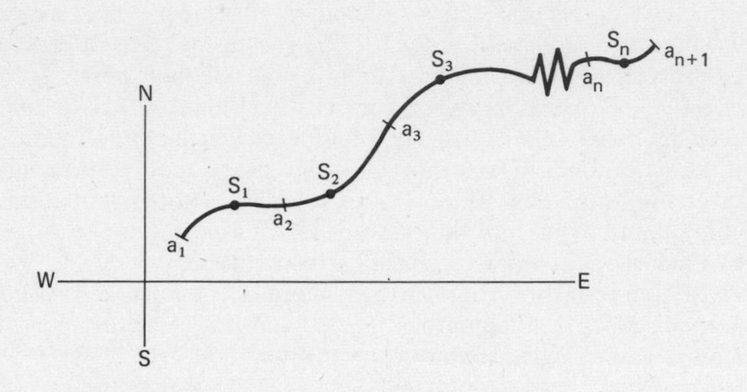

Figure 3-4. Franchise Boundaries and Store Location.

may turn out to be, they may not all seem intuitively reasonable. All that can be claimed is that they follow from the particular franchising model that we have been considering.

One characteristic of an optimal (to the franchisor) franchise contract is that it will siphon from each franchisee any surplus of profits over and above what would be required to induce an optimal number of entrepreneurs to serve as franchisees. To see why this is so, recall from the previous section that it is only the royalty fee that influences the price and output policy of the franchisee. Whatever the royalty, the fixed cost coefficient γ, which includes the licensing fee, does not appear in either (2.8) or (2.9), the equations explaining the output and pricing policy of the optimizing franchisee. This means that without influencing price or output behavior, an annual license fee (or the amortization cost of the franchise grant) can be raised to that point at which the franchisee is drained of any return in excess of that required in order to induce him to remain in the industry.

A second characteristic follows immediately, for an indirect proof suffices to establish that the *median rule* yields the franchise location that is optimal from the point of view of the franchisor as well as the franchisee. To see why this must be so, consider the contrary situation. Suppose that the franchise prescribed some alternative location; then the franchisor could do better by rewriting the contract to maintain the same retail price, but permitting the franchisee to relocate at the median. Then the licensing fee could be raised so as to siphon off at least a portion of the resulting rise in profits realized by the franchisee. This means that given the boundaries of the marketing area, any disagreement concerning the optimal retail location is likely to be the result of alternative conceptions concerning the nature of market conditions. Alternatively, it may be part of a bargaining strategy in which the franchisee hopes to obtain an enlarged marketing area or a reduction in royalty fees. But there is no genuine conflict of interest with regard to franchise location, for the same location is optimal for both franchisor and franchisee.

A third characteristic of the optimal franchise contract concerns the magnitude of the royalty fee when the franchisee is allowed to determine price and sales volume. Assume that in an optimal franchise contract the royalty fee per item sold will just cover the incremental costs of the franchise headquarters. In order to permit a rather general formulation of the problem, write the profit of the ith franchisee as

$$\pi_i = R_i(q_i) - P_i(q_i) - L_i(q_i) \qquad (3.1)$$

where $R_i(q_i)$ denotes revenue as a function of sales, $P_i(q_i)$ denotes production costs as a function of sales, and $L_i(q_i)$ denotes royalty and licensing fees to be paid to the franchisor. If the franchise is held by an optimizing franchisee, the first derivative of (3.1) is zero, as this is a necessary condition for profit maximization:

$$\frac{\partial \pi_i}{\partial q_i} = \frac{dR_i}{dq_i} - \frac{dP_i}{dq_i} - \frac{dL_i}{dq_i} = 0. \qquad (3.2)$$

Now the profits of franchise headquarters are

$$\pi = \sum_i L_i(q_i) - E^*(q_1, q_2, \ldots), \qquad (3.3)$$

where the first term denotes total licensing and royalty receipts and the second total operating costs incurred by franchise headquarters. Substituting from (3.1) into (3.3) yields

$$\pi = \sum_i [R_i(q_i) - P_i(q_i) - \pi_i] - E^*(q_1, q_2, \ldots, q_n). \qquad (3.4)$$

For a solution that is optimal from the point of view of franchise headquarters, the first derivative of this last expression with respect to each q_i must be zero:

$$\frac{\partial \pi}{\partial q_i} = \frac{\partial R_i}{\partial q_i} - \frac{\partial P_i}{\partial q_i} - \frac{\partial \pi_i}{\partial q_i} - \frac{\partial E^*}{\partial q_i} = 0. \tag{3.5}$$

But since we are dealing with optimizing franchisees, (3.2) must also be satisfied, and a comparison of that equation with (3.5) reveals that both conditions hold simultaneously only when

$$\frac{dL_i}{dq_i} = \frac{\partial E^*}{\partial q_i}. \tag{3.6}$$

Thus, the incremental royalty paid by the franchisee on each additional unit he sells must just equal the resulting incremental cost incurred by the franchisor.

A fourth characteristic of optimal franchise contracts is illustrated on Figure 3-5. One retail outlet is located at point S_1, a second at point S_2; point a_2 indicates the border separating the two regions. As in Figure 3-2, we have two price funnels indicating how delivered price varies with distance from the store. Note that the situation pictured is one in which certain customers in the territory reserved for the first franchisee would do better to purchase at S_2. Obviously, this situation is one offering a temptation to the second franchisee to cut into his neighbor's territory in violation

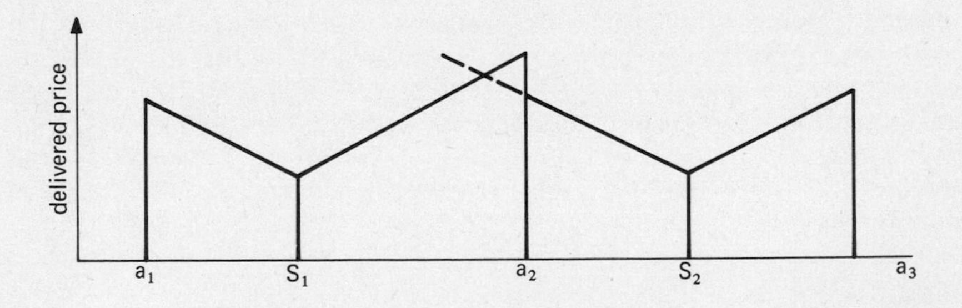

Figure 3-5. A Suboptimal Franchise Contract.

of the franchise contract. From the point of view of all concerned (other than the customer), this situation can spell disaster. The franchisor will have to devote time and energy to make sure that such an exclusive provision of the contract is observed, for otherwise there is a danger that the situation will deteriorate into a succession of price wars.[6] It is easily shown that the situation pictured in Figure 3-5 cannot characterize contracts that are optimal from the point of view of the franchisor, if each store has the same price markup. To see why this is so, suppose that the contract was redrawn so as to enforce current retail price and location, but the boundary point a_2 was moved to the left. The switched customers would purchase more, and since markups are identical, there would be a net increase in combined profits that could be partially siphoned off by the franchisor.[e]

An Optimal Franchise Contract

Although we have seen that it is possible to specify certain characteristics of the optimal franchise contract under quite general conditions, solving for the optimal boundaries of a franchise seems impossible without further information restricting the generality of the problem. A special case of the problem has been solved elsewhere;[7] it will be instructive to summarize certain salient features of the model. For one thing, it reveals certain properties that are *not* necessarily possessed by optimal franchise contracts.

One simplification to be invoked is the assumption that the distribution of customers over the road is uniform, as was illustrated by Figure 3-3a. That is, we suppose that $c(a) = c$, a constant. Under this simplification all market territories should be the same size, and a fundamental question involves solving for this optimal market breadth. If we use the symbol m to denote this common market breadth ($m = a_{i+1} - a_i$), the total number of customers serviced by a franchise will be $C = mc$. Integration reveals that with a uniform customer distribution, $M = cm^2/4$ and $M/C = m/4$, and the optimizing franchisee will locate halfway between a_i and a_{i+1}. Further, the optimizing franchisee will set price so as to achieve average sales per customer[f] of

$$q_a = q/C = (\alpha - \beta\delta)/2 - \beta\sigma m/8 \qquad (4.1)$$

as may be seen on substitution into (2.8).[8]

---

[e] Prices and δ_i may be the same, but it will suffice if the excess of price over marginal cost is the same at both outlets.

[f] Customers located close to the store purchase more; those further away purchase less than q_a.

The downward sloping straight line on Figure 3-6 is (4.1); given the size m of the franchise area, we can read off of this line average per customer sales achieved by the optimizing franchisee. The price charged by the optimizing franchisee is

$$p^o = (\alpha/\beta + \delta)/2 - \sigma m/8, \tag{4.2}$$

as may be seen from (2.9). But what is the optimal value of m, from the point of view of the franchisor, given that the straight line on Figure 3-6 reveals the response of the optimizing franchisee to changes in m? It turns out that the optimal point is e, where the two curves cross. To see why this is so, note that the total profits generated per customer mile are

$$\pi_a = \frac{\pi}{C} = (p^o - \delta)q^o_a - \gamma/C = q^{o2}_a/\beta - \gamma/mc. \tag{4.3}$$

Here δ is the sum of the incremental costs incurred by the franchisor and franchisee and γ is the sum of fixed costs.[g] The second equality follows on substitution form (4.2). Setting the first derivative of (4.3) equal to zero, we obtain

$$\frac{\partial \pi_a}{\partial m} = \frac{2q_a}{\beta}\frac{\partial q_a}{\partial m} + \frac{\gamma}{m^2} = -\frac{\sigma q_a}{4} + \frac{\gamma}{cm^2} = 0 \tag{4.4}$$

where the fact that $\partial q_a/\partial m = -\beta\sigma/8$ is exploited in obtaining the last equality. Solving we find as the expression for the optimal m:

$$m = \sqrt{4\gamma/c\sigma q_a} \tag{4.2}$$

which is the curved line passing through point e.[h]

How the optimal solution is affected by changes in cost and demand conditions is determined from inspection of Figure 3-6. First of all, an increase in fixed costs (γ) will move the dashed curve toward the east. But since the straight line is unchanged, the net effect must be a reduction in sales volume as well as an increase in m. While these effects are hardly surprising, it is of interest to note from (4.2) that the net effect will be a reduction in the price charged by the store. Second, consider δ; the straight line on Figure 3-6 will be lowered by half of any increase in incremental costs, but the dashed curve is unaffected. This means that an increase in δ causes retail outlets to be located further apart in the long run because point e will have slid southeast along the straight line. This causes a further reduction in sales. Further, observe from equation (4.2) that in the long run the increase in price is less than fifty percent of the increase in incremental cost. Third, consider an increase in popula-

---

[g] Maximizing (4.3) is optimal from the point of view of the franchisor, who—if successful—siphons off excess profits.

[h] For a road of finite length, or a loop, this is only an approximate solution, for there are end point problems to worry about.[9]

tion density (c). This according to (4.2) will shift the dashed curve on Figure 3-6 to the west. Point e slides to the northwest; average sales per customer increase, and retail outlets are located closer together. Since m falls, we see from (4.2) that price must fall. Thus, a population explosion not only leads to a more profitable franchise operation; it can also benefit the consumer by leading to a price reduction and more conveniently located retail outlets.

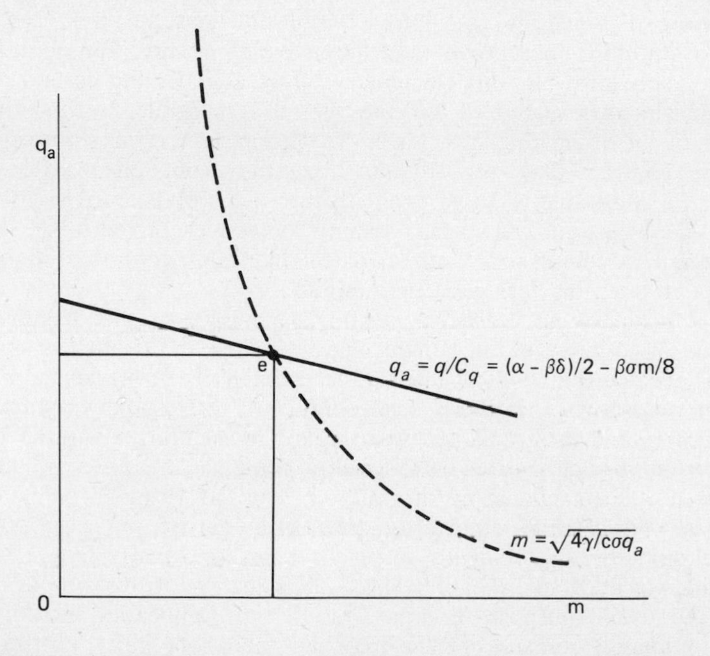

Figure 3–6. Simultaneous Marketing Area and Output Determination.

Of course, the analysis is subject to serious qualification if the degree of market protection provided by the franchise contract is only partial. The possibility that rival firms may be tempted to market a closely related commodity deserves consideration. Behavior must be appropriately modified if it seems likely that the oligopolistic threat will materialize. Entry may be forestalled by conservative pricing and the dense location of retail outlets. While this will undoubtedly be costly, it may still be possible to realize substantial profits without attracting rivals if potential entrants can be convinced that the present market is so close to saturation that an additional layer of suppliers selling a closely related product would not be viable. Entry is less likely to represent an attractive proposition if the franchisor has a reputation of responding to the appearance of new rivals with aggressive price cuts.[10]

Summary and Conclusions

It can hardly be claimed that the theory of optimal franchising presented in this paper is realistic. The argument was simplified by assuming that demand is linear in price. While this has an advantage in that it facilitates the task of estimation in practical applications, there certainly are situations in which it would be necessary to relax the assumption of linearity. Further, the argument is static. Worse, it assumes perfect foresight. In any specific application, it would be useful to explore the consequences of relaxing those assumptions that prove most offensive to reality. But tentative as the theory obviously is, this elementary effort at modeling certain aspects of franchising has served to indicate that it is possible, by invoking the concept of an optimizing franchisee, to determine certain features of the franchise contract that serve to maximize the profits of the franchisor. Indeed, we were able to solve explicitly for the optimal provisions of the franchise contract under a specific assumption concerning customer density; the optimal franchise size, optimal price and sales volume, and optimal royalty and licensing fees were determined.

The concept of an optimizing franchisee facilitates the diagnosis and treatment of certain types of conflict that may arise in a franchise situation. Conflict may be the result of alternative evaluations of market conditions. Thus, it was shown that there is no conflict of interest between franchise headquarters and the franchisee with regard to location, given the boundaries of the franchise area. Presumably, conflict of this type may be minimized by the exchange of information. This is fortunate, for the desires of the franchisee with regard to store location are not susceptible to manipulation through changing either licensing or royalty fees, given the boundaries of the franchise area. Thus, identification of this type of conflict serves the useful purpose of indicating that the allocation of additional effort to market research would improve the profitability of the entire operation. There are other types of conflict that cannot be resolved by improved knowledge—but may be eliminated to mutual advantage by adjusting certain terms of the franchise contract. For example, we saw that appropriate adjustment of royalty and licensing fees will induce the franchisee to want to charge whatever price the franchisor deems most appropriate. Another arena of potential conflict involves the interaction among franchisees. We found that a certain form of rivalry between neighboring franchisees is symptomatic of a poorly drawn franchise contract that fails to maximize the profits of the franchisor. Here again the existence of conflict, for from being dysfunctional, can serve a positive purpose by focusing managerial attention on a suboptimal condition demanding correction.

The concept of an optimizing franchisee is not only useful in determining a profit maximizing strategy for the franchisor and in diagnosing certain types of conflict; it is of help also in analyzing certain issues of public policy. Consider, for example, the assertion that franchises are socially detrimental in that they cause higher prices by injecting an element of monopoly into the market place. It may be true that reserving exclusive trading areas for franchisees serves at times to reduce the number of retail outlets. But the analysis given above indicates that exclusive areas may lead to a lower rather than a higher price. Under the conditions specified earlier, an increase in the exclusive trading area induces the optimizing franchisee to charge a lower price.[i] This confounds the task of evaluating the social contribution of franchising, for although some customers are inconvenienced and indeed may pay a higher delivered price as a result of the reduction in the number of retail outlets, those who are so fortunate as to be located close to the franchisee obviously gain from the reduction in price. While an analysis of the pros and cons of franchise operations is beyond the scope of this paper,[11] the analysis suffices to show that any argument based on the presumption that franchisees charge more than unconstrained retail outlets must be fallacious.

Notes

1. Martin Beckmann provides a lucid introduction to the first field in *Location Theory,* New York: Random House (1968). For a pioneering paper in the theory of teams see J. Marschak, "Towards an Economic Theory of Organization and Information," Chapter 14 in R. M. Thrall, Coombs and Davis, ed., *Decision Processes,* New York: John Wiley and Sons, Inc. (1954). The current development of the theory of teams is revealed by inspecting Marschak and Radner, *Theory of Teams,* New Haven: Yale University Press (1970). For a related and readable contribution on conflict resolution see C. H. Kriebel and L. B. Lave, "Conflict Resolution in Economic Organizations," *Behavioral Science,* 8 (May, 1969), 183–96.

2. For a pedantic development spelling out the constraints see M. Lovell, "Product Differentiation and Market Structure, "*Western Economic Journal,* 8 (June, 1970), 120–43.

3. Harold Hotelling, "Stability in Competition," *Economic Journal,* 39 (February, 1929) as reprinted in *Readings in Price Theory* (Boulding & Stigler, editors), Homewood: Illinois, Richard D. Irwin (1952).

4. M. Lovell, *Differentiation.*

5. For a discussion of the optimal variety of products for a retailer to stock see William J. Baumol and Edward A. Ide, "Variety in Retailing," *Management Science,* 3 (October, 1956), 93–101.

6. For a discussion of how price and location are determined under competitive market conditions within the context of this model see Lovell, *Differentiation.*

7. See Lovell, *Differentiation.*

---

[i] The argument may seem plausible to anyone concerned about the opportunity provided for spreading the overhead. An exception to the rule is presented in note [d].

8. Alternatively, see Lovell, *Differentiation*.

9. See Lovell, *Differentiation,* Section 3, for further discussion.

10. A more detailed discussion of oligopolistic complications appears in Lovell, *Differentiation,* Section V.

11. The problem receives further discussion in Sections VI and VII of Lovell, *Differentiation*.

Part Two
Minority Group Capitalism through Franchised Business

4 The Feasibility of Minority-Group Capitalism through Franchising

E. Patrick McGuire*

Franchising has been heralded by many, in both industry and government, as one of the primary vehicles in the development of black capitalism. But experience indicates that there are some serious obstacles to the utilization of franchising to achieve this goal. This paper examines some of those obstacles and discusses the feasibility of the franchising approach to black capitalism.

Introduction

During the presidential campaign of 1968 speech writers, reaching for phrases and expressions that would gain support from the black community, popularized the phrase black capitalism. In a surprisingly short period of time, this expression came to have widespread support among conservatives, liberals, blacks, whites, militants and moderates, and large segments of the academic community. But as it turned out, *black capitalism* meant different things to the different groups involved. For some in the business and political community, the concept produced the comforting theory that the ills of the black community could be substantially alleviated through a self-help program which would be catalyzed by black ownership of business establishments within the ghetto. But while many agreed on the desirability of blacks owning ghetto businesses, there remained a great deal of vagueness and confusion over exactly how this goal was to be attained. To a large degree, this situation still exists. Indeed, we have recently witnessed some serious dissent from the black capitalism approach itself.

Andrew S. Brimmer, black member of the Federal Reserve Board, told the American Economic Association that the best chance for blacks to become capitalists was to "acquire yourself some marketable skills, get to be an officer of a corporation, and own a block of stock." Other observers, such as Richard N. Farmer of Indiana University, noted that "it is highly unlikely that any black capitalism program, however developed in financing, will ever make much of a dent in our overwhelming urban problems."[1]

Administrative strategists in both the Johnson and Nixon administrations have long recognized that the problem of creating black capitalists is far from simple. To begin with, there is little existing precedence for a black

* The Conference Board, New York City, and Rutgers University, Newark.

entrepreneurship. In New York City, for example, where one out of every four white male residents is some variety of business proprietor, professional, or manager, only one out of every thousand blacks occupies a similar position. With a black population of approximately 1,100,000, the city has less than 30 black business enterprises which individually employ as many as 10 persons.

In addition, educated blacks have traditionally oriented themselves towards teaching or the professions. On a per capita basis, blacks achieve far better representation in medical schools than they do in business schools (although business school representation has improved markedly during the past two years).

Franchising provides both financial and managerial support to the franchisee, coupled with the protection of a national brand umbrella. Thus, it has been concluded that franchising offers an excellent device to convey blacks into the economic mainstream.

Franchisors point out that new black entrepreneur is unlikely to have had previous managerial education or experience. He is also vulnerable to financing difficulties and faces the task of entering a marketplace which is already highly structured and competitive.

Franchising's Record

The Small Business Administration recently completed a survey of 138 franchising companies.[2] The latter organizations had over 27,155 franchised outlets. Only 354 of these outlets were owned or leased by minority group members (black, Mexican Americans, Puerto Ricans or Indians, according to SBA definition). Of the 354 units, 114 were within a single company (Mr. Softee). Only five of the companies had as many as ten minority-group franchisees, and seventy of the firms, more than 50 percent, had no minority-group franchisees at all.

Separate investigations in the retail automotive sector of franchising also confirm a paucity of minority group participation. At the start of 1970, less than one tenth of one percent of the 34,000 plus retail automotive dealerships were owned by minority entrepreneurs. Not even in the retail gasoline sector, which is characterized by relatively easy entry and high franchisee turnover, do we find very many black franchisees; however, there is evidence that the petroleum refiners are actively seeking black franchisees. American Oil Company reports over 500 black franchisees within its organization and is attempting to place black gasoline dealers in all ghetto neighborhoods. But with over 200,000 retail gasoline outlets in the United States, blacks have still failed to achieve even one percent representation in this easy-entry sector of franchising.

Stirrings of Company Activity

Franchise organizations, pressed by the demands of both government agencies and community groups, are actively seeking minority-group franchisees. Automobile manufacturers are purposefully attempting to transfer some of their ghetto dealerships to black entrepreneurs; the progress is painfully slow.

In the fast-food field, firms such as McDonalds, International Industries, and Bonanza International are pressing to increase the number of their minority franchisees. In some cases, they are graduating black employees into franchisee positions. In other cases, they are supporting modest training programs specifically designed to provide potential black franchisees with actual operating experience, gained as employees of the franchisor, prior to launching them on the franchising path.

In the personal-service sector, companies such as Dunhill Personnel Systems have been successful in attracting black franchisees. The latter firm has seven black employment service franchisees in the New York area. The mobile franchisors, such as soft ice cream or hand tool marketers, also seem to be more successful in recruiting minority entrepreneurs.

In addition to the efforts of white-owned franchising companies, black-owned and managed franchising firms are experiencing a small measure of success in creating black entrepreneurs. Firms such as All-Pro Chicken, Jet Foods, Rib Cage International, and Village Maid Services, which are black-owned and oriented, are contributing to the pool of black franchisees. Although most of the latter companies are still very modest-sized business organizations, some observers believe that their contribution to the pool of black franchisees may be relatively substantial. Within a few years these firms may be producing more black franchisees than are the white-owned and managed companies.

Impediments to Black Franchising

Many franchisors feel that in order for franchising to become feasible as a primary medium for black capitalists, it will be necessary for the industry to first overcome some serious obstacles which currently restrict the implementation of a black franchising program. These obstacles are not necessarily unique to black entrepreneurs, but because of the particular circumstances of the black entrepreneurs, they achieve critical significance. Among the obstacles to be overcome are problems of financing initial franchise fees, recruiting motivated franchisees, training the new black entrepreneur, and locating and maintaining the ghetto-based franchisor unit.

Financing the Franchise Fee

The purchase of a franchise (by minority-group members or anyone else) usually requires the payment of an initial franchise fee. (Although there are some franchises which do not require initial fees, these generally tend to be in lower profit margin and borderline opportunity areas.) The amount of initial franchise fees have accelerated sharply during recent years. Now, even some of the most modest retail operations require initial franchise fees of $25,000 or more. It is not unusual for one of the major fast-food franchises to cost up to $100,000.

While the franchisee may not be expected to have the total amount of the initial franchise fee, he nonetheless is usually required to have 10 percent to 20 percent of it. The latter amount is over and above the cash base which he must have to sustain him during the first several months of operation.

There seems little likelihood that the black community unaided by industry or government subsidies, will produce many would-be-franchisees who possess the financial resources for even the most minimal initial fee. The median family income for blacks is approximately $5,600, and only

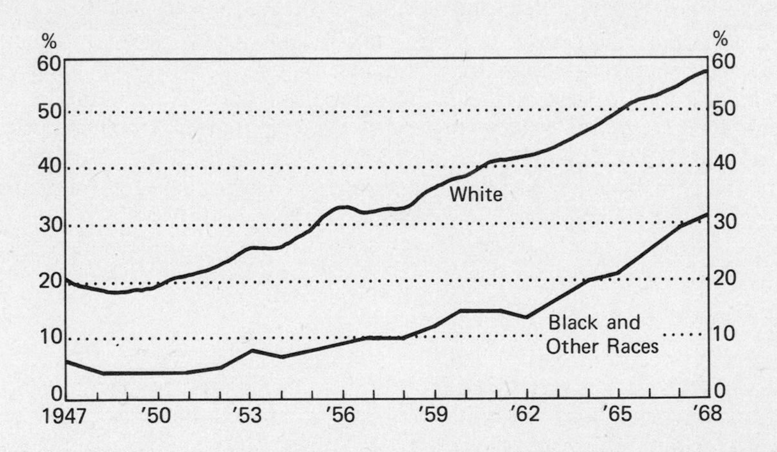

Figure 4–1. Percent of United States Families with Income of $8,000 per Year or More. (Adjusted for price changes, in 1968 dollars). Source: National Industrial Conference Board, *Road Maps of Industry, No. 1643.*

32 percent of black families achieve income levels of $8,000 or more.[3] A community with these economic dimensions does not produce appreciable surplus capital for entrepreneur investment opportunities.

In some cases franchise companies, to gain minority-group entrepreneurs, have reduced the initial franchise fee and extended the time period during which the franchise may be repaid. However, most franchisors are inhibited from reducing the total cost of the franchise because of legal considerations.[a]

Serious doubts have been expressed about the ability of franchising companies to engage in the broad-scale deferment of franchise fees for minority entrepreneurs. These doubts are based on a variety of factors—with company size and financial strength among the most prominent.

The franchise industry, with the exception of automotive and petroleum marketers, is characterized by a plurality of medium and small enterprises. While there are reputed to be over 1,200 companies engaged in various types of franchising, a closer examination of industry statistics reveals that there are no more than 250 to 300 firms which have gross annual revenues of over one million dollars, and even among this segment the total value of corporate revenues is often surprisingly modest (see Table 4-1).

Table 4-1
Percentage Distribution of Company Size in Conference Board Survey

Gross Income in Millions of Dollars	All Companies	Fast Food	Type of Franchisor* n = 193 Nonfood Retail	Personal Services	Business-Industrial
Under 2.0	60.7	50.9	53.3	66.7	78.5
2–4.9	17.4	18.9	15.6	15.8	14.3
5–19.9	14.8	18.8	20.0	12.3	3.6
20–49.9	3.3	7.6	—	1.8	3.6
50–99.9	1.0	0	2.2	1.7	—
100–199.9	1.7	3.8	2.2	—	—
Over 200	2.1	0	.6	1.7	—

* Survey of 193 franchising companies. Ten companies failed to report gross sales volume. Panel includes 53 fast-food companies, 45 nonfood retailers, 57 personal service franchisors, and 28 business-industrial franchisors. Column totals may not add to 100% due to rounding.

When a franchising company takes on a minority-group applicant it almost always involves itself in a greater financial risk and expenditure than it does with white applicants. SBA statistics indicate that the failure rate for black franchisees is nearly twice that for white franchisees. In

[a] Franchisors may be restricted from reducing the total cost of the franchise for minority-group applicants because of the equal pricing considerations contained in the Robinson-Patman Act, and because of possible adverse interpretations of the unfair competition provisions of the Federal Trade Commission Act.

addition, the franchisor who engages minority-group applicants, even if they do have the ability to obtain initial franchise fee financing, must usually commit himself to proportionately greater expenditures of time and money in the training and support of the new entrepreneur.

Current evidence seems to indicate that the vast majority of franchising companies, including some of the most well-recognized roadside names, lack either the financial or managerial resources to engage in more than a token minority-group franchise program. Indeed, the financial structure of many franchising companies allows little space for marginally profitable corporate activities. Between 5 percent and 6 percent of all franchising companies ceased franchising operations during the single year of 1969.[5]

The problem of securing satisfactory financing for minority-group entrepreneurs has many franchise executives concerned. James W. McLamore, president of Burger King Corporation, states that:

> I feel that the financing issue must be resolved. Obviously, blacks do not generally have sufficient capital to consider business opportunities. White businessmen, and I include franchisors, do not have sufficient capital to support them either. Besides, I consider that an undercapitalized business is quite undesirable. It puts too much pressure on the businessman. It is one of the seeds of failure. A great need exists in our country to involve blacks in our economic mainstream and it is indeed unfortunate that adequate financing is not available.

Various government agencies, but principally the Small Business Administration (SBA), have sought to overcome the financing difficulty by becoming guarantors of minority-group loans. The SBA, which up until 1968 was not interested in franchise loans (because they did not consider franchising within the realm of small business), has accelerated its activity in this area.

The SBA reports that in the 21-month period between March 1967 and December 1969, it made a total of 2,611 franchise loans (total of all loans regardless of borrower's race). The latter loans represent 7 percent of the total SBA dollars allocated during the period. Approximately one-third of all the loans were for automotive or automotive-related activities. Fifteen percent were allocated to retail stores, 12½ percent to fast-food restaurants, and 10 percent to service stations. The dollar value of loans provided to minority-group franchisees averaged only 50 percent of the value of loans provided to white franchisees, and many of these loans were in the retail gasoline sector. It would appear that SBA-financed black entrepreneurs are acquiring lower cost—and lower profit—franchises.

The Office of Minority Business Enterprise (OMBE) has also initiated a franchising program which is designated as the "25 × 25 × 2" plan. The latter program, begun in July 1969, was intended to enroll 25 franchising companies who would in turn pledge to acquire 25 minority franchisees during a two-year period. By the fall of 1969, the OMBE announced that it was expanding this program to include 200 franchisors. But by March 1970, only 78 franchisers were active in the program. Franchisors report that difficulty in obtaining minority loan financing was a principal factor in the program lag.

There is one aspect of government-backed franchise loans that invites examination. This factor involves the element of time. A number of franchise executives have complained of bureaucratic delays in SBA loan procedures. They pointed out that governmental procrastination has dulled the appetite of both would-be minority franchisees and franchisors alike. One New York State based franchisor cited delays of up to a year in getting minority franchisee loans approved by the New York SBA office; the Denver, Colorado, SBA office had delays of up to seven months. Some southwestern United States SBA offices have similarly modest records of minority-group loan approvals. In part, the latter difficulties reflect the realities of a decentralized agency which places substantial policy autonomy in the hands of regional SBA administrators. In part, it reflects what has come to be regarded by some disillusioned franchisors as the inevitable effect of governmental involvement in a business program. This situation has improved noticeably with the SBA's 3-Day loan approval program, but some franchisors still have a bad taste in their mouths from previous loan delays.

Difficulties in Recruiting Minority Franchisees

Conference Board interviews with franchising industry executives reveal that franchising companies are experiencing difficulty in not only finding reasonable numbers of qualified minority-group applicants, but in some cases in finding any applicants at all. A few companies reported that their franchise opportunity advertisements, geared for and placed in minority media, had failed to elicit a single response. Executives from these firms were perplexed over just how to reach the potential black entrepreneur.

Conference Board research in franchise recruiting indicates that most franchisees select their franchise on the basis of personal observation (as a customer) and experience with the franchise unit, rather than on the basis of exposure to franchisor advertisements (see Table 4-2).

Franchisors who have been successful in attracting black franchisees report that they resort to a number of different techniques. They recommend the employment of black advertising agencies who can prepare copy which will be most effective with minority-group members who may be converted into franchisees. They utilize literally every contact with the minority community. For example, one SBA officer related that he personally persuaded one black mechanic who worked on his car to take on

Table 4-2
Sources of Franchisee Interest in Franchise Offering

	Percentage Distribution *				
Source of Information	All Franchisees	Fast Food	Retail Automotive	Retail Gasoline	Personal Services and Nonfood Outlets
Newspaper advertisement	13.4	11.9	—	16.6	48.6
Radio TV advertisement	—	—	—	—	—
Magazine advertisement	0.9	0.8	2.4	—	—
Personal referral **	54.6	62.5	43.9	46.2	40.5
Call by franchisor representative	11.7	5.5	17.0	33.3	8.1
Franchise show	0.7	0.8	1.2	—	—
All other sources	18.3	18.2	35.3	3.7	2.7

* Survey of 430 franchisees with 22 N.A. Group includes 235 fast-food, 82 retail automotive, 54 retail gasoline, and 37 personal service or nonfood franchisees. Column totals may not add to exactly 100% due to rounding.

** Personal contact as a customer of franchisor or personal referral from friends, family or business associates.

one of the Washington, D.C., Midas Muffler franchises. Chick-n-Joy, a fast-food franchisor, found black franchisees amongst the deliverymen who trucked chicken parts to their plants. In other cases, the shortage of individual black entrepreneurs has forced franchise companies to reconsider their policies with regard to granting franchises to a group. Ordinarily, franchisors are loathe to engage in the latter practice. The companies feel that it is much more difficult to maintain control over a franchise owned by a group than it is one owned by an individual. Recently, however, Singer Sewing Machine Company granted a franchise to a Harlem community group, and McDonalds sold two of its units to the Hough Development Corporation.

Even when black franchisees do inquire about franchises in response to franchisor advertisements or publicity, they are not always met with open arms. SBA loan officers in one northeastern city reported that they had several black investors who inquired about a well-publicized minority-group franchising program initiated by a fast-food firm. These investors were contacted, but when it was known that they wished to locate their units in the city in question, they were discouraged from further application.

Training Problems

Some cases of black franchisee failure result in part from inadequate training. A number of franchise companies, their claims not withstanding, do not provide extensive periods of work training. In fact, a majority of them provide less than 12 days initial training to their franchisees (see Table 4-3).

Table 4-3
Franchisee Failure Rates in Relation to Initial Training Received

Days Initial Training Provided	Percentage Distribution * Annual Failure Rate Percentage Ranges: Less Than 1	1–4	5–9	10–14	15 or more
0–5	12.1	6.8	30.0	18.2	33.3
6–10	9.1	25.0	10.0	9.1	23.3
10 or more	72.7	61.4	60.0	63.6	33.4
Not available	6.1	6.8	—	9.1	—

* Survey of 193 franchising companies.

Some critics of franchising question whether this degree of training is sufficient to overcome the limited work experience and managerial deficiencies that many entrepreneurs, black or white, possess.

The relatively meager initial training might be compensated for if franchisor field support programs were providing extensive follow-up and assistance. But many franchising company field supervisors, the personnel who provide the day-to-day training support, visit their units on an average of only once per quarter. These visits, which may last from an hour to a full day, cannot always overcome the obstacles of insufficient experience and nonentrepreneurial outlook (see Table 4-4).

Table 4-4
Franchisee Failure Rates in Relation to Field Supervisor Visit Frequency

Frequency of Field Supervisor's Visit (weeks)	Percentage Distribution * Annual Failure Rate Percentage Range: Less than 1%	1–4%	5–9%	10–14%	15 or More %
0–2	14.1	13.6	10.0	—	16.7
2–4	23.2	9.1	15.0	18.2	16.7
4–6	8.1	6.8	5.0	—	16.7
6–8	9.1	6.8	10.0	—	16.7
8–10	3.0	6.8	—	—	—
10–12	12.1	11.4	30.0	9.1	—
12–14	6.1	9.1	10.0	18.2	—
14 or More	24.3	36.4	20.0	54.5	33.2

* Survey of 193 franchising companies. Table indicates frequency with which field supervisors visit franchisees in each of the five ranges of franchisee failure (less than 10%, etc.).

The problem of occupational outlook is one of the most serious in franchisee training. Franchise training executives point out that their principal difficulty is not providing the technical or managerial skills requisite to their operations, but in changing the would-be franchisee's outlook from that of an hourly or salaried employee to that of an independent entrepreneur.

Most franchisee training programs rely on on-the-job training techniques for a major portion of the program. Experienced franchisees feel that on-the-job training techniques, to be successful, must simulate the work environment the franchisee is likely to encounter. There is some question whether the simulated environment used by franchisors in company-maintained flagship stores, is sufficiently realistic to prepare the minority entrepreneur for the exigencies of ghetto retail operations. In fairness to some franchisors, it should be noted that the firms are not inexorably committed to placing minority franchisees in minority community locations. But the de facto effect of many of their programs does lead to the same result.

The Placement and Operation of Ghetto Franchises

Franchising companies may be many things, but most of all they are pragmatists and their experience has taught them where a retail business will succeed or fail. In general, they have honed the tools of site selection to a fine edge. It is not surprising, therefore, that numerous companies are reluctant to locate franchise units in or on the periphery of ghetto areas.

Franchisors have closely examined the operating record of retail units within the ghetto and have often found the record wanting. Independent evaluations of the chances of business success have confirmed their expectations. For example, Gordon S. Bloom of MIT notes that "the record of black-owned supermarkets to date has been largely one of losses, sales below expectations, and, in a few cases, scandalous mismanagement."[6]

Franchisors have experienced difficulty in obtaining insurance for ghetto locations and in achieving satisfactory profit levels in many of the units based in these areas. Some companies candidly admit that the latter difficulties may arise in part from franchisor misconceptions about the product and its suitability for the ghetto market, and in part from the practical operating experiences (high employee turnover, vandalism, and so on) incident to ghetto operations.

Franchisors, like all businesses, come to recognize, and be enamored of, repeatable patterns of business activity. They sometimes expect these patterns of activity to be equally applicable within ghetto environments. For example, a fast-food franchisor, specializing in doughnut products, found that most of his unit sales took place during the early evening hours. The franchisor installed a unit within a northeastern city ghetto area and watched in dismay as his business volume actually ebbed during the peak sales period. In the latter case, the high incidence of crime in the area discouraged normal pedestrian activity during the evening shopping hours and forced a rearrangement of marketing strategy in order to market more of the product during daytime shopping hours.

Franchisors also experience difficulty when they attempt to transplant units or franchise concepts which are highly oriented towards automobile-borne patronage. A few of the fast-food franchises, which normally depend heavily on drive-in customers, have attempted to graft their units and concepts on to ghetto markets. They have not always been successful in achieving satisfactory gross sales volumes due to the inadequate transportation facilities, both personal and public, which normally exist within the ghetto. They have found that their market simply cannot get to them.

Psychological Impediments to Minority Group Franchising

Minority-group entrepreneurs who would enter the so-called economic mainstream are burdened with enough real financial and operational difficulties without being further encumbered by franchisor-harbored psychological impediments. But a number of franchisors do seem to add to psychological problems. The companies do not deliberately set out to erect psychological hurdles, but the net effect of their activities is much the same. While there are many minor impediments, the major psychological obstacles center about minority franchisee perceptions of profit, business direction and control, and business success and failure.

The single most dominant theme in franchising advertising is the *profit* theme. An analysis of several hundred franchise advertisements, plus franchisor responses themselves, confirms the preference for this theme.

Table 4-5
Franchisor Recruiting Theme Preferences

Recruiting Theme	Weighted Ranking All Mfgs.	Frequency of Mention Percentage Distribution * Ranking 1	2	3	4	5
Income-profit potential	1	47.1	35.8	12.1	6.7	4.7
Independence-security	2	22.7	23.5	24.3	26.2	28.5
National reputation of franchisor	3	13.6	19.4	29.0	31.3	23.8
Investment potential-capital appreciation	4	12.5	14.7	29.0	31.3	14.2
All other factors	5	3.9	6.4	5.4	4.2	28.5

* Survey of 193 franchising companies with 176 companies providing ranking data. Column totals may not add to 100% due to rounding. Weighted ranking computation provides for most important source cited by respondent receiving a weight of five, the second most important a weight of four, etc.

Personal profit, arising from the proposed purchase of a franchise, is the most dominant theme in franchisor recruiting; it is not unusual for one to encounter exaggerations of this theme. Governmental investigators point out that there are any number of franchise advertisements, accepted by some of the nation's leading newspapers and financial media, which deliberately overemphasize the profit potential of franchise opportunities. This overemphasis has been denounced by both industry executives and government agencies. John Y. Brown, Jr. president of Kentucky Fried Chicken, notes that:

> . . . why you can pick up the *Wall Street Journal* this morning or *The New York Times* or *The Washington Post* and you will see a number of franchise ads promising a man can make $50,000 on a $10,000 or $20,000 investment . . . . They overexaggerate performance statements when in fact they have no stores in operation. There are numerous instances of fraudulent misrepresentation and nondisclosure in advertising that must be cured if you are going to save many aspects of our (franchising) industry.[7]

Separate examinations of franchisee recruiting have also provoked comment that this advertising may be misleading in appearance and content. A report to New York State Attorney General Louis Lefkowitz, on the advertising practices of over 500 franchising firms, reports that:

> In almost 100% of the cases where the Attorney General's (New York) investigators have obtained the literature used to promote sales (involving approximately 500 franchising companies) the special study group concluded the offering literature is either grossly inadequate, misleading, insubstantial, or nonexistent as to material facts and in general presents a danger to the investing public, particularly to persons of low and moderate income who would be interested in bettering themselves from such investments.[8]

Conference Board surveys amongst a national group of franchisees also confirmed that franchisee profit attainments are frequently below the levels projected by the franchising company (see Table 4-6). Failure to achieve projected business volume and profit levels is a practical and psychological hazard for all franchisees, but minority-group entrepreneurs seem to be particularly vulnerable to this obstacle.

To begin with, the minority entrepreneur may enter franchising with some trepidation. Franchise training executives report that for a majority this is probably their first entrepreneur venture and for many it may be the first experience in a nonemployee role. The franchisee enters the arrangement with a built-in insecurity which stimulates a continuous self-reappraisal of his performance.

When profit performance is misleading or overstated it can lead the franchisee to a sense of futility and despair which will inhibit, and may actually prevent, the successful operation of the franchise. Failure to meet

Table 4-6
Franchisee Net Income Evaluation by Class of Franchisee

	Percentage Distribution by *				
Income Evaluation	All Classes	Fast Food	Retail Automotive	Retail Gasoline	Personal Services and Nonfood Outlets
Equal to franchisor projections	30.1	32.3	31.9	20.8	26.9
Above franchisor projections	24.5	25.8	22.2	22.9	24.4
Below franchisor projections	45.3	41.9	45.9	56.3	48.7

* Survey of 371 franchisees. Group includes 210 fast-food, 72 retail automotive, 48 retail gasoline and 41 miscellaneous franchisees.

projected profit levels produces discouragement. Discouragement can spiral into despair and subsequently to the collapse of the franchise unit. While this effect is not unique to minority franchisees, it does seem to have more pronounced effect with minority entrepreneurs.

Franchisors sometimes also discover that franchise advertisements promising that you can be your own boss later backfire among black franchisees. The new minority entrepreneur, already sensitive to paternalism, may believe such advertisements to the point where he bridles at practically any franchisor advice or control. A major gasoline company watched in dismay as one of their new black dealers went $7,800 in debt, despite all offers of company aid and advice. Eventually, the dealer was forced into bankruptcy by his creditors.

When minority franchisees fail, and they do fail, it can come as a bitter shock to both the franchisee and the minority community at large. Some minority community members have come to believe that major franchises are fail-proof. While experienced businessmen would regard such a view as naive, it is nonetheless widely held by black proponents of franchising. The latter group tends to believe that a major franchisor can't afford to let a black franchisee fail. An examination of many franchise company finances and policies would indicate that the franchisor can hardly afford to maintain a failing franchisee regardless of racial considerations.

Group Support

Franchise directors state that nearly all franchisees—but particularly those of minority-group origins—seek to establish how they are doing. They desire reference standards to gauge their relative performance and to determine whether or not they are in trouble. In some franchise systems, the individual franchisees have little if any contact with their brother franchisees and have little information available to them to indicate their own relative performance.

During the past several years, franchisors have moved to overcome this problem and, through formation of company-sponsored franchisee associations, annual franchise meetings, quarterly district meetings, and so forth, they have brought franchisees into social and professional contact. However the minority-group entrepreneur sometimes has a little more difficulty in bridging the interpersonal gap that may exist between himself and other franchisees within his company's system. Franchisors who recruit minority entrepreneurs should make a special effort to bring these new members into the franchisee family. The group morale and support that originates from such contacts proves a valuable bulwark against the success-failure malaise that normally occurs during a franchise start-up.

Franchising's Contribution to Black Capitalism

Each year approximately 400,000 new business concerns are started, and between 350,000 and 400,000 entities are discontinued.[9] Starts for new franchising operations average between 13,000 and 14,000 units per year.[10] Thus, franchising starts as a percentage of all business starts account for little more than 3 percent of the total each year. Yet the importance of these businesses (and of all franchising businesses) as a measure of their contribution to the Gross National Product is substantial. It is estimated that franchised businesses accounts for roughly 10 percent of the GNP and for 25 percent of the retail dollar transactions.

Minority entrepreneurs entering franchising will have to do so by either starting a new franchise unit or purchasing one already in operation. The opportunities for the purchase of existing units are relatively low—with annual turnover rates averaging less than 5 percent per year.[11] For many franchise organizations, with a median size of 500 or so franchised units, this means that no more than 25 units per year will be available for resale. In addition, the company may wish to purchase some of these units itself in order to strengthen its own earnings ratio.

For the vast majority of minority entrepreneurs, the road to franchising will lie through the openings of new units. Even if minority entrepreneurs were provided with new unit opportunities in a proportion equal to their representation in the population, fewer than 1,400 units per year would be available. On a more practical basis, it is doubtful that more than 300 or 400 units per year would be available to minority franchisees. The Small Business Administration, the prime loan guarantor source for the vast majority of minority group-franchisees, reports a total of only 400 minority-group franchise loans during the past two years. The majority of these loans were for retail gasoline outlets, an activity which does not generate appreciable amounts of capital for reinvestment in the ghetto community. The minority community (blacks, Mexican Americans, Puerto Ricans, or Indians) with over 25,000,000 persons, is certainly capable of absorbing more than 400 or 500 business opportunities per year.

The incremental income addition, as represented by these new franchise units, would represent no more than $5,000,000 or $6,000,000 per year [median franchisee net income of $10,000 × 500–600 new units per year].[12]

In summary, the total real economic contribution of franchising, as a vehicle for black capitalism, tends to be exaggerated by both government and industry proponents. Franchising can and should make a contribution to improving the integration of minority groups into the economic system; but it may be unwise (if one is seriously concerned about implementing black capitalism goals) to rely on new black franchisees as a principal vehicle for black capitalism.

Notes

1. Richard N. Farmer, "The Pro's of Black Capitalism: A Modest Program Can Pay Dividends," *Business Horizons* (February 1970), 37.

2. Arthur McZier and Roger Ralph, *Minority Franchising: Its Development, Prospects and Problems* presented at the Sixth Annual International Management Conference on Franchising, Boston College, April 3, 1970.

3. See Conference Board Report, *Roadmaps of Industry, Nos. 1643 and 1644.*

4. Data from recently completed Conference Board survey of 193 franchising companies in the fast-food personal service, and retail nonfood sectors.

5. Data derived from Conference Board examination of 1200 franchise companies, 57 of whom ceased operations during calendar 1969.

6. Gordon S. Bloom, "Black Capitalism in Ghetto Supermarkets: Problems and Prospects," *Industrial Management Review,* Massachusetts Institute of Technology (Volume 2, No. 3), 38.

7. Testimony of John Y. Brown, Jr., *hearings* before the Subcommittee on Urban and Rural Economic Development, United States Senate, *The Impact of Franchising on Small Business,* 91st Cong., 2nd Sess., Part 1, 190.

8. Report to Honorable Lewis J. Lefkowitz, Attorney General, State of New York on *Franchising*—January 7, 1970, by David Clurman, Assistant Attorney General in Charge.

9. *The Failure Record Through 1968—A Comprehensive Study of Business Failures,* New York: Dun & Bradstreet, Inc. (1968), 2.

10. Donald N. Thompson, *Quantitative Approach to Franchising,* a paper presented to the Sixth Annual International Management Conference on Franchising, Boston College, April 4, 1970.

11. Data derived from Conference Board survey of franchising companies as previously cited.

12. Median net incomes computed from Conference Board survey of 437 franchisees in fast-food, personal service, nonfood retail, business and professional, retail gasoline, and retail automotive fields.

5 Franchising and the Inner-City

Roger Dickinson*

The Challenge

No successful franchise patterns appear to have evolved for the economic development of the inner-city. Furthermore, the limitations in applying franchising to the inner-city appear to be quite substantial. Probably as a result of these limitations, new institutions have been developing within the inner-city to overcome the disadvantages of the franchise relationship while preserving some type of constrained decision making and the common-pattern-of-doing-business characteristic of franchising.

The inner-city and its development offer a distinct challenge to the marketing community. To some extent, the marketing academic community appears to have striven for irrelevance in treating the problems of the inner-city. Little has been done by marketers to analyze the problems of high retail prices, of entrepreneurial development, institutional alternatives, and so on. The challenge would appear large in a number of areas.

For example, marketers might attempt to outline some alternative patterns of economic development in the inner-city, with an indication of the ramifications of each alternative, and perhaps borrow from some of the work done for underdeveloped countries.[1] A number of questions might be considered. Can small-scale retailing be part of an efficient channel system for most product classifications? What are the economics of scale for retail organizations in an inner-city environment? If there are substantial economies of scales in retailing and wholesaling, is there any priority of sequence in which the two sectors should be developed? Should large-scale retailing precede large-scale manufacturing? What facilitating organizations need to be established or fostered to encourage the necessary changes?

Marketing scholars might also be useful in conceptualizing some new institutions for development of the inner-city, or in assisting old institutions trying to solve problems in new ways. For example, what type of retail food store is viable in the inner-city? Should drug stores be integrated with supermarkets in the inner-city to provide a new hybrid retail institution?

Other efforts might be directed toward the setting up of institutions

---

* Rutgers University, Newark.

whose primary purpose is the creation of yet other new institutions and firms. Examples of such intermediaries will be offered later in the paper. Marketing expertise might be quite useful in helping to create new institutions with a higher probability of success than is found with conventional institutions. Academicians might also evaluate and test the implications of the institutional alternatives offered by others.

Intermediary institutions create a great many problems that may be amenable to analysis by channel observers. For example, traditional channel analysis assumes that channel members are trying to maximize their long-term profits either individually or collectively. Many intermediary institutions being created in the inner-city appear to have a different set of goals, with profits at the most a constraint and (if more than zero) perhaps irrelevant. Even if one assumes that the goals *are* primarily economic, how is total society to be considered in these goals? In many ways, society is paying the bill for the creation of inner-city intermediary institutions, and the needs of society thus should enter into the objective function. The creation of institutions that aid in creating new firms may have particular significance in light of the finding that the rate of change of institutional life cycles is increasing.[2]

Marketers might study the impact of such intermediary institutions (and other developments on control and efficiency of the channel) from the perspective of society as well as that of the individual channel participants. What are the channel alternatives among higher prices to consumers, higher wages to employees, and the success of enterpreneurial endeavors for short- or long-run inner-city development?

The lack of research, and of understanding, is implied in the failure of franchising in the inner-city, and in the general lack of development of inner-city areas. The inability of the marketing system to develop acceptable alternatives for the inner-city has lead many to question the entire marketing structure in its present form.

This paper considers the present situation, some reasons for the lack of success of franchising in the inner-city, the environment, a definition of franchising and possible ramifications of the definition, and certain intermediary marketing institutions.

The Present

More than five years after a task force of the Department of Commerce reported that franchised business offered members of minority groups an advantage in going into business for themselves (and the Department started publishing *Franchise Company Data for Equal Opportunity in Business*),[3] franchising was still of little significance for the minority community. This is so despite several aggressive programs developed by the Small Business Administration and other government organizations. The lack of success of franchising for minority individuals in and out of the inner-city has been indicated by McZier and Ralph,[4] by the report of the National Industrial Conference Board,[5] by a small study by the author in Newark and New York City, and by the author's interaction with observers of inner-city development.[a] The historical development of minority franchising (from a government perspective) has been outlined by McZier and Ralph.[6]

The lack of success has been true of members of the minority community as franchisor as well as franchisee, and both in and out of the inner-city. Thompson suggests that as of January 1970, there were only eight inner-city franchisors.[7] Despite the lackluster performance of franchising, articles are still being written by ostensibly informed individuals about the bright potential of franchising for minority individuals.[8] Recent programs such as the Department of Commerce "25 × 25 × 2" indicate that government agencies still regard franchising as a valuable element in black capitalism.[b] Indeed, it has been argued that franchising is still in its infant stage of growth and that the full impact of the vitality of franchising will be seen in the inner-city in the future. Whether this is true remains to be seen.

Reasons for Franchising's Lack of Success

Franchising in the inner-city has been questioned by many on various grounds. The inner city has been held not to be suitable for those franchises which were created mainly with the needs of a suburban community in mind. Perhaps white institutions are in general not appropriate for minority areas.

The inner-city, typically with a high store-vacancy rate, many not be an appropriate area for any franchise operation that has a high break-even point. The initial costs of a franchise in the form of new fixtures, high franchise fee, land costs, and so on create high break-even points which may be difficult to meet in areas with low consumer mobility, high store-vacancy rates, and generally low per capita and per store dollar sales. A study of black-owned businesses in Washington, D.C., indicated that median sales for the black-owned business were well under $25,000.[9] Similar results were obtained by a National Business League study in Atlanta, Cleveland, Durham, Jackson, Los Angeles, Norfolk, and Richmond. Average receipts per store in these cities were $19,147.[10] As misleading as

[a] Inner-city is defined as that area between suburbia, and the central business district. The focus of this paper is on those areas of the inner-city that have large minority populations. A more appropriate term might be ghetto.

[b] "25 × 25 × 2" means that as a pilot program, 25 franchisors would try to develop 25 new minority franchisees each within two years. This program has been expanded and as of March 20, 1970, 78 franchisors were participating in the program.

averages may be, and as dated as this information is, the figures do suggest what most observers believe they know. High dollar volume sales are unusual in inner-city areas; low break-even points may be essential in the early stages of inner-city development.

Franchising has been regarded by many as a type of servitude relationship in which the larger franchisor imposes its desires on the smaller franchisee—and thus deprives both the individual and the minority community of many of the indirect advantages of ownership.[11] A report by Brimmer and Terrel has highlighted the belief that the contribution of entrepreneurship to minority employment and to increased standards of living may be small.[12] Even if this hypothesis were correct, it would still be important to have blacks purchasing from minority-owned stores and to have individual entrepreneurial successes within the community that the young could identify with. Franchising is not seen by many as contributing to these latter dimensions.

In addition, there appears to be a tendency for large franchisors to buy back their franchises. Indeed, there is evidence to support the hypothesis that the larger and more financially sound the franchisor, the more probable is the eventual conversion of the franchise system to an ownership integrated system.[13] Thus, there is the chance that much of the benefit to the community will be lost in the long run, although not in the short run.

Franchising is thought by many to be too expensive for most minority participants in that the franchisor charges high initial fees for the services he offers. These services are made to appear all the more exorbitant, because there are organizations in the larger cities that both offer and represent that they offer somewhat equivalent free business services.

The relative advantage of franchising over other types of ownership alternatives in the inner-city may not be as great as in noninner city areas. In the last few years, there have been large numbers of white, small businessmen who are interested in leaving the inner-city, primarily for safety reasons. The large number of businesses thus available for sale tends to create a low price-earnings ratio, that is, high earnings relative to the price being asked for the enterprise. Most of those extolling the advantages of franchising have compared new franchise enterprises with similar nonfranchise alternatives. The more relevant comparison would appear to be between an inner-city enterprise with an operating history being purchased by an individual with some experience in that industry, and the new franchise opportunity, either with or without experience on the part of the buyer. Data on these kinds of alternatives appear to be totally lacking.

The potential inner-city entrepreneur may secure business advice from consultants in one or more nonprofit organizations. A Small Business Administration (SBA) official estimated that about 75% of the minority loans processed from the city of Newark were forwarded by only two organizations. These organizations (composed of blacks and whites) do not appear to recommend franchising alternatives very aggressively. This lack of enthusiasm stems from the factors previously mentioned, as well as the fact that franchise opportunities appear to return lower wages-per-hour than comparable salaried jobs.[c]

Financing is also a problem. For example, economic opportunity loans have been limited to $25,000, and this is often not sufficient to purchase some of the better known franchises. In addition, while a number of financial alternatives may be available to a minority individual, he is seldom aware of all his options.

The Environment

A discussion of the future of franchising within the inner-city should include at least an indication of the environment in which any development would take place. The following set of assumptions, three in number, is perhaps overly short; others could certainly be added which would be relevant.

First, black ownership of many small enterprises is going to have to be a part of any substantial black economic movement. Black ownership of enterprises in and out of the inner-city is essential to the psychological development of the black community; is necessary to provide outlets for qualified individuals who do not desire, or are not capable psychologically of fitting into the corporate mold; and is necessary for the development of future large corporate entities with large scale nonwhite ownership or management.

Second, the inner-city, defined as that area between the central business district and suburban areas (and particularly that element of the inner-city with a large minority population) is an appropriate environment for substantial economic development. This assumption is based in part on the author's feelings that opportunities within this area will increase as individual incomes and government subsidies of various types increase. In part, it represents the author's conviction that the question is only how we as a society should revive the inner-city community; not if we should do so. Thus, Brian Berry's statement of several years ago that the store-vacancy rate in many inner-city areas stabilizes at 20 percent of total retail establishments is not seen as relevant to inner-city areas of the future.[d]

Third, most black economic development, large or small, is going to be

---

[c] A comparison between chain store supermarkets and franchises indicated a decided advantage for the latter.[14]

[d] Berry's assumption is highly debatable. One observer recently suggested that the faster the firms (presumably small retail firms) leave the inner-city area, the better. The inference is that remaining units will be more economic, and that prices may be reduced.[15]

guided development: by government programs, by corporations, and/or by private consultants. This guidance will entail constrained decision making over most of the key decision variables of the enterprise. Indeed, most of the minority alternatives developed in the inner-city today are guided to some degree in this way.

What is Franchising?

Many definitions of franchising are possible; several are presented in a book by Donald N. Thompson.[16] The definition accepted is important, because definitions (and names) appear to influence behavior. One marketing professor suggested that if we called a supermarket "a store in which a customer generally shops once a week," that we would over time actually change the merchandise mix handled by the store, and customers perception of that store.

The definition of franchising with regard to the inner-city seems to have been unnecessarily limiting, and indeed leads McGuire to conclude that on the basis of his analysis on NICB data that the incremental income addition from a successful minority franchise program would be no more than $5,000,000 to $6,000,000 a year.[17] It is the belief of the writer that a redefinition of franchising would broaden the scope of government programs, offer much greater potential for inner-city development, and direct academic research to a much broader potential set of topics.

It would appear that four components are necessary for franchising in the inner-city in addition to the existence of at least two somewhat independent parties, and some available potential market.

1. The organizing party must have a proven successful record of directing business which is relevant to the proposed enterprise. Historically, many franchise operations have been direct extensions of existing operations of the larger firm. Thus, a firm in the restaurant business (if it gets involved in franchising at all) tends to develop franchise operations in the restaurant field. In today's inner-cities, organizations such as the Urban Coalition and Interracial Council for Business Opportunities, are developing experience related to different types of enterprises, but without ever being involved in an ownership capacity.

2. The organizing party must be capable of aiding the new business in such aspects as site location, personnel training, and so on, where relevant.

3. There must be a continuing relationship in which all parties expect to benefit.

4. The organizing party is the dominant nonmanagement[e] influence in the decision making of the newcomer, and has an active part in the opera-

---

[e] Dominant ownership interests are also included in management although this need not be so.

tion of the firm. The activity of the newcomer must frequently be constrained in important ways by the organizing party. The relationship involved may be formal or informal.

Many elements of a normal franchise (such as the existence of a formal legal contract) are not thought necessary aspects of the inner-city franchise, although they may be desirable in some instances. Enterprises such as Hallmark would meet the four listed criteria, even though not normally considered part of present-day franchising.

Possible Types of Operations

Many other types of enterprises would fall under the above definition that normally would not be thought of as included in franchising. The following types might be particularly useful in inner-city development.

A new enterprise might be developed as a sponsored manufacturing entity. For example, a medium-size manufacturing corporation with marginal sales volume in a distant geographic area could be used as a parent-sponsor for an independent manufacturing venture in that area. The parent-sponsor might retain 40 percent or so of the proposed venture, and the government and/or members of the community would have options on 60 percent. Convertible debentures guaranteed by the government could be issued at low interest rates, and government contracts (perhaps 8A contracts) that favor small businesses, or perhaps partial requirements contracts of five years or so in duration, generated by students from schools of businesses in the designated geographic area, could be obtained.[18] The manufacturer-sponsor would agree to provide a specific percentage of minority managers for the new venture within a certain stipulated time period, as part of the package.

The availability of computer banks of data on potential customers would aid in encouraging firms to consider this type of expansion. If business schools or alternative organizations such as the various purchasing associations could develop sizeable puchase commitments for such new operations, substantial efforts might be forthcoming from all organizations involved to match supply with demand. This type of geographic interchange seems to have been impeded by the local nature of most organizations designed to aid minority communities.

New enterprises could be developed under the sponsorship of larger, existing ones in related industries, but with different product mixes. Such new enterprises could be of many types. Two possible reasons why this apparently obvious development has not yet occurred to any great extent may be (1) lack of interest on the part of both parties, and (2) fear of competition by the sponsoring company.[19] The following types of sponsored enterprises are suggested as being feasible.

A new corporation might be developed in which the new (or restructured) enterprise has distinct competitive advantages over the sponsor firm. For example, a corporation might be developed, under rigorous government regulation and with the active sponsorship of a reputable financial institution, to offer ghetto residents lower-priced credit, perhaps with emphasis on consumer credit. There appears to be a ready market for such credit in the inner-city. Judging from such evidence as is available, profitable inner-city financial institutions with reasonable loss ratios could be established with black management and control.

Such a venture should have low initial marketing expenses, because ghetto residents presently utilizing credit appear eager to shift away from establishment financial enterprises. Others, not presently using established credit channels, could be induced to utilize the facilities of the new venture. Such an organization would appear to have many advantages in establishing meaningful credit procedures in the inner-city, as well as in establishing acceptable credit collection procedures.

A second type of new corporation might be developed to exploit situations where established corporations have rejected business alternatives which, while projected as profitable, have expected return rates below the return on investment required by those corporations. Thus, a firm may reject an alternative that offers a projected rate of return of 18 percent, even though the 18 percent may be a conservative projection because of great variation in the estimates of expected payoffs. Several such projects in one industry might be the basis for a new firm to be sponsored or aided by larger, existing firms. The cost of capital for the new firm might be lower than for existing firms, because government can either offer loans at low interest rates, or offer investors various types of guarantees or risk underwriting. Government may also increase the projected payoff by changing cost factors: through liability or fire insurance, for example. This second type of new corporation may not be popular with existing companies, but it may be more palatable than other alternatives, for example those proposed by Richard F. America, Jr.[20]

A third and related type of new firm might be created to undertake certain long-term endeavors that do not offer immediate potential profit, again under the secondary control of another firm or group of firms. COMSAT, at the time it was established, might have offered such possibilities. Many of these alternatives will not be in highly labor-intensive industries; however substantial entrepreneurial possibilities are present.

Arrangements might be developed for inner-city operation by leading food, department, or discount stores. Such new enterprises, with increased local identification, might develop more customer loyalty, have a lower stock shortage rate, and perhaps a lower rate of accidents than do existing establishments in the ghetto. The government might provide low-cost insurance and/or partial funding for such an enterprise. This type of enterprise could be viable in situations where a retailer without professional guidance plus resident advantages would not. Such an alternative has been proposed most recently by Little and Spralen.[21]

One tends to think of this as a White Front (West Coast discount operation) sponsoring a minority-owned discount store in areas where the trade name is reasonably well known. It could also be a way by which an A&P gains some market share participation in the San Francisco Bay area.

Corporate spinoffs of various types might also be considered. Assume a corporate subsidiary currently earning a substandard rate of return on invested capital. Ownership and/or management of the subsidiary by minority individuals might increase profits through some of the competitive techniques previously discussed. Therefore, spinoffs might be attractive for all concerned. One large bank recently suggested that this appeared to be a key solution for the development of black-run, neighborhood banks. Apparently this bank is examining the feasibility of spinning off some branches in this way.

One element of inner-city entrepreneurship that must not be overlooked is the encouragement of *existing* minority-group entrepreneurs. The chances of the third pancake house succeeding in the long term under an entrepreneur with two successes already to his credit are rather high. It may be better from most perspectives to support the existing ghetto entrepreneur with a proven success record. This means that in changing the inner-city, one need not wait for entrepreneurs to walk in with ready-made plans, but should make a dynamic effort to locate entrepreneurs and inform them of additional existing opportunities. Unfortunately, a number of studies conducted, including those mentioned earlier, indicate that the number of successful black entrepreneurs is not large.

Intermediary Institutions

Of particular significance to the development of the inner-city are the newer types of institutions which serve as intermediaries in the channel. Some of these may be considered as part of franchising, according to the previous definition. Indeed, it can be argued that many intermediary institutions are evolving because of the inadequate inner-city performance of franchise-type firms. These intermediaries are of several types, including the following.

Advisory Services. The Interracial Council for Business Opportunities, Urban Coalitions, and so on, which are advisory to their clients, usually do not charge for their services. These organizations may develop and promote patterns of doing business that have proven successful in existing industries, for example dry cleaning. They can become quite sophisticated in site selection, as they participate in opening more and more of a specific type of outlet in an area. They may participate financially in opening retail or service stores, or develop a continuing relationship in which they have no ownership interest. In most instances, such organizations are solely advisory in function, so that they would not qualify under the previous definition of franchising.

Advisory service organizations are becoming a potent force in the development of the inner-city, and are an aspect of the channel of distribution that cannot be overlooked. They provide an important communication link in the channel, absorb some of the costs otherwise borne by the financial institutions and/or the Small Business Administration, and represent community interests in a variety of ways. Their development raises a number of questions of how such intermediaries should be treated from various channel perspectives.[22] It is possible that advisory service organizations, or adaptations of them, could come to control large sectors of specific marketing channels within the inner-city.

Venture Management Companies (VMC). The concept of the VMC combines features of regular franchising, with a principal who sets policies and provides management assistance—all the while maintaining the independence of management of the inner-city enterprise. The major features of a VMC, as conceived by PACT in San Francisco, are as follows: (1) a contractual relationship exists between the businessman and the VMC which includes some element of compensation to the VMC; (2) the VMC retains the right to repossess the business under specified conditions; (3) the VMC has some ultimate control over financing disbursements by the business; (4) the VMC provides, or assists in providing, on-the-job managerial training; (5) The VMC provides financial reporting and monitoring services; (6) the VMC provides consultant services in defined areas of management; (7) the VMC provides bail-out assistance in case of emergencies; (8) the VMC provides continuing educational programs; and (9) the ultimate financial responsibility for the business remains with the entrepreneur, so long as he fulfills the terms of his contract with the VMC.

A discussion of how such VMCs should and would work is beyond the scope of this paper.[23] The VMC as envisioned is a combination of franchising as it now exists, and the advisory organizations outlined above. The combined organization, if successful, could develop new patterns of doing business in several industries, and would have numerous ramifications for channel management and performance, and for overall business viability in the inner-city.

Notes

1. See Charles C. Slater, "Contractual Interdependence . . .", *infra.*
2. William R. Davidson, "Changes in Distributive Institutions," *Journal of Marketing* (January 1970), 7–10.

3. U.S. Department of Commerce, *Franchise Company Data For Equal Opportunity in Business* (July, 1969).

4. Arthur McZier and Roger Ralph, *Minority Franchising, Its Development, Prospects, and Problems,* a paper presented at the Fifth Annual International Management Conference on Franchising, Boston College (April 3, 1970).

5. E. Patrick McGuire, "The Feasibility of Minority Group Capitalism," *infra.*

6. McZier and Ralph, *Minority Franchising.*

7. Donald N. Thompson, "Contractual Marketing Systems: An Overview," *infra.*

8. "Minority Franchising Boom or Bust," *Black Enterprise* (August, 1970), 50–55.

9. Maury Seldin and Michael Sumichrast, "Negro Entrepreneurship in the District of Columbia," *SBA Economic Review* (Spring-Summer, 1969), 11.

10. *Project Outreach,* Washington, D.C.; The National Business League (June, 1969).

11. Robert W. Little and Thaddeus Spratlen, *Alternative Ownership Forms for Inner-City Businesses,* unpublished manuscript (1969).

12. Andrew F. Brimmer and Henry S. Terrel, *The Economic Potential of Black Capitalism,* a paper presented at the 82nd meeting of the American Economic Association (December 28, 1969).

13. See Alfred R. Oxenfeldt and Anthony O. Kelly, "Will Successful Franchise Systems Ultimately Become Wholly-Owned Chains?," *Journal of Retailing* 44 (Winter, 1969), 69.

14. See National Commission on Food Marketing, *Organizations and Competition in Food Retailing, Technical Study No. 7,* Washington, D.C.: U.S. Government Printing Office. (1965) 330.

15. Brian J. L. Berry, *Commercial Structure and Commercial Blight,* Department of Geography Research Paper No. 85, Chicago; University of Chicago (1968).

16. Donald N. Thompson, *Franchise Operations and Antitrust,* Boston, Mass.: Heath Lexington Books (1971), esp. Chapter Two.

17. E. Patrick McGuire, *infra.*

18. For some indications on how business schools may help, see Roger Dickinson, "New Frontiers in Encouraging Minority Entrepreneurship—The Role of the Business School," *Journal of Small Business* (April–July 1969), 14–16.

19. Robert R. McKersie, "Vitalize Black Enterprise," *Harvard Business Review,* (September–October, 1968), 88–89.

20. Richard F. America, Jr., "What Do you People Want?," *Harvard Business Review* (March–April, 1969) 103–112.

21. Little and Spratlen, *Alternative Ownership.*

22. For example, Louis Stern's perspectives of the intermediary would appear to be relevant. See Louis Stern, "Potential Conflict Management Mechanisms . . .", *infra.*

23. For a discussion of the VMC, write Mrs. Del Behrend, PACT, 593 Market Street, San Francisco, California 94105.

Part Three
Conflict and Conflict Resolution in Contractual Marketing Systems

Potential Conflict Management Mechanisms in Distribution Channels: An Interorganizational Analysis

Louis W. Stern*

Introduction

The purpose of this paper is to suggest potential mechanisms that might be employed to manage, reduce, or resolve conflict in distribution channels. Very little work has to date been done in applying to the field of marketing the findings of sociologists, labor relations experts, or political scientists on resolving conflict. Conflict in distribution may be viewed behaviorally as a form of opposition which is opponent-centered; based on incompatibility of goals, aims, or values of opposing firms; direct; and personal; in which the opponent or opposing firm controls the goal or object desired by both parties.[1] Such conflict—behavior which thwarts, injures, or destroys an opponent—is present in all socioeconomic systems, including channels of distribution.

For any given socioeconomic system, some degree of conflict may be highly functional for the long-term viability of the system.[2] At some point, excessive conflict becomes dysfunctional and produces adverse effects on the system. Conflict should not be treated as all good or all bad. Boulding nicely characterizes the view taken here:

> We are not "against" conflict. It is indeed an essential and for the most part useful element in social life. There is, however, a constant tendency for unmanaged conflict to get out of hand and to become bad for all parties concerned.[3]

It would be desirable to develop confiict-resolution machinery which would prevent system participants from making pathological moves toward each other in a conflict situation.[4] A distribution channel would likely exhibit chronic conflict even in the context of a relatively stable relationship among the firms comprising it.[5] Our main concern is with impeding the possible dysfunctions of social and economic conflict within channels of distribution;

---

* The Ohio State University: during the 1969–70 academic year, Visiting Associate Professor of Business Administration, University of California, Berkeley. The author acknowledges the contributions of his research assistants, Charles S. Snow and David E. Keefe, to the preparation of this paper. Research and clerical support was provided by the Institute of Business and Economic Research, University of California, Berkeley.

that is, those consequences which make for a decrease in the adaptation or adjustment of particular social relationships.[6]

Change frequently produces conflict. Change-induced conflict occurs when two parties try to maintain their traditional relationship in the face of changes in the underlying basis for that relationship. Efficiency in the economy calls for technological advancement leading to lower production costs. It also calls for efficient distribution of products to users. Here we are studying devices to minimize disruption in distribution, which is a part of achieving efficiency in distribution but obviously not all. If the underlying basis of technology and market demand shifts in an industry, the most efficient distribution system might also have to change. In most cases, the traditional or established parties in the distribution channel will be the best ones to accommodate the new distribution system. But if a channel member does not feel it should have to change, it will either be bypassed and thereby eliminated from the system, or else the disruption will be postponed until the situation deteriorates to the point where action from outside the system (for example, government intervention) is needed.

This does not reflect an interest in defending the status quo or impeding change. Beyond those generally exogenous shocks which bring conflict but which produce social benefits far beyond the costs of the disruptions they cause, there are a multitude of situations where the reduction, management, or resolution of conflict could increase the efficiency of distribution. Certainly, a system cannot bear continuous dysfunctional conflict among its components unless such conflict is consistently regulated or resolved. As Assael has put it:

> If commonly accepted procedures for conflict resolution can be developed, then the system can establish a degree of stability, despite the competing self-interest of its members.[7]

Several broad strategies for dealing with various types of conflict are available. The first approach assumes that the system itself is not wrong, rather that the participants in the system are just not working it properly. The second approach to dealing with conflict involves the creation of additional conflict-resolution machinery. The third approach requires alteration of the institutional structure so that there is less built-in conflict.[8] Although the last of these approaches is extremely appealing, this discussion will concentrate mainly on the first two in an attempt to propose mechanisms that will preserve the system, and by so doing, accent its positive attributes. The mechanisms suggested can operate in two ways: (1) on the situation within which channel members act (or on their perceptions of the situation); and/or (2) through direct appeal to the values and attitudes of the participants in the system.[9] However, one must continually grapple with the problem of how best to coordinate channel activities in order to make the channel into a highly rational unit—while simultaneously maintaining social integration, the normative commitments of the members, and their motivation to participate.

Two general limiting conditions on conflict resolution within distribution channels are the nonpermanency of the channel relationships and the asymmetric interdependence of the members on each other. Even though any given channel for a product, service, or individual brand has a tendency to persist over a long period of time, there still may be very little member loyalty to the channel over the long run. The greater the frequency and duration of the interactions among channel members, the greater the likelihood that institutionalized resolution processes will emerge.[10] Obviously, the ephemeral nature of many distribution channels militates against such institutionalization.

Also, it is observed that channel members exhibit various degrees of reliance on each other. Conflict may impinge upon the very autonomy of one organization but have only marginal effects upon another. Similarly, the mutual benefits seemingly derived from cooperation may be minute for one unit and of survival impact for the other.[11] It is recognized that these limitations do, in fact, exist, and an attempt is made to account for them in the following discussion.

This paper draws heavily from the literature on political science, international relations, sociology, organizational behavior, and industrial relations for insights into possible ways of managing conflict in distribution channels. Although there are certain risks in applying the findings and concepts of one field to another, it is the author's opinion that marketing in general—and distribution channel analysis in particular—suffer from a serious paucity of concepts and models by which we might seek to describe, explain, or predict with fullness and clarity. Our conceptual poverty strikes this writer as perhaps the greatest single handicap to the development of everything from basic empirical generalizations to a major theoretical scheme. Some judicious and selective borrowing and adaptation from the behavioral sciences is definitely in order.

In this paper, the potential conflict management mechanisms suggested are organized into categories which are consistent with the various degrees of perceived vertical interdependence among channel members. Viewing vertical interdependence on a continuum from high to low, the categories and the specific mechanisms discussed under each can be outlined as shown in Figure 6-1, p. 114.

As is pointed out below, certain mechanisms facilitate the implementation and reinforce the effectiveness of others (for example, establishing superordinate goals facilitates conciliation and mediation). In addition, productive bargaining and negotiation underlie and make possible the enactment of almost all of the mechanisms proposed.

It is important to note at the outset, however, that if dysfunctional conflict within distribution channels is to be managed, reduced, or resolved, it will be essential for the members involved to come to grips with the

Degree of Perceived Vertical Interdependence

High ⟷ Low

Category	Supraorganizational	Interpenetration	Bargaining and Boundary Negotiation
Specific Mechanisms	superordinate goals; conciliation and mediation; arbitration; special-purpose mechanisms: (1) commissions of inquiry (2) observers	membership: exchange-of-persons programs; ideological: (1) education, (2) propaganda; membership *and* ideological: cooptation	diplomacy bargaining strategy

Figure 6-1

underlying causes of the conflict issues which arise among them. And the specific mechanism employed will depend not only on the cause of the conflict but also on the structure of the channel itself. The scope of this paper is, nevertheless, limited to suggesting potential conflict management mechanisms irrespective of issues, causes, or channel structure.

Supraorganizational Mechanisms

In channels of distribution characterized by a high degree of interdependence and interaction among members, we might expect to come upon fertile ground for the institutionalization of supraorganizational conflict resolution mechanisms. The supraorganizational mechanisms discussed below are: (1) establishing superordinate goals; (2) employing conciliation and mediation; (3) submitting to arbitration; and (4) establishing special-purpose mechanisms. In order to implement such instruments, channel members would have to view themselves as part of a channel *system* and thereby recognize, overtly, their functional interdependence. Even in these situations, however, members will generally have different sets of active goals (or at least different preference orderings for the same set of goals), and thus the conditions for conflict will continue to exist among them.

Establishing Superordinate Goals

Superordinate goals are those ends greatly desired by all those caught in dispute or conflict, which cannot be attained by the resources and energies of each of the parties separately, but which require the concerted efforts of all parties involved.[12]

If a superordinate goal or goals could be established within a channel of distribution, this would not only lead directly to a reduction in conflict among members but would provide the motivational basis for adopting other resolution mechanisms. More than any other device, superordinate goals could facilitate functional accommodation. Thus, mediation between groups or organizations in conflict is likely to be most beneficial when effective appeal can be made to a superior value-consensus which transcends group or organizational differences (for example, the preservation of the system itself, common larger interests, shared norms, and so on).[13] Superordinate goals can also provide the foundation for meaningful contacts, communication, and negotiation—as well as interorganizational problem-solving.[14]

Conflict resolution requires an integration of the needs of both sides to the dispute so that they find a common goal without sacrificing their basic economic and ethical principles.[15] The difficult task is, obviously, to articulate a goal or common interest on which all parties can agree.

Disregarding the social merits of certain goals for now, it is possible to provide two pertinent examples. In the television receiver industry, the desire for stabilized prices has served as a superordinate goal for certain manufacturers, distributors, and most retailers.[16] Similarly, in the liquor industry, distillers and small retailers have established the superordinate goal of preventing large discount retailers from gaining a significant market share. "Small retailers have endorsed price controls in order to prevent price competition. Distiller support for the small retailers is provided to resist the power of larger retailers and to insure continued channel leadership."[17] It is doubtful, however, whether a defensive goal would be as effective, over the long run, in maintaining a viable channel system as one that would increase the efficiency of moving a product through the channel, with the result that greater sales volume would be obtained at lower, or at least stable, distribution costs. This latter goal might require shifting functions within the system, but would result, over time, in higher rates of return for all participants.[18]

The establishment of a superoordinate goal requires equitable participation and contribution from all parties in interdependent activities. In his experiment utilizing such goals, Sherif found that "ways of doing things, of meeting problems, of behaving under certain conditions were standardized, permitting variation only within limits."[19] Such standardization or routinization of behavior within channel systems is a prerequsite to effective channel performance.[20] Likewise, it is possible that the establishment of such goals will encourage implicit mediation[21] within a channel of distribution. As is shown later, one of the mediator's tasks is to articulate systemic demands or those values which might be realized if the system is to survive. With the existence of superordinate goals, such demands may interpose themselves between conflicting channel members without recourse to the services of a third party. Conflicts may be indefinitely suspended in the interest of values which transcend immediate, parochial concerns.

The notion of implicit mediation is similar to the concept of encapsulated conflict in which feelings of hostility, differences of belief or interest, and a mutually agresssive orientation might well continue—but where the sides rule out certain modes of conflict.[22] Since a universal superior authority does not generally exist within a channel system, the participants, acknowledging superordinate goals, are more likely to work out self-imposed limitations on the means of conflict without employing referees.

If the establishment of superordinate goals is going to lead to effective problem-solving among organizations in a channel, mutual identification must be high among the participants. As Parsons observes: "The focus of the integrative problem on a trans-organizational level . . . is the problem of the determination of the loyalties of the participants. . ."[23] Clearly, then, the varied loyalties of channel members are limiting factors to the establishment of superordinate goals.

As indicated above, a superordinate goal can be an explicit desire by channel members to resist a threat to the channel's survival or growth from some outside pressure (for example, competitive, legal). In such situations, the channel members set aside their differences for the sake of defense. The threat of government investigation has encouraged large manufacturers and chains to use their power to resolve conflicts internally in the food,[24] automobile, farm equipment,[25] liquor, and television receiver industries[26]—as pointed out previously. To some extent, it makes no difference if the threat from the outside is real or is simply perceived; it will tend to increase cohesion within the channel. Not only is it likely to result in the reduction of minor conflicts within the channel, but also it may lead to a heightened sense of identity as an interorganizational system and a greater degree of consensus of opinion and purpose.[27]

It is also likely that the process of meeting a threat external to the system will serve to displace or transfer hostility between and among channel members to the common enemy.[28] However, a major question remains: When the outside threat is removed, will the internal conflicts return? In other words, is the cohesion ephemeral and is the prior conflict among channel members merely postponed?

The unified reaction on the part of channel members to an outside threat can be viewed as a behavior change, and as behavior changes, attitudes are usually altered to become more consistent with the new behavior. These new attitudes may remain once the threat is removed. In addition, during the process of countering the threat, information will be exchanged, some of which may have a bearing on sources of conflict beyond that posed by the threat. Because of the information exchanged and because of the monetary and psychological costs jointly borne by the parties during the time of combating the threat, future relationships between the parties may be significantly different than they were during previous interactions.[29] Channel members may gain empathy by seeing, perhaps for the first time, other channel members' points of view even though these viewpoints are presented in a different context than under normal circumstances. Finally, the original conflict issues—prior to the threat occurrence—may decay over time as energies are directed at the outside threat.

On the other hand, there is a good possibility that the prior conflict will reemerge, unaffected by the temporary unity of the parties. Blake, Shepard, and Mouton have observed that:

The condition under which superordinate goals will produce cooperative effort, *without resolving the intergroup relations problem,* is when the assumed *superordinate goal is really a superordinate threat* . . . In this circumstance, the groups put aside their own conflict until the greater enemy has been annihilated. But, the differences that were set aside earlier, return once the threat or superordinate need has been removed. In truth, then, the problem has not been solved. It has only been deferred under conditions of more pressing need for cooperative effort.[30]

Research by Stouffer on army personnel[31] supports Blake, Shepard, and Mouton's conclusion.

In addition, while channel members are coalescing to combat the threat, it is unlikely that they will tolerate more than limited departures from the unity which they establish. Needed innovation and change, apart from that used in combating the threat, may be stultified during the time of unified action; the only way the channel members can solve the problem of dissent within their ranks at this time is, presumably, through the dissenter's voluntary or forced withdrawal.[32]

Thus, establishing superordinate goals on the basis of threats from the outside, whether real or perceived, can be a double-edged sword. Extended periods of integrated effort may be achieved only when the institutions and conflict and attempt to resolve them. This task may be advanced by the agencies within a given channel uncover the underlying causes for their supraorganizational mechanisms of conciliation and mediation.

Employing Conciliation and Mediation

The process of reconciliation presumably leads to the convergence of opposing images held by the conflicting parties.[33] In theory, conciliation is the passive role of attempting to bring harmony and a spirit of cooperation to a negotiation over conflicting issues and primarily involves adjustment of the dispute by the parties themselves.[34] It may be broadly defined as:

> . . . the non-regulatory process of effecting agreement, compromise, or the reconciliation of differences between disputing parties through the action of a third party. The third party—a conciliator or intermediary—takes part in the settlement process by bringing the disputing parties together to resolve their differences.[35]

It is likely that, in many distribution channels, independent wholesalers serve as conciliators between their suppliers and their customers and may occasionally serve as mediators. Here, the term intermediary has a double meaning, pertaining to marketing tasks assumed as well as to conciliatory functions performed.

Mediation implies more active intervention by the third party than does conciliation.[36] Mediation is the process whereby the third party attempts to secure settlement of a dispute by persuading the parties either to continue their negotiations or to consider procedural or substantive recommendations that the mediator may make.[37] Thus, conciliation is primarily adjustment of the dispute by the parties themselves, while mediation is guidance by a third party to an acceptable accommodation.[38] In the following discussion, unless otherwise stated, we concentrate on the more intricate process of mediation.

Functional Attributes of Mediation. Mediation essentially involves operating on the field of the conflicting parties in such a way that opportunities or trading moves are perceived which otherwise might not have been perceived. Solutions might be given an acceptability simply by being suggested by the mediator and hence acquire a degree of saliency which is important in making them mutually acceptable. One party often finds it difficult to accept a proposal suggested by an opposing party, whereas if the same proposal is suggested by a neutral mediator, it can be accepted without difficulty.[39] Effective mediation succeeds in clarifying facts and issues, in keeping parties in contact with each other, in exploring possible bases of agreement, in encouraging parties to agree to specific proposals, and in supervising the implementation of agreements.[40] The National Agricultural Chemicals Association (NAC) serves not only as a conciliator but as a permanent mediator between manufacturers and distributors on the entire range of conflicts in the pesticide industry. NAC has been effective in helping to resolve inventory level, distributor representation, price maintenance, and advertising allowances conflicts within pesticide channels.[41]

Primarily, mediation in distribution channels is likely to be of a strategic nature, that is, concerned with creating a favorable environment within which the parties to the conflict can interact. Such mediation aims at reducing the incidence of conflict and channeling it along nondestructive lines of development.[42] In the food industry, many conflicts (for example, over bypassing wholesalers, price discrimination, advertising allowances, private brands, shelf-space allocations, and loss-leader selling) have arisen from society's increased affluence which has changed the economic basis of the industry. According to Adler, Johnson, and Meschio, an advertising agency based in Chicago has acted as a mediator for a multitude of problems in the industry by setting up a committee of six leading grocery chain executives, wholesalers, and manufacturers. The committee reviews merchandising ideas and programs and provides an apparatus whereby industry problems and conflicts can be considered by all segments concerned.[43]

The Mediator's Role. In large part, a mediator of channel conflicts should concern himself with getting the conflicting parties together (perhaps over some noncontroversial procedural problem, such as types of forms used in billing), deflating the conflict situation by providing pertinent facts, raising doubts about positions already assumed, and expanding the area of agreement by suggesting alternate solutions to the problem.

Kerr has emphasized that a mediator's role may be to reduce irrationality, to remove nonrationality, to explore solutions, to assist in the graceful retreat, and to raise the cost of the conflict.[44] The latter tactic would not generally be pursued in the mediation of channel conflicts and would likely be reserved for cases of great public concern. In such cases, the government may act as mediator and, perhaps, as arbitrator (for example, in dealers' rights situations).

Another function of the mediator is to restructure conflict situations by isolating nonrealistic elements of aggressiveness so that the contenders can deal directly with the divergent claims at issue.[45] Once he has ascertained the real as opposed to the stated positions of contending parties, he can suggest proposals in the area of the real demands or leak information to the various sides about what each side will settle for.[46] Through control of the communications structure, the mediator can reinforce or minimize the intensity of the position of one party as it is transmitted to the other. Here, again, the possibilities of utilizing an independent merchant middleman as a mediator are seen, for such middlemen undoubtedly form a key link in the communications network between manufacturers and retailers and may control communications to some extent. (The ability to control communications has obvious implications for the power structure within the channel, however.) The role of the mediator in the communications process is even more crucial when viewed in the light of Blake and Mouton's findings.[47] They have determined that:

> When competition is between groups, each of which has developed its own fixed position, the identification of an individual with his group makes it difficult, if not impossible, for him to penetrate the content and to comprehend the position represented by the opposition to the same degree he grasps the content of his own group's product.
>
> This study suggests that under competitive conditions members of one group perceive that they understand the other's proposal when in fact they do not.

Groups tend to act toward one another's solutions as though they had "blinders" on.[48]

To the extent that a mediator exercises independent initiative (as in the case of McKinsey and Company or other consultants), he becomes an entrepreneur of ideas and may, as such, play an extremely important role in structuring the network of interorganizational relationships.[49]

Early in 1970, the Ford Foundation allocated $1.1 million to finance a Board of Mediation to solve disputes among New Yorkers. In supporting the establishment of the Board, Mayor John Lindsay stated that "Men and women of the community will find new avenues for resolution of conflicts."[50] Although most conflicts among members of a distribution channel are less heated than those which one might expect to find before this particular board, a worthwhile investment in industries with a record of distribution conflicts might be the establishment of similar boards, whereby respected individuals (for example, retired judges, professors, and consultants) are held on retainer to aid in mediation with the consent of the parties. Many trade associations attempt to play the role of mediator, but their usually slanted interest makes them inappropriate for the task (aside from the possible antitrust implications of their actions). Operating executives of neutral firms may not have the time or inclination to help mediate distribution conflicts in which their firms are not involved. Nevertheless, the history of distribution in the United States has shown that, if the disputants allow the conflict to continue long enough, the federal or state government will assume the mediator's role. In the latter case, mediation can rapidly lead to compulsory arbitration or adjudication in the guise of legislation which all parties might find difficult to live with over the long run (for example, the Robinson-Patman Act).

Submitting to Arbitration

Arbitration is another supraorganizational conflict management mechanism which can be applied to channel situations. It is felt to be inferior to the mechanism of conciliation and mediation for the resolution of conflict in distribution channels, because imposed resolution often leaves each disputant feeling that his position was poorly understood. The "solution" may be viewed as inequitable, and the dispute may easily surface again in slightly different form.

Arbitration can be compulsory or voluntary. Compulsory arbitration is a process wherein the parties are required by law to submit their dispute to a third party whose decision is final and binding.[51] In a channel context, the government (or the courts) have served to settle disputes, as was the case when the automobile dealers and manufacturer clashed publicly over certain distribution policies and when fair trade pricing was a conflict issue between resellers and manufacturers.

Voluntary arbitration is a process wherein parties voluntarily submit their dispute to a third party whose decision will be considered final and binding.[52] Examples of such arbitration are found by reviewing the Trade Practice Conferences of the Federal Trade Commission. One case occurred in the television receiver industry. In 1955, the Federal Trade Commission, in concert with television set manufacturers, distributors, and dealers, set up 32 industry rules to protect the consumer and to reduce distributive conflicts. Five distribution conflict areas were arbitrated: (1) tie-in sales; (2) price-fixing; (3) mass shipments used to clog outlets and foreclose competitors; (4) discriminatory billing; and (5) special rebates, bribes, refunds, and discounts.[53]

Conflict resolution through voluntary arbitration requires at least three prior commitments among the disputants:

1. They have to agree that some form of settlement—even one involving the loss of a position—is preferable to continued conflict.
2. They have to agree to resolve the conflict on the basis of legal standards rather than according to political, economic, or social criteria.
3. They have to agree to the jurisdiction of a specific court, commission, or committee.[54]

Thus, in arbitration, a preliminary bargain must be struck, in the sense that the parties have to agree to submit to arbitration. It is hoped that channel members would, in the process of undertaking such a bargain, understand that the whole question of relying on law and law enforcement to truly resolve conflicts among them is suspect, because it is doubtful whether permanently legislated solutions can be equitably applied to future conflicts in different channel contexts. As Assael has found, internal (intrachannel) conflict resolution has proven, historically, to be more satisfactory, from both a micro and a macro viewpoint, than external or legally imposed resolution.[55]

Establishing Special-Purpose Mechanisms

Two intriguing supraorganizational mechanisms are suggested in the political science literature. Brief mention is made of them here, because they could prove useful in helping to resolve, manage, or reduce conflict in distribution channels.

Commissions of Inquiry. Although such commissions are frequently slow in operating, have no effective sanctions, and sometimes serve only as a substitute for action,[56] it is likely that, in situations of considerable friction in the channel, the need for in-depth information, independently gathered, might warrant their establishment. One issue of importance in the drug industry involves the problem of physicians owning pharmacies. The National Association of Retail Druggists (NARD), the American Pharmaceutical Association (APhA), and the American Medical Association (AMA) formed the Commission on Medicine and Pharmacy to resolve this problem.[57] Although the recommendations of the commission's work were not widely accepted, it is possible that they might result in more viable long-term channel relations than state laws passed at the request of independent pharmacists aimed at preventing physician ownership of pharmacies.

Observers. The dispatch of neutral observers to the scene of hostilities by, say, trade associations comprised of the channel members in dispute might be useful in verifying disputed facts and in acting as a restraining influence. Although such a mechanism is similar to conciliation, the information received about the conflict might be reported to the trade association and published in a factual manner in the trade magazine of the association. With the supposedly fresh insight generated by the information, especially as it relates to the various positions taken on the issue, conciliation may be facilitated.

Interpenetration Mechanisms

Organizations with frequent interactions may be more likely to develop patterns of conflict resolution or management in their interrelationships than those whose relationship consists of only occasional events.[58] Interpenetration mechanisms provide means for increasing the number of meaningful interactions among channel members and, concomitantly, for reducing conflict within the channel. In this section, we suggest two primary approaches to interpenetration—membership and ideological.

Membership

According to Lasswell and Kaplan, conflict among groups varies inversely with their mutual permeability. "The permeability of a group is the ease with which a person can become a participant."[59] Thus, in a specific channel context, it has been found that meetings between the National American Wholesale Grocers' Association (NAWGA) and the Grocery Manufacturers of American (GMA)

> . . . provide an opportunity to exchange ideas on better methods available to manufacturers and distributors for improving market and distribution functions.

Members of the trade associations involved see these meetings as an opportunity to resolve many distributive conflicts which normally could not be resolved by individual trade associations.[60]

An even more explicit example of membership interpenetration is found in the television receiver industry.

As recently as 1960, the lack of communications in the channel of distribution was one of the major dealer complaints. Another was the lack of product knowledge and the lack of understanding of the dealers' problems on the part of the distributor salesmen.

The approach used to correct the lack of communications was to invite the manufacturers to become members of the National Appliance and Radio-TV Dealers Association (NARDA). Twelve of the major manufacturers are now members, and representatives of these and other companies now attend NARDA conventions. Manufacturers' relations meetings are a regular convention feature. Executives of manufacturing organizations are regular speakers at NARDA training seminars and at the annual convention.[61]

Despite the applicability of these examples, interaction among the various representatives in trade association-sponsored events is undoubtedly infrequent. What is even more desirable is the creation of a network of primary relations among channel members. The possibility for creating such a network is present within many channels because the relations formed within a channel are functionally important to the members; therefore, as Galtung suggests, their conflict-preventing value may be considerable.[62] But even on a relatively infrequent basis, the arranging of inter-organizational collaboration on a common task jointly accepted as worthwhile and involving personal association of individuals as functional equals should result in lessened hostility among the organizations.[63] Perhaps one of the most meaningful interpenetration mechanisms, in this respect, might be an exchange of persons program among channel members, similar to those implemented in international relations.

Exchange of Persons. In distribution channels, exchange of persons could take place on several different levels of an organization or at all levels. Thus, as part of his initial executive training program, the recruit (perhaps fresh from college) could spend a prescribed period of time working in the organization of suppliers, middlemen, and/or customers. A salesman employed by a manufacturer could, on a periodic basis, spend a specified period of time as an employee of a wholesaling or retailing firm selling the latter's assortment of products of which the original manufacturer's product may be only one of several. In like fashion, traffic and inventory personnel could be exchanged as well as other line and staff personnel. For certain types of employees, such as relatively prominent executives, it might even be possible to work out a sabbatical system similar to that at universities, so that these executives could replenish themselves by taking positions either closer to or farther away from the ultimate market in which the product of the particular channel is sold.

Persons participating in such exchanges would no doubt take back to their home organizations a view of their job in an interorganizational context and a personal and professional involvement in the channel network, as well as added training. In addition to learning something of the complexities of another channel member's organization and mission, participants in such programs would have the opportunity of coming together with channel counterparts who share specific tasks, professions, and interests. These shared tasks could form the basis of continuing relationships that are extraorganizational in content and perhaps interorganizational (or even supraorganizational) in commitment.[64] It is highly likely that positive changes in attitudes toward other channel members would occur.[65]

Taking the notion of intertransfer of personnel one step farther, it might also be possible to establish a more or less permanent representative or presence in another channel member's organization as an expression of concern and to exert a restraining influence over conflicts which might arise. In lieu of this mechanism, many manufacturers probably view their agent middlemen, their salesmen, or the merchant wholesalers whom they supply as permanent representatives in a given market. The role of the independent merchant wholesaler as a possible conciliator and mediator has already been mentioned. The use of salesmen as conflict managers is discussed in the section entitled "Boundary Mechanisms."

Membership interpenetration is presently employed in some channels of distribution, but on a relatively haphazard basis. Thus, in the electrical equipment industry, conference booths at distributor conventions manned by manufacturers' executives permit direct discussion of distributive conflicts and may be viewed as a form of membership interpenetration. Another example is the use of factory specialists provided by the manufacturers to distributors in this industry; when technical problems arise, the factory specialist permeates the distributor's organization.[66] This type of activity is common in many industries. However, approaches to conflict resolution through membership interpenetration of this type are not believed to hold the promise, over the long run, of the exchange-of-persons programs suggested above, because the interaction is infrequent and there is less likelihood of attitude change.

An exchange-of-persons program in a distribution channel would be of little significance, however, if the only individuals with which the exchangee comes into contact are no potential threat to channel cooperation or are already converted to an interorganizational view of channel relations. Furthermore, the best type of exchange might involve not merely a transfer of persons but common enterprises, jointly initiated and carried out on a relatively large scale.

Ideological

Basically, ideological penetration refers to informational, propaganda, and educational activities aimed at managing, resolving, or reducing conflict. Some of the aims of such activity may be: (1) simply to enhance knowledge and understanding; (2) to cultivate goodwill among channel members, gain prestige, and perhaps to undermine the goodwill and prestige of a competitor or competitive channel; and (3) to shape attitudes among the personnel of another channel member so as to influence its management to follow a certain course of action.

Effective ideological penetration, independent of kind, should lead to a reduction of bifurcation of images and to the definition of common symbols among conflicting parties. What the channel propagandist (or educator) may be seeking is some sort of ideological conversion. For example, the effort by many manufacturers and wholesalers to influence retailers to think in terms of return-on-investment criteria rather than in terms of gross profit margins would, if accomplished, represent an ideological conversion, as well as result in changes in retail operating methods. In order to achieve such a conversion, it would be wise for the channel member performing the educational role to:

1. avoid actions that would have the effect of humiliating the target organization(s);
2. attempt to achieve a high degree of empathy with respect to the values of members of the target organization(s);
3. adopt a consistent attitude of trust toward the target organization, including an open statement of one's own plans and intentions;
4. make visible concessions for one's cause and maintain a consistent set of positive activities which are an attempt at the explicit realization of the goals of the organizations involved and, hopefully, of the channel as a whole.[67]

Specific Mechanisms. We have already mentioned the sales training programs conducted by manufacturers for their middlemen's salesforces. Another specific mechanism that has often been employed to achieve ideological penetration is the wide dissemination of trade publications and reprints. In the electrical equipment industry, for example, the National Association of Electrical Distributors (NAED) publishes two monthly magazines, *The Electrical Distributor* and *Electrical Wholesaling,* which have large circulations among both manufacturers and distributors.

> Articles are published on distributor operations, industry trends, and distributor-manufacturer dialogues which provide information and an exchange of ideas leading to better understanding of the problems facing both supplier and distributor. Legal information, government legislation affecting members, and association activities are frequent topics. In addition, articles on operating, financing, and sales management are included.[68]

Also, the development of professional ethics in an industry, either through interactions among trade associations or the Trade Practice Conferences of the Federal Trade Commission, may often serve as a normative structure through which increased coordination is achieved among channel members. Similarly, channel members can coalesce to achieve public relations ends. Such a phenomenon occurs regularly in those industries where the retailers are small and the manufacturers and distributors are large. In the drug, petroleum, and grocery industries, small businessmen have attempted to influence the public in order to gain regional or national sympathy for their plights. Obviously, this method of ideological penetration of manufacturing and/or wholesaling organizations is indirect, but it has proven to be effective in a number of cases. The issue must, however, be fairly simple in order for the generally disinterested public to understand and favor action on it.

All other things being equal, educational programs will have maximum effects when information is presented as part of the ordinary action of a group or organization carrying out its usual socioeconomic function.[69] Thus, it would appear that ideological conversion, if that is the aim, would be easier in on-the-job training situations where channel members interact directly with one another in the performance of a common task than through trade publications or other general information programs. A unique approach, which is somewhat in between the on-the-job and the general information approaches, might be the establishment of either libraries or training schools or both by channel members, either individually or collectively. In the case of collective efforts, this would take the form of a supraorganizational mechanism; individual efforts would be an ideological penetration mechanism.

Perhaps ideological penetration can be best accomplished through the process of uncertainty absorption by one channel member for others in the system. This mechanism has been described elsewhere in a channel context[70] and is, therefore, only briefly discussed here. Uncertainty absorption takes place when inferences are drawn from a body of evidence and the inferences, instead of the evidence itself, are then communicated.[71] All channel members face uncertainty in their respective task environments and, as Cyert and March point out, "firms will devise and negotiate an environment so as to eliminate the uncertainty. Rather than treat the environment as exogenous and to be predicted, they seek ways to make it controllable."[72] There is, however, little likelihood that such a situation will occur. One can expect a high degree of uncertainty to prevail in almost all commercial situations. The problem is to reduce the uncertainty to the point where meaningful predictions are possible, based on probability distributions, and to achieve at least some degree of consensus on a realistic perception of the environment in which firms operate. Once this realistic perceptual consensus is established, one can expect at least some reduction in conflict that was based on incongruent views.

Several examples of uncertainty absorption can be cited. In the electrical equipment industry, conflict has arisen between a manufacturer and a distributor over a manufacturer's nebulous, unwritten sales policy. All subareas of conflict (for example, number of distributors in a territory, discount structure, pricing policy, inventory, and so on) would presumably be dealt with less antagonistically when policies are written out and agreed upon in advance, at least in outline.

To improve distributive relations, NAED maintains a file of representative policies currently in use by manufacturers. Manufacturers who are interested in formulating a new policy, amending one which appears to be ineffective, or aligning their policy with acceptable ones in their industry, may use this information.[73]

In the often conflict-ridden automobile industry, the automobile manufacturers have combined membership and ideological penetration (uncertainty absorption). The manufacturers send business management specialists to dealers facing problems; these specialists are called upon to analyze the dealerships thoroughly and to make recommendations to the individual dealers which would improve their management practices. In order for such an approach to be effective, it must not degenerate into a feedback system whereby the specialists report adversely on dealers who do not follow their suggestions. Otherwise, trust will collapse and the approach will be ineffective and most likely generate rather than reduce conflict. Another means of absorbing uncertainty in this industry has been employed by General Motors and Ford. Both of these companies feed back to individual dealers and area sales managers statistical averages and other data on sales volumes and profit margins useful for comparisons by dealers. The data provide the dealer with norms to strive for in altering his sales policies. Through his actions, he may thereby negotiate his environment in a more realistic and calculated manner. Undoubtedly, the information explosion has had a major impact on the capability of firms to deal with uncertainty.

Combinations of Membership and Ideological Penetration

Perhaps the most effective type of interpenetration in terms of changing the goals, attitudes, or behavior of the target organization occurs when the penetration involves both membership and ideology.[74] An important mechanism in this respect is cooptation.

Cooptation is the process of absorbing new elements into the leadership or policy-determining structure of an organization as a means of averting threats to its stability or existence.[75]

Cooptation may be a response to the pressure of specific centers of power within a channel of distribution.

The functional attributes of cooptation as a conflict resolution mechanism are many. Cooptation may permit the achievement of ready accessibility among channel members in that it requires the establishment of routine and reliable channels through which information, aid, and requests may be brought. Administration of the channel may become more centralized so that the execution of a broad policy is adapted to local market conditions by utilizing the special knowledge of individuals attached to distributive organizations located in diverse markets. Cooptation also permits the sharing of responsibility so that a variety of channel members may become identified with and committed to the programs developed for a particular product or service.

A channel member, given a position of power and responsibility with regard to the generation of policy decisions throughout the channel, should gain increased awareness and understanding of the problems which the channel as a whole faces. Also, as Thompson and McEwen observe, "By providing overlapping memberships, cooptation is an important social device for increasing the likelihood that organizations related to one another in complicated ways will in fact find compatible goals."

> By thus reducing the possibilities of antithetical actions by two or more organizations, cooptation aids in the integration of the heterogeneous parts of a complex society. By the same token, cooptation further limits the opportunity for one organization to choose its goals arbitrarily or unilaterally.[76]

It might also be said that cooptation of channel members encourages their ideological transformation, so that they subsequently tend to carry the ideology of the coopting unit into their other membership groups.[77]

Selected examples of cooptation (or methods approaching cooptation) are available. As previously mentioned, the membership structure of the National Agricultural Chemicals Association (NAC), which serves the pesticide industry, consists of representatives of both manufacturers and distributors. Wesson has found that:

> In its informal role as discussion leader seeking a common ground, NAC utilizes the "team approach" in which member companies work together in a coordinated effort to develop a workable compromise acceptable to both its manufacturer and distributor members. This sophisticated approach to problem resolution has the additional advantage of being both a time and money saving device. If there were two associations (one to represent each party), both manufacturer and distributor would be forced to spend considerable time and money "counterbalancing" the opposing efforts of the other association. By utilizing the unique approach of NAC, the entire pesticide industry (and the food and fiber industry as well) avoids the built-in provincialism so inherent in other industries.[78]

In the food industry, retailers were coopted by wholesalers in forming voluntary cooperatives. Dealer councils which have been established in the television receiver and automobile industries were promoted, to some extent, by manufacturers and represent another situation of cooptation on an informal basis.

There are some real dangers in implementing this device, especially for the coopting organization. Selznick states:

> The significance of cooptation for organizational analysis is not simply that there is a change in or a broadening of leadership, and that this is an adaptive response, but also *that this change is consequential for the character and role of the organization or governing body.* Cooptation results in some constriction of the field of choice available to the organization or leadership in question. The character of the coopted elements will necessarily shape the modes of action available to the group which has won adaptation at the price of commitment to outside elements.[79]

Thus, cooptation makes inroads on the process of deciding goals and means. Not only must the final choice be acceptable to the coopted channel member(s), but to the extent that cooptation is effective, it places an outsider in a position to determine the occasion for a goal decision, to participate in analyzing the existing situation, to suggest alternatives, and to take part in the deliberation of consequences.[80] When an established organization is coopted, the coopting organization becomes in some measure dependent upon the coopted organization for administration. Using the administrative machinery of the coopted organization requires one to pursue the interest and goodwill of those who control it, the leaders of the coopted organization.[81] And, finally, as Etzioni observes, cooptation may be used to create a semblance of communication from others to those in control without effective communication really existing. Manipulated or fictitious cooptation only conceals the need for real communication and influence.[82] It is perhaps for this latter reason that the term coopted has fallen into such disrepute among students seeking change on college campuses today. The same reaction could easily occur in distribution channels.

It may not, of course, always be feasible or desirable to institute penetration processes similar to those mentioned in this section. If this is the case, channel members may have to rely heavily on activities taking place at the boundaries of their various organizations if conflict is to be reduced or resolved. The following section turns to a discussion of possible boundary mechanisms for resolving conflict or for, at least, coming to grips with conflict situations.

Boundary Mechanisms

For the purposes of this section, assume that the relevant boundary of an organization is its legal boundary. Given this assumption, a boundary position can be defined as one for which some role senders are located in other organizations.[83] The personnel of an organization who are concerned primarily with foreign (external) affairs are called, in this context, boundary persons. Thus, in the role-set of a boundary person are his role-partners in other organizations. Within a channel of distribution, two key classes of boundary personnel are, obviously, salesmen and purchasing agents.

Activities between and among personnel operating at the boundary of organizations within distribution channels may be significant in reducing conflict just as they are significant in creating it. Their boundary roles make these persons continual mediators between organizations, for they should be able to justify the position of either side to the other and thereby should be instrumental in bringing about compromise.[84] Whether the existing boundary people in many channels are the most appropriate to *manage* conflict is a question that is taken up later in this section. What is being sought in a normative sense are boundary persons who can serve as "liaison officers" for channel members. In the long run, the roles of these boundary specialists should become routinized through the emergence of opposite numbers, thereby reducing the likelihood of interorganizational conflicts accruing from threats to the status of organizational representatives.[85] What is suggested as a conflict resolution mechanism, then, is the institutionalization of some form of channel diplomacy.

Diplomacy. Using an analogy from international relations, channel diplomacy is the method by which interorganizational relations are conducted, adjusted, and managed by ambassadors, envoys, or other persons operating at the boundaries of member organizations. Channel members must persuade, negotiate with, and exert pressure upon each other if they wish to resolve conflict, because, with the exception of the government, there is generally no superior above them that can impose a settlement. Therefore, they must engage in, cultivate, and rely upon diplomatic procedures. Taken in its widest meaning, the task of diplomacy is fourfold:

1. Diplomacy must determine its objectives in the light of the power actually and potentially available for the pursuit of these objectives.
2. Diplomacy must assess the objectives of other members and the power actually and potentially available for the pursuit of their objectives.
3. Diplomacy must determine to what extent these different objectives are compatible with each other.
4. Diplomacy must employ the means suited to the pursuit of its objectives.[86]

The tasks involved in the implementation of diplomatic procedures and processes are similar to those involved in the implementation of negotiation and bargaining discussed later. The functions of a channel diplomat would, again in the widest interpretation, be to help shape the policies he is to follow, to conduct negotiations with channel members to which he is assigned, to observe and report on everything which may be of interest to the firm employing him, and to provide information concerning his firm to the operatives in counterpart channel organizations.[87]

The presence of individual or of diplomatic committees is frequent in distribution channels. We have already referred to the use of business management specialists in the automobile industry and of factory specialists in the electrical equipment industry. The National Association of Wholesale Druggists has a Manufacturers Relations Committee which meets with manufacturers in joint seminars to resolve conflicts which arise, for example, over problems of direct sales to retailers.[88] Perhaps the best example of channel diplomacy can be found, however, in the food industry. Manufacturers appoint liaison men who represent and interpret company policy to wholesalers and retailers. According to an official of one major grocery manufacturer, the use of liaison executives has resulted in a resolution of many conflicts before they have matured.[89] Adler, Johnson, and Meschio point out that

> . . . by the use of direct executive contacts and controls, many wholesalers and retailers achieve a greater degree of communication than was previously obtainable. The activity of liason men has proved to be very advantageous to the industry in improving relationships.[90]

In this and other situations where diplomacy is employed, communication —or the transmission of messages, impressions, and interpretations from one human source to another—is crucial. The channel diplomat is, or can become, a key link in this human network.

Strains on Boundary Personnel. Individuals who operate at the boundaries of organizations are subject to important strains which tend to impede their ability to aid in the resolution of conflict. In a study of such boundary personnel as salesmen, credit expediters, and traffic managers, Kahn, et al., concluded that:

> Lacking formal power over role senders outside his work unit, a person at the boundary has a reduced ability to guarantee that the performance of these outsiders will be as he needs and wishes. In compensation for this lack of formal authority, a boundary person relies heavily on the affective bonds of trust, respect, and liking which he can generate among the outsiders. But these bonds are unusually difficult to create and maintain at the boundary. For the outsiders, the failings of a person's unit are all too easily identified as failures of the person, thus weakening their affective bonds with him.
>
> [A consequence of the role senders' inadequate understanding of boundary positions] is the failure of role senders, especially in other departments, to appreciate the urgency or necessity of a boundary person's requests to them. They are likely to present him with self-interested demands and to be intolerant if these demands are not met.

A person in a boundary position is faced, therefore, with a sizable body of role senders whose demands are hard to predict and hard to control . . . Most difficult of all, the boundary person faced with such demands has at his disposal only limited power resources with which he may attempt to induce their modification.[91]

This extended quotation shows clearly the problems that are likely to face the channel diplomat.[92] (As a result of these problems, it is possible that boundary personnel can become "marginal men.")[93]

Assuming that all boundary personnel face strains similar to those enumerated above, the question remains: Who are the most appropriate individuals within an organization to assume the role of diplomat in resolving channel conflicts? It is essential that the status of the diplomat be high enough so that the power which the diplomat holds is at least relatively obvious to the parties with whom he interacts. A suggestion by Kahn, et al., appears appropriate to the concept of creating diplomat positions:

With respect to the liaison of the organization with the outside world, create specialized positions for which liaison is the major and continuing function. Provide strong support for such positions, in terms of power, ancillary services, and organizational recognition.[94]

These authors further suggest that the organization should create multiple rather than single liaison arrangements whenever the workload justifies; as they point out, "all truth is seldom contained in one channel." Finally, they urge that formal procedures be built into the organization for maintaining agreement and understanding between the boundary personnel and those personnel within the organization who are inwardly oriented.[95]

To prepare the channel diplomat for this role, it would seem important that he be given thorough indoctrination in and knowledge of organizational procedures and operations if he is to resolve the uncertainty which his role prescribes. In addition, to prevent occupants of these positions from developing too strong an identification with specific channel members, it might be wise to periodically shift such boundary persons among the different members of the channel.[96]

Bargaining and Negotiation

It might be reasonably argued that no matter what conflict management mechanism is adopted by policy-makers within a channel, resolution is always the result of bargaining—the making of commitments, offering of rewards, or threatening of punishments or deprivation—between and among the members. Insights into effective bargaining and negotiation should facilitate the employment of the mechanisms suggested previously. And, channel members often can be viewed as interest groups in opposition over scarce resources. If channel members do not (or only vaguely) perceive themselves as part of a distribution system and, instead, take the position of interest groups,[97] then a bargaining model is more appropriate to deal with the conflict which arises among them.[98]

In a channel context, the term bargaining refers to the negotiation of an agreement for the exchange of goods or services between two or more organizations. Negotiation is a process through which the parties interact in developing potential agreements to provide guidance and regulation of their future behavior.[99] Here, the two terms will be used interchangeably, unless otherwise noted.

Within a channel, the bargaining may at first appear to be a fixed-sum game, that is, whatever solution is arrived at will yield the same total benefit, even though the division of returns will vary. However, solutions frequently yield a greater total benefit to the channel in, say, the form of higher sales or lower costs. Bargaining, under these conditions, takes on the characteristics of a variable-sum game. In addition, there is, within a channel:

> . . . a curious mixture of cooperation and conflict—cooperation in that both parties with a certain range of possible solutions will be better off with a solution, that is, a bargain, than without one and conflict in that, within the range of possible solutions, the distribution of the total benefit between two parties depends on the particular solution adopted.[100]

The functional qualities of recurrent bargaining are pointed out by Thompson and McEwen:

> Even where fairly stable and dependable expectations have been built up . . . the organization cannot assume that these relationships will continue. Periodic review of these relationships must be accomplished, and an important means for this is bargaining, whereby each organization, through negotiation, arrives at a decision about future behavior satisfactory to the others involved.[101]

On the other hand, bargaining almost necessarily places strains on the status and power systems within a channel of distribution. If those members who are more powerful prevail, this may result in a more forceful perception of status and power differences throughout the channel. If they do not prevail, their position is weakened. Also, bargaining probably acknowledges and legitimizes heterogeneity of goals throughout a channel.[102]

The Strategy of Bargaining. Two questions appear central in developing a bargaining strategy: (1) How much is it necessary to concede? and (2) How can the other side be induced to accept less favorable terms than it wants? Schelling notes that "to 'win', a party must make his commitment appear irrevocable to the other party." On the other hand, if one party can demonstrate to the other that the latter is not committed, or that he has miscalculated his commitment, the former may undo or revise the latter's commitment.[103] If bargaining is going to be effective in leading to integrative problem-solving, it is essential to prevent the other party from holding a committed position in order to claim a disproportionate share of the joint gain. In other words, it is important to attempt to keep the other party flexible or to help him abandon a committed position once it has been taken, because integrative or cooperative bargaining[104] requires free and open exploration without preconceived ideas or dogmatic positions.

Unfortunately, in distribution channel situations, such flexibility is rarely present. In dealing with retailers handling multiple brands of one product, a manufacturer, in his attempt to solve a distributive conflict, may find that the retailers jealously safeguard their autonomous positions by arguing that they are manifestly unable to satisfy the expectations of one supplier without arousing the enmity of another. This excuse (which is a commitment to the status quo) can be used by all members of the channel of distribution and is probably a primary reason for resisting change.

There is also a tendency on the part of some commercial organizations to attach symbolic value and importance to conflicts arising from rather simple sources, as when retail druggists continually employ the small business ethic in attempting to come to grips with conflict situations between them and the larger firms with whom they compete or from whom they buy. This technique of escalating issues into matters of principle is useful in establishing a commitment to a bargaining position, but it is a double-edged sword which can also cut off escape routes and destroy bargaining flexibility.

A stable bargaining situation depends on the development and maintenance of trust and mutual respect between bargainers. One obvious reason for trusting another channel member is the awareness that this member has incentives for behaving in a trustworthy fashion and that its leaders recognize these incentives. In some cases, trust or distrust is based on what is known about another member's past behavior. Trust is likely to develop if the other member has engaged in helpful behavior (as defined by the furtherance of the goals of the affected member), distrust if it has engaged in harmful behavior.[105]

If a channel member wants to be trusted, it should demonstrate that its helpful actions are freely taken and that it adopts policies harmful to the interest of other channel members only when compelled to do so by forces beyond its control.[106] The relatively beneficial relationships within the food industry between grocery manufacturers and food chains have no doubt been a result of the development of trust through this approach while the relationships between automobile dealers and manufacturers have been continually strained by actions taken by the manufacturers that could only breed distrust, such as the inequitable sales quotas levied in the early 1950s. One would therefore expect to find integrative bargaining in the former industry and an abundance of distributive or competitive bargaining in the latter.[107] The element of trust in negotiations is maintained by:

> . . . scrupulous observance of certain unwritten rules, including the avoidance of lies, misrepresentation, and impugning of motives; the execution of all verbal or written agreements; the payment of debts of gratitude; and the maintenance of procedures which facilitate rather than block easy communication.[108]

Some suggestions which seem useful for establishing trust in channel relations come from the political science literature. One suggestion is the taking of unilateral steps to reduce tension. Adapting Osgood's theory to a channel context, one could say that for such a unilateral act to be effective in inducing another channel member to reciprocate, it should (1) be clearly disadvantageous to the member making it, yet not cripplingly so; (2) be such as to be clearly perceived by the other member as reducing his external threat; (3) be such that reciprocal action by the other member is available and clearly indicated; (4) be announced in advance and widely publicized to all channel members (its nature, its purpose as part of a consistent policy, and the expected reciprocation); and (5) not demand prior commitment to reciprocation by the other member as a condition of its commission.[109] Etzioni has shown actual support for such a theory in international relations. He points out, however, that critics of unilateral moves have argued that there are several dangers involved: (1) the recipient of the move will be able to distinguish between real and symbolic moves; and (2) the recipient might reciprocate below par and thus accumulate an advantage.[110] Boulding also observes that unilateral peaceableness may become too costly for the peaceable, especially in the face of genuinely pathological behavior on the part of the "nonpeaceable."[111] Despite these dangers, judicious unilateral moves may prove to be highly beneficial in moving a conflict situation away from dysfunctional stalemate and into multilateral negotiations based on trust.

Compromise, like trust, is a prerequisite in successful bargaining. Negotiations are possible only if each side is prepared to give up something in order to gain some of its objectives. Thus, compromise requires that:

> Both parties must initially agree that a partial withdrawal of demands or positions is preferable to continued conflict, and only after this decision has been reached can they begin discussing the substantive terms of a compromise agreement.[112]

The difficulty with the compromise outcome is that the basic problem may not be solved and may continue to be a source of tension.[113]

The willingness to negotiate a compromise depends, of course, on correct assessment of the conflict situation. Such assessment and the following accommodation is possible only if each party is aware of the relative strength of the others.[114] If implicit assessment is difficult, mediation may help, for one of the key functions of the mediator is to make such indices readily available to [the] parties. The conflicting parties will be able to negotiate to the extent they share a common system of symbols allowing them to arrive at a common assessment.[115]

Trade associations have an important role to play in generating such symbols and in facilitating strategic bargaining. For example, one of the most important contributions of the National Association of Electric Distributors and National Electrical Manufacturers Association in encouraging cooperation and resolving conflict in distribution in the electrical equipment industry is in maintaining a dialogue between manufacturers and distributors through meetings, conventions, and industry trade publications.[116] Similar activities also take place among channel members in other industries through their trade associations. Bargaining or negotiation is performed by the individual channel members; however, the trade associations facilitate the development of appropriate symbols. For example, the National Automobile Dealers Association appointed a Task Force Committee to discuss and negotiate mutual problems and their solutions with manufacturers. According to Buob, Sacks, and Seckler:

> This committee has been successful in convincing manufacturers to maintain elected dealer councils, to cooperate in promoting ethical advertising, to make adjustments on warranty parts and allowances, and has encouraged the manufacturers to inaugurate intensive business management programs.[117]

Within channels of distribution, it is likely that there will be considerable problems in selecting the appropriate negotiators for any given conflict issue. The obvious answer would seem to be that, if the issue is of major importance, the chief executive officer or, at least, the vice-president in charge of marketing or procurement (in the case of large organizations) should act as negotiator. Such individuals have the unique advantage of being best able to commit their companies, but they often suffer from lack of time, lack of specific experience, and undue pressures to produce results.[118] The extreme visibility and pressure when top executives negotiate may make the desire to avoid loss of face a principal motivation. This may also be used as a bargaining tactic, but if employed by both executives, it appears likely to result in stalemate.

With regard to the loss of face problem, the logic of bargaining and compromise is not appropriate for the settlement of ideological differences. The negotiators cannot bargain over an ideological principle, as might be represented by the small business ethic versus the desire for efficiency on the part of large businesses, without compromising their moral position. There is, as Katz observes, an "all-or-none quality to moral principles."[119]

Thus, in order to prevent the two types of differences from getting confused, it may be best to send to the channel bargaining table pragmatic, task-oriented men (rather than ideologues, as some top corporate executives must be) with at least some system perspective and intimate understanding of the nature of the channel structure, so that the members can avoid bargaining over ideological issues.

Several major problems face the negotiator, however, even if he is vested with appropriate authority. Blake and Mouton point out that:

> . . . in the negotiation situation, logical considerations may require that a representative renounce his group's prior position in order to gain a valid resolution of the intergroup problem. But acting against the exercise of a logical and factually analytical attitude are group ties that require him to gain victory and, at whatever cost, to defend a point of view which protects his membership position.[120]

Thus, negotiators face the dual problems of (1) securing consensus among the operating executives within his own firm; and (2) compromising between the demands for flexibility by conflicting channel members and the demands for rigidity by the executives in his own firm. These same problems serve to place constraints and limitations on negotiation as a conflict resolution mechanism in distribution channel relations.

Constraints and Limitations. We have already mentioned one major limitation on the scope of negotiation in channel relations—the difficulty of settling ideological differences through bargaining. In fact, it is likely that establishing superordinate goals is the only means to settling ideological differences. We have also noted that negotiation is governed by, and operates within, bounds acceptable to the firm from which the negotiator comes. In this respect, leaders on each side in the bargaining situation must avoid courses of action which threaten the leadership positions of their counterparts. Where there is genuine interest in maintaining the bargaining relationships, studies indicate that leaders on both sides clearly take into account the limitations that their opposite numbers must contend with and minimize behaviors that produce embarrassment or problem-creating consequences for them.[121]

Clearly, there is no point in negotiating in the absence of some possibility of success. The problem is more complicated, though, if the purpose of one or more of the parties is not agreement but rather the pursuit of a side effect. Such side effects can be positive or negative, for example, to maintain contact (to keep channels of communication open), to gain more knowledge of the other party's true position, to reveal the intentions of the other side, to deceive (to buy time, for example), to permit a forum for propaganda, or to affect a third party (the government, consumers, suppliers, middlemen outside the negotiation, and so on).[122]

Lastly, although this list is not exhaustive, public debate among the channel members is likely to hurt the chances of achieving an effective accommodation through negotiation. Taking a public position in advance of negotiation lays the groundwork for competition to enter, even when the firms would be expected to interact in a collaborative manner. Taking a public position intensifies the problems mentioned above, for when a negotiator deviates from a fixed public position, it means that he is openly going against the desires of his firm. As we have already taken pains to point out, compromise is a prerequisite to bargaining, and therefore, it may be impossible to negotiate successfully in channel situations if one side takes a specific and adamant public position.

Other Mechanisms

We have not discussed the conflict resolution mechanisms of (1) avoidance or withdrawal (sometimes referred to as conflict denial or passive settlement); and (2) the use of force, counter-threats, and deterrence (balance-of-power mechanisms). We have also not explored fully the use of law and law enforcement or the creation of authority in a supersystem. These mechanisms have been placed outside the scope of this paper because they are either (1) obvious and may require no purposive effort on the part of channel members to institute; (2) dependent for their initiation on some manifest coercive power on the part of members; or (3) maintain the conflict in a suspended and oftentimes unstable state. Nevertheless, by omitting an examination of them, we do not mean to imply that they are unimportant.

Summary and Conclusions

At some point in time, dysfunctional conflict is expected to occur in channels of distribution, as it does in all social systems. This paper has suggested potential mechanisms which might be employed by channel members to manage such conflict. It draws heavily on the literature from fields where conflict has been most intensively studied. While it is understood that there are dangers in transferring findings from one context to another, the insights generated by a selective adaptation of the behavioral sciences to distribution channel analysis can prove highly useful for improving intra-channel relations and for increasing the efficiency of distribution.

The paper lists four main categories of conflict management mechanisms: supraorganizational, interpenetration, boundary, and bargaining and negotiation.

The specific supraorganizational mechanisms examined were (1) establishing superordinate goals; (2) employing conciliation and mediation;

(3) submitting to arbitration; and (4) establishing special-purpose mechanisms, such as commissions of inquiry and a system of observers. The institutionalization of these mechanisms is greatly enhanced when the channel members view themselves as having a high degree of vertical interdependence, that is, as being components of a channel system. Under such circumstances, the establishment of positive superordinate goals is expected to be highly beneficial in itself as well as in facilitating effective conciliation, mediation, negotiation, and joint problem-solving. However, it is questionable whether superordinate goals which take the form of defenses against the threat of a force outside a channel will enhance the long-term viability of that channel.

The interpenetration conflict management mechanisms were divided into three groups: (1) membership; (2) ideological; and (3) combinations of membership and ideological. Suggested as the most functional form of membership penetration for distribution channels was exchange-of-persons programs among channel members. Ideological penetration is accomplished by informational, propaganda, and educational activities. The primary mechanism proposed for the combination of membership and ideological penetration was cooptation. While cooptation involves the formal or informal inclusion of channel members into the decision-making apparatus of the focal organization—thereby leading to a fuller understanding of common problems in the distribution of the focal organization's goods or services—it places constraints on the policy-makers of that organization. The coopted members will generally insist on having some influence over policy-setting for the channel by the focal organization; otherwise, the cooptation is merely symbolic in nature and is likely to be discredited quickly.

The primary boundary mechanism advanced was the appointment of channel diplomats. There are, however, considerable strains on individuals operating at the boundaries of organizations which are produced by, and also cause, considerable role conflict. The selection of the appropriate individual(s) within a firm for the position of channel diplomat is, therefore, crucial to the effectiveness of this mechanism.

Bargaining and negotiation, the fourth major category put forward, underlies all of the other suggested mechanisms. Their functional attributes would be difficult, if not impossible, to obtain without effective bargaining. The paper discusses the strategy of bargaining, including the concept of commitment, the development of trust, and the use of compromise. It indicates some of the desired characteristics of a negotiator while examining the pressures which he must face during negotiation. Lastly, it suggests that bargaining cannot be used to settle ideological differences and that negotiation is governed by and operates within bounds acceptable to the organizations or groups from which the negotiators come. These latter factors, among others, place important limits on negotiation as a conflict management device in distribution channels.

Several means for achieving conflict resolution were purposively omitted from the discussion, either because their employment would not lead to an effective grappling with the issues at conflict in the channel, or because they were too obvious to examine in detail. For these reasons, there is no exploration of avoidance, withdrawal, conquest (for example, vertical integration), the use of force, counterthreats, or deterrence.

In order to manage, reduce, or resolve dysfunctional conflict within distribution channels, it is essential that the issues and causes of conflict, as well as channel structure, be analyzed in conjunction with the various conflict resolution mechanisms. Here are suggested a number of such potential mechanisms. It will be the task of future theoretical and empirical research to link issues, causes, and structure to the mechanisms proposed.

Notes

1. Louis W. Stern, *A Sociological Interpretation of Competition, Conflict, and Cooperation in the Marketplace,* Working Paper No. 54, Berkeley, California: Institute of Business and Economic Research, University of California (January, 1970), 4–7.

2. Lewis A. Coser, *The Functions of Social Conflict,* Glencoe, Illinois: The Free Press (1956).

3. Kenneth E. Boulding, "Opening Remarks," in Elise Boulding (ed.), *Conflict Management in Organizations,* Ann Arbor, Mich. Foundation for Research on Human Behavior (1961), 1.

4. Kenneth E. Boulding, "A Pure Theory of Conflict Applied to Organization," in Robert L. Kahn and Elise Boulding (eds.), *Power and Conflict in Organizations,* New York: Basic Books, Inc. (1964), 136–145.

5. See, for example, Henry Assael (ed.), *The Politics of Distributive Trade Associations: A Study in Conflict Resolution,* Hempstead, New York: Hofstra University (1967), and "Constructive Role of Interorganizational Conflict," *Administrative Science Quarterly,* XIV (December 1969); Eugene Litwak and L. F. Hylton, "Inter-Organizational Analysis: A Hypothesis in Coordinating Agencies," *Administrative Science Quarterly,* VI (March 1962), 395–426; Joseph C. Palamountain, Jr., *The Politics of Distribution,* Cambridge, Mass.: Harvard University Press (1955); and William M. Evan, "Toward a Theory of Interorganizational Relations," in Louis W. Stern (ed.), *Distribution Channels: Behavioral Dimensions,* Boston, Mass.: Houghton Mifflin Co. (1969), 73–90.

6. Coser, *Social Conflict,* 8.

7. Assael, "Constructive Role," 580.

8. Daniel Katz, "Approaches to Managing Conflict," in Kahn and Boulding, *Power and Conflict,* 107–8.

9. Robin M. Williams, Jr., *The Reduction of Intergroup Tensions,* New York: Social Science Research Council, Bulletin No. 57 (1947), 17–18.

10. Harold Guetzkow, "Relations Among Organizations," in Raymond V. Bowers (ed.), *Studies on Behavior in Organizations,* Athens, Georgia: University of Georgia Press (1966), 22, 24–25.

11. *Ibid.,* 28.

12. Muzafer Sherif, *Social Interaction,* Chicago, Ill.: Aldine Publishing Company (1967), 457; see also Muzafer Sherif, O. J. Harvey, B. Jack White, William R. Hood, and Carolyn W. Sherif, *Intergroup Conflict and Cooperation: The Robbers Cave Experiment,* Norman, Oklahoma: The University of Oklahoma (1961), 202.

13. Williams, *Intergroup Tensions,* 75.

14. William M. Evan and John A. MacDougall, "Interorganizational Conflict: A Labor-Management Bargaining Experiment," *Journal of Conflict Resolution,* XI (December 1967), 399.

15. Kurt Lewin, *Resolving Social Conflicts,* New York: Harper and Brothers (1948), 59.

16. Robert G. Biedermann and Richard L. Tabak, "The Television Receiver Industry," in Assael, *The Politics of Distributive,* 278.

17. John Mingst and Robert A. Soriano, "The Liquor Industry," in Assael, *Constructive Role,* 369.

18. Louis W. Stern and J. L. Heskett, "Conflict Management in Interorganization Relations: A Conceptual Framework," in Stern, *Distribution Channels,* 295.

19. Sherif, et al., *Intergroup Conflict,* 206.

20. Wroe Alderson, *Marketing Behavior and Executive Action,* Homewood, Ill.: Richard D. Irwin, Inc. (1957).

21. Michael Barkun, "Conflict Resolution Through Implicit Mediation," *Journal of Conflict Resolution,* VIII (June 1964), 121–30.

22. Amitai Etzioni, "On Self-Encapsulating Conflicts," *Journal of Conflict Resolution,* VIII (September 1964), 242–3.

23. Talcott Parsons, *Structure and Process in Modern Societies,* Glencoe, Ill.: The Free Press (1960), 47.

24. Albert Adler, Herbert Johnson, Jr., and William Meschio, "The Food Industry," in Assael, *The Politics of Distributive,* 200.

25. John C. Buob, Robert M. Sacks, and Robert P. Seckler, "The Automobile Industry," in *ibid.,* 299–350; and Everett Rashotsky, "The Farm Equipment Industry," in *ibid.,* 387–412.

26. Mingst and Soriano in *ibid.;* and Biedermann and Tabak in *ibid.*

27. Coser, *Social Conflict,* 95.

28. Amitai Etzioni, "The Kennedy Experiment," in Louis Kriesberg (ed.), *Social Processes in International Relations,* New York: John Wiley and Sons, Inc. (1968), 431.

29. George C. Homans, *Social Behavior: Its Elementary Forms,* New York: Harcourt, Brace and World (1961).

30. Robert R. Blake, H. A. Shepard, and Jane S. Mouton, *Managing Intergroup Conflict in Industry,* Houston, Texas: Gulf Publishing Co. (1964), p. 89.

31. Samuel A. Stouffer, et al., *Studies in Social Psychology During World War II: The American Soldier,* I and II, Princeton, N.J.: Princeton University Press (1949).

32. Coser, *Social Conflict* 103.

33. Kenneth E. Boulding, *Conflict and Defense,* New York: Harper and Brothers (1962), 310.

34. Charles M. Rehmus, "The Mediation of Industrial Conflict: A Note on the Literature," *Journal of Conflict Resolution,* IX (March 1965), 119.

35. Paul P. Tinning, "Conciliation of Labor Disputes and Civil Rights Disputes," *Labor Law Journal,* XIX (September 1968), 563.

36. Rehmus, Mediation, 119.

37. Vernon H. Jensen, "Bibliography on Dispute Settlement by Third Parties," *Labor Law Journal,* VI (August 1955), 572.

38. Clark Kerr, "Industrial Conflict and its Mediation," *American Journal of Sociology,* LX (November 1954), 230–45.

39. Kenneth E. Boulding, "A Pure Theory of Conflict Applied to Organizations," in Elise Boulding, *Conflict Management,* 50.

40. Robert H. Cory, Jr., "Conflict Resolution in the United Nations: A Review of Three Studies by the Brookings Institution," *Journal of Conflict Resolution,* II (June 1958), 615.

41. Robert W. Wesson, "The Pesticide Industry," in Assael, *The Politics of Distributive . . . ,* 76.

42. Kerr, *Industrial Conflict,* 236.

43. Adler, Johnson, and Meschio, in Assael, *The Politics of Distributive,* 163.

44. Kerr, *Industrial Conflict,* 236–39.

45. Coser, *Social Conflict,* 60.

46. Daniel Katz, "Nationalism and Strategies of International Conflict Resolution," in Herbert C. Kelman (ed.), *International Behavior* (New York: Holt, Rinehart and Winston, 1965), 384.

47. Robert R. Blake and Jane S. Mouton, "Comprehension of Own and of Outgroup Positions Under Intergroup Competition," *Journal of Conflict Resolution,* V (September 1961), 304–10.

48. *Ibid.*, 309.

49. Guetzkow, Organizations, 22.

50. "$1 Million for 'Persuaders,'" *San Francisco Chronicle* (January 7, 1970), 9.

51. Jensen, *Bibliography*, 573.

52. Jensen, *Bibliography*, 573.

53. Biedermann and Tabak, *Television*, 280–82.

54. K. J. Holsti, "Resolving International Conflicts: A Taxonomy of Behavior and Some Figures on Procedures," in Kriesberg (ed.), *Social Processes,* 550.

55. Henry Assael, "The Political Role of Trade Associations in Distributive Conflict Resolution," *Journal of Marketing*, XXXII (April 1968), 21–8.

56. Evan Luard, *Conflict and Peace in the Modern International System*, Boston: Little, Brown, and Co. (1968).

57. George E. Prochaska and Joseph J. Schramek, "The Drug Industry," in Assael, *The Politics of Distributive*, 45–6.

58. Guetzkow, *Organizations,* 14.

59. Harold D. Lasswell and Abraham Kaplan, *Power and Society*, New Haven: Yale University Press (1950), 35.

60. Adler, Johnson, and Meschio, in Assael, *The Politics of Distributive* . . . , 192.

61. Biedermann and Tabak, in Assael, *ibid.*, 287.

62. John Galtung, "Pacifism From a Sociological Point of View," *Journal of Conflict Resolution,* III (March 1959), 74.

63. Williams, Intergroup Tensions, 69.

64. Anita L. Mishler, "Personal Contact in International Exchanges," in Kelman, 552.

65. See Jeanne Watson and Ronald Lippitt, "Cross-Cultural Experience as a Source of Attitude Change," *Journal of Conflict Resolution,* II (March 1958), 61–6.

66. Paul Kurland, Paul Malecha, and John Zerbo, "The Electrical Industry," in Assael, *The Politics of Distributive* . . . , 231.

67. Katz, in Kelman, *International Behavior,* 381.

68. Kurland, Malecha, and Zerbo, in Assael, *The Politics of Distributive* . . . , 235.

69. Williams, *Intergroup Tensions,* 65.

70. Stern and Heskett, in Stern, *Sociological Interpretation,* 288–305.

71. James G. March and Herbert A. Simon, *Organizations,* New York: John Wiley and Sons, Inc. (1958), 166.

72. Richard M. Cyert and James G. March, *A Behavioral Theory of the Firm,* Englewood Cliffs, N.J.: Prentice-Hall, Inc. (1963), 120.

73. Kurland, Malecha, and Zerbo, in Assael, *The Politics of Distributive* . . . , 240.

74. Guetzkow, *Organizations,* 17.

75. Philip Selznick, *TVA and the Grass Roots,* Berkeley, Calif.: University of California Press (1949), 13.

76. James D. Thompson and William J. McEwen, "Organizational Goals and Environment," in Amitai Etzioni (ed.), *Complex Organizations: A Sociological Reader,* 2nd Edition, New York: Holt, Rinehart and Winston, Inc. (1969), 195.

77. Guetzkow, *Organizations,* 18.

78. Wesson, in Assael, *The Politics of Distributive* . . . , 80.

79. Selznick, *TVA,* 15–16.

80. Thompson and McEwen, in Etzioni, *Complex Organizations,* 194.

81. Vernon Dibble, "The Organization of Traditional Authority," in James G. March, *Handbook of Organizations,* Chicago: Rand McNally and Co. (1965), 884.

82. Amitai Etzioni, "Administration and the Consumer," *Administration Science Quarterly,* III (September 1958), 261.

83. Robert L. Kahn, Donald M. Wolfe, Robert P. Quinn, and J. Diedrick Snoek, *Organizational Stress: Studies in Role Conflict and Ambiguity,* New York: John Wiley and Sons, Inc. (1964), 101.

84. Fred H. Goldner, "Organizations and Their Environment: Roles at Their Boundary," paper read at the meeting of the American Sociological Association, New York, 1960, in Peter M. Blau and W. Richard Scott, *Formal Organizations: A Comparative Approach*, San Francisco: Chandler Publishing Co. (1962), 197.

85. Guetzkow, *Organizations*, 19.

86. Hans J. Morgenthau, *Politics Among Nations*, 4th Edition, New York: Alfred A. Knopf (1967), 519.

87. Vernon Van Dyke, *International Politics*, 2nd Edition, New York: Appleton-Century-Crofts (1966), 252.

88. Prochaska and Schramek, in Assael, *The Politics of Distributive . . .*, 47.

89. Adler, Johnson, and Meschio, in *ibid.*, 195.

90. *Ibid.*

91. Kahn, et. al., *Conflict and Ambiguity*, 123–4.

92. See also Stouffer, *American Soldier.*

93. Lewin, *Resolving Social Conflicts*, 180.

94. Kahn, *et. al.*, *Conflict and Ambiguity*, 393.

95. *Ibid.*

96. Guetzkow, *Organizations*, 21.

97. See Phillip McVey, "Are Channels of Distribution What the Textbooks Say?" *Journal of Marketing*, XXIV (January 1960), 61–5.

98. Louis R. Pondy, "Organizational Conflict: Concepts and Models," *Administrative Science Quarterly*, XII (September 1967), 296–320.

99. Jack Sawyer and Harold Guetzkow, "Bargaining and Negotiation in International Relations," in Kelman, *International Behavior*, 466.

100. Boulding, *Conflict and Defense*, 314 (adapted from Schelling; see footnote 102).

101. Thompson and McEwen, in Etzioni, *Complex Organizations*, 193.

102. Adapted from March and Simon, *Organizations*, 131.

103. Thomas C. Schelling, *The Strategy of Conflict*, Cambridge, Mass.: Harvard University Press (1960), 28.

104. R. E. Walton and R. B. McKersie, *A Behavioral Theory of Labor Negotiations*, New York: McGraw-Hill (1965).

105. Dean G. Pruitt, "Definition of the Situation as a Determinant of International Action," in Kelman, *International Behavior*, 408.

106. *Ibid.*, 409–10.

107. Walton and McKersie, *Behavioral Theory.*

108. Holsti, in Kriesberg, *Social Processes*, 549.

109. C. E. Osgood, "Suggestion for Winning the Real War with Communism," *Journal of Conflict Resolution*, III (December 1959), 295–325.

110. Etzioni, in Kriesberg, *Social Processes*, 423–24.

111. Boulding, in Kahn and Boulding, *Power and Conflict*, 143.

112. Holsti, in Kriesberg, *Social Processes*, 546.

113. Katz, in Kelman, *International Behavior*, 385.

114. Lewis A. Coser, "The Termination of Conflict," *Journal of Conflict Resolution*, V (December 1961), 352; and Coser, *The Functions*, 137.

115. Coser, "The Termination," 352.

116. Kurland, Malecha, and Zerbo, in Assael, *The Politics of Distributive . . .*, 237.

117. Boub, Sacks, and Seckler, in *ibid.*, 347.

118. Sawyer and Guetzkow, in Kelman, *International Behavior,* 508.

119. Katz, in *ibid.*, 383.

120. Robert R. Blake and Jane S. Mouton, "Loyalty of Representatives to Ingroup Positions During Intergroup Competition," *Sociometry*, XXIV (June 1961), 177–83.

121. Robert Dubin, "Leadership in Union-Management Relations as an Intergroup System," in Muzafer Sherif (ed.), *Intergroup Relations and Leadership*, New York: John Wiley and Sons, Inc. (1962), 87.

122. Van Dyke, *International Politics,* 255.

The Development of Conflict in Contractual Marketing Systems: A Case Study

Larry J. Rosenberg*

Introduction

Since the publication of Palamountain's work on *The Politics of Distribution* in 1955,[1] interest in conflict within and between distribution channels has markedly increased. Channels are being viewed as systems in which interdependent members at two or three structural levels of distribution act more or less in concert for their mutual benefit. For the channel systems to remain viable and thus to effectively compete against rival channel alliances, cooperative interactions must predominate. However, many marketing scholars since Palamountain have emphasized the presence of conflict and have described several of its dimensions.[2] While these and other studies have combined descriptions of channel conflict and concepts from the behavioral disciplines, they have largely neglected the measurement of conflict and its dynamics of development.

This paper explores the emergence of the conflict process from underlying causes to overt behavior in a given distribution arrangement, which in many respects can be considered a contractual marketing system. The research approach represents an initial attempt at the measurement of conflict in both the attitudes and acts of channel members toward each other. The empirical findings from the case study channel system include conflict issues (covert) and conflict incidents (overt). They can be analytically linked to demonstrate the development of conflict. From this perspective, implications for those interested in channel management will be presented. While the results of this case study are hardly generalizable to other channel alignments, the research approach described and tested may be applied in other channel settings to generate more knowledge about the emergence of conflict.

Concepts and Model

Several concepts regarding intrachannel conflict are operationally defined in this section. They provide the theoretical framework upon which the research approach is based.

* New York University. The author acknowledges the support during the research stage of the Division of Research, College of Administrative Science, The Ohio State University, and the Distribution Research and Educational Foundation of the National Association of Wholesalers.

Within any system, interdependence among the components may be observed. Interdependence means that two or more units must take each other into account if they are to accomplish their respective goals. This line of thinking leads to the acceptance of a distribution channel as a *behavior system.* In this regard, McCammon and Little have depicted the channel as structured of interrelated components, striving for mutually acceptable objectives, sequencing activities and flows, participated in voluntarily, usually administered by one firm, and regulated by a code of behavior or group norms.[3]

This conception excludes consumers from the organizable components of the behavior system. Unless a channel is a loose, fragmented network of relatively autonomous firms, it is a system in which the mode of organization is, to some degree, vertically aligned and horizontally coordinated. Arrangements usually encompass the allocation of functions and geographical coverage. Davidson identifies three types of distributive systems: corporate, contractual, and administered.[4] *Corporate* systems are ownership-integrated networks, in which the authority hierarchy assures control among the various divisions. *Contractual* systems involve voluntary but contractual integration, as in franchise arrangements. *Administered* systems refer to a channel relationship covering a line or classification of merchandise. When the line accounts for a significant portion of a firm's sales and profits, the distinction between contractual and administered systems becomes blurred.

Conflict may be viewed as the following state or situation:

> A social relationship between two or more parties (persons, empirically distinguishable entities) in which at least one of the parties perceives the other as an adversary engaging in behaviors designed to destroy, injure, thwart, or gain scarce resources at the expense of the perceiver.[5]

The several types of channel participants possess different goals and values, often incompatible or mutually exclusive. It is inevitable that one party will try to impose barriers against a rival to improve its chances of attaining either economic goals (for example, sales, profits, return on investment) or social goals (for example, prestige, autonomy, leadership).

The relevance of intrachannel conflict relations is not solely as a state, but also as a *process.* Stern and Gorman[6] postulate that the presence of conflict is due to certain causes. While the conflict may remain convert, potentially to emerge at a later time, it may overtly manifest itself in the form of behavioral changes. These may be the exercise of power or the response of intraorganizational adjustments which may serve as modes of conflict resolution. Finally, outcomes of the conflict process result. Their conception parallels Pondy's "stages of conflict episode," originated in an intraorganizational context: latent (conditions); perceived (cognition); felt (affect); manifest (behavior); and aftermath (conditions, again).[7] It is in the progression from one stage to another, from covert to overt, that the impact of the conflict process may be better understood.

Combining and modifying the Stern-Gorman and Pondy typologies produces an operational model of intra-channel conflict development,[8] depicted in Figure 7-1. In terms of the *process,* basic member and system *causes,*[a] which yield specific *issues,* may induce *behavioral changes* on the part of the participant firms. The behavior, which is a mixture of incidents of adversary interaction and of conflict resolution mechanisms, contributes to the occurrence of consequences, inducing financial performance and behavioral outcomes for channel members. The consequences, in turn, affect the basic causes of conflict.

The conflict process may be explained by the level of conflict, for which means of measurement may be devised for different stages of conflict development. The issues which are expressions of the conflict causes may be latent, perceived, or felt. As such, the conflict may be identified as to the issues and measured as to intensity, but it remains covert with little direct impact on intrachannel relations and performance. The behavioral changes are *manifest* forms of conflict which involve the channel members in confrontations. In the aftermath, the consequences may be assessed. Whether they are disruptive or constructive to the channel system bears on the survival and viability of the channel.

The model of conflict development furnishes the foundation for the research design and field study. To operationalize the model further, the following assumptions are necessary:

1. The channel system is composed, for all practical purposes, of those firms exchanging title and possession—manufacturer, distributors, and dealers.
2. Relevant interaction patterns in the channel system involve three dyads —manufacturer-distributor, distributor-dealers, and manufacturer-dealers.
3. Organizations can be conceived of as members of a channel system, that is, they comprise the unit of analysis.
4. The attitudes and behavior of firms may be reported by key spokesmen—top executives for complex organizations and owner-operators for simple organizations.

Case Study Channel

The case study channel is a three-level contractual marketing system of a specific branded product, hereafter referred to as Brand X. (Because of the confidential nature of the data collected, the product, brand and

[a] One example of a typology of conflict causes between channel members is posited by Stern and Heskett: goal incongruity, domain dissensus, and perceptual differences.[9]

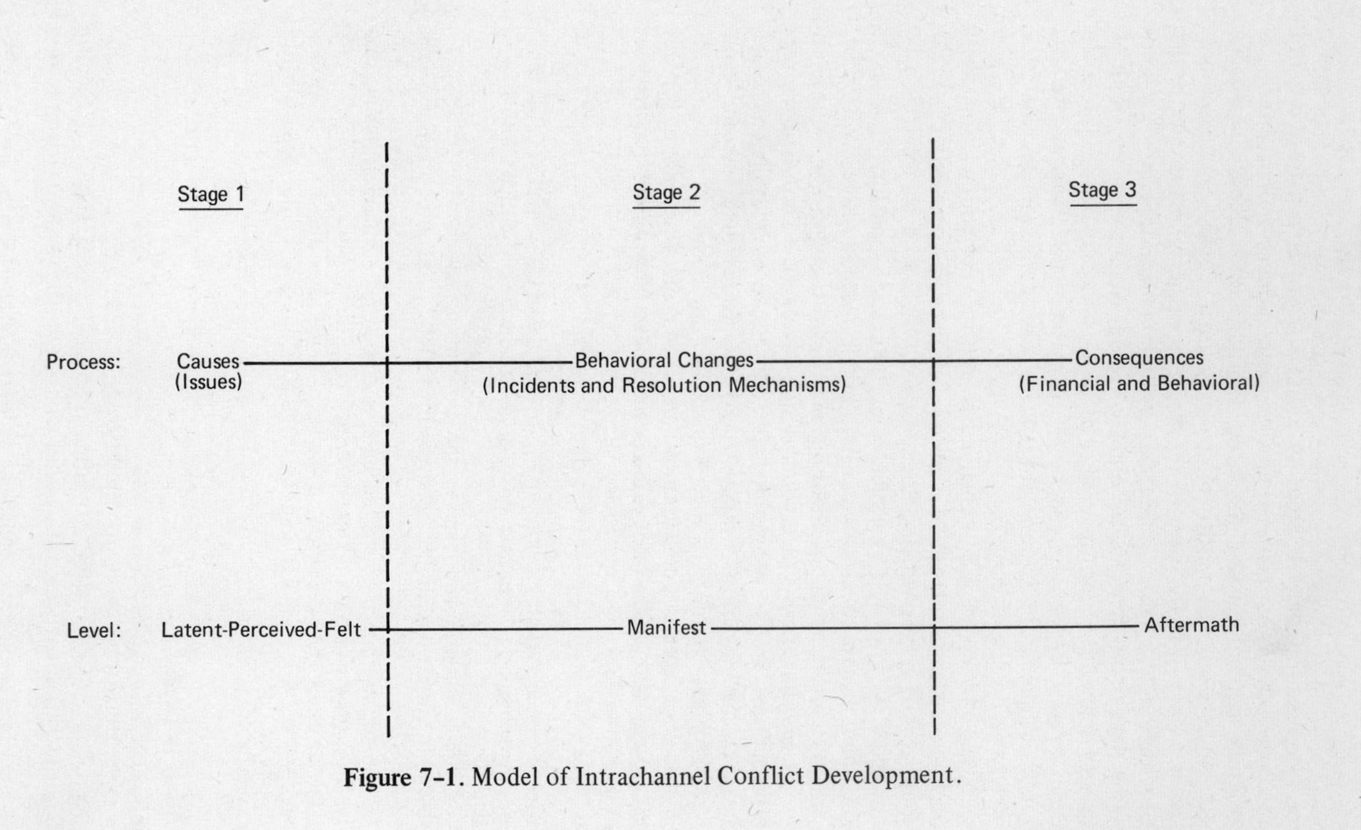

Figure 7–1. Model of Intrachannel Conflict Development.

firms must remain anonymous.) Brand X may be operationally described as the branded line of an expensive (generally above $500) household durable good. Brand X is one of the leading nationally marketed lines in its industry. The components of this channel system consist of the manufacturer, a set of distributors within a specific geographical region of the company's operations, and a set of dealers within that region.

The manufacturer is a major decentralized operating division of a large parent corporation, and produces a complete line of branded products. The manufacturer markets its many product lines to various markets—residential, commercial, institutional, and defense. Only the trading path of the residential Brand X through distributors and dealers is covered by the case study. The manufacturer may be structurally differentiated into its headquarters marketing personnel and its several regional field office staffs.

The manufacturer maintains an exclusive distribution policy, in which independently-owned distributors are designated to sell Brand X (along with a commercial line of the product) in restricted territories. Although some of the distributors carry noncompeting products of other producers and all handle the manufacturer's commercial line, a sizable percentage of their total sales are in the Brand X line. The manufacturer tends to control its distributors through the implied threat of franchise termination, and through informal persuasion. Manufacturer's and distributor's reciprocal rights and obligations are not specifically detailed in the franchise contract.

In its territory, each distributor supplies Brand X to selected, independent dealers. The designation of dealer is based (1) on the substantiality of Brand X sales, relatively or absolutely (although competing brands are carried); or (2) on dealing exclusively in Brand X. A few of the distributors franchise their dealers to sell Brand X exclusively, and restrict the number of dealers. Most distributors want to secure as many sound dealers as possible, and thus allow these dealers to handle competing brands.

Within the channel system, the vast majority of the dealer's interactions are with his distributor. However, there is a clear community of interest between dealers and manufacturer. First, this is apparent when the manufacturer and a distributor sever their relationship, and most of the distributor's dealers remain manufacturer-loyal rather than distributor-loyal. In other words, the dealers chose to join the manufacturer's newly appointed distributors in order to continue carrying Brand X, as opposed to dropping Brand X and adopting another brand for which the former distributor may have been franchised. Second, manufacturer-dealer contacts often result during dealer incentive trips, factory tours, dealer association meetings, and manufacturer field representatives' visits on dealer premises.

It may be argued that the contractual system definition should not be applied to this case study channel because lines or brands other than Brand X are handled by many distributors and dealers. Two points counter this contention. A contractual agreement, augmented by many rigid industry and channel rules, affects member expectations. And, a high degree of commitment exists on the part of participating firms because of the significant or majority extent of sale and profits which Brand X generates. On balance, the behavioral characteristics of this case study are relevant to scholars of contractual marketing systems and of the conflict inherent in them.

Methodology

Research Instrument

A field instrument, with several modifications for each class of organizations in the case study channel system, follows from the following research objectives: (1) to obtain attitudinal data on conflict issues; (2) to devise an operational measure of the intensity of conflict; and (3) to secure descriptions of overt conflict behavior. The questions to each channel segment are similar in content and format, since the instrument must satisfy both mail and personal interviewing requirements.

Three versions of the research instrument, one for each class of members, each contain two major sections: (1) two sets of conflict issues; and (2) a conflict incidents reporting form. In the first section, two conflict issue sets for each organization are selected from the three sets available for all intrachannel dyads—manufacturer-distributors (Appendix 7-A), distributors-dealers (Appendix 7-B), and manufacturer-dealers (Appendix 7-C). Each firm completed those two sets applicable to the two dyads of which it is a member.[b] Each question set contains 32 conflict issues about which both organizations in the dyad would have an opinion. The respondent can state his opinion, which he believes to be in his company's best interests, on a Likert-type scale of five choices: *strongly agree, agree, neutral, disagree,* and *strongly disagree.*

While the first major section of the instrument treats conflict issues which may be covert, the second contains an open-ended part in which the respondent is asked to recall three important disputes with the two reciprocal channel organizations. These descriptions are intended to spotlight overt episodes of conflict. A disput is denoted as a complaint, discussion, or demand concerning an issue or problem about which the respondent became actively involved along with either of the other two firms. Descrip-

[b] The distributor interacts with one manufacturer of Brand X and the dealer with one distributor and one manufacturer of Brand X. Because the manufacturer interacts with all the distributors and dealers in the region and the distributor with all the dealers in its trading area, the single firm's opinion regarding the counter component of the dyad must be expressed vis-à-vis the typical one among the many firms, that is, a reflection of the majority of the collectivity.

tions of disputes, at best, include who participated, nature of disagreement, why it came about, and how it was or was not resolved. Along with the description of the incident, the tension level of the participants is recorded on a five-point scale: *very high, high, medium, low* and *very low*. The tension level is designed to reflect the perceived magnitude of the disputed issue, and the emotional feelings generated through direct involvement.

Sample and Respondents

For the manufacturer, two types of personnel concerned with distribution are included: (1) key headquarters executives; and (2) members of a regional field office staff.

The major headquarters executives selected as respondents consist of the marketing director, field sales manager, marketing services manager, and Brand X product sales manager. A single regional office was chosen for the following reasons: (1) it is the focus of interaction between the manufacturer field personnel and a given set of distributors and their dealers; (2) nearly the entire universe of distributors could be sampled; and (3) distributors and dealers are geographically homogeneous yet varied on other dimensions. Among the channel relevant positions in the regional field office are the regional manager, assistant manager, account manager, consumer marketing managers, and service engineering supervisors.

The four marketing headquarters respondents and the eight regional channel-related respondents comprise the majority of relevant personnel of one region of the manufacturer. The manufacturer represents, although with clear bias, other of its regions and other competing producers. In another sense, these headquarters and regional respondents comprise a small, but identifiable, population universe.

One of the manufacturer's regions was selected for study; 11 of the total 14 distributors there agreed to be interviewed. These distributors may be considered as either a biased representation of all Brand X or industry distributors, or as a population universe bounded by one region. The owner-operator, usually the chief executive, or the sales manager for Brand X, served as the respondent for the distributors.

According to the manufacturer's list, a total of 250 Brand X dealers were in the territories of the 11 distributors, or 15 to 30 dealers per distributor. The dealers were either residential (Brand X) or full-line (Brand X plus the manufacturer's commercial line). Full-line annual sales ranged from $10,000 to $100,000. Completed returns were received from 87 dealers, or 35 percent. A shortened follow-up questionnaire to non-respondents and some information on the dealer population vis-à-vis the sample failed to establish the representativeness of the sample.

Interview Procedures

The research instrument was administered to the manufacturer's regional field and distributor respondents in person, and to the manufacturer headquarters and dealer respondents by mail. Personal interviews with the regional field staff were conducted individually on the respondent's premises, and took approximately one hour each. The respondent completed the first section of the questionnaire on conflict issues by himself. As his familiarity with the variety of issues increased, his subsequent descriptions of overt instances of conflict were recorded by the interviewer. Headquarters executives were reached by mail. The personal interview situation for the 11 distributors was largely identical to that for the manufacturer regional field group.

A pretest comparision of mailing and personally administering the instrument to dealers disclosed few significant differences in response patterns. Although rate of dealer returns was only adequate and some open-ended questions suffered from brevity, there was little difference with the interview instrument concerning responses to major question sets. In order to obtain a larger number of completed questionnaires, the mail approach was chosen.

The questionnaire was sent to 250 dealers and a follow-up letter was sent to all nonresponding dealers. An abbreviated version of the instrument was mailed to 50 (or one-third) of subsequent nonresponding dealers, and 20 replies resulted.

Analysis of Data

Data analysis consisted of the statistical testing of conflict over issues within channel dyads, and the content analysis of conflict incidents. In a macroscopic approach to issue conflict, the channel system positions are regarded as categories and the respondents are grouped to represent the manufacturer (8 respondents), distributors (11), and dealers (87). Computing the means for each issue in the set of 32 for all respondents in the category permits comparisons of the grand means of the common issue sets in each dyad (manufacturer-distributors, distributors-dealers, and manufacturer-dealers). The operational measure of conflict between the organizations in each dyad is the difference on the Likert-type scale for each conflict issue, to a maximum of four points (2 to -2). As each group of firms may be considered as samples of the larger universes of which they are a part, the t-test as a measure of significance was employed. To describe overt conflict incidents, a content analysis of frequency, intensity (according to tension levels), causation, conduct, and outcome was used.

Limitations of Study

There are several constraints upon the study which influence interpretation and evaluation of the results and conclusions. The research instrument was designed for and tested in a field setting, affording less rigor than a laboratory experiment. Only tentative generalizations can be made because one channel system was investigated, and reseller firms were drawn from one geographical region, with no assurance that the responding dealers are representative of the dealer universe. The study was conducted during a single and brief time interval, mid-1969, during which the channel members were enjoying marked prosperity. Therefore, issues and incidents that registered high conflict levels in harder or crisis times might have been deemed minor irritants.

Although the respondent's personality was disregarded, it probably influenced both attitudinal data and reactions to open disputes. The willingness and difficulty in expressing conflict incidents and of separating out multiple brand recollections were also problematic.

Results—Conflict Issues

The surface issues provide the foci of intrachannel conflict insofar as they reflect the fundamental conflict issues. An analysis of the 32 issues and their conflict levels was conducted for the macro dyads, with significant differences noted.

In Table 7-1, the greater agreement of the manufacturer in the manufacturer-distributors dyad applied to its belief in manufacturer dominance

Table 7-1
List of Ten Highest Conflict Issues between Manufacturer and Distributors

Rank	Item No. [a]	Issue	t [b]
1	13	Manufacturer's profit expectations	4.8077 [c]
2	29	Distributor's competitive vigor	3.6079 [c]
3	16	Knowledge of industry problems	3.5720 [c]
4	6	Distributor's payment of freight costs	2.5760 [c]
5	3	Dominance of manufacturer	—2.5643 [c]
6	18	Quantity discounts to distributor	2.2978 [c]
7	5	Distributor's independence	2.1534 [c]
8	19	Manufacturer's product shortages	—2.0381
9	32	Manufacturer's accounting system for distributor	1.9311
10	22	Share of dealer training	1.8707

[a] For full wording, see Appendix 7-A.
[b] A positive sign indicates that distributors agreed with the item more than the manufacturer; a negative signifies that the manufacturer agreed more than distributors.
[c] Significant at .05 level (P = 2.080, df = 21).

in the relationship and to justification of product shortages on its part during the peak season. Distributors held that they are willing to compete vigorously for the manufacturer, but desire to maintain their independence and identity. Distributors agreed more that the manufacturer should accept a reduction in profits if it means higher profit for distributors, that distributors should not pay freight costs when the manufacturer is out of stock and the item is shipped from another distributor, that the manufacturer's suggested accounting system for distributors keeps tabs on the latter, and that the manufacturer should shoulder more dealer training. Distributors conceded that the manufacturer knows more than they about industry problems.

The distributor-dealers high conflict issues are reported in Table 7-2. Distributors contended that they have the right to set quotas on dealers and that dealers will obtain greater profit if they accept advice from their distributors. Distributors saw dealers as not promotional minded enough and as trying to perform fewer functions to reduce costs. Dealers agreed more that they should set their minimum inventory level, that they should go over their distributor's head when complaining, and that in returning defective product, no additional handling or product replacement costs should be incurred. Also, dealers regarded distributors as inflexible and as securing a higher net profit on sales than did dealers.

Within the manufacturer-dealers dyad, reported in Table 7-3, the manufacturer registered greater agreement that it should expand sales to maintain industry leadership, that it should obtain increased information regarding dealers, and that its recommended accounting system for dealers should be universally adopted. On the other side, dealers firmly believed that they sacrifice independence when handling Brand X, that it is advantageous to sell related sidelines rather than to concentrate on Brand X,

Table 7-2
List of Ten Highest Conflict Issues between Distributors and Dealers

Rank	Item No. [a]	Issue	t [b]
1	10	Distributor's product return policy	6.0130
2	25	Dealer's avoidance of functions	—5.7565
3	26	Distributor's sales quota setting	—5.3918
4	8	Net profit of dealer and distributor	4.6735
5	7	Dealer's promotional mindedness	—4.4693
6	14	Dealer's inventory level	4.2113
7	2	Dealer's complaint solving	3.8082
8	22	Distributor's return goods policy	3.7456
9	27	Value of distributor's assistance	—3.6810
10	15	Distributor's inflexibility	3.5486

[a] For full wording, see Appendix 7-B.
[b] A positive sign indicates that dealers agreed with the item more than distributors; a negative signifies that distributors agreed more than dealers. All are significant at .01 level (P = 2.6390, df = 90).

Table 7-3
List of Ten Highest Conflict Issues between the Manufacturer and Dealers

Rank	Item No. [a]	Issue	t [b]
1	14	Defect allowance for dealer	6.9227
2	32	Dealers showroom quality	4.6046
3	29	Installation vs. product quality	4.0903
4	25	Manufacturer absorbing repair costs	3.5273
5	5	Manufacturer's sales expansion	−3.1878
6	20	Dealer information for manufacturer	−2.9836
7	17	Dealer's sidelines to Brand X	2.8738
8	10	Manufacturer's product mix authority	2.7550
9	21	Dealer's individuality	2,2795
10	28	Accounting system for dealer	−1.9101

[a] For full wording, see Appendix 7-C.
[b] A positive sign indicates that dealers agreed with the item more than the manufacturer; a negative signifies that the manufacturer agreed more than dealers. All but #10 are significant at .05 level (P = 1.9901, df = 90).

that dealer premises are well maintained for customer demonstrations, and that their performance in installation and service outweighs in importance the manufacturer's product quality. Dealers asserted that the manufacturer should pay both a labor and materials allowance when the product defect is the manufacturer's fault, and that when the breakdown responsibility is indeterminant, the manufacturer should still bear repair costs. Dealers conceded that the manufacturer should make final decisions concerning product design and output.

In summary, some key issues of high conflict appeared in more than one dyad. These included warranty administration; dominance, independence, identity, initiation, flexibility, and status in the relationship; product shortages and inventory problems; expanding sales, profit levels and vigor of competition; and information and communication.

Results—Overt Conflict Incidents

The previous section on conflict covered issues, some salient and others subtle or latent. This section seeks to analyze, from open-ended discussions by the respondents, those issues which are not merely perceived by the channel participants but which have generated enough tensions to be manifest in open disputes. The issues were foci of conflictful interactions; the underlying attitudes, tensions, and behavioral responses within the channel dyads are explored in the following content analysis.

Manufacturer-Distributors

The nature of the overt conflict incidents is depicted in Table 7-4. The leading conflict incident for both manufacturer and distributors was product unavailability in the face of high demand. The manufacturer acknowledged the existence of product shortages. Promises to deliver goods to

Table 7-4
Issues Embodied in Conflict Incidents Occurring in the Manufacturer—Distributors Dyad

	Tension Level					
Reported by Manufacturer regarding Distributors	Very High	High	Medium	Low	Very Low	Total
1. Equipment unavailability and allocation	2	3	1			6
2. Product quality and defects	1	2	2	1		6
3. Service problems by distributor's personnel	1	3				4
4. Ineffective communication—verbal and computer	1	1	1			3
5. Warranty administration			2			2
6. Distributor cash flow tightness				2		2
7. Documenting rebates and payments		1				1
8. Loss and damages in delivery		1				1
9. Competition with manufacturer's sister corporation		1				1
10. Documenting advertising expenditures		1				1
11. Weak market penetration by distributor		1				1
12. Violation of sales policy			1			1
13. Price protection policy			1			1
14. Incentive trip payment			1			1
15. Gaps in product line			1			1
Total	5	14	10	3	0	32
Reported by Distributors regarding Manufacturer						
1. Product unavailability	1	3	2			6
2. Inadequacy of new products	1	3	1			5
3. Ineffective communication for problem solving	1	2	1			4
4. Product quality and defects	2	1				3
5. Unavailability of special parts	2					2
6. Faulty sales forecasting	2					2
7. Pricing and bidding matters	1		1			2
8. Competition from manufacturer's sister corporation	1					1
9. Unmet rural distributors' needs			1			1
10. Damages due to packing				1		1
11. Off-season financing burden				1		1
Total	11	9	6	2	0	28

distributors had been made which could not later be honored; this impaired distributor trust. The manufacturer admitted its production capacity was the bottleneck because of the difficulty in predicting and responding to rapidly expanding demand. While the manufacturer had to inject considerable judgment into its computer estimates, it felt distributors made inadequate reports upon which estimates were in part based. The manufacturer stressed how distributors aggravated the situation. Some prestocked many units because of foresight. The manufacturer was forced to allocate on an equitable basis the existing products among distributors. The complaints were especially loud from some who had promised delivery to their dealers. While distributor sales of Brand X were up substantially over the previous year, lost sales hurt. To the contemplation by some distributors of temporarily handling competing equipment during the production shortage, the manufacturer objected on family and future grounds, although the practice was not forbidden.

Distributors saw no reasonable justification for unavailable product. They placed the blame on the manufacturer's poor long-range planning. The manufacturer had not believed his own estimates of soaring demand. Besides this conservatism, the parent corporation was funding acquisitions of companies rather than capitalizing the manufacturer's expansion of capacity. This lack of the manufacturer's growth led to several distributors taking on additional noncompeting product lines—which diminished their dependence on Brand X sales.

The second most serious cause of open disputes with the manufacturer was product quality; this was registered as fourth by distributors. The manufacturer confessed to the epidemic of product defects which had occurred the previous year and its adverse effect on sales and channel relations. It had waited until dealer complaints forced distributors to demand corrective action, and then agreed to absorb most of the repair costs. Because the manufacturer had not faced the situation immediately, openly, and totally, it lost goodwill and damaged its high product quality reputation. Distributors had lost dealer sales and, in some cases, dealers themselves as Brand X outlets. Several distributors were aware that the manufacturer had eased its usually strict quality control standards in order to speed production. Distributors blamed the manufacturer not for the defects *per se,* but for being slow to anticipate them and for withholding any early suspicions from distributors. Distributors were thus caught without any knowledge or answers when confronted by enraged dealers concerning the wave of product breakdowns.

Distributors' second most frequent discussion of conflict incidents centered on the inadequacy of new products from the manufacturer, who rated this problem at the very bottom of its list. Handling the manufacturer's Brand X line exclusively, distributors admitted to being particularly vulnerable to gaps in the product line in satisfying customer segments. Distributors made requests of the manufacturer, but felt the new products were too little, too late, and often poorly designed. They believed the manufacturer should be the industry leader in product innovation, should anticipate new market opportunities, and should develop new products much faster than had been its practice. Conservatism in introducing new products was a common allegation against the manufacturer. Another was that the manufacturer lacked flexibility because of its organization structure, and of constraints that the parent corporation imposed as it divided market opportunities among the manufacturer and its sister companies. Although the manufacturer had recently introduced a major and unique new product that was selling well, distributors recalled gaps that had existed or that were filled by inadequate products. Since distributors felt they were footing the bill for the manufacturer's research and development (R & D) through the price of the product, they expected a better product line. At the time of the questioning, the manufacturer was reorganizing its R & D department.

The third most serious cause of overt conflict reported by the manufacturer was service problems involving distributor personnel. This was not even mentioned by distributors.

Ranking third for distributors and fourth for the manufacturer was the situation of ineffective communication between the participants on routine and strategic matters. There were several phases to this problem. First, information from manufacturer headquarters intended for distributors at times failed to reach them. Accounting for this, the manufacturer contended, were growing paperwork flows, overworked executives at headquarters, and a lack of knowledgable personnel there. Distributors were apt to point to the slow reorganization occurring at manufacturer headquarters and its inability to attract outstanding personnel because salaries tended to be inadequate. Second, distributors found it difficult to communicate with manufacturer headquarters. Even its regional field staff concurred with this complaint. With neither enough authority or information, field men experienced delays in handling distributor requests. Distributors were disappointed that key headquarters personnel rarely visited them to learn of their individual problems. There were regional distributor councils and a national executive committee to bring issues to the manufacturer. Some distributors doubted the effectiveness of this sounding board since the manufacturer usually already knew what could and should be done.

Increased sales volume, bureaucratic complexity, and the introduction of the computer contributed to frequent routine problems. Distributors were angered over how the computer had altered the communication relationship. Along with technical bugs and inadequate routines, the largely impersonal and arbitrary process made longer delays and bigger errors all the more frustrating. Being dependent on a low-level clerk on the other end of the TWX line in the computer network contrasted with the prompt, personal service most distributors claimed they used to enjoy.

The remaining foci of overt conflict incidents registered concern among few respondents and typically generated less tension.

Distributor-Dealers

In Table 7-5 are enumerated those issues which resulted in open conflict between distributors and dealers. Product unavailability was ranked most serious by distributors but numbered fourth by dealers. While dealers preferred or were under instructions to install a Brand X unit, its unavailability was not automatically a total loss since dealers could substitute another brand handled. On the other hand, to distributors this situation always meant lost sales. Neither dealers nor distributors were comforted by the blame actually falling on the manufacturer's inability to deliver the product.

Dealers' primary complaint regarding credit allowances may be related in part to distributors' problem of the slow receipt of dealer payments. The epidemic of product failures created a great burden for dealers. Although distributors and the manufacturer provided a materials allowance, dealers had to absorb labor charges for repairs. Besides credit allowances being inadequate, their receipt by dealers was often delayed or in error. Dealers balked particularly at the complicated and time-consuming paperwork involved in handling credit allowance claims. Distributors felt that dealers contributed to this problem by not following procedures properly, by having inadequate help, and by sometimes requesting credit although the fault was the dealer's rather than the distributor-manufacturer's.

Distributors felt they too often had to wait beyond the normal 30-day period to collect on accounts receivable from dealers. Cash flow problems occurred as sales volume grew, increased working capital was needed, and interest rates rose. Distributors were compelled to have on hand adequate inventory when dealers wanted Brand X and to stock preseason inventory at the manufacturer's request. Because the manufacturer had decided to use funds to expand productive facilities rather than to finance distributors and had priced to dealers on 30-day terms, the distributors required prompt payment. Dealers, however, had been accustomed to regarding their distributor as their bank, especially since some disliked relating to banks. Dealers felt particularly justified in delaying payments when their customers had not yet paid their bills. Since dealers were experiencing delays in receiving credit allowances due them, they seemed to feel it was right to slow their bill-paying pace, especially for items ordered as replacements to defective goods. The red tape orientation of distributors was not shared by the less business-sophisticated but more rationalizing dealers.

Product quality was of second most serious concern to dealers, but fifth to distributors. Aside from the related problem of credit allowance for defective products, dealers were bothered by failures of Brand X *per se*. In times of rising sales, dealers' installation activities had been severely hampered by the upsurge of breakdowns of recently installed product requiring extensive repair service. Distributors appear to have regarded

Table 7-5
Issues Embodied in Conflict Incidents Occurring in the Distributors—Dealers Dyad

	Tension Level					
Reported by Distributors regarding Dealers	Very High	High	Medium	Low	Very Low	Total
1. Product unavailability	3	2				5
2. Dealers' slow payment of bills	2	2		1		5
3. Poor business skills of dealers		4		1		5
4. Limited extent of dealer loyalty	1		2	1		4
5. Product quality and defects	1	1	1			3
6. Addition of more dealers		2				2
7. Dealers' demand for technical service		1				1
8. Manpower shortage for dealers		1				1
9. Fixing responsibility for product defects			1			1
10. Damage in shipping				1		1
11. Dealers' unwillingness to disclose information				1		1
Total	7	13	4	5	0	29
Reported by Dealer regarding Distributors						
1. Problems with credit allowances for defective parts	2	3	4	4		13
2. Product quality and failures	1	1	4	5	1	12
3. Delivery—delays, damages, and errors		1	4	4		9
4. Product unavailability		1	3	3		7
5. Ineffective communication with distributor	1	1	4			6
6. Advertising allowances and content disputes	2	1	1	1		5
7. Distributor's assistance to competing dealers	1	1	1	2		5
8. Financial issues—discounts, charges and pricing		1	1	3		5
9. Product line gaps		1	1	2		4
10. Distributor circumventing and interfering dealers	1	1	1			3
11. Record keeping inaccuracies						2
12. Inequity of incentive trips				2		2
13. Manufacturer's constraints on distributor			1			1
Total	8	13	25	27	1	74

product defects as beyond their control, being the fault of either manufacturer production or dealer installation.

The poor skills of many dealers qualified as distributors' third most problematic issue leading to overt conflict. This admission by dealers about themselves did not occur. The great majority of dealers came from technical-mechanical backgrounds. Because capital and personnel requirements for entry were low and sales volume was flourishing, these dealers easily established a viable business. Distributors claimed that many of these dealers were unable to merchandise properly, too prone to cut price to make sales, reluctant to hire additional sales manpower, unwilling to be guided by accounting procedures, and unfamiliar with bank financing. Contrary to dealer contentions, distributors asserted that they could demonstrate that the dealers were not making adequate, if any, profits. Distributors would drop dealers who were impossible to upgrade. But a distributor's need to secure as many minimally sound dealers as possible in the face of growing demand compelled it to try to train and develop dealers. The reaction of some dealers that they did not want or need this type of assistance usually precipitated further efforts at distributor persuasion.

Once a dealer was given some assurance by his distributor that the product was available, then delivery became the problem. For dealers this as a cause of overt conflict ranked third, just above product unavailability, but it was almost never mentioned by distributors. Dealers considered the violation of the distributor's promise of delivery of the right product, at the right time, and in the right condition as a great sin. Many dealers were sensitive to expecting delivery because they had, in turn, already promised installation dates to customers.

To distributors the fourth most serious cause of open disputes was the lack of dealer loyalty exhibited. Because distributors depended so much upon dealer loyalty and worked so diligently to earn it, they reacted to threats which might diminish such loyalty. When product line gaps existed or product unavailability occurred, both in large measure the fault of the manufacturer, dealers turned to a supplier of an alternative brand. Also, to distributors providing dealer training and a full range of services, a dealer's desire to buy from other suppliers on the basis of a lower price was particularly upsetting.

Other major foci of overt conflict, in the dealer's viewpoint, included ineffective communication with its distributor, advertising disagreements, distributor's discriminatory assistance to rival Brand X dealers, and a range of financial matters.

Manufacturer-Dealers

Table 7-6 contains those issues which brought forth overt conflict behavior between manufacturer and dealers. The leading problem for both parties was product quality discussed above. When failures of Brand X units occurred, the manufacturer paid material allowances for repair but left dealers to absorb labor costs. While dealers argued the fairness of this decision, most complied. But the distrust which was created could haunt the manufacturer in the event of a future problem of any magnitude.

The second most serious producer of open disputes was the same for both parties—product unavailability. The manufacturer had been informing dealers that product shortages were lessening and dealers had accepted

Table 7-6
Issues Embodied in Conflict Incidents Occurring in the Manufacturer—Dealers Dyad

	Tension Level					
Reported by Manufacturer regarding Dealers	Very High	High	Medium	Low	Very Low	Total
1. Product quality and defects	3	4	1			8
2. Product unavailability	1	1	2			4
3. Service problems and misapplication		2				2
4. High price of product		2				2
5. Skilled manpower shortage			1	1		2
6. Increasing number of dealers	1					1
7. Competitive pressures felt by dealers	1					1
8. Territorial dispute between dealers	1					1
9. Damages in delivery		1				1
10. New product introduction problems			1			1
11. Dealers as poor businessmen			1			1
Total	7	10	6	1	0	24
Reported by Dealer regarding Manufacturer						
1. Product quality and defects			3	1		4
2. Product unavailability			2	1		3
3. Dispute over advertising control			1	1		2
4. Failure of manufacturer recommended promotion			1			1
5. Unkept delivery promises			1			1
6. Poor quality of manufacturer training of dealers			1			1
7. Ineffective communication procedures			1			1
8. Manufacturer's service representative's visit				1		1
9. Warranty administration				1		1
10. Service department policy				1		1
11. Complicated accounting system					1	1
12. Incentive trip policy					1	1
Total	0	0	10	6	2	18

the information. In the face of increasing demand, little actual improvement was discerned by dealers.

Of the many conflict incidents listed by both channel members, what stands out is the breadth of topics rather than the depth of seriousness, as expressed by the frequency of mention and the tension generated. Most of the conflict issues developed into more pronounced disputes in the manufacturer-distributors and distributors-dealers dyads, where the vast majority of channel interactions occur.

Conclusions and Implications

The development of conflict in a three-level contractual marketing system is a complex phenomenon. One dimension of this complexity is the relationship between conflict issues and incidents over time within each channel dyad. This was spotlighted in the model of intrachannel conflict development. Another dimension is seen in the interdependence of system members as indicated by similar and related issues and incidents *across* channel dyads. These two dimensions, forming a time and participant matrix for the empirical results of this study, emerge as the major conclusions. Each conclusion yields implications for channel management regarding conflict resolution.

Development of Conflict

According to the intrachannel conflict model presented earlier, issues and incidents comprise two important aspects of the conflict process. While they are stages in sequential order (that is, issues are escalated into incidents), they may be related concomitantly and in reverse order. The results disclosed regarding issues and incidents lend support to these three relationships.

Several of the issues can be seen as the latent or perceivable forerunners of the later full-blown incidents. In the descriptions of many of the incidents, member attitudes toward salient issues contributed to the conflict becoming an open dispute. A longitudinal study of specific conflict situations might be conducted to seek further verification of this perspective. As this study was made during one brief time span for the respondents, several issues reflect in intensity the serious incidents that were extant during that interval. By the time of the study, some incidents that were recalled had already been resolved to varying extents; some of the issues probably express the aftermath of the overt conflict.

From the three relationships between issues and incidents, implications for channel management are suggested. They center around the contentions that conflict develops over time from antecedents to actions and that conceptually distinct aspects of conflict may be measured. Grasping the nature and intensity of a range of conflict issues may provide an early warning system, revealing the disputes that may be incipient. Lead time may permit channel members to take resourceful and immediate steps to mitigate the festering conflict. Where the issue and incident conflict concomitantly escalate, the crisis proportions of the conflict can be more concretely gauged. Priorities may be established along with some insight into the underlying dimensions of a deteriorating situation. When the conflict level for issues is viewed as an effect of an improving or fully settled situation, a longer-run and learning approach is available for the managers of system conflict. The data on issues are considered to be feedback which may be useful in evaluating aspects of a recently past crisis —its causes, means employed to reduce conflict, and the consequences. This may facilitate the use of long-range planning as an alternative to the more prevalent approach of conflict management. Of particular interest from these postmortems would be whether the incident was a unique or recurring event for the channel system.

Although the above benefits might well flow from periodic measurement of issues and incidents, two problems may be noted. First, what should be the frequency of the research? Instructing respondents to submit to a questionnaire at short intervals, for example, every month or quarter, would generate adequate and current data, but would become a task increasingly resented and decreasingly effective. The benefits of the information to the channel must be determined in relation to its cost. However, the infrequent conduct of the research, for example, every six months or annually, would provide insufficient and dated information for understanding the development of conflict. Second, who should be conducting the research? Who designs, administers, summarizes, and uses this information system would significantly affect its value to the channel. The channel leader or contractual administrator would have the greatest need and ability to innovate such a research approach. While an outside agency may be hired, the problem of sponsorship still remains. All channel participants must be involved in the preparation and the use of the research in order to assure their commitment and cooperation.

Interdependence of Conflict

The condition of high interdependence in a contractual system is heavily intertwined with the development of conflict. Conceptually, the conflict process can be studied and measured within one dyad of channel members. Actually, the entire interaction system of the channel comprises the arena in which conflict is inherent and pervasive. Relations between two organizations can be investigated only if the relations with other dyads are held constant.

The data indicate that a firm takes certain stands on issues vis-à-vis another firm because it is influenced by its involvement with other system members. The greater business sophistication of the manufacturer and distributors cause them to line up against dealers over certain issues. The relatively larger size and power of the manufacturer often separates it from distributors and dealers regarding issues of autonomy and flexibility.

This perspective serves as background for another observation on interdependency buttressed by the results of this study: conflict issues and incidents are shared by all channel participants. Each may be affected by the same problem (in this study, notably product shortages and defects). The high conflict issues tend to be diffused among the several dyads, rather than localized within given dyads.

Some conflict involves informal coalitions of channel members; other conflict is common to the entire system. Both these conclusions, characteristics of structural and goal interdependence, point to the necessity for a unified approach to conflict management in the channel. To leave the handling of conflict within the dyad in which it is part of the interaction patterns, would be a suboptimizing solution to the problem. The interactions to facilitate performance of the distribution process have traditionally evolved in the case channel as the manufacturer-distributors and distributor-dealers. Contracts and custom perpetuate this myopic arrangement.

With structure and behavior recognized as interrelated, modifications in the channel structure would contribute to a more suitable means of managing systemwide conflict. Contractual agreements may specifically provide for mechanisms by which members might jointly cope with the development of conflict and attempt to avoid its disruptive effects.

Appendix 7-A
Manufacturer-Distributors Issue Set

1. Distributor wants to work harder for his supplier (Manufacturer) than he wants to support his Dealers.
2. It is solely Manufacturer's responsibility to project the product mix for the coming year and to base production schedules upon it.
3. Manufacturer is dominant in the relationship between Manufacturer and Distributor and that is the way it should be.
4. Manufacturer continues to hire away some of the better personnel of Distributors.
5. As a part of the Manufacturer's selling thrust, Distributor does not want to sacrifice his independence and discretion over his own business.
6. When Manufacturer is out of a specific product, Distributor should not have to pay freight costs when the product is sent from another Distributor.

7. Manufacturer is rapidly approaching the day when product quality and shortage problems will be eliminated.
8. Manufacturer's computer facilities have confused and delayed order processing.
9. Distributor should be willing to sacrifice some of his short-run profits (one-year basis) by following Manufacturer's recommendations for the opportunity of making more profit several years in the future.
10. Distributor has the right to suggest product design changes to Manufacturer and to get his suggestions accepted.
11. Manufacturer is inflexible when Distributor comes to him with a special problem and desires action.
12. Manufacturer's order correspondent needs more authority to handle effectively the problems of Distributor.
13. Manufacturer should want to settle for a somewhat reduced profit if it means his Distributors can obtain an increased profit figure.
14. When offering his funds for a joint promotion campaign, Manufacturer is justified to specify the exact and only ways in which funds may be spent by Distributor and his Dealers.
15. The less is Distributor's Brand X share of market in his territory, the more Manufacturer should be dissatisfied with Distributor's performance.
16. Manufacturer has a significantly higher concentration of knowledge and experience in industry problems than does Distributor.
17. Distributor is firmly committed to helping Manufacturer's Brand X become the largest selling line in the industry.
18. Distributor should be entitled to higher quality discounts on very large orders.
19. During the peak sales period of the summer months, shortages in the Manufacturer's supply of Brand X are justified.
20. The introduction of new systems for ordering and inventory routines are inadequately planned.
21. It is a prime goal of Distributor to always be increasing his sales volume.
22. Manufacturer should bear a greater share of the burden of training Dealers than Manufacturer is now doing.
23. When there are changes in Manufacturer's personnel who contact Distributor, the result is less efficiency in Distributor's operations.
24. Manufacturer withholds marketing research data from Distributor which could benefit Distributor.
25. The status and prestige of being a Brand X Distributor are enough to make Distributor satisfied with less than the highest profits possible from other brand lines.
26. Because of the high demand for Brand X during the summer months, Distributor should prestock more.
27. Manufacturer is more willing to try new ideas in selling and sales promotion strategy than is Distributor.

28. Distributor often encounters difficulties in communication with Manufacturer and other Distributors in order to obtain rapidly items needed for inventory.
29. Distributor is willing to compete vigorously to increase Brand X's share of market in Distributor's territory.
30. It should fall to Manufacturer to initiate all major policies and programs of Distributors and Dealers toward Brand X and be sure they comply.
31. Too much national advertising ties up funds which could otherwise be better spent at Distributor's discretion in his territory.
32. Manufacturer has established an accounting system for his Distributors in order to obtain information so as to keep tabs on them.

Appendix 7-B
Distributors-Dealers Issue Set

1. The higher the gross margin, the more is Dealer satisfied to be handling the Brand X line.
2. When Dealer has a serious complaint, he has the right to go over the Distributor's head and discuss the matter with Manufacturer.
3. When Dealer has large discretion over his advertising, there is the tendency for inconsistency over time in advertising and for funds to be ineffectively used on odd-ball promotions.
4. Dealer does not implement all the training received from Distributor.
5. Dealer has little desire to establish himself among his consumers as an authority in this product line.
6. Distributor should delay his placement of Dealer's order because Distributor is waiting to place a sizable enough order with Manufacturer to obtain a higher quantity discount.
7. Dealer is not promotional-minded enough in his pursuit of business.
8. Distributor's net profit as a percent of sales of Brand X is higher than Dealer's.
9. Dealer's complaints to Distributor are caused by Dealer's desire to be able to satisfy fully his customers.
10. When Dealer returns a defective product, Dealer should not have to incur any cost, like payment of handling charges.
11. Distributor is too strict on the enforcement of credit terms and discounts involving Dealer.
12. Dealer uses advertisements and merchandising plans of Brand X to get customers, but then may sell them on another (usually cheaper) line.
13. Dealer should be striving to make Brand X the largest selling brand in the Dealer's area of competition.
14. In setting the minimum level of inventory to be carried by Dealer, the Dealer should make the final decision.

15. Distributor is inflexible in that he does things by the book with little regard for exceptions.
16. Distributor makes promises of delivery to meet Dealer's request just to get past current problems, even at the risk of not being fully sure that Distributor can make good his promises.
17. Dealer should prefer to tie up as little of his working capital as possible in equipment and part inventory.
18. Distributor should have full responsibility in the setting of advertising funds to which Dealer is entitled.
19. Dealers are better technical people than they are businessmen.
20. Distributor almost always exhibits the highest integrity in responding quickly and decisively to Dealer when Dealer lodges a complaint.
21. Distributor is justified in inducing Dealer to sell the greatest volume possible of Brand X.
22. When Dealer returns a defective part to obtain credit, he should not have to pay the bill for the replacement part when it is due.
23. Frequent visits of Distributor's salesmen to Dealer builds confidence in Dealer that Distributor is there to help him.
24. The incentive trip award is increasingly becoming a less and less successful means of making Dealer increase his sales of Brand X.
25. Dealer is always pressuring Distributor to do more for him, because Dealer wants to avoid some responsibilities and the costs incurred when Dealer performs them.
26. Distributor has the right to set sales quotas on Dealer and to hold Dealer accountable for meeting them.
27. The more Distributor helps Dealer run his business, the greater will be Dealer's sales volume.
28. Distributor's salesmen like to make frequent visits to Dealer, but generally have little information for Dealer's use.
29. Dealer is basically a rugged individualist who wants the challenge of running his own business as he sees fit.
30. Distributor should not just help Dealer with bidding (or quoting), but also assist Dealer with closing the sale.
31. The funds that Distributor is now spending on incentive trips for Dealer could be better spent on advertising.
32. Distributor's salesmen are typically pleasant when taking orders, but less cooperative when complaints are made.

Appendix 7-C
Manufacturer-Dealers Issue Set

1. Dealer greatly desires the high status and prestige of handling Brand X.
2. Manufacturer should be doing something to ensure Dealer an adequate supply of skilled manpower for Dealer's technical and sales needs.

3. Manufacturer has nearly always proved trustworthy in introducing policies and programs which are of mutual advantage to Dealer and to Manufacturer.
4. In sending promotional materials to Dealer, Manufacturer provides too many, too often, and with inadequate instructions to be fully understood by Dealer.
5. If Manufacturer is to be the leader in the industry, he should be constantly expanding his sales volume.
6. Manufacturer should set and enforce standards for Dealer, to be sure the ultimate consumer is getting a fair value for his purchase of a Brand unit.
7. Brand X is *the* prestige line among the several lines of equipment which Dealer handles.
8. There now is less loyalty by Dealers toward manufacturers' brands because the large corporation has displaced the family-owned firm.
9. Manufacturer's adoption of national policies (planned by Manufacturer's personnel and outside expert agencies) is to be preferred to local flexibility and discretion of Dealers.
10. Manufacturer should be the one to have full and final say, because of his expertise, as to what to make, how many to make, and the design of what is made.
11. Dealer's success is more assured if he is tied to Brand X than if Dealer handled any other brand.
12. The complicated paperwork and mechanics of returning defective items of obtaining credit under the warranty protect the interests of Manufacturer more than they help Dealer.
13. Dealer often sells more Brand X in order to obtain incentive trips, even though Dealer may not make any profit on the extra sales.
14. Where breakdowns can be traced to Manufacturer's fault, Dealer should receive both a labor and materials allowance from Manufacturer.
15. Although Manufacturer's policies toward Dealer are introduced to help Dealer, they often end up having the opposite impact.
16. When Manufacturer changes the specifications of a product, Manufacturer is slow to inform Dealer about the new product details.
17. It is to Dealer's advantage to add major sidelines to its business, rather than to concentrate fully on the primary product of Brand X.
18. It is Manufacturer's responsibility to educate the consumer in the necessity and adequacy of Brand X.
19. Nearly every major manufacturer's technological capability to produce a good product is about equal in this industry.
20. Manufacturer should have detailed and timely information about his Dealer's business.
21. Dealer sacrifices his identification and individuality when he joins Manufacturer's distribution system.
22. Dealers have a right to register opinions to Manufacturer regarding product design features, *and* to get these suggestions incorporated into the product.

23. What Manufacturer intends as incentives to make Dealer sell more, Dealer views as added pressures to work harder.
24. Manufacturer encourages Dealer to offer comments regarding the programs which Manufacturer has introduced.
25. When it is difficult to determine who was responsible for the product's breaking down, repair costs should be absorbed by Manufacturer (who is best able to assume them).
26. Dealer deserves extra assistance from Manufacturer in the face of vigorous competition from public utilities and mass merchandising chains (like Sears and Penney's).
27. Manufacturer changes models and specifications of Brand X items too often.
28. Manufacturer's suggested accounting system for Dealer should be used by all Dealers.
29. Dealer's ability to install and service a Brand X unit for the customer is more important than Manufacturer's ability to produce the best quality brand in the industry.
30. Manufacturer's incentives for Dealer to buy more inventory are pressures on Dealer to load up and thus be forced to work harder to sell more.
31. Manufacturer has designed a warranty which is fair and adequate from Dealer's point of view.
32. Dealer's showroom area is very well maintained for customer demonstrations.

Notes

1. Joseph C. Palamountain, Jr., *The Politics of Distribution*, Cambridge, Mass.: Harvard University Press (1955).

2. Valentine F. Ridgway, "Administration of Manufacturer-Dealer Systems," *Administrative Science Quarterly*, I (March, 1957), 464–483; Bruce Mallen, "A Theory of Retailer-Supplier Conflict, Control, and Cooperation," *Journal of Retailing*, XXXIX (Summer, 1963), 24–32; Louis W. Stern and Ronald H. Gorman, "Conflict in Distribution Channels: An Exploration," in Louis W. Stern (ed.), *Distribution Channels: Behavioral Dimensions*, Boston: Houghton Mifflin Company (1969), 156–175; and Louis W. Stern and J. L. Heskett, "Conflict Management in Interorganization Relations: A Conceptual Framework," *ibid.*, 288–305.

3. Bert C. McCammon, Jr., and Robert W. Little, "Marketing Channels: Analytical Systems and Approaches," in George Schwartz (ed.), *Science in Marketing*, New York: John Wiley and Sons, Inc. (1965), 330.

4. William R. Davidson, "Changes in Distributive Institutions," *Journal of Marketing*, XXXIV (January, 1970), 7–8.

5. Ralph M. Goldman, "A Theory of Conflict Processes and Organizational Offices," *Journal of Conflict Resolution*, X (September, 1966), 335.

6. Stern and Gorman, *Conflict*.

7. Louis R. Pondy, "Organizational Conflicts: Concepts and Models," *Administrative Science Quarterly*, XII (September, 1967), 300–306.

8. For a somewhat different version of an intrachannel model in which the variables are explained in detail, see Larry J. Rosenberg and Louis W. Stern, "Toward the Analysis of Conflict in Distribution Channels: A Descriptive Model," *Journal of Marketing*, forthcoming.

9. Stern and Heskett, *Conflict*, 293–294. This was supported by Larry J. Rosenberg, "An Empirical Examination of the Causes, Level, and Consequences of Conflict in a High Stake Distribution Channel," unpublished Ph.D. dissertation, The Ohio State University, 1969.

Conflict and Its Resolution in a Franchise System

Jerry S. Cohen*

Franchising has been referred to both as "the last frontier of the independent businessman," and as a "cruel hoax."[1] The debate which has gone on in Congress and other forums as to which of these propositions is most correct serves no useful purpose except to indicate that there are problems. But effort does need to be directed toward determining how to make the franchise method of distribution function more equitably, efficiently, and economically.

It is my contention that there is a basic flaw built into the structure of this form of marketing. That flaw is the continuing and destructive conflict between franchisor and franchisee which I believe is inherent in the system itself.

It exists because the franchisor generally is able to maximize his profits through the efforts of the franchisee, rather than solely through the success of his own operation. His basic goal may may not be to make his profit as an organizer, a seller of expertise, or the seller of a product. Rather, the franchisor may be reaching into the pocket of his franchisee to extract earnings which in a normal competitive relationship would not belong to him. The franchisor, in effect, may be able to maximize his profits by causing the franchisee to make decisions and follow policies which do not maximize franchisee profits. The franchisor, then, desires not a profitable business for the franchisee, but a profitable business for himself. The two are not the same.

At the same time that the franchisor is trying to influence or control franchisee decisions, the franchisee is seeking a greater measure of independence in his economic decision making in order to maximize his own profits (which may mean less profit for the franchisor). A collision course is inevitable because of the opposing goals of the participants.

While the franchisor is seeking, and can often obtain, the same degree of control he could achieve through vertical integration, he is receiving immeasurably greater benefits. Contractual vertical integration through franchising provides the capital needed to establish the distribution system through the use (or misuse) of the franchise fee. Yet the franchisor need assume none of the financial risks of vertical ownership. It is the franchisee who must assume such risks and burdens as taxes, tort liability, insurance, workmen's compensation, labor negotiation, and adherence to

* Attorney, Washington, D.C.

local ordinances—which ordinarily the integrated marketer would have to assume himself. In addition, the franchisor often is getting labor at bargain rates—franchisees working long hours for low pay, often with "free" family help. More important, the retail franchise operation need not make a profit in order for the franchisor to make a profit. The reason is that many franchise agreements include as a monthly royalty a percentage of revenue based on gross income rather than net income. In an average fast-food franchise, five percent of gross is a common monthly payment to the franchisor.

Therefore, the concern of the franchisor at the retail level is with volume, not profit. Many franchisors in this business advertise specials or give aways which the franchisee is bound to honor. The franchisor may attempt to set retail prices by the preprinting of menus, or may require the franchisee to stay open longer hours than can possibly be profitable to the franchisee. In the petroleum business, for instance, some stations are required to stay open 24 hours a day. If the petroleum company owned the station itself, simple economics would not allow it to operate at more hours than were profitable. But with a franchisee operating the station, such a requirement adds a small amount to volume, while greatly increasing overhead, therefore increasing the royalty to the franchisor while decreasing the total net profit of the franchisee.

Petroleum companies often overbuild, knowing the incremental outlets will make little if any net profit. However, the royalty is based on gallons pumped, which has the same effect as basing it on gross income. The greater the volume, the greater the income to the franchisor, regardless of the profit or lack of profit to the franchisee. If a franchisee goes bankrupt, another can always be found to fill the breach. What is not profitable for the franchisee can be very profitable for the franchisor.

These considerations explain, at least in part, why such gigantic industries as petroleum have utilized franchising as their preferred method of distribution, and have along the way acquired such substantial real estate holdings.

Other forms of maximizing the profits of the franchisor at the expense of the franchisee are built into the franchise agreement. Most such agreements require the franchisee to buy all his equipment and supplies from the franchisor or from designated or approved suppliers. The purported reason for this is to give the franchisee the advantage of mass purchasing. In actual practice, it works generally to the franchisee's disadvantage. The reason is that many franchisors receive overrides from suppliers on equipment and supplies sold or leased to franchisees. The higher the price of equipment, the greater the amount of the override. Therefore, it is often to the franchisor's own economic advantage to arrange for equipment at higher than competitive prices in order to increase his income. The highest —and not the lowest—bidder may get the business.

Because the franchisee is required to pay whatever price is charged by the designated or approved supplier, he does not have the alternative of seeking a better price in the marketplace. He is tied in to an economic practice which the Supreme Court has said generally "has no redeeming features."[2] I have seen actual situations where a franchisee could have bought equipment of equal quality in the marketplace for one-third to one-half less in price, yet the power of the franchisor prevents the franchisee from exercising this economic sanity. Keeping the franchisor deeply in debt may simply act to reinforce the power of the franchisor.

A franchisor may also sell products related to the franchise, but not required to be sold by the franchise agreement. It is to the franchisor's advantage to require the franchisee to handle such products exclusively. The franchisee may feel that he can sell competing products more profitably. To the extent that the franchisor can coerce the franchisee not to handle competing products, he gains an advantage (and the franchisee suffers a disadvantage) not anticipated in the franchise agreement. Auto manufacturers, for instance, prefer dealers to use their brand of parts, even though replacement parts of another manufacturer may meet all their specifications and have equivalent or better quality, and allow the franchisee a better margin of profit.[3] A petroleum company also in the fertilizer business (and that business has almost been taken over by the petroleum companies) may request a gasoline franchisee to handle his fertilizers exclusively.

Other common requirements (written or unwritten) in franchise arrangements which may maximize profits for the franchisor while minimizing them for the franchisee are the following:

(1) Site Location. This must generally be approved by the franchisor. Thus, the franchisee is not free to use a site which he believes to be to his best advantage. The franchisor may be interested in keeping competition away from a company-owned store. He may want a site near a franchisee with whom he is dissatisfied, to utilize the threat of competition to keep this or other franchisees in line. He may want to blanket an area in a certain pattern, even though the franchisee's location in the pattern would not be advantageous to that franchisee's operation.

(2) Rental of Signs from the Franchisor. In many cases, identical signs meeting the franchisor's specifications could be purchased from an independent source at a much lower cost to the franchisee.

(3) Paying A Percentage of Gross for Advertising. In most cases, the franchisee has no voice in how or where the advertising will be spent, or indeed, even that it will be used entirely for advertising purposes.

(4) Approval of the Franchisor Before the Franchisee Can Sell Any Part of His Business. At the same time, the franchisee has no veto of a sale by the franchisor. In view of the fact that the franchisee primarily is paying for expertise, he may find himself dealing with a new franchisor who has little experience in the business. This is particularly true as the conglomerates move to take over franchising.

The kinds of controls which allow the franchisor to insist on practices which will maximize his own profits at the expense of the franchisee exist both inside and outside of the contract.

Most contracts provide for termination for violations of any of the clauses. These may range from complying with local ordinances to minimal sales objectives. The minimal sales objective is the most invidious of the devices. Generally, it is established at unrealistic levels which subjects the franchisee to cancellation almost at the will of the franchisor. This has been particularly prevalent in automotive franchise agreements.[a]

The most effective method by far for controlling franchisees is the short-term real-estate lease, or even the long-term lease without a right of renewal. The standard lease in the petroleum industry, for instance, is one year. Unless the franchisee accepts the conditions imposed by the franchisor he simply is not renewed. It is not surprising that the turn-over among gasoline station dealers is almost thirty-five percent yearly. The threat of nonrenewal also is a potent weapon to force the franchisee to sell at recommended prices—or to sell only the products distributed by his franchisor. Even where a five-year lease is involved, as in many fast-food contracts, it generally takes a number of years to build up a business. The danger of losing the fruits of this labor is never forgotten by the franchisee.

Another method by which profit is maximized at the expense of the franchisee, and control is maintained at the same time, is the interest of the franchisor in the lease of property to the franchisee. Many franchisors either lease, lease-back or guarantee the lease (with options to select the tenant and use) for the property where the franchise is located. Therefore, upon a violation of the contract or the imposition of conditions which a franchisee may not wish to accept, the franchisee may not only lose his franchise, but he may not continue doing business at the same location. Thus, he is not able to go into business for himself or work out an arrangement with another franchisee at a location where he is known; his alternatives are greatly restricted, making him more receptive to suggestions of the franchisor. The relationship between landlord and tenant traditionally has been one of tension and conflict; this becomes more acute where the landlord also is the franchisor.

A final method of control is to build a company-owned store in close proximity to the franchisee. In such a situation, the company-owned facility can be used to impose on the franchisees in the area whatever policies in

[a] Chrysler attempted to cancel a dealer who did not meet minimum sales standard. The Court found that approximately 50% of the other dealers were not able to perform according to the standard established.[4]

regard to pricing, specials, or other selling devices the franchisor feels are in his best interests.

Another aspect of the total problem is the policy of certain franchisors of allowing the franchisee to take the initial risks, then once the business becomes highly profitable, failing to renew and taking over the business. This practice occurs only where a business becomes so profitable that it makes more sense to maximize profits at the retail level than through the franchisee. Certain petroleum companies, for instance, take over stations after they start pumping in excess of 40,000 gallons per month.[5] The moral, of course, is not to work too hard or become too successful. The franchisee who does is in danger of losing his business.

At this point, the reader may assume that I have a prejudice against franchising as a form of distribution. This is not the case. I strongly believe that the franchising concept makes good sense not only for the franchisor and franchisee, but for our competitive system as well. What bothers me is the gulf between concept and reality.

At the outset, the franchisee has been sold on the advantages of being an independent businessman, even though he has no experience or expertise. How well he has been sold, not only by the franchisor, but by the media and the government as well, can be demonstrated by the prices he pays for the right to operate a franchise. In order to operate a Jerry Lewis Cinema, over 700 franchisees have paid a minimum of $15,000 each. Most of these franchises were sold before a single Cinema was in operation. Yet what the franchisee has bought, basically, is the right to use a well-known name, pay eight percent monthly royalties on gross sales, and pay an override on a lease while at the same time giving up all rights to select his own pictures. In this instance, the franchisor has produced a large income from the franchise fee alone—$10,500,000. Even if not a single theater makes money, the franchisor may have achieved his financial goal.

To the extent that an effective and independent distribution system can be established, that new competition can be induced where needed, that untrained persons utilizing the expertise and trade names of others can become effective competitors, then the consumer and the economy will benefit from franchising. This is particularly true as the production end of the economy becomes more and more concentrated. Two hundred corporations already control almost two-thirds of manufacturing assets in this country. Many industries with high concentration ratios engage in the most rigid kind of lock-step pricing. The consumer often can find competition only at the retail level. In automobiles, for instance, whether demand rises or falls, prices charged by manufacturers go up each year apparently in unison. Only competition at the retail level reflects the condition of the market place. If General Motors, Ford, and Chrysler owned all their retail outlets, one could reasonably expect the same price rigidity at the retail level which exists at the production level.

So franchising makes good sense for the economy and the buyer. It is an excellent method of inducing new competition into the market place. But it will recognize its true potential only when the franchisee can make independent decisions. Because of the inherent conflict in the system, and bargaining power heavily favoring the franchisor, the system will work without distortion only when two events take place: (1) control by the franchisor is relaxed; and (2) certain of the basic causes of conflict are removed. For this to come about will require, in my opinion, both greater use of present laws and the passage of new laws.

One method of attacking the problem is that of the Canadian courts which have chosen to accept the system as it is and have imposed a fiduciary obligation on the franchisor in his dealings with the franchisee.[6] This approach may assist the franchisee on occasion. However, it runs contrary to the concept of the system and does not help the competitive structure of the economy.

The better approach, I believe, is that contained in the antitrust laws which generally condemn vertical price fixing, tie-in sales, and full-line forcing requirements.[7] The most recent case which met the problem head on is *Siegel* v. *Chicken Delight*. This case deserves special mention. The Federal Judge in the *Chicken Delight* case, ruled that some tie-ins were illegal as a matter of law and others were up to the jury to decide. The Court, in determining that paper packaging requirements were illegal as a matter of law, said:

Defendants' showing on paper packaging is nothing more than a recitation of the need for distinctive packaging to be used uniformly by all franchisees in identifying the hot foods. This was not contested. However, the admissions in evidence clearly demonstrated that the tied packaging was easily specifiable. In fact, the only specifications required were printing and color. Moreover, defendants have admitted that any competent manufacturer of like products could consistently and satisfactorily manufacture the packaging products if defendants furnished specifications. Those suppliers could have sold to the franchisees through normal channels of distribution. As a matter of law, therefore, this paper products tie-in cannot be justified on any grounds within the contemplation of acceptable authority.

In regard to those products which might be considered unique to the trademark, the Court said:

The dip and spice mixes are alleged to be secret and to impart a unique and distinctive flavor to the final products. Likewise, the cooker is alleged to be unique and to prepare the food in a special manner. Contradictory testimony has been offered on this aspect of the litigation. As such, a question of fact exists for the jury to determine.

In regard to this fact question, the jury found (after being out only two hours and after only one ballot) that the special batter, and the cookers and fryers, could be purchased from other sources than the franchisor without damaging the quality of the product or the goodwill of the franchisor's name.

Summarizing, the Court said:

The Court finds as a matter of law that there is an unlawful tie-in arrangement; that sufficient market control exists; that a 'not insubstantial' amount of interstate commerce is affected; that no justification exists with respect to the continuity of supply of paper products; that neither the alleged justification of convenient accounting device nor continuing source of supply are defenses in this litigation; that the new business justification is clearly inapplicable to this case; and that the fact of damages is established.

The law has seldom been stated as clearly and as bluntly.

The implications of a court decision have also never been so readily apparent and blunt. One entire range of franchising practices are legally suspect, and several others are subject to potential attack. The economic implications of the decision are also far reaching. Basically, the *Chicken Delight* case holds the prospect of shifting the brunt of interbrand competition from the franchisee to the franchisor, while also stimulating intrabrand competition among franchisees by minimizing franchisor imposed vertical market restrictions upon franchisees.

For example, it may well be illegal for a major petroleum company to tie the sale of its own gasoline to its trademark and lease, if in fact reasonable specifications can be established for gasoline which is similar to the trademarked item. From a practical point of view, major petroleum companies exchange regular gasoline as a matter of course, and tests run by the Senate Antitrust Subcommittee and some state agencies indicate that there are no significant chemical differences between branded and unbranded gasoline.

If such tie-ins could be eliminated, it would narrow the area of possible conflict and force the franchisor to be more concerned with the interests of the franchisee. In the gasoline example, it would force him to compete for the franchisee's business, instead of telling him what to sell and at what price. Interbrand price competition would be faced directly by the producers and the oligopolistic gasoline industry could feel the warm breath of competition for the first time in several decades.

The antitrust laws also condemn price fixing in any form. Even when a major petroleum company went to a consignment system of selling in order to dictate price, the Court found it was only a subterfuge to circumvent the law.[8] The petroleum companies are now experimenting with a manager-consignment contract which would maintain control over prices and TBA without the company accepting the actual responsibilities of management. Such decisions should help free-up the operation of the franchisee, and promote rational intrabrand and interbrand competition free of artificially imposed restraints. The magnitude of the problem, however, has frustrated a realization of the full potential of the franchise system.

One of the difficulties has been reluctance by, or lack of manpower in the antitrust agencies to enforce the laws. However, the advantages of the class action are being more fully understood, and it is developing as a potent weapon in private hands for the enforcement of the law. Private antitrust litigation has been on the upswing but new remedies must be found to mitigate the cost and delay of this form of litigation if it is ever to fulfill the potential of effective self-help.

There are other new developments on the legal horizon which also may assist the franchisee. For instance, the use of the "attempt to monopolize" provisions of the antitrust laws is being expanded to include a company attempting to monopolize its own system of distribution. While the law is still vague in this area, it has great potential for reaching certain forms of franchisor activity, such as undercutting his own franchisee for a particularly desirable piece of business, or cancelling a successful operation in order to run it himself.[9]

Yet to be fully tested, but on the horizon, is a private action for violation of Section 5 of the Federal Trade Commission (FTC) Act which forbids "unfair trade practices in commerce." If the Supreme Court ultimately holds that there is not a private right of action to enforce the prohibitions of Section 5 of the FTC Act, I am confident that legislative attempts to spell out such a right will occur.

But even accelerated use of the antitrust laws by government and private litigation will not solve the entire problem. Legislation is needed in at least two areas:

A full disclosure bill patterned after the one introduced by Senator Harrison Williams of New Jersey, is needed to protect the potential franchisee from fraud and misrepresentation.[10] That bill would give the Securities and Exchange Commission the same authority to compel disclosure and prohibit fraudulent practices that it now has in the securities field. At the least, it would assure the franchisee that he knew what he was buying.

More important is legislation to prevent unfair cancellation and nonrenewal. Regardless of the outcome of the lawsuits, the franchisee faced with nonrenewal lives with a club over his head, which he ignores only at the price of a terrible headache. It is this kind of threat, implied or actual, which has diminished the force of the cases which have been decided in the franchisee's favor. Any franchisee considering a lawsuit to assert his legal rights, must do so with varying degrees of fear and trepidation about his future.

The answer here, I believe, is the Hart "Fairness in Franchise" bill[11] which provides a cause of action for money damages for termination or nonrenewal without good cause. So far the bill has been bottled up in Subcommittee, but inevitably it must become law if only because (and, perhaps, naively) it makes good sense and good justice.

While it would not solve all problems, the bill would at least give the franchisee some incentive to resist pressure which is contrary to his own economic interest. More importantly, such legislation would improve the balance of negotiating power between franchisor and franchisee, which, in turn, should considerably improve the fairness of franchise contracts.

Finally, in industries which are highly concentrated, the production of a product should be divorced from its distribution. Separation would have the effect in several industries of preventing the use of the company-owned store as a source of coercion, of forcing the distributor to identify more closely with the interests of his franchisee, and of removing a weapon which has frequently been used for disciplining recalcitrant franchisees.

Another development, particularly in the brewing industry, is the use of arbitration clauses in franchise agreements. In the past, they have generally proven unsuccessful. Although, they should be encouraged, they do not deal with the basic problems as I have attempted to outline them.

I do not believe that franchising will ever reach its potential while present practices exist. Destructive conflict in the structure can only be resolved by revising the structure. Franchising will work effectively only when the interest of the franchisee and franchisor have more in common. That is not the case today.

Notes

1. See generally, "Franchise Legislation," *Hearings* before the Subcommittee on Antitrust and Monopoly of the Committee on the Judiciary, U.S. Senate, 90th Congress, 1st Session (1969).

2. *Northern Pacific Railway Company* v. *United States,* 356 U.S. 1 (1957).

3. A good example of this type of practice can be found in *Automatic Radio Manufacturing Co., Inc.* v. *Ford Motor Co.,* 272 F. Supp. 744 (D.C. Mass., 1967).

4. See *Madsen* v. *Chrysler Corporation,* 261 F. Supp. 488.

5. See testimony of H. C. Thompson, President, Congress of Petroleum Retailers before the U.S. Senate Antitrust and Monopoly Subcommittee, *Hearings on Methods of Distribution and Pricing of Gasoline* (July 14, 1970).

6. *Jirna Limited* v. *Mr. Donut of Canada, Limited,* decided July 28, 1970.

7. See *Northern Pacific Railway Co.* v. *U.S., supra; Fortner Enterprises* v. *U.S. Steel,* 394 U.S. 495 (1969); *Advanced Business Systems Supply Co.* v. *SCM Corp.,* 415 F.2d 55 (1969); *Siegel* v. *Chicken Delight,* 311 F. Supp. 847 (1970).

8. *Simpson* v. *Union Oil Co. of California,* 377 U.S. 13 (1963).

9. See generally, E. Zimmerman, "Attempt to Monopolize: The Offense Redefined," *Utah Law Review,* Vol. 4 (September, 1969).

10. S. *3844,* introduced in 1970.

11. *S. 1967,* introduced by Senator Philip A. Hart, (D) Michigan on April 25, 1969.

Part Four
The Development of Contractual Marketing Systems Outside of the United States

9 The Internationalization of Contractual Marketing Systems

Stanley C. Hollander*

The article "the" and the preposition "of" are probably the two most definite and concrete words in the title of this paper. All of the others are fuzzy, susceptible to multiple definitions, embrace more subject matter than can be handled satisfactorily in a reasonably short document, and will be defined on a more or less *ad hoc* basis as we go along. Many of the definitional problems are relatively trivial, at least from a conceptual point of view, but even these tend to illustrate the variety of institutional and operational elements that may be involved in internationalized contractual marketing systems.

Definitional Questions

The term "internationalization" lacks definitiveness in several respects. The demarcation between "inter-" and "intra-national" becomes hazy in the case of systems that embrace various portions of a commonwealth or that reach from a protecting power to its protectorates. Thus, a trade paper article argued some years ago that Puerto Rico was a good training ground for American retailers who eventually wanted to venture further abroad. Even though at least technically domestic, mainland-Puerto Rican systems involved some of the problems of cultural adjustment, language barriers, and other pressures associated with internationalization.[1]

Another definitional question asks what aspects of the system or its related elements have to be international (however defined) before the system itself is international. Often the contract is a purely domestic instrument between, say, an indigenous franchisee and the local subsidiary of a foreign principal. Thus, Volkswagen dealers in the United States normally contract with an American subsidiary rather than with the German parent. In this case, the total system is rather clearly international since it is controlled from Germany and is designed to move a German-made product. Another instance is somewhat more confusing. W. R. Grace & Co., an American conglomerate, has acquired a French company, Jacques Borel which, among other activities, franchises fast-food establishments in France. (Borel happens to operate this business as a sublicensee of a

* Michigan State University. A generous grant from the Midwest Universities Consortium for International Activities supported the collection of some of the data reported in this paper.

British firm, Pleasure Foods, which holds its master license from an American firm, but that chain of relationships is essentially independent of Grace). Putting aside the origin of the franchise, is the Grace-Borel-franchisee concatenation an international system?

Questions of individual firm nationality and of contractual jurisdiction can be nettlesome in specific cases. For example, the Philippine Retail Trade Law, which confines certain types of distributive business to Philippine nationals, is subject to a treaty exemption in favor of United States firms. Some Philippine courts have tried to restrict this exemption to corporations that can prove United States nationality for 100 percent of their stockholders, including trust accounts. This interpretation apparently is still being tested in the higher courts. A related, often-tragic, nationality question tends to rise in those countries and areas where marketing activities are normally concentrated within ethnic minorities. Contractual, as well as fully, integrated systems that draw their members from these groups are always in danger of being branded as foreign, even though all the members may actually be nationals and long-time residents of the country involved. Thus, the question of who is foreign and who is indigenous is not always resolved easily or equitably.

The term "internationalization" can apply to both specific systems and to concepts. The multicountry flow of ideas, methods, and techniques is at least as significant as the fact that some particular contractual organization happens to reach across national boundaries. We will return to these types of flows later on.

One can also ask what is meant by the term "contract" or "contractually." One aspect of this question is illustrated in a description of Wehkamp, N.V., a large Dutch mail-order firm owned by Great Universal Stores, Ltd., a British firm. The description says that Wehkamp's "agents do not act as representatives of the company to whom they are not bound by any type of commercial contract."[2] This apparently self-contradictory statement arises from the fact that Wehkamp uses a mail-order technique that has become very popular in Britain and differs substantially from what we normally expect of Sears, Roebuck and Montgomery Ward types of businesses. Instead of mailing its catalogs directly to its customers, Wehkamp sends the books to agents who then solicit orders from friends and neighbors. This approach has become very popular in Britain and also in many European countries, and demonstrates the international transfer of operating methods.

The mail-order firms that use this technique, as well as most other direct (home) selling companies (except Singer), emphasize the supposedly complete autonomy of their representatives. Various tax, social security, and liability advantages flow from this sort of detachment. Hence, the claim that no contractual system exists. But some type of implicit contract would seem to prevail if both parties, the firm and the agents, have and act upon a set of mutual expectations concerning each other's behavior.

Implicit dimensions may also be added to even an explicit contract by operation of law. In many countries, agents acquire vested interests in their agency regardless of the contract wording, and substantial indemnification often has to be paid if the principal terminates the relationship. The American Automobile Dealers Franchise Act provides our closest domestic approximation to this rule, but the foreign regulations are often much stricter.

Finally, we came to the question of what is a "marketing system?" For this purpose let us confine ourselves to microsystems and avoid the debate expressed in Alderson's *Dynamic Marketing Behavior* as to whether the macrosystem is a useful, analytic concept.[3] In any event, so long as we remain within the context of relatively free enterprise or competitive marketing, contractual integration is almost entirely a micro concept. (It might be fascinating to look at the use of contractual linkages in more totalitarian systems, but that is another topic.)

Three subquestions remain: (1) How tightly do the units have to be tied together before we can say that a system exists? (2) How do we differentiate marketing systems from other systems? (3) Who are the system members?

The degree of articulation varies greatly among international groupings. For example, the International Association of Department Stores is primarily a highly prestigious agency for research and information exchange among a group of selected European (and Japanese) stores. Is it an integrated system?[4] A French government study reports that RIMPU, which ties together nine major variety and junior department store chains in as many countries, is also primarily an informational agency. But some of its members, such as Standa (Italy) and Monoprix (France), exchange buying services for each other and Standa carries some of Monoprix's private brands.[5] Is this an integrated system? The members of the Intercontinental Group of Department Stores undertake to do considerable buying for each other. Is this an integrated system?

If we then ask which small-scale systems are marketing ones, we come back to the thorny problem of defining marketing. Certainly most international groupings of firms tend to have marketing effects. Perhaps we would be justified in excluding purely financial or investment consortia from the term marketing systems. For example, General Shopping, S.A., a Luxembourgese holding company backed by Swiss funds, has made substantial investments in Swiss, Austrian, German, and Spanish department store groups, an Italian variety chain, a German newstand organization, some industrial and credit subsidiaries, and a Curacoa-domiciled automatic vending complex operating in Britain, Belgium, France, and Germany. Is this a system? Would we consider it a system if General Shopping exercised little or no influence over its holdings? Would we consider it a marketing system if the investment was primarily in manufacturing or processing rather than in distribution? In the same vein, are patent, process, and trademark licensing agreements part of marketing? Certainly they are often considered and adopted as low-risk, low-effort means for deriving some benefits from foreign markets.[6]

Similarly, we sometimes tend to think of contractually integrated marketing systems as forward or downward organizations, primarily intended as outlets. The alternative term franchising, certainly implies such a direction. But as some of the earlier illustrations indicate, many contractual marketing channels are really supply systems. It has become commonplace for writers on marketing and economic development to point to the beneficial impacts that Sear's subsidiaries have had upon their indigenous, and often quasicontractually integrated, suppliers. (This relationship is, of course, an example of intranational linkage within an international system.) The European and Asian buying services that Metasco, an Allied Stores' subsidiary, sells to about twenty American department stores outside the Allied chain, and Jewel (Tea) Companies' participation in a Mexican vegetable-growing joint venture are both examples of more directly internationalized procurement systems.

Procurement systems obviously vary in some significant respects from sales-oriented ones. Many operating details differ. Some of the revenue arrangements used to compensate suppliers in franchise systems, for example, would appear inappropriate for the quasicaptive supply units in procurement systems.[7] Immediate objectives also obviously differ, and quite possibly growth expectations (at least at the channel captain position) may be different as well. Nevertheless, theories at some reasonable level of abstraction may apply equally well to both types of systems. For example, tendencies towards or away from complete integration may quite probably be explained as functions of perceived risk, capital and size imbalance, legal restraints and incentives, and life goal patterns of the participants in either system type, rather than as a function of the direction in which decisions flow.[8]

The discussion, so far, has concentrated on vertical linkages, but a considerable number of horizontal contractual relationships have also become important in international distribution. The joint venture type of association in international retailing is exemplified by such well-known chains as Simpson-Sears (Canada), Kresge-Cole (Australia) and Super Bazaars (Jewel Companies and several Belgian associates). A bewildering variety of such ventures are emerging in Europe. For example, both Metro, a German firm, and Carrefour, a French one, are now each working with other European partners in developing chains of giant self-service stores. Another type of horizontal linkage, already mentioned, is the buying pool or group which may bring together a number of individual stores or chains. At least some of the European pools are binational or multinational in scope, although of course, small stores normally participate in such multinational groups only through some type of affiliated chain intermediary.

The horizontal contracts probably exhibit somewhat different power distribution characteristics than the vertical ones. The notion of a channel captain, which is a vertical concept, implies a strong power imbalance. Some vertical contracts in international marketing, such as perhaps one between an automobile manufacturer and the dominant export-import trading agency in a given African country, may exhibit more signs of countervalence and bilateral oligopoly than of clear-cut dominance. Nevertheless, the idea of dominance or leadership does seem inherent in many vertical plans. The power distributions in the horizontal plans appear much more random, with possibly some tendency to cluster near to equivalency.

Other types of transnational contracts are more difficult to categorize as either horizontal or vertical, and to some extent raise the question of who should be considered as system members. The leased chain operator who contracts for space and services on premises maintained by other merchants probably represents the interaction of two or more systems: one designed to provide a specific commodity or service category, and the others designed to provide generalized retailing mixes at specific locations. One such internationalized interface that astonishes a layman unversed in the mysteries of hairdressing is beauty salon operation. Two American firms, Seligman & Latz, and Glemby Corporation, each with over 400 leased units, now include a number of Latin American, British, and European department store salons on their rosters.[9]

The management contract is another type of arrangement that has some application in distribution even though it is more commonly used as a means of extending manufacturing, rather than retailing, expertise across national boundaries. To cite one complex example, Booker McConnell, Ltd., a British conglomerate with substantial interests in Africa and the Caribbean, recently sold its Zambian retail chains to the government-owned Zambia Consumer Buying Corporation. Part of the compensation was used to purchase a minority interest in the expanded ZCBC, and Bookers has undertaken a ten-year contract to act as managing agent for the entire ZCBC. The arrangement appeared to work so satisfactorily that Bookers established a similar relationship in Malawi, a neighboring country.[10] Other management contracts, such as those which have been used in the European mail-order trade, may involve less complex political considerations, but they still present problems in tracing the flow of authority and responsibility through the system.

Somewhat similarly, many franchise-based systems are complicated through the use of master franchisees or licensees who then establish subfranchisees, just as procurement systems may be complicated through the use of subcontractors. One specialist argues that the use of a licensing program is the most practical approach for most American franchisors who seek foreign expansion, a market he most earnestly recommends to their attention.[11] The master licensee is at least directly involved in the core flow, the basic raison d'etre, of the franchise system, whether that flow consists of the right to an identity, an operating technique, specific merchandise, or some combination of all three.

Most franchise systems also involve a host of auxiliary flows. The original franchisor may provide buildings (or building designs) and merchandising concepts, with the actual merchandise, supplies, promotional services, financing arrangements, repair work and/or other items and services coming from a multitude of affiliated, quasiaffiliated, approved, or totally independent suppliers.[12] The facilitating agencies and the analysis of auxiliary flows probably should receive more academic attention than they normally do, and these agencies must be considered as part of the total system. Often the major channel can take the form that it does only because other elements of marketing can be delegated out to warehousemen, banks, advertising specialists, and the like. One of the problems of extending contractual systems to other countries, particularly to the less developed nations, is the relative dearth of some types of auxiliary institutions in the places where they are needed to complete the system.

The extent to which the ultimate consumers can be, or should be, considered as channel members is also an intriguing question. Some years ago Donald Blankertz wrote that: "Since nothing in the household's activities corresponds to the selling function (creation of demand, location of a buyer, negotiation of terms, or transfer of title) it cannot be, by definition, a marketing unit."[13] He did hold that consumer participation in the management and work of a cooperative was a distinct form of economic activity, distinguishable from both consumption and marketing.[14] But whether we call the activity marketing or something else, the contractual or quasi-contractual participation of the consumer in a marketing system, as some versions of British and European cooperative theory contemplate, is obviously relevant to our topic here.

The Topic Unbounded and Then Restrained

As the preceding discussion indicates, internationalized contractual marketing systems can be stretched to cover a wide variety of arrangements and institutions. Although international marketing differs from intranational primarily in degree, practically all of those differences tend to encourage relatively increased use of contractual (as distinguished from outright ownership) ties when the system is designed to cross national boundaries. Several problems contribute to the risk and difficulty of operating fully-owned international systems.

Essentially Xenophobic Barriers. These include customs, tariff, licensing, import quota and similar burdens and restrictions on importation of both merchandise and supplies, and the always-present danger that those barriers may increase at some future date. Current or future legal requirements or extralegal pressure (customer resistance, boycotts, violence, and so on) may demand nationalization of ownership, of management, of personnel in general, or of other phases of the operation. Currency controls and profit repatriation restrictions may hinder revenue flow from foreign branches.

These problems are by no means omnipresent—nor are they always severe enough to preclude international investment. In at least some cases, they have had beneficial long-run effects. Unanticipated restrictions on merchandise importation and profit repatriation are reported to have structured some of Sear's of Mexico's profitable internal growth.[15] But a marketing system, and especially its retail components, are highly visible institutions. Consequently, wisdom sometimes cautions against expatriate ownership of the final links in the chain. Thus, many of the British and European trading companies that once actively engaged in all phases of African import and export commerce are now trying to turn much of their small-scale back-country upriver retailing over to indigenous ownership. The companies still maintain their automobile dealerships and their European style major outlets, such as the Kingsway Department Stores (United Africa Co.) in Nigeria and the Chaine-avion self-service markets (S.C.O.A.) in the Ivory Coast. But they would like to see the smaller stores become locally-owned voluntary affiliates.

Socio-cultural Differences. These may limit the market or require greater degrees of adaptiveness than a totally-owned system exhibit. Language differences complicate promotion and communication in an internationalized system. Tastes, shopping habits, and living patterns often vary considerably. Some American fast-food franchises, for example, are designed for a drive-in trade or for an urban clientele that has a relatively brief lunch period away from home. Considerable adaptation may be required to meet the needs of different customer groups, although increasing urbanization and rates of car ownership are now reproducing American market conditions in many parts of the world.

Legislation. Even legislation that is not ostensibly or intentionally discriminatory against foreign-owned retailing may encourage the use of independent ownership at the retail level. Chain store taxes, wage and hour controls, and social security legislation have encouraged franchising, rather than refiner-ownership of American gasoline stations. In many other countries, social and labor legislation and mandatory fringe benefits play an even more significant role in large-firm labor relations. The more or less unregulated small enterprise, often even the franchised outlet, thus derives a competitive advantage over the larger, integrated firm.

Besides xenophobic regulation and sanctions against large business, the international marketing system, like any other enterprise, must also face all special rules that may arise with regard to its intrinsic operation. Thus in some countries, hamburger-stand systems, which normally depend upon supplies of ground meat patties from central sources, have come into conflict with local public health regulations that prohibit transportation of ground meat. The burden of such regulations can fall differentially upon total and quasi-integrated systems with the advantage probably usually going to the partially integrated ones.

In contrast, some regulation actually favors total integration. We have already noted termination restrictions which can make a franchise a more substantial commitment than the franchisor desires. In some countries, legislation imposes more liability upon the franchisor for the acts of his franchisees than is usually the case in the United States or Canada.[16] Some of the new Common Market antitrust regulations, particularly restrictions on exclusive contracts, may also provide inducements towards total ownership. Nevertheless, on balance, the legal problems of contractually organized systems are probably considerably less severe than those of comparable fully-owned international marketing agencies.

Currency fluctuations. These add another element of risk to the international venture and thus tend to retard investment commitments.

Long-distance Control. Finally, in spite of jet-age communications improvements, management at a distance still has its difficulties. Even though some fully-owned international retailing systems have been able to display amazing degrees of control over foreign branches, foreign marketing operations normally demand at least somewhat more decentralization than is necessary in purely domestic business.

All of these factors, and undoubtedly many more, are conducive to the use of contractual ties, which minimize investment and risk, in international marketing systems. Nevertheless, the contractual systems—and particularly franchising arrangements—will also face some special difficulties.

We have already noted the ways in which law may sometime favor outright ownership instead of contractual ties. Restrictions on cancellation or termination of established agency relationships definitely (and perhaps quite properly) discourage the use of contractual systems as trial balloons, or as transitional arrangements in the growth of wholly-owned systems.

The market for franchises (that is, the supply of suitable franchisees) may be more of a problem than the market for the final product. Mendelsohn comments that an Englishman who has $12,000 to $25,000 to invest in a business is usually not willing to work in that business the same way an American franchisee would.[17] The dealer or agent recruitment problem seems to be a severe one in many organizations. The basic concept of franchising itself is likely to arouse suspicion in many markets. And potential franchises may be inclined to evaluate foreign franchisors in terms of questionable national stereotypes.

The international franchising firm faces a number of other problems. Many franchisors claim real-estate advice and assistance as one of the major services they render in return for their fees and commissions. But locational knowledge is a delicate wine that seems to travel poorly, and international retailing firms do appear to suffer many site selection difficulties.[18] (Of course, the contractual system shifts the loss to the agent.) So-called celebrity franchising may be limited by the parochial nature of the celebrity's fame. Finally, the contractually organized firm loses some opportunities and has to forego some flexibility in transferring funds, equipment, and personnel between countries of operation. However these disadvantages have not been serious enough to preclude the widespread use of contractual arrangements in international marketing systems.

The Franchising Plot Thickens

One fascinating aspect of most franchising discussions is the extent to which the quoted figures, for example on total volume of business, usually include all of the old established traditional franchisors, particularly the automobile manufacturers, the petroleum refiners and the soft-drink syrup refiners. But the textual comments normally concentrate on newer developments and institutions, such as fast-food franchisors. It is important to remember that much international franchising is still in the traditional automotive, automotive-related, and soft-drink bottling fields.

The extent of internationalization among the newer franchisors is unclear and subject to contradictory reports. Curry and his associates commented in 1966: "Franchising's relative failure in penetrating the international market is surprising for several reasons." Yet in 1967, *Business International* published a report entitled "The New Wave in Marketing: Worldwide Franchising."[19] Thompson and Oxenfeldt concluded that: "Franchisors have not penetrated foreign markets to any appreciable degree in spite of their demonstratably large potential sales and considerable rate of growth."[20] *Marketing in Europe*, a highly useful monthly report prepared by the Economist's Intelligence Unit, commented in December, 1968: ". . . U.S. operators are increasingly using 'export franchising' to extend into European and Latin American markets"; but in January 1970, the same publication discussed "Franchising's Slow Progress in Europe."[21]

Any census of internationalization among the newer franchisors would encounter many problems. The difficulties might be exacerbated by the penchant the founders of those firms seem to have for grandiose names, such as "Global. . . ," "Worldwide. . . ," and "International . . ."—though such words might help identify some of the newer firms. The contrast between the publicity given to fledgling foreign branches and the obscurity that normally surrounds any subsequent demise complicates analysis of growth. Fundamental definitional questions, such as "what is a franchise, as distinguished from say a voluntary chain membership?" and "what trades belong in the newer categories?" would complicate matters. And attention must be given to an often-overlooked distinction between the number of firms that have internationalized and the percentage of their volume they do abroad. To cite a related example, the attention and discussion that has been devoted to Sears' branches outside the United States and Canada is highly disproportionate to the approximately two percent that those branches contribute to Sears' total sales volume.

But even in the absence of such a census, certain types of businesses can be distinguished as centers of contemporary action in the establishment of wide-ranging franchised and other contractually integrated systems.

Travel-serving Systems. The enormous increase in foreign travel on the part of both Europeans and North Americans since the end of World War II has very naturally stimulated the development of systems to serve that trade. Entirely apart from the intrinsic quality of the services offered by any particular organization, international travel is an obviously fertile field for the creation of international plans. In spite of his wanderlust, the traveler often looks for the assurances of the familar, the home away from home; and he often wants to, or has to, make his arrangements and reserve his accommodations before he reaches his destination. The travel agency industry has evolved complex channels, with various degrees of integration and articulation between retail and wholesale agents and branch, correspondent, or representative agencies abroad, to serve at least part of this demand. The airlines, amalgamated into the I.A.T.A. cartel, have a complex system in which each will act as ordertaker for any other member anywhere in the world. In addition, individual sets of carriers have often worked out their own agreements for more active off-line representation.

But the most spectacular growth of travel-serving franchise systems has been in hotel, rental car, and related fields. The American traveler has been, and will become, accustomed to seeing both wholly-owned and contractually tied Hiltons, Sheratons, Intercontinentals, Holiday Inns, Travelodges, Howard Johnsons, and the like in an increasing number of countries.[22] A Howard Johnson hotel in Bali may seem a contradiction in terms, or at least in images, but is already under construction. Relais Routiers, a highly successful French operator of inexpensive hotels, has now licensed the construction of a British chain under the control of Bass Cherington, a major brewer and pub franchisor.[23] The Fortes chain, which originated in Britain, is now participating in hotel ventures in France, Bermuda, Malta, Sardinia, Cyprus, Guyana, Ceylon, and Jamaica. The European Hotels Corporation, a consortium of European airlines and banks, is planning twenty hotels in major European centers. UTA, a French airline, currently participates in five African and three South Pacific hotels, Lufthansa has been involved in Kenyan hotel development, and Japan Air Lines now has plans for properties in Southeast Asia, Honolulu, and Paris.[24] Sightseeing and other travel-related organizations are also developing or extending international systems, along with Avis, Hertz, and Budget Rent-A-Car.

Designer and Luxury Boutiques. The trade in de luxe or high-priced goods has always had a strong flavor of internationalism. Customers are likely to be more widely traveled and to have more cosmopolitan living styles than average. Imported goods, so long as they escape the pejorative connotations of cheap manufacture, are often especially prized or assumed to have a special flair in design and execution. Consequently, it is not surprising that some portion of the retail trade in fine jewelry, expensive household goods, de luxe clothing, art objects, and the like, is carried on by firms that have either ownership or contractual horizontal and/or vertical international connections.

The last few years particularly have supported a wave of international boutique systems operating under the name and aegis of famous couturiers and designers. These people have created perhaps the only viable international celebrity franchise system. The sports figures who have played an important role in American franchising are often unknown outside the country. After all, how many of the readers of this paper could name the captain of the Argentine national soccer team, or the leading batter in British cricket circles? But the relevant markets around the world seem to know the designers to whom *Womens Wear Daily* refers as "Monsieur X" and "Monsieur Y."

Designer boutique systems sometimes operate as free-standing shops (in the sense of not being part of another store rather than in the sense of isolated location)—but in many other cases they are conducted as distinctive franchised units within large department and specialty stores. As in other franchise systems, the degree of franchisor control and the requirements imposed upon the franchisee undoubtedly vary from system to system and perhaps sometimes from location to location.

The introduction of these self-contained departments within larger stores would seem to present many problems to the store management. In the typical case, where the designer's line is only part of the store's offering in a particular merchandise category, the creation of autonomous boutiques complicates shopping and comparison. In this respect, the designer boutiques constitute organization by source rather than by customer-use patterns, even though the marketing concept would argue for the latter approach.[25] Moreover, promotional activities invariably tend to feature the designer somewhat at the expense of the store's own image.

Nevertheless, the last few years of economic expansion and the prestige stores' desire for every approach that would differentiate them from mass over-the-counter retailing, has fostered the growth of many such systems. The fortunes of design houses always wax and wane with changes in styles and fashion trends. They are also more or less captive to fluctuations in the creativity of their principals. But whether the basic concept of these systems is itself ephemeral or incapable of resisting economic decline is something that only long experience will tell.

One organization that has attracted considerable attention is the chain of Rive Gauche womenswear boutiques operated by the French couture house of Yves St. Laurent, itself a subsidiary of an American complex, Lanvin-Charles of the Ritz. At the end of 1969, the chain included 28 units in France, Switzerland, Italy, Venezuela, Spain, Germany, and the United States. A Parisian shop and one free-standing store in New York are wholly owned, all of the others are franchised. St. Laurent controls the design of both the separate shops and the in-store boutiques, and strives for considerable uniformity of appearance.[26] Another French designer, Pierre Cardin, has been active in the styling of mens-, womens- and childrenswear, textiles and house furnishings, and is reported to have contracts with 186 retailers in many countries in the Americas, Europe, and Japan.[27]

The list of other European designers and stylists whose names suggest swank, chic, and rather frightening price tags, and who control identified-name boutiques and departments in American stores includes, in womenswear: Barocco (Italian), Nino Cerruti (Italian), Carol Chombert (French, furs), Finn Birger Christensen (Danish, furs), Courreges (French), Christian Dior (French), Eres (French, swimwear), Katja (Swedish), Hubert de Givenchy (French), Marimekko (Finnish), Patou (French), Sonia Rykiel (French), Gunther Sachs (operating a French firm, Mic Mac), Tiktiner (French), Emanuel Ungaro (French), and Valentino (an Italian subsidiary of an American firm, Kenton). Some of those operating in other merchandise fields include Robert Carrier (British, high-style cookware), Mr. Fish (British, menswear) Dunhill (smoking accessories and leather goods), Godiva (Belgium, candy), Hermes (French, leather goods luggage), Kids in Gear (British, childrenswear), Mallett & Son (British, antiques), Palazzi (Italian, menswear), Pucci (Italian, menswear), Turnball & Asser (British, menswear), Louis Vuitton (French, luggage), Zolotas (Greek, jewelry), Giaconda (Italian, jewelry).

While some of these outlets are confined to New York, many of the others have spread elsewhere in the United States and Canada. Many are also represented in more than one European country and also often in Japanese stores. A few American designers, such as John Weitz (mens clothing) have established similar units in Europe. A number of manufacturer-operated international franchises for such things as fine shoes (Bally and Salamander) and modern tableware (Rosenthal A.G.'s Studio Haus franchise) seem analogous to the designer systems.

The luxury trades are one of the few sectors in which promotional emphasis upon foreign connections is a generally advisable managerial practice. Pseudo, and sometimes even bona-fide, internationalism are coming to play increasing roles in fast-food franchising, which two perceptive writers have labeled as a major lower-income luxury.[28] Caution often demands de-emphasis of expatriate affiliations in other product and service sectors. One wonders, for example, whether some of the United States-based international hotel groups have always followed the wisest path in so clearly publicizing their American, rather than their indigenous, participants and associations.

But both the luxury and the foreign-travel categories of international franchising must be placed in perspective. International travel is always delightful to read about and usually fun to experience. Luxuries are nice. Nevertheless, most people are at home, rather than abroad, most of the time. And almost by definition, most purchases fall outside of the upper echelon, snob, luxury bracket. Consequently, these two categories can only constitute a limited share of total market operations.

General Merchandise Retailing Through Gasoline Stations. Both types of internationalization, that is, exemplification of foreign systems and the use of connections with international companies, are present in another type of franchise system that is also still small in absolute volume but which may promise great growth. Merchants and marketing pundits have long felt challenged by the captive audience sitting in the automobiles parked at the gasoline pumps of America. E. B. Weiss has ruefully commented that his forecast for general merchandise retailing through the gasoline station, made repeatedly since 1954, has been one of his most unfulfilled prophecies.[29] Numerous attempts have been made (Spiegel once even tried placing its catalog on display stands in a selected number of stations), but practically all have withered away. One firm, Northwestern Refining Co. of St. Paul, now reports success in selling about 2,000 miscellaneous items at its discount Super-America stations, but this is an exception to the general rule.[30]

Several refiners operating in European markets, including both domestic and international firms, are now mounting substantial efforts at adding extensive general lines to their franchised outlets. In Italy, Rinascente-Upim, a department and variety store firm, is franchising its Autobazaar stores which share highway locations with stations of a gasoline chain, but which operate through entirely separate staffs and organization.[31]

Other firms are trying more closely integrated operations. One international oil company official says that his dealers in Scandinavia, Italy, Austria, Japan, and the Philippine Republic, and to some extent elsewhere, have had good results from separate profit center kiosks handling dairy items, confectionary, magazines, and newspapers. Shirts, socks, games, and other lines sell well in Japan and the Philippines. He claims that his marketing divisions supply none of this merchandise for the dealers, but the company likes the arrangement because of the resultant improvement in station atmosphere and service. The dealer's wife usually manages the kiosk; she drives away the loiterers who might otherwise congregate at the station.[32] An executive in another company sees nonautomotive merchandise as a means for offsetting the low profitability of gasoline retailing, and thus it both attracts better dealers and reduces the general level of dealer-company hostility.[33]

The Heron company in Britain, which has been absorbed by one of the majors, has tried to develop rather elaborate subscription plans in addition to sales from its display cases.[34] Shell has a large number of "Shell Boutiques" at its French stations. Esso of France is now doing much the same thing; approximately 2,000 of its stations will have shops selling a mixture of automotive and nonautomotive items. It also maintains or is opening similar shops in its dealer network in Belgium, the Netherlands, Germany, Italy, Austria, and Switzerland. It has made a particularly heavy investment in this type of outlet in Britain, but business is reported as being slow.[35]

Whether or not, and the degree to which, these European systems will succeed also remains to be seen. Whether if successful they will become prototypes for similar American operations is also an open question. But at least the European ventures are struggling more heroically than their American counterparts with two problems of scale or critical mass. The European essays have typically been mounted simultaneously in enough stations to make a strong consumer impression. Instead of an isolated test station or two, which might appear as purely deviate retail outlets, European efforts have been conducted at substantial numbers of locations. And the merchandise selection has been wide enough to demand special attention and often special salestaff. This counteracts the usual dealer tendency to treat general merchandise as simply an unwelcome distraction from his normal automotive interests.

Other Types of Systems. A number of other important clusters of internationalized systems (identified in part on the basis of kind-of-business, and in part on the basis of operating method) should receive at least passing notice.

Direct selling. Direct-selling firms that use autonomous or quasiautonomous agents for consumer sales solicitation in a number of countries include several reference book and encyclopedia firms, Caxton, Encyclopaedia Brittanica, Grolier, and Crowell Collier Macmillan; cosmetics houses such as Avon and Dart Industries (Rexall Drugs) Beauty Counselors, and household supply organizations such as Dart's Tupperware Division, Stanley Home Products, Watkins Products, and Fuller Brush. Some of these have been very successful (Avon for example, had about $130 million sales outside the United States and Canada in 1967), while others have encountered various degrees of resistance in different markets. Other direct selling companies with international ties include Singer, as well as Electrolux and Spirella Corsets. However, Singer representatives are usually company employees rather than agents, and at least some of the international ties in Spirella and Electrolux (originally a Swedish corporation) have been loosened or dissolved. The experience of many of the companies cited here, as well as of the British-type mail-order firms mentioned earlier, does show that direct selling is exportable to many countries, and even to markets that *a priori* might appear to regard such techniques as improper invasions of domestic privacy.

Multilevel plans. The controversial multilevel direct-selling plans, in which agents recruit successive levels of subagents, have also internationalized. Holiday Magic, a new cosmetics firm that has enjoyed spectacular success during the last five years, now has subsidiaries in Canada and Mexico as well as franchised operations in Australia, Great Britain, Germany, Norway, Sweden, and Denmark. The corporation president reported $250,000 sales during the first three months of operation in Australia.[36] Another multilevel plan, reportedly originating with an American firm, Homecare (a subsidiary of Chemical Associates of Houston), recently enjoyed meteoric success in promoting a multipurpose cleaner called "Swipe" throughout France. Advertising was confined to lapel badges, car stickers, and signs reading "J'aime Swipe," displayed by the agents with the aim of provoking curiosity and inducing conversations that could lead to ultimate sales. The agents ranged from consultants, with a required investment of only 12 bottles up to distributors who had to take 1,800 to 3,600 bottles. Compensation was based in part on sales to consumers and to subordinate levels of agents, and in part on rewards for agent recruitment. However, the campaign's pyrotechnical expansion rather quickly turned into an equally dramatic collapse. The teaser promotional campaign eventually lost its capacity to invoke curiosity after "Swipe" became a household word, and the market for both users and subsidiary sellers of the high-priced cleanser became completely saturated. The French company is now in bankruptcy.[37]

Miscellaneous Franchisors. At least some American producers and packagers have maintained well entrenched and successful networks of franchised outlets abroad. The Dr. Scholl's footcare organization, whose yellow storefront signs are displayed in many European countries, and Helena Rubenstein's deluxe beauty salons are two examples of such operations. Arthur Murray Dance Studios and Sonotone Hearing Aid Stores are established abroad. More recently, they have been joined by some of the newer service and product franchisers. In the fast-food field, Carrol's, Kentucky Fried Chicken, Lum's, Shakey's Pizza, and Wimpy's have been reported outside United States and Canadian borders. Culligan, Inc., Martinizing Dry Cleaning, Weight Watchers International, and Servicemaster also claim foreign affiliates. Mattel's British subsidiary now plans to license toy stores that carry specified minimum inventories of Mattel products.

A relatively limited amount of franchising moves in the opposite direction. Crowell, Collier, and Macmillan, for example, acts as the United States (and also Canadian, Mexican, and Japanese) licensee for Berlitz

Language Schools. A French operating concept, Le Drugstore is a feverish assemblage of an a la carte restaurant and lunch counter bar, and moderately expensive cosmetic, clothing, phonograph record, gift, and other boutiques that constitutes an almost caricatured exaggeration of an American pharmacy. Le Drugstore has spread throughout Europe and has been introduced in New York. It does not seem to have had the same impact here as it enjoyed abroad, possibly because the food service arrangements are much less novel in the American scene. Attempts to introduce British pubs into the United States have foundered on the complexity of the American liquor laws. In general, much European franchising into the United States belongs in the luxury category discussed earlier.

The Retailers Unite

The distinction between a franchise system and a voluntary chain is, at best, thin and indistinct. Some of the organizations listed above might well be placed in the voluntary chain category; many of those mentioned below could easily be called franchise systems. But the label is not nearly as important as the fact that the retailers in many Western industrial countries are uniting, or being united, in comprehensive and articulated systems that often reach across national boundaries. As might be expected, a variety of arrangements are being used for this purpose.

Private Brand Exportation. Some merchants with reputations for outstanding private brands are now exporting this merchandise to correspondent retailers in other countries. Standa's use of Monoprix' lines has already been mentioned. Some J. C. Penney items are now being sold in Selfridge's and other major British department stores owned by Sears Holdings, Ltd.[38] (Sears Holding is not affiliated with Sears, Roebuck). Britain's enormously popular variety chain, Marks & Spencer, now exports some of its St. Michaels products to department-store operators in Sweden, Finland, Denmark, and France. The degree of control varies between exporting chains. In many instances the Marks and Spencer merchandise is placed in separate, even free-standing, St. Michael shops and boutiques.[39]

Affiliated or Agency Stores. A number of European corporate chains also supply affiliated or agency stores in just the same manner that some American chains unite wholly-owned and contractually associated outlets. Many of these systems are wholly intranational, but at least some are multi-country in scope. The Etam lingerie and womenswear cluster of national chains use some very modern merchandising methods, and some very old-fashioned display techniques, in approximately 700 stores in Britain, France, Belgium, Holland, Germany, and South America. About three-quarters of the stores are wholly owned, with the others franchised.[40] Foto

Quelle GmbH, a subsidiary of Germany's multinational mail-order house, Die Quelle, has agencies in France, Luxembourg, Austria, and Switzerland.[41] Prisunic, the dominant French variety chain and a part of the Prisunic-Printemps-Sapac complex, has an organization chart that rivals any American conglomerate for complexity. It is a participant in joint ventures in Greece and Spain, is involved with Belgian interests, holds a minority share in some of SCOA's African enterprises, is reported to have had an unhappy participation in a Brazilian chain, and operates wholly-owned and affiliated stores in much of the French-speaking world.[42] Prenatal, a French chain specializing in maternity and infants items, has licensed national chains rather than individual stores. It holds a substantial interest in the Belgian and Dutch licensees, Achat & Distribution Belge and Moeder en Kind, and has also licensed a British organization, Mothercare, which has set up its own stores in Scandinavia, Austria, and Switzerland. Again these are only examples; many other names could be added to the list.

Voluntary Chains. Several United States voluntary chains, such as Western Auto, Rexall Drug, Pro-Hardware, I.G.A., Red & White Stores, and Clover Farms have substantial Canadian operations. A few also have established affiliations, with varying degrees of integration, elsewhere in such countries as Australia, Spain, and South Africa. But the most striking post-World War II development in voluntary merchandising has been the growth of the large-scale European voluntary food chains.

These pan-European organizations are essentially super-federations of national federations of wholesaler-retailer groups. They represent their constituent national units before multicountry bodies such as the Common Market authorities; they engage in considerable research and information exchange; and they transfer food-marketing technology from country to country through their advisory work. Several of them are encouraging increased pooled or reciprocal buying on the part of wholesaler members in different countries, and at least some tentative efforts are being made towards international financing and lending arrangements. Those chains, such as SPAR, VeGe, ViVo, and Centra, that use the same name in every country of operation have been developing international private brands and have been working towards increased uniformity of display insignia and image-building materials. Each of these chains serves between 15,000 and 35,000 food retailers in perhaps ten to fifteen countries. SPAR, which is generally considered to be the leader, was originally established by a Dutch wholesaler in the early 1930s and to a considerable extent was patterned on the American Red & White stores.[43] Three other multinational voluntary groups, A & O International, E. O. Organisation Europeene, and IFA-Farchring, operate through national chains that have different names from country to country. Although the voluntaries have achieved by far their greatest prominence in the food field, some other fields are also represented. Euro-Seldis is a major international textile chain, and Catena is of considerable significance in European hardware retailing. It had assembled 1,350 stores in eight countries by 1963 and has grown since then with considerable encouragement of joint buying and improvement in members' management methods.[44] The Jarnia hardware voluntary group of over 500 stores in Sweden, Denmark, Norway, and Finland has had great success in implementing standardized store design, merchandising, and promotional programs.[45]

Cooperative Chains and Buying Groups. As noted, the voluntary chain concept developed in the United States and then spread to Europe via Holland. The idea of the retailers' cooperative chain traveled in the opposite direction, having been brought to the United States by a group of emigre grocers from Germany. These retailers had originally participated in the Edeka chain there and they used that organization as a model in developing what is generally regarded as the pioneer American cooperative chain, the Frankford Grocery Company of Philadelphia.[46]

Although the retailer-sponsored cooperative chains preceded the development of wholesaler-sponsored voluntaries in Europe, they typically have not achieved nearly as much integration or internationalization as the voluntaries. Nevertheless, some international linkages have emerged. In the food field, Edeka has sponsored Intereinkauf to unite retailer cooperatives in ten countries; Rewe, another German chain, has established Eurogroup International with French, Dutch, British, Swedish, and Danish associates to develop common private brands. Gedelfi, a German cooperative composed of corporate chains, has set up linkages with its French counterpart, Paridoc. A number of international informational and buying pools have formed among retailer cooperatives and buying groups in hardware, variety, and textile lines.

The increasing integration and rationalization of private sector European retailing have triggered similar developments on the part of the consumer cooperatives. Nordisk Andelsforbund, a long-existing joint-buying agency for the Scandinavian consumer societies, has taken on increased importance and now undertakes at least some purchases for non-Scandinavian societies as well. The Co-operative Wholesale Committee, representing fourteen societies and one Israeli national society, maintains fruit-buying offices in California and in Australia. It is also developing international trademarks, such as the CIRKEL brand for coffee purchased through Nordisk Andelsforbund's Santos office.[47]

Why the Systems Flourish

The postwar growth of the foreign and international consumer goods and service systems rests, directly and indirectly, upon much the same economic base that has supported American systems. Rising prosperity, increased specialization in economic life, increased urbanization, and increased consumption have provided fertile ground for new marketing systems. The traditional European independent small stores simply were not prepared to handle the desired volume of goods. Increased foreign travel and increased cosmopolitanism undoubtedly also contributed some increased receptivity for foreign-based systems and ideas.

But to some extent, these forces operated upon the contractually affiliated systems quite indirectly. Economic growth in Europe, and elsewhere, lead to reductions in, and elimination of, many restrictions on large-scale distribution. On one hand, consumers wanted better and more efficient retail institutions. On the other, the widespread availability of nonretail employment and the opportunities in augmented markets removed the most strident and effective pressure for the preservation of protectionism. Consequently, the large-scale, fully integrated organizations could, and did, flourish. The growth of contractual systems, then, was a natural and healthy competitive response. The reactive nature of much of the contractual growth can be seen in the recent history of the consumer cooperatives. The revitalized Co-operative Wholesale Committee, the expansion of Nordisk Andelsforbund, the growing tendencies towards rationalization, centralization, and international linkages among and between the various national societies, and the emphasis upon efficiency rather than ideology, have all been part of a response to increased large-scale competition and, in many countries, to declining market share.

Other factors, such as the withering away of some international trade barriers, have contributed to the growth of international systems. But the basic forces have been the push and pull of competitive pressure and economic opportunity.

A Final Puzzle

Both total and contractual vertical integration are normally considered in terms of various pairings of primary suppliers, manufacturers, and intermediate dealers. The final consuming units, whether called part of the system or not, are usually presumed to deal with the rest of the channel only at an arm's length removed. The puzzling questions are why this presumption is usually valid, and why the consuming units are not (more) closely integrated into the total marketing organization.

Yet many economists now treat the household as a small factory that performs the businesslike function of combining capital goods, raw materials, labor, and consumption time to create utility.[48] Similarly, Marketing Science Institute's presentation of its CRIM model (Customer-Retailer Interaction Model) emphasized the symmetry of customer-retailer and retailer-supplier interfaces. As CRIM depicted it, both the consumer-customer unit and the retailer had highly similar informational, decisional, and inventory-holding tasks. Moreover, MSI hypothesized that this relationship might be generalized to all levels of channel interaction.[49]

If vertical integration presents efficiencies and advantages at the levels preceding final purchase, and if the final purchase interaction is essentially analogous to these earlier levels of trade, then it would seem to follow that some form of at least quasi-integration would be advisable at the consumer purchase stage. In fact many writers have predicted increased consumer participation in contractual linkages with their suppliers, so as to routinize transactions and to minimize search and negotiatory effort. For example, Ferdinand Mauser noted in 1963:

> One of the more promising approaches to spending family income in committed amounts is either to lease merchandise or to sell it on a replenishment contract basis.
>
> Many steps in the direction of contractual selling and leasing are already in evidence . . . .
>
> Indeed . . . savings dividends would be wholly practical since renewal sales costs would be small. . . .
>
> This method of advance ordering would create the ideal situation manufacturers have dreamed about since the beginning of mass production, for it enables the manufacturer to plan production on a long-range basis. Certainly greater facility in planning ahead would lead to cost reductions that could be passed on to consumers.[50]

Both domestic and foreign marketing history do provide numerous examples of successful and unsuccessful individual systems that linked consumers with their suppliers on some type of subscription or long-run contractual basis. Buying-club plans that provided a type of one-way contract, under which suppliers agreed to give club members special discounts in return for an expected but not legally obligated concentration of purchases, have frequently emerged—and just about as frequently disappeared in American marketing history. One now-completely forgotten club of this sort, the confusingly named Association of Army and Navy Stores, Inc., sold 275,000 memberships during its period of operation from 1916 to 1952, and in its heyday could claim discount privileges for its members at many of America's department and specialty stores. Even Sears, Roebuck once gave discounts to consumers who had purchased membership in the Association.[51] Many other, usually smaller and more homogeneous clubs, have come and (usually) gone. Groups of fellow-employees, members of fraternal orders, student associations and, some years ago, even the fledgling automobile clubs promulgated this type of buying plan.[52] In April 1970, *Home Furnishings Daily* reported a new group, The Buying Power Club, in New York with a claimed affiliation of 1,200 stores that had agreed to give 5% discounts to the Club's members, then numbering 27,000.[53] Similar clubs have appeared in Britain and elsewhere, and with some modifications in concept have apparently played significant roles in marketing in some parts of South Africa.[54]

The closed-door discount house method of retailing also suggests a semi-integrated system, at least in concept. The operators often claim that the membership plan facilitates inexpensive direct mail promotion and also tends to create a homogenous market with a consequent reduction in merchandising problems. Nevertheless many operators would probably also admit that the so-called membership plan is often primarily a promotional gimmick that makes customers feel they have access to unusual privileges.

Subscription plans have had more success in the United States and abroad in some limited segments of marketing, such as book and phonograph record distribution, where preselection is often a substantial service to the consumer. Leasing plans have been used with some substantial success, although not with the degree of general acceptance once predicted, in American automotive marketing. Television-set rental, instead of sale, is now widely accepted in much of Europe, and a number of the major rental firms are operating internationally.[55]

But by far the most substantial examples of consumer-linked systems are provided by the consumer cooperative organizations which are still of great importance in Britain, Scandinavia, and to some extent in other parts of Europe. Technically speaking, membership in a cooperative society imposes no contractual obligation to purchase from that society. But it seems clear that many of the pioneers and developers thought in terms of the member's moral commitments to the groups. The references to member's loyalty to the organization that abound in the early writings on cooperation have a strong normative connotation and are laden with much more intense value judgments than we would put into comparable terms such as brand or store loyalty. Arnold Bonner's definitive history of British consumer cooperation echoes this recurrent theme of mutual interaction and obligation in the title of his summary chapter: "Towards the Co-operative Commonwealth."[56]

Yet when all is said, these examples suggest relatively little, surprisingly little, consumer-supplier linkage. The buying clubs have usually proved to be ephemeral; the closed-door discount houses are relatively minor elements in American marketing and have often converted to conventional open-door operations. The successful long-term leasing and subscription plans have typically been restricted to limited product and service categories. In Europe, control of the cooperatives is rapidly passing out of the hands of the philosophers and ideologists and into the efficiency models of the engineers and technocrats. The societies are becoming much more centralized, much more power is being transferred to the national wholesale bodies, and international linkages are being strengthened. The co-operative societies have concluded that they must fight rising competitive pressures on market terms and in the market arena, rather than on the basis of sentiment or emotional attachment. They have been willing, or forced, to sacrifice the traditional methods of customer attachment in order to achieve the rationalized operations necessary for effective market competition.

Which then leaves us with the fundamental, unanswered question: Why are contractual linkages so much more effective at trade-supplier levels than at the customer-dealer level? Thus confusion remains compounded.

Notes

1. "Puerto Rico: Prelude to American International Retailing," *Progressive Grocer* (September, 1961), 86ff.

2. "Mail Order in the Netherlands," *Marketing in Europe* (November, 1968), 23.

3. *Dynamic Marketing Behavior,* Homewood, Ill.: Richard D. Irwin, Inc. (1965), 13.

4. Derek Knee, "European Retail Trade Associations Come of Age," *Journal of Retailing* (Spring, 1968), 26.

5. France, Centre National du Commerce Exterieur, *Le Commerce d'Alimentation Integre ou Organise en Italie.* Paris: CNCE (1967), 28–29.

6. See Jack Baranoff, "Technology Transfer Through the International Firm," *American Economic Review* (May, 1970), 437–40, for a discussion of the considerations influencing the choice between licensing and direct investment.

7. Milton Woll, "Sources of Revenue to the Franchisor and Their Strategic Implications," *Journal of Retailing* (Winter, 1968–69), 14–20.

8. Alfred R. Oxenfeldt and Anthony O. Kelly, "Will Successful Franchise Systems Ultimately Become Wholly-Owned Chains?" *ibid.,* 69–83.

9. "Setting Coiffures of Women Abroad Big Business For U.S. Firm," *Business Abroad* (December, 1969), 17; "The Sun Never Sets on Clemby's Beauty Salons," *New York Times* (September 3, 1969), 46.

10. "British Trading Giant Rides High on Changing Tide," *Business Week* (November 16, 1968), 120–27; "State Parties Ride Out Zambia Takeover Storm," *The Sunday Times* (London) (April 21, 1968), 31.

11. Robert A. Weaver, Jr., "International Licensing," in Charles L. Vaughn & David B. Slater (editors), *Franchising Today—1966–1967,* Albany, N.Y.: Matthew Bender (1967), 62.

12. "Franchising's Busy Helpers," *Business Week* (February 21, 1970), 132–33.

13. "Consumer Actions and Consumer Nonprofit Co-operation," in Wroe Alderson & Reavis Cox (editors), *Theory in Marketing,* Chicago: Richard D. Irwin, Inc., (1950), 166.

14. *Ibid.,* 174.

15. William R. Fritsch, *Progress and Profits: The Sears, Roebuck Story in Peru,* Washington: Action Committee for International Development (1962); Richardson Wood and Virginia Keyser, *The Case Study of Sears, Roebuck de Mexico, S.A., Washington: National Planning Association* (1953).

16. J. A. H. Curry *et al., Partners for Profit.* New York: American Management Association (1966), 122.

17. M. Mendelsohn, *The Guide to Franchising,* Oxford: Pergamon Press (1970), 79.

18. Stanley C. Hollander, *Multinational Retailing,* East Lansing: Division of Research, Graduate School of Business Administration, Michigan State University (1970), 138.

19. "The New Wave In Marketing: Worldwide Franchising," *Business International* (February 17, 1967).

20. Donald N. Thompson and Alfred R. Oxenfeldt, "Franchising in Perspective," *Journal of Retailing* (Winter, 1968–69), 10.

21. "Marketing Review," *Marketing in Europe* (December, 1968), 3; (January, 1970), 3.

22. "Hotel Game Better: Now Everybody's Playing," *The Magazine of Wall Street* (August 3, 1968), 9–11.

23. "U.K. Targeted for Network of Economical Restaurants, Hotels," *The Travel Agent* (April 20, 1970), 40.

24. William D. Patterson, "The Big Picture," *ASTA* [American Society of Travel Agents] *Travel News* (May, 1970), 124ff.

25. I am indebted to Mr. Stephen Flaster for this observation.

26. Annual report, Lanvin-Charles of the Ritz, Inc. (1969), 5.

27. "Lucky Pierre," *Womens Wear Daily* (July 16, 1968), 4; International Association of Department Stores, Retail Newsletter, #138 (May, 1969).

28. D. Halas & S. Halas, "Hamburgers, 18¢ Food Franchise Business," *Esquire* (July, 1968), 80–82.

29. "A New Hope for Food and Gas Stores?" *Marketing Insights* (April 1, 1968), 18.

30. "SuperAmerica Gas Stations Really Sell Home Goods," *Home Furnishings Daily* (January 30, 1970), 6.

31. "Audience Discussion," in A. L. Trotta (editor), *Retailing International 1969–1970,* New York: National Retail Merchants Association (1970), 137.

32. *Interview* in New York (March 19, 1968).

33. *Interview* in London (June 11, 1970).

34. International Association of Department Stores, *Retail Newsletter* #117 (June, 1967).

35. *Ibid.,* #139 (June 1969).

36. "Holiday Magic," *Womens Wear Daily* (February 6, 1970), 22.

37. "Swipe Is Sweeping French Marketing Scene," *New York Times* (December 13, 1969), 51; "French Cleaning Product Is Wiped Out by Success," *ibid.* (March 5, 1970), 15.

38. International Association of Department Stores, *Retail Newsletter* #146 (February, 1970).

39. *Ibid.*, #142 (October, 1969).

40. *Ibid.*, #146 (February, 1970).

41. *Marketing in Europe*, #71 (October, 1968), 60.

42. See: "Personality A Plus for Prisunic's Image," *Womens Wear Daily* (December 30, 1969), 1; "Conran Chairs at the Prisunic" *Sunday Times* (London) (February 18, 1968), 25.

43. Christina Fulop, *Buying by Voluntary Chains*. London: George Allen and Unwin, Ltd. (1962), 42.

44. International Association of Department Stores, *Retail Newsletter* #73 (June, 1963).

45. Erik Elinder, "Voluntary Single Line Chains in Sweden," in A. L. Trotta (editor), *Retailing International 1969–1970*, New York: National Retail Merchants Association (1970), 67.

46. Russell L. Childress, *Trends and Prospects for Affiliated Food Retailers*, Newark, Delaware: University of Delaware for the U.S. Small Business Administration (1962).

47. Portions of this and the preceding section have been excerpted or paraphrased from Hollander, *Multinational Retailing*, 56–60, 71–74.

48. See A. K. Cairncross, "Economic Schizophrenia," *Scottish Journal of Political Economy* (February, 1958), 15–21; Gary S. Becker, "A Theory of the Allocation of Time," *The Economic Journal* (September, 1965), 493–517.

49. Michael Halbert, *The Meaning and Sources of Marketing Theory*. New York: McGraw-Hill Book Company (1965), 37–44.

50. "The Future Challenges Marketing," *Harvard Business Review* (November-December, 1963), 178.

51. See Stanley C. Hollander, *The Rise and Fall of a Buying Club* (Marketing and Transportation Administration Paper #3), East Lansing: Michigan State University Bureau of Business and Economic Research (1959).

52. *Ibid.*, and F. W. Gilchrist, "The Discount House and Channels of Distribution," in S. Rewoldt (ed.), *Frontiers in Marketing Thought*. Bloomington: Indiana University Bureau of Business Research (1955), 55.

53. "N.Y. Co-op Buying Plan Called 'Whopping' Success," *Home Furnishings Daily* (April 21, 1970), 6.

54. See T. Van Waasdijk, "A Functional Analysis of Retail Buyers' Associations in the Union," *South African Journal of Economics* (June, 1957), 124–29.

55. International Association of Department Stores, *Retail Newsletter* #144 (December, 1969).

56. Arnold Bonner, *British Co-operation*. Manchester, England: Co-operative Union, Ltd. (1961). See also: Robert Kohler, "The Concentration Trend Among Co-operative Enterprise Groups," *Annals of Public and Cooperative Economy* 41 (January-March, 1970), 33–35.

10 Contractual Interdependence in Marketing Processes of Developing Latin American Communities

Charles C. Slater*

This paper aims to illuminate the role of backward vertical market coordination in selected developing Latin American communities.[1] It is important to recognize first a constraint and then a goal.

The constraint is that, unlike several other papers in this collection, this paper does not consider forward vertical market coordination activities such as franchising, or government acquisition contracting such as defense purchases. Only one aspect of contractual marketing is explored in depth—backward vertical market coordination. The goal is to demonstrate the role of marketing in economic development, specifically the influence of market coordination on producer decisions to change the effectiveness with which they utilize their available capital and other resources. In developing these concepts, two topics are explored: first, a review and assessment of the role of marketing in economic development with reference to Latin American experience; second, a contrast between traditional and modern marketing institutions, particularly contractual marketing schemes.

At the outset it may be useful to provisionally define backward vertical market coordination. The coordination of a market articulates the behavior and expectations of institutions and operators to reduce the cost of achieving a given level of throughput in a channel sequence from producer, assembler, shipper, storage and process center, wholesaler, retailer and finally, to the consumer. Improvement in market coordination reduces the perceived risk attendant to the acquisition of inputs and the sale of product and service, and thus, changes the level of investment that the operator will risk on a given transaction. Indirectly, then, capital is made more efficient as less of it needs to be held back for security against possible adverse demand and price changes. With backward vertical market coordination, the impetus for change occurs at steps closer to the final consumer, and works back up the channel. Changes by retailers to increase consumer purchases usually are consumption expanding, and not as often restrictive as the profit maximizing of producers or others further up the channel.

A Framework

Economic development has long recognized the categorical imperative of development—a shift in population and income from the rural to the

* University of Colorado.

urban sector. Noted by A. G. B. Fisher,[2] and partially developed in Colin Clark's influential *Conditions of Economic Progress,*[3] this has been an important aspect of Simon Kuznets' work concerning the three sector economy—agriculture, manufacturing, and service industries.[4] Kuznets notes that in a developing country there is a negative correlation between income level and the proportion of income directed to the agricultural sector, and a positive correlation between income level and the manufacturing sector. In his studies, no consistent pattern emerged for the way in which services varied with per capita income. Later, an attempt will be made to indicate that it is the changing character of the income of the service industries that is critically important to the development process.[5]

This phenomenon has given rise to a number of attempts to interpret the process. Lewis and Owen have enunciated models concerned with a two-sector agriculture approach, where a subsistence or traditional sector is allowed to languish while a modern or capitalist sector of the developing economy is oriented to serving the urban sector.[6,7] Virtually all economists who have considered this problem have placed heavy emphasis on the importance of rising real incomes of urban consumers as the principal driver to the development of the two-sector economic model. Johnston very ably summarizes the research in agricultural and structural transformation in developing countries in a current *Journal of Economic Literature* article.[8]

> Particular emphasis has been given to the fact that income elasticity and demand for food is almost always less than one—as implied by Engel's law—and that it tends to decline as higher levels of per capita income are attained. Chenery suggests, however, that changes in supply conditions resulting from changes in factor costs associated with the increases in the size of the country's domestic market are also highly important. The changes in costs are attributed primarily to scale effects and externalities. The increase in the size of the market is, of course, a function of rising per capita incomes and increased specialization and exchange as well as population growth.[9]

Kuznets has also suggested that the very process of industrialization and urbanization has required changes on the supply side.

> Especially relevant in this regard is the large increase in "marketing services" included in retail outlays for food in a high-income urbanized society. Data that Kuznets presents for the U.S. and Sweden show a very sharp decline in the percent of income devoted to food in terms of its primary cost—its value at the farm gate or point of import—whereas there has been a considerable increase in the share of income spent on the processing, transportation, and distribution of food products.[10]

At a later point, Johnston reveals a bias by suggesting that "although some of the additional costs associated with these services were 'imposed' upon consumers, the growth of demand for processing, transportation, and distribution services was also a result of various technical innovations and other factors that influenced consumer preferences.[11]

Johnson proceeds to point out that critical issues in development policy revolve around interpretation of the process of structural transformation involving the decline of agriculture relative to secondary (manufacturing) and tertiary (service) sectors. To some, he notes, this structural transformation is simply a consequence of development. To others, the structural transformation is not merely a consequence of development, but a process that can be deliberately fostered by policy measures to accelerate development. It is at this point that marketing specialists are, in my opinion, critically important to the development of strategies for development. Detailed and explicit study of marketing as a social process is a requirement for the elucidation of theories of economic development.

Marketing channel coordination and its impact on development involves *increasing the level of income within a community and its related food shed* and also *equalizing the distribution of that income within the community to expand the consumption of the lower-income elements of the society.*[12] Thus, development is given a twin set of goals. It is important to appreciate that there is conflict inherent between equalizing distribution and increasing the level of income.

It has been universally observed that saving is indulged in by the wealthier members of the community. Thus, to increase the level of savings in the community, it is usually necessary to increase the concentration of income. Therefore, the second goal of increasing the consumption potential of low-income people by redistributing income is in contradiction to the goal of increasing the level of income through increased savings. A redistribution of income to the lower-income groups in a society, which have a very low propensity to save, results in an increase in the proportion of the income devoted to consumption—but a decrease in the proportion of income available for savings.

The political art of development consists of balancing capacity-expanding income-concentrating activities with demand-expanding income-redistributing or unconcentrating activities. It is precisely because the financial markets in less developed communities are often inefficient in translating private savings into effective income-expanding investment that improvement in the efficiencies with which marketing channels operate may be crucial in improving the reinvestment process.

Improvement in the vertical coordination of marketing channels through contractual marketing can induce the entrepreneurs operating in these distribution channels to become more efficient, by increasing their output through utilizing more efficiently their present capacity with small increments in capital. The argument also suggests that horizontal improvement in the coordination and efficiency with which market channels operate can be important in the demand-expanding side of the equation of development. To the extent that market channel coordination fosters fuller utilization of the productive capacity of the community, it contributes to increased output.

Market Process Coordination

One can postulate certain behavioral assumptions regarding consumers' propensities to consume, save, and shop, as well as producers' attitudes toward risk and uncertainty in relation to their output levels. A limited theory can be suggested:

1. Income redistribution as a goal of development can be stimulated by lowering the relative prices of necessities such as food, since these necessities absorb a very large share of low-income family purchases.
2. Prices of necessities in large, rapidly growing, urban centers can be lowered by inducing two changes in retail marketing:
   a. increases in scale of markets from individuals each selling a single line of product, to a supermarket selling over 1,000 items; and
   b. variations in pricing so that selected high volume necessities are sold at lower margins, while less frequently purchased items usually purchased by higher-income families are sold at higher margins.
3. In order to secure the larger quantities of the commodities sold at lower prices, coordination vertically between retailer and suppliers becomes necessary. Reduction in market risk associated with contract purchase by retailers as well as increases in scale of assembly, transport, and wholesale breakdown functions can contribute to output and efficiency and thus, to lowered costs.
4. Selected producers, given the greater assurances of contractual marketing arrangements through the discount supermarket, will in some cases elect to expand their production by adopting changes in technology.
5. Given the atomistic market structure at retail and wholesale for foods in some large, low-income areas, the reduction in retail prices for selected commodities consumed by low-income families will induce limited price reductions by all retailers. Because the margins of small retailers are also small, they must achieve price reductions by improving their buying capability. Retailer cooperative buying programs can achieve some of the risk reduction and channel simplification that the large retailer enjoys.

Thus, the twin goals of development—increased level of real income and redistribution of income—can be fostered by marketing reforms. Income increases as producers respond to the more certain market opportunities of contract production, and income is redistributed through consumer price reductions for necessities.

Typical Behavior Patterns

The average propensity to consume food in the less developed community is as high as .7 for lower-quartile-income consumers, and is often below .3 for the upper quartile. Often the upper quartile has a propensity to save of .05 or greater. Given these propensities, reductions in food prices will redistribute real income, thereby expanding effective demand. The total product society will be shifted more to consumption because the lower-income people have a lower propensity to save, and they are enjoying a slightly larger share of total income. The reduction in savings may have limited effect upon investment because of increased producer and channel member market participation yielding an expansion in effective investment at critical points in the internal economy. The losses in savings due to price cuts on food may affect the savings of the rich—but not too likely the investments of merchants and small market farmers.

Producers often take a low-risk, low-output option, given the risks and uncertainties of the traditional market and technologies of production available to them. When a reduction in market risk occurs such that the quantity of easy-to-produce products demanded can be assured at dependable prices, producers will move toward technologies that carry greater risks and demand fuller use of available resources. Critical to this notion is the inducing of producers to expand output by low-cost fuller utilization strategies, rather than the inducing of new institutions of production to expand capacity.

Capacity may not be fully utilized by producers and distributors, and small changes in capital frequently can induce fuller use of available capacity of production in the less developed community. Labor is similarly in surplus so that wages are not driven up by output changes. Instead, more people are employed a greater amount of time. Increases in real wages for the community thus occur even though the wage rate is not affected by changes in output.

These conditions are at some variance with the traditional stagnation thesis offered by Schultz. The stagnation equilibrium implies that capacities are presently utilized so that increases in demand would increase the prices of the presently scarce resources. Even though many areas are tilled, the poor and limited uses of nonlabor inputs imply a low rate of use. Given the low rate of capacity utilization characteristics of many less developed communities and the high rate of unemployment, the postulated conditions of the stagnation equilibrium seem inappropriate.[13]

A Market Coordination Theory

With the above conditions characterizing the less developed community, horizontal market coordination is a critical first step in the market integration process. Horizontal coordination is defined as a consolidation of distribution from the atomism that is the hallmark of merchants in less developed communities the world over. Horizontal coordination implies larger-scale retail outlets selling several products—including necessities to low-income people—and following "modern" practices of charging low margins for high turnover staples and higher margins on low turnover luxury goods. The scale economies due to increases in the sales per worker cut costs of operation of such horizontally integrated retailing institutions somewhat, but the key reductions in costs result from the opportunities created to vertically coordinate the marketing system through contract supply arrangements which cut the cost of acquisition, particularly for low priced consumption goods that are the leader items.

Vertical coordination of the marketing system reduces the risks of intermediaries associated with transactions. The capital available to the intermediary is expanded because of the dependability of the order placed by the horizontally integrated, larger-scale retailer. The vertically coordinated market of stable demands of the horizontally integrated retail operations creates a set of producer expectations that result in fuller utilization of presently available productive capacity. The increments in investment that are necessary to utilize more fully the productive-distributive system can often be paid for by reduced transaction costs of the better capitalized system.

A necessary but not sufficient condition to induce the process of horizontal and vertical coordination are public facilitative changes to improve market environment:

1. better producer market information through government communication services concerning price, product, and terms of sale;
2. improved transportation facilities including penetration roads to reach more producing areas rather than reduction in the cost of importation of goods and services by installing trunk roads or import harbor facilities;
3. improvement of locally understood product specifications and grading;
4. extension and marketing services to provide for application of improved technologies; and
5. improved credit facilities and technical assistance through supervised credit.

These public facilitative changes are themselves not a sufficient condition to induce change unless market coordination is a practical option for a selected few progressive operators in the system. The thesis suggests a sequence of priorities for internal market process improvement as an aspect of the overall task of development.

1. *Describe the marketing system,* first, in order to know the average propensities to consume, the average propensities to save, the shopping mobility and potential shopping mobility of all income groups; second, to appreciate the expansion opportunities and problems for horizontal market coordinating institutions; third, to learn of the special problems of vertical market coordination; fourth, to learn of the needs perceived for facilitative changes that may best be carried forward by government action.
2. *Induce or encourage horizontal market coordination in the private sector* by encouraging innovative operators with modern ideas and basic faith in the expansibility of income to create or expand low-price multiproduct outlets.
3. *Vertical market coordination can be fostered at the retail level initially,* when horizontal market coordination is underway and discount supermarkets are selling necessities to low-income people. It is important to note that suboptimal maximization is often associated with producer vertical market coordination. Dairy marketing in the United States has been a prime example of producers increasing their income at the expense of the ultimate consumer. Frequently, however, forward vertical market coordination is associated with export commodity promotion schemes, and marketing boards with the aim of foreign exchange expansion.
4. *A selective development of facilitative reforms can foster the improvement of horizontal and vertical coordination.* Communication, transportation, commodity exchange, and public storage regulation are examples. The facilitative reforms are, however, no substitute for market reforms internal to the system.
5. A concomitant reform needed when market integration is fostered is to *redeploy distribution labor as improvements in efficiency cut distribution labor costs.* A careful appraisal is needed of the benefits through increases in real income and redistribution of income to lower-income groups versus the offsetting costs associated with displaced distribution labor. A general systems simulation model appears to be an efficient mechanism for assessing the benefits and costs associated with an ongoing program of internal market reforms.

It is in the third step of this five step strategy for development that vertical market coordination through contractual arrangements becomes a critical step in the total operation. Later, evidence will be presented to show the far-ranging impact of reforms that achieve this third step in the process.

Cases Illustrating the Evolving Pattern of Contractual Market Interdependencies

The author has been privileged to study in some detail the marketing systems for food products serving San Juan, Puerto Rico; Recife, Brazil; and La Paz, Bolivia; with a less thorough examination of the marketing systems serving Santo Domingo, Dominican Republic; Panama; and Bogota, Colombia.[14] These cities are a mixture of traditional and modern marketing systems. At one extreme, San Juan possesses an extremely modern and sophisticated food-marketing retail facility. This facility supplied at the time of study approximately 40 percent of the food requirements of the metropolitan San Juan area. In contrast, some of the other cities analyzed—such as La Paz—had no modern food-marketing outlets, and possessed some extraordinarily primitive supply channel systems. The range of degrees of market channel coordination found in these communities was indeed substantial.

It is useful to look at some limited statistical evidence concerning the typical pattern of food-marketing practices and to contrast the impact of contractual marketing schemes. Several aspects of the traditional market processes will be explored including land tenure, assembly practices, communication patterns, interpersonal trust, and the price and other responses of producers to vertical marketing programs.

Land Tenure Patterns

In traditional agricultural marketing, sharecropping contracts and the sale of crops prior to harvest represent two of the most fundamental contractual marketing schemes. Surveys conducted in Northeast Brazil show the widespread use of sharecropping practices (see Table 10-1).

Table 10-1 shows that sharecroppers are most important in rice growing in the relatively poor Codó area in the cotton areas northwest of Recife. When these agricultural practices are analyzed in relation to the size of farm cash income and of farm and land values by commodity group, a picture of the character and efficiency of these farming practice arrangements can be appreciated.

Table 10-2 shows the size, income, and livestock assets of the same grouping of farms. The Codó farms are an extreme case of latifundia. A 444 hectare farm supports on the average, 27 sharecroppers plus the owner—28 families of five to six people, a total of 167 people or 2½ hectares per capita. This farm yields an average of 2,100 NCr$ per crop year. Based on the typical division between farm owner and sharecroppers, the 28 sharecropper families have 75 NCr$ cash income of $15

Table 10-1
Land Tenure Arrangements in Farm Survey, by Commodity, 1967*

Producer Group	Percent Land Owners	Percent of Landowners with Renters or Sharecroppers	Percent of Landowners with Relatives Using Land Free	Average Number of Sharecroppers per Landowner Having Sharecroppers	Percent of Landowners with Sharecroppers Who Used a Half-Share Arrangement
Rice:					
Codó	59.3	48.2	29.6	27.0	7.7
São Francisco	86.6	19.7	18.1	13.3	91.2
Beans:					
Irecê	98.0	12.3	10.2	2.5	100.0
Al-Pe	99.2	7.0	18.7	3.9	22.2
Manioc	91.4	10.0	15.2	2.8	40.0
Cotton	92.1	29.1	18.8	3.7	64.6
Milk	97.6	N.A.	0	N.A.	N.A.

* Source: SUDENE/MSU Farm Survey (1967).

U.S. per household per year! These people are barely in the market economy.

Analysis of the São Francisco farms yields an average sharecropper income in cash of 480 NCr$ or at .20 exchange rate, about $96 U.S. per year (see Table 10-2).

Table 10-2
Size of Farm, Cash Farm Income, and Land Values by Commodities Studied, 1966*

Commodity and Area	Average Farm Size in Hectares	Average Total Cash Income Per Farm [a]	Average Value of Land Per Farm [b]	Average Value of Livestock and other Capital Goods [c]
		NCr$	NCr$	NCr$
Rice:				
Codó	444	2,100	12,840	13,761
São Francisco	96	6,255	55,767	
Beans:				
Irecê	74	2,803	11,286	8,371
Al-Pe	81	1,835	11,030	
Manioc	19	1,505	7,094	2,105
Cotton	104	1,463	11,084	6,392
Milk	170	11,593	37.383	23,137

[a] Average total cash income per farm was obtained by asking farmers their sales of the major crops which they produce, sales of livestock, sales of livestock products, and sales of other crops produced. The income figure is limited to those farms selling more than NCr$100.00 in 1966.

[b] Value of land was determined by asking producers what total sales price they would be willing to accept for their farm at the time of the interview.

[c] Estimates were obtained by multiplying the number of ox plows, tractors, jeeps, scales, cattle, hogs, and other production goods for each commodity group by a constant estimated value for each of the items and dividing the results by the subsample size. The resulting values were summed to give an average value for each commodity group.

* Source: SUDENE/MSU Farm Survey (1967).

The most common sharecrop arrangement was equal shares—in other words, the sharecropper in Northeast Brazil gives half his production to the land owner and keeps the remaining half for himself. The usual arrangement also requires the sharecropper to sell to the landowner any part of his share which is not consumed. The sharecropper must sell his part at harvest time when prices are lowest. If the sharecropper does not sell to the landowner, he will generally be removed from the land the following year.

While the sharecroppers' plight is indeed tragic, the evidence shows also the rising income pattern of farmer-owned rice and dairy farms in São Francisco. These farmers are entering the market economy and responding to the developing channels serving Recife and other large cities of the area.

Assembly Practices

The agricultural commodities of Northeast Brazil that were studied are for the most part produced on small farms widely scattered geographically, poorly linked with urban consuming centers and with other rural consumer markets. Assemblers perform the function of combining small lots of commodities, assembling them for sale in local markets, and for forwarding to distant markets. In carrying out these functions, assemblers assume the risk of ownership and add to the value of the commodity by creating place utility. Assemblers also contribute time utility through storage activities, and many add form utility by sorting, grading, and processing commodities. Assemblers are also deeply involved in providing credit to both producers and small assemblers.

Assemblers are relatively heterogeneous in their operating characteristics. It may be helpful to roughly classify them into separate groups based on the nature of their activities. Categories described here apply mostly to rice and bean assembly operators, but they also are partially applicable to other commodities such as manioc and cotton.

Gatherers. They are often farmers who buy from their neighbors and add these products to their own before going to local trading centers. Also included in this category are ox cart owners or mule runners, who pick up bags of products as they pass small farms on their way to the local village.

The Country Store. It is located at the crossroads of a small village and may buy commodities or trade basic necessities such kerosene, salt, and matches for the commodity. These are the dealers who most often buy crops that are still unharvested in exchange for commodities that are essential. Parenthetically, the author had the opportunity to observe the practice of buying corn in tassel in the Dominican Republic. It was the common practice for farmers to sell their crops halfway through the growing season when the corn had tasseled and to use the credit extended at the general store to buy rum and necessities for survival. This too, is backward vertical coordination—but in a primitive transactional system. There is little evidence that this induces expanded production.

Feira (Outdoor Markets) Assemblers. They buy commodities in small quantities at rural feiras and resell locally. They may also rent a truck together with other assemblers to sell their merchandise in the city.

Truck Assemblers. These people travel from market to market, using either their own or rented trucks, dealing in six to eight ton lots, buying in rural areas and selling in cities.

Local Assemblers or Town Buyers. These are specialized commodity buyers with established places of business in a local trading center. These buyers are most likely to extend credit to producers and to store significant quantities of commodities.

Large Coordinated Assemblers. These workers are usually headquartered in conversion centers. They buy principally from assemblers and rural trading areas that can provide relatively large lots of products.[15]

Communication Practices

The communication attributes of farmers and assemblers are important in their marketing role. Table 10-3 shows that assemblers are more frequent readers of magazines and newspapers, and are more likely to possess a functioning radio. They watch television and attend movies. However, it's interesting to note that a smaller percentage of manioc and cotton assemblers listen to the radio than do their farmer counterparts. Similarly, a smaller percentage of cotton assemblers watch television than do cotton farmers. The high percentage for these farmer groups may be due to respondent bias or, more likely, is due to the fact that they visit friends and relatives to listen to their radio or watch their television.

Only 14 percent of the farmers in the sample had ever attended a farm extension meeting. Rice farmers in São Francisco, bean farmers in Irecê and milk producers had the highest percentage of participation in some kind of extension program. Rice, bean, and cotton producers most frequently obtain market news from their buyers. Manioc farmers usually gather market information by personal observation at the feiras. The major news source for milk producers are their neighbors. Assemblers also obtain market information most frequently from their assembler colleagues or from neighbors. In all cases, personal observation in the markets or feiras was a close second in terms of percentage response.

It is clear that most market information in the system is transmitted by word of mouth with all the inefficiencies and errors related thereto. It is also apparent that a high percentage of all farmers—57.9 percent —relied principally on their buyers for market news. This potentially gives the assemblers a significant information advantage over the farmer. However, assemblers themselves have only indirect and infrequent news from larger markets, and are thus handicapped in their business operations as well.

The survey results suggest that radio is the most important mass com-

Table 10-3
Communication Characteristics of Farmers and Assemblers by Commodity, 1967*

	Communication Characteristics											
	Percent Read Magazine or Newspaper Lately		Percent Having Functioning Radio		Percent Listen to Radio Sometimes		Percent Watch Television Sometimes		Percent Attend Movies Sometimes		Percent Attended Extension Meeting Before	
Commodity	Farmer	Assem.	Farmer	Assem.	Farmer	Assem.	Farmer	Assem.	Farmer	Assem.	Farmer	Assem.
Rice:												
Codó	33.3		51.9		81.4		66.7		33.3		7.4	
		55.4		98.3		100.0		81.7		90.3		N.A.
São Francisco	38.2		76.4		89.4		40.6		57.7		19.5	
Beans:												
Irecê	36.7		65.3		91.9		38.8		26.5		26.5	
		40.0		84.7		93.4		56.1		79.1		N.A.
Pe-Al	35.2		50.8		82.9		28.2		27.3		16.4	
Manioc	23.3	44.6	56.7	79.6	87.4	66.6	65.6	91.7	17.3	80.6	10.7	N.A.
Cotton	21.2	52.4	52.7	86.0	95.2	51.6	72.7	66.6	27.3	82.9	9.7	N.A.
Milk	50.5	[b]	88.8	[b]	97.5	[b]	84.1	[b]	44.4	[b]	44.8	N.A.
All [a] (Total)	29.4	47.7	58.7	87.4	88.9	99.1	40.2	73.4	28.0	82.9	14.3	N.A.

[a] Milk excluded.
[b] Interviews were not conducted among milk assemblers.
* Source: SUDENE/MSU Surveys (1967).

munication medium both for farmers and assemblers. This medium might be effectively utilized to provide crop forecast information, day-to-day market news, information on modern farm methods and inputs, and other related information. At present, little or no such farm information is disseminated through radio broadcasts.

The limited use of public media to communicate public business, e.g., agricultural practices, scheduling of production, and market prices seems to be a generalized problem in less developed countries. From studies in Bolivia the problem appears to be common.[16] Thus, one of the policy implications for development is the creation of more efficient programs, principally for radio. Another implication for development strategy is that vertical coordinators with market and production information can be effective. If they can be induced to avoid short-run monopolistic exploitation of their market information, significant development gains can be achieved. Public broadcast of market news can help prevent monopolistic exploitation.

Interpersonal Trust

Economic growth and the private enterprise system are affected by the degree of trust held by businessmen in each other and in the government agencies, laws, and other institutions set up to facilitate economic exchange and to encourage business confidence. Improvements in marketing efficiency often hinge on the willingness of participants to accept without personal observation another's word on quality, price, or market conditions. Moreover, the pooling of resources into partnerships, corporations, or cooperatives is an important way of capturing economies of scale in production and marketing that require more capital than most individual businessmen or farmers could muster. But the formation of such groups and the formation of vertical contracts are difficult and unlikely when men are unable to trust one another to be honest.

Table 10-4 shows the percentage of farmers agreeing with three statements directed toward different aspects of interpersonal trust. For all three statements, assemblers indicate less willingness than farmers to trust others, especially those outside the family. Among assemblers, it is difficult to identify the group with the smallest trust propensity, though rice assemblers show considerably less trust than others on the first and third statements, while showing the highest agreement that one can join partnerships with nonrelatives.

While a strong correlation had been expected among the responses to the three statements, it is not surprising that such relations did not exist. Each question focuses on a slightly different aspect of trust, which itself is a many-faceted concept. Hence, a person may respond in one way to a general statement about trust in others, but feel quite differently about investing in a partnership. It is significant that assemblers exhibit less

Table 10-4
Percentage of Farmers and Assemblers Agreeing with Selected Attitude Statements about Interpersonal Trust, by Commodity, 1967*

Commodity	Statements					
	One can trust equally in relatives and in other people (Percent)		One can join in partnerships with other people even if they are not members of our family (Percent)		One may lose much money when working with others (Percent)	
	Farmers	Assemblers	Farmers	Assemblers	Farmers	Assemblers
Rice:						
Codó	70.0		63.0		52.0	
		26.3		66.9		52.0
São Francisco	44.0		71.0		42.0	
Beans:						
Irecê	51.0		82.0		40.0	
		56.6		64.8		37.8
Pe-Al	57.0		68.0		33.0	
Manioc	45.3	33.3	74.7	45.1	43.3	34.0
Cotton	69.7	51.2	66.1	59.7	43.0	46.5
Milk	51.6	N.A.	73.0	N.A.	53.2	N.A.
All	55.1	42.0	70.4	60.4	41.2	42.7

* Source: SUDENE/MSU Surveys (1967).

willingness to trust others than do farmers. These results suggest that assemblers' lack of confidence in others may be holding back marketing improvements.

Recalling that the São Francisco rice growers were among the most progressive, Table 10-5 shows the yields per hectare for the various growing areas. The low productivity for the Northeast is evidenced by contrasting it with the averages for Brazil.

Table 10-6 reports the results of questioning farmers about how they would go about increasing their production without planting more land. Two response categories stand out—"use fertilizer" and "don't know." The percentage responding "don't know" ranges from 24 percent for São Francisco rice growers to 49 percent for A1-Pe bean producers. It is significant that such large numbers of farmers have no idea how to go about improving yields, even if they could afford to.

Producer Price Responsiveness

To estimate supply responsiveness, a series of questions was asked to determine what might be the most likely producer response to different

Table 10-5
Average Yields, by Commodity*

Commodity and area	Average yields on farms of the Northeast in survey areas			Average yields for all Brazil, outside the Northeast, 1965
	1965	1966	% change	
Rice: [a]				1,679
Codó	1099	1095	−0.3	
São Francisco	1904	1981	4.0	
Beans: [b]				800
Irecê	488	516	5.7	
Al-Pe	464	658	41.8	
Manioc [c]	N.A.	1971	N.A.	3,560
Cotton [d]	317	247	−22.1	832
Milk [e]	N.A.	4.25	N.A.	N.A.

[a] Kilos unhulled rice per hectare.
[b] Kilos of beans per hectare.
[c] Kilos of manioc flour per hectare.
[d] Kilos of unginned cotton per hectare.
[e] Liters of milk per cow per day.
* Source: SUDENE/MSU Farmer Survey (1967) and Anuário Estatístico do Brasil (1965).

price conditions. A base price was determined for each commodity (usually the minimum government price stabilization price). Producers were then asked whether they would try to increase or decrease production if the expected market price went up or down to a specified level. They were also asked what they would do if, before planting, they were sure of receiving a specified price. The hypothesized prices for each commodity are given in Footnote A of Table 10-7.

A high percentage of Northeastern producers would increase planted acreage in response to a price increase. Most farmers are inclined to expand acreage in response to higher and more dependable prices than to reduce acreage in response to lower prices. A guaranteed price set at or slightly below the current year average price would induce more than one-third of the farmers to expand output.

Parenthetically, a similar pattern of traditional food producer response to price dependability can be documented in studies of Puerto Rican egg and milk agriculture[17] as well as rice production in eastern Bolivia.[18] These cases show both production increases in response to price dependability and, in Moran's work, the decline in production with a loss of dependability of the government price support program.

To gain insight into whether the indicated Northeastern Brazilian production response to a guaranteed price has merit in a development strategy, one must consider the in-system margins from farmer to consumer. One

Table 10-6
Farmer Opinions on Ways to Increase Yields, by Commodity, 1967*

Commodity	Percent Responding								
	Other	Use Fertilizers	Narrow Plant Spacing	Crop Specialization	Insecticides	Irrigation	Better Seed	Mechanization	Do Not Know
Rice:									
Cadó	.0	11.1	.0	7.4	.0	7.4	3.7	33.3	37
São Francisco	.8	46.8	3.1	2.4	.0	6.3	1.6	12.6	24.4
Beans:									
Irecê	2.0	4.1	.0	20.4	.0	8.2	4.1	14.3	46.9
Al-Pe	.0	32.0	4.7	2.3	.8	1.6	2.3	7.0	49.2
Manioc	.7	52.0	.7	2.7	.7	2.7	1.3	2.0	37.3
Cotton	20.6	7.9	1.8	6.7	4.2	3.0	3.6	12.1	40.0

* Source: SUDENE/MSU Farmer Survey (1967).

Table 10-7
Average Producer Response to Hypothesized Price Changes, by Commodity, 1967*

Commodity	Percent who would increase acreage if price increased [a]	Percent who would increase acreage if government offered guaranteed price [a]	Percent who would decrease acreage if price decreased [a]
Rice:			
Codó	66.7	55.6	11.1
São Francisco	51.2	33.9	15.0
Beans:			
Irecê	[b]	38.8	20.8
Al-Pe	71.1	28.1	35.2
Manioc	48.0	36.0	35.0
Cotton	84.0	48.5	33.0
Milk	73.0	50.0	38.9

[a] Hypothesized prices were:

	Hypothesized Prices NCr$		
	Increase	*Guaranteed*	*Decrease*
Rice per 60 kg. bag	14.00	11.00	10.00
Beans per 60 kg. bag	20.00	15.30	14.00
Cotton per 15 kg. unginned cotton	7.00	5.20	4.50
Manioc flour per 50 kg. bag	8.00	6.00	5.80
Milk per liter	.28	.23	.18

[b] The hypothesized price increase to NCr$20.00 per 60 kg. bag in Irecê was actually below the market price and thus is not valid for this analysis.

* Source: SUDENE/MSU Farmer Survey (1967).

must determine where and when these margins can be reduced sufficiently to sell the increase in output occasioned by a dependable price.

Contractual Marketing of Rice in Brazil

In the distribution of rice from the São Francisco area, a significant marketing breakthrough occurred in the Recife urban area. The flow of rice through the market system serving São Francisco is presented graphically in Figure 10-1. Circles on the map indicate the transaction points in the channels, and the percent of product handled is indicated. The relative importance of each flow is represented by the width of the connecting lines. Also, the percent of product movement through each channel is indicated numerically within the connecting line. The SUDENE-MSU field surveys of producers, assemblers, wholesalers, and retailers provided most of the data used in constructing the channel map. These survey data were supplemented by follow-up interviews of selected market operators, direct observations by researchers, and the use of secondary data. The resulting channel map is a reasonable approximation of the market relationships for the specific areas studied for the conditions that existed during 1966.

A relatively small number of firms buy rice in the lower São Francisco valley. There are about 158 rice assemblers of all sizes in the São Francisco rice area. Table 10-8 shows the number of different types of assemblers operating in the region.

Table 10-8
Estimated Number of Assembly Firms by Types for the Two Areas under Study, 1967*

Type of Assembly Firm	São Francisco	Codó
Large coordinated millers	2	1
Other millers	33	N.A.
Medium-sized assemblers	25	N.A.
Small assemblers	95	360
Itinerant trucker-assemblers	3	N.A.

* Source: SUDENE/MSU Survey (1967).

There are 35 mill owners operating in the area of the São Francisco River valley that was studied. Two of these are large-scale mills that have developed direct sales agreements with large-scale retailers. This is one of the first examples in the Northeast of market channel simplification through both vertical integration and internal market coordination. That is, one retail firm chose to bypass intermediaries in the marketing system by purchasing and managing its own rice mill, which purchases directly from larger farmers.

In the other case, the miller chose to bypass wholesalers and attempt to market his product direct to retailers through informal supply arrangements. These amounted to backward vertical contract purchasing programs. These efforts to simplify the rice channel appear to have been successful for the firms involved. There is also evidence that total marketing cost has been reduced through such efforts.

There is evidence to suggest significant spatial differences in the intensity of competition among rice assemblers. In particular, the competition seems to be greater among assemblers and millers who are located in the market convergence centers such as Penedo and Propria. Small assemblers and millers in villages and rural areas often find themselves competing directly with only a few other buyers. In such cases, informal market-sharing arrangements often evolve. Assemblers also avoid direct competition through supplying credit to and developing close ties with their farmer suppliers, either tacitly or through overt collusion.

There appears to be excess rice milling and assembly capacity in the area studied. Rising production may offset this trend to some extent. How-

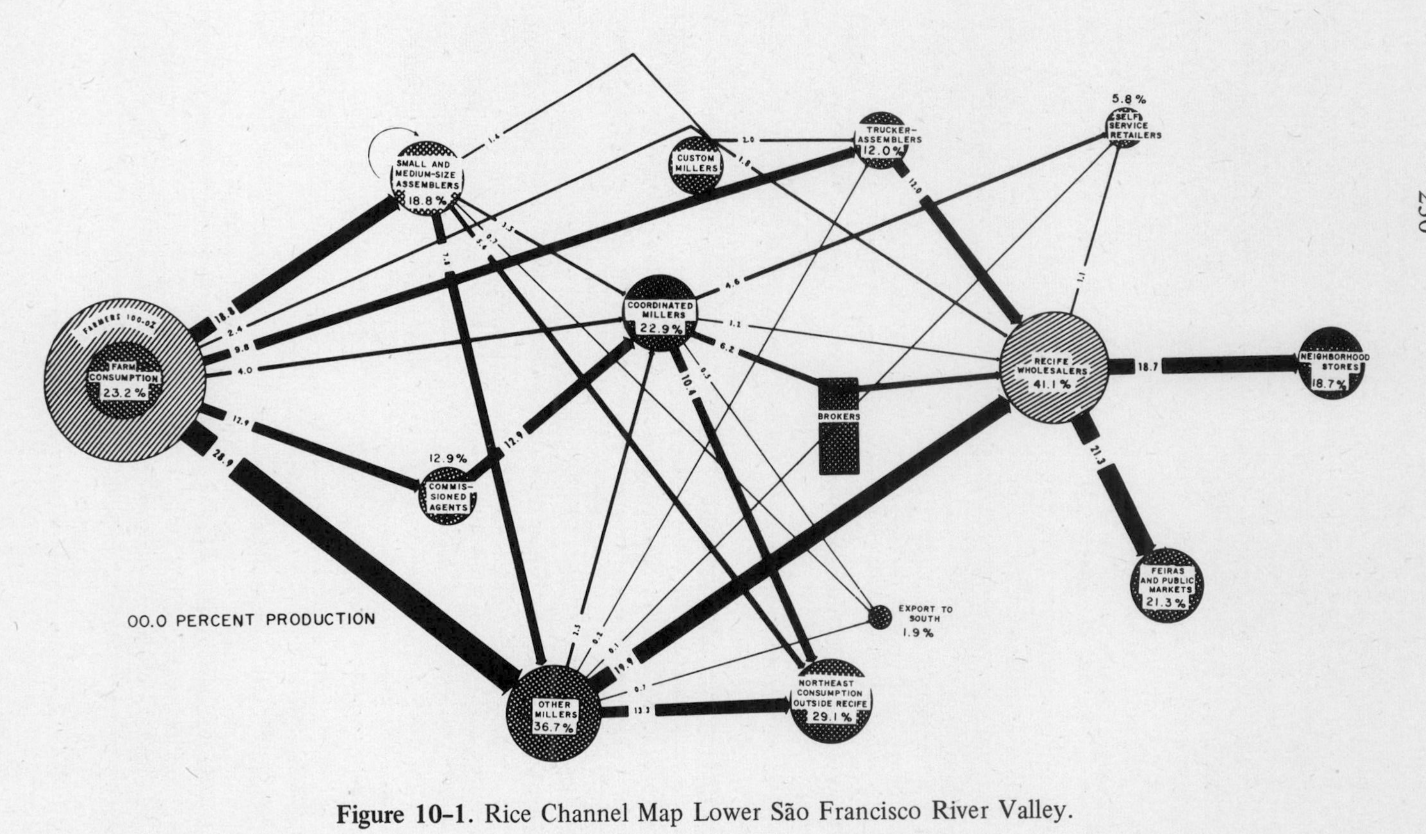

Figure 10-1. Rice Channel Map Lower São Francisco River Valley.

ever, it seems apparent that nonmilling investment opportunities for possible entrants are greater today than when the average small mill entered the market about fourteen years ago. It is interesting to note that excess capacity at the milling and processing level is characteristic of the conditions which made private label marketing programs effective in the United States in a variety of products.

Other Producer Responses to Vertical Marketing Coordination

The Puerto Rican study revealed two very interesting cases of vertical coordination of marketing activities.[19] The Lajas Valley Egg Producers Association, with technical assistance from poultry specialists and an assured market from Pueblo Markets' contract purchase arrangements, increased output from 311,000 dozen eggs in 1963 to 546,000 dozen in 1965. Price was held from one to three cents below certain other brands marketed on the island. Pueblo and the Association cooperated periodically to reduce prices during periods of excess supply. The government agencies responsible for developing the Lajas Valley have subsequently sought to apply the approach to other commodities in other producing regions.

The dairy industry of Puerto Rico has also prospered as a result of both market coordination and stimulation of production by technical assistance. The dairy industry grew from 9.9 percent of gross farm income in 1951 to 20.7 percent in 1965, while sugar cane dropped from 50.1 percent to 30.1.[20,21]

The seasonal fluctuations in production coupled with inadequate market coordination created in Puerto Rico the typical problems of the dairy industry—supply cycles of surpluses and shortages. In 1954, industry agitation for a two-price system began; voluntary industry schemes failed. In 1957, a two-price milk marketing law was passed. Details of these problems were described in Harrison's thesis, previously cited. Retail prices were fixed and discounts were allowed only if given to the entire class of customers. A consumer promotion campaign was part of the program. Since then production has increased steadily at stable prices. This is a case of effective vertical market coordination where government played a key technical assistance role, while the market process was kept in private hands.

Of course, the lowering of prices for goods with elastic demand schedules will only dry up flows through the market channel unless there are supply-expanding responses in the system. The Puerto Rican milk case stands out as an example of supply elasticity when necessary technical assistance and market assurances were offered farmers.

A further example of producer responsiveness to technical assistance and market assurance is found in rice marketing in Bolivia. Moran indicated that rice production responded to a series of technical assistance activities during the ten years from 1957 to 1967, and to a changing price support program during some of these years. Production increased threefold over the decade, and Bolivia shifted from being an importer to an exporter of rice. In part because of the shifting market expectations of farmers, rice production fell off after the 1960 to 1963 government price support program collapsed in 1963.[22]

Output increased rapidly when prices were supported at a high level, even though only six percent of the rice production of the Santa Cruz region was at any one time under contract with government agencies. When the price support program collapsed, output was reduced by about one-third. With resumption of price supports in 1966 and 1967, rice production again increased.

Summary of Response to Market Opportunity

Some tentative conclusions emerge which support the thesis that traditional farmers will respond to market opportunity. These can be enumerated:

1. Some traditional farmers lack information as to how to expand their output—even if the funds were available. Thus, technical assistance is a precondition to market participation.
2. Traditional farmers and market channel participants can be reached by radio, even in extremely primitive areas of Latin America. Technical and market information can be supplied to farmers via radio.
3. A small but economically significant proportion of the producers and market participants have sufficient interpersonal trust to accept business opportunities.
4. Market coordinating programs such as egg and milk marketing in Puerto Rico and rice marketing in Northeast Brazil and Bolivia have at various times proven effective.

Thus, the case can be made for adding to the usual technical assistance efforts, marketing institutional analysis, and reform as a key precedent condition in the increase of productivity of indigenous internal market participants. To those experienced in marketing, this may seem obvious; to economists responsible for development strategy, this may be quite novel. Let us turn to the specific institutional reforms which have induced changes in marketing productivity and caused the sequences of desired changes in urban consumption patterns, for example, lowered food prices, redistributed income and for the lower two-thirds of urban society, increased real income.

Necessary Changes in Retail Marketing

The necessary preconditions for retailing organization to provide a backward vertical marketing coordination capability through contractual supply arrangements need to be specified. In addition to aiding in the smooth flow of food products into La Paz, the introduction of larger-scale retailing and wholesaling institutions reduced the price of food in that city.

While retail gross margins in La Paz are generally reasonable, margins of 17 to 20 percent on staples such as bread and beef (which account for approximately 20 percent and 10 percent, respectively, of the food budgets of low- and middle-income families) are higher than for slower-moving items such as canned milk and vegetable oil. Gross margins of 15 to 17 percent on potatoes are lower than for most fruits and vegetables, but are high for a staple item. The merchandising policy suggested is one of mixed margins, with high-volume staple items carrying a low margin, and slow-moving specialty items carrying high margins. However data developed in this research clearly show that present food retailers are in no position to follow a mixed-margin policy. At existing sales levels, any substantial reduction in margins on staples would severely cut an already low level of return. Substantial changes in capital, technical, and managerial inputs are needed before any entrepreneur could gain the increase in market share which would make low margins on staple items economically possible.

Increases in scale of operations at the retail level would permit vertical coordination of the system, reducing the cost of acquisition, and thus the final price to the consumer. In some products, for example, bread, pasta, sugar and soft drinks, large-scale retailers should be able to obtain quantity discounts on the order of two to five percent by virtue of their increased bargaining power. While such savings may not appear high, they apply to products comprising approximately 20 percent of the food budget of low- and middle-income families.

Points of aggregation for the key staples of potatoes and rice occur sufficiently early in the channel to permit large-scale retail units to reduce acquisition costs by bypassing intermediate institutions in existing distribution channels. For example, rice production and milling are geographically centered in the Santa Cruz area. At present, milled rice is purchased in Santa Cruz by merchants who then arrange for its transport to La Paz, where it is sold to wholesalers. These wholesalers sell to retailers and consumers. Approximately 25 percent of the retail price of rice is added by these intermediaries. A large-scale retailer could purchase directly at the mill and (absorbing the freight costs himself), reduce his acquisition cost by 15 to 20 percent.

Cost reductions on the order of 20 percent for potatoes could be effected through direct purchases at early aggregation points in the channel. *Tambos* in the Cochabamba area provide readily accessible assembly points for substantial volumes of potatoes. Transport costs for rice and potatoes could be reduced by contracting with a trucker to haul rice from Santa Cruz to Cochabamba, pick up potatoes in Cochabamba, and deliver both commodities in La Paz.

Beef purchases direct from the larger cattle producers are feasible for very large-scale retail operations. If the government were to relax its regulations on beef prices, retailers capable of instituting new cutting methods and providing assured outlets would almost surely receive the cooperation of large cattle producers in filling their purchase needs. It is likely that new entrants into large-scale retailing will continue to obtain their beef supplies from existing wholesalers. However, the quantity which they buy should permit two to five percent reductions in the cost of acquisition. As retailers develop more familiarity with beef operations, integration further back into the channel may be possible.

A key question, of course, is the degree of scale needed to achieve the mixed-margin and direct acquisition policies suggested above. Since no large-scale retail units existed in La Paz at the time of this study, it is not possible to give a definitive answer to this question. However, reasonably accurate pro forma financial statements can be projected to permit analysis of the feasibility of large-scale retailing in La Paz.

Table 10-9 gives data for low- and middle-income families of La Paz, Bolivia on their weekly purchases of foods and nonfoods in large-scale retail outlets. No fresh fruits and vegetables are recommended for the product mix in these proposed retail outlets; the inclusion of highly perishable produce items would undoubtedly overtax the managerial capabilities of these new entrants into food retailing. Also, the political implications of competition with market women in the sale of perishables can thus be avoided.

Table 10-10 shows suggested gross margins for the various product categories, as well as expected gross profit per family. With the exception of rice, beef, bread, and potatoes, on which mark-ups have been reduced to ten percent, all gross margins for food are maintained at existing levels. No increases in food margins are proposed.[a]

A low-income family purchasing the listed items exclusively at a large-scale retail outlet would spend $7.74 per week, resulting in gross profit to the outlet of $1.00. The comparable figures for middle-income families are $12.72 and $1.71. Overall gross margin for the retail outlet is thus

[a] A number of nonfood items are suggested for inclusion in the product mix. A gross margin of 20 percent is proposed on these items. We have no data on existing margins on these items and have therefore chosen a figure corresponding approximately to margins on food items.

Table 10-9
Weekly Expenditures on Selected Food and Nonfood Items by Low- and Middle-Income Families, La Paz, Bolivia*

	Weekly Purchases By:	
	Low-Income Families	Middle-Income Families
Cereals		
Rice	$0.23	$0.32
Bread	0.92	1.33
Other Cereals	0.79	1.10
Meat and Poultry		
Beef	1.74	2.62
Other	0.29	0.90
Fats and Oils	0.48	0.77
Milk and Eggs	0.44	1.12
Potatoes	0.89	1.17
Sugar and Spices	0.68	0.93
Tea and Coffee	0.36	0.53
Soft Drinks	0.11	0.29
Total Food Expenditures	$6.93	$11.08
Non-Foods [a]	$0.81	$ 1.65
Total	$7.74	$12.73

[a] The nonfood items suggested for sale are soaps and detergents, personal care articles, plastic shoes, and underwear.
* Source: MSU Consumer Survey (1967), Bolivia.

Table 10-10
Suggested Gross Margins and Gross Profits by Product and Income Level, La Paz, Bolivia*

Product	Suggested Gross Margin	Low-Income Family Gross Profit	Middle-Income Family Gross Profit
Cereals			
Rice	10%	$0.023	$0.032
Bread	10	0.092	0.133
Other	15	0.119	0.165
Meat and Poultry			
Beef	10	0.174	0.262
Other	20	0.058	0.180
Fats and Oils	13	0.062	0.100
Milk and Eggs	12	0.053	0.134
Potatoes	10	0.089	0.117
Sugar and Spices	13	0.088	0.121
Tea and Coffee	15	0.054	0.079
Soft Drinks	20	0.222	0.058
Non-Foods	20	0.162	0.330
		$0.996	$1.711

* Source: MSU Retailer Survey (1967), Bolivia.

projected at 12.9% for a low-income family's market basket and 13.4% for a middle-income family's market basket.

On the basis of the suggested product and gross margin mix, pro forma profit and loss statements for a large-scale retail outlet servicing low-income consumers, and projected return on investment at weekly sales volumes of $5,000, $10,000, $15,000, and $20,000 are shown in Table 10-11. Operating expense estimates are based on data for equivalent-sized stores in the United States.[23] Bolivian wages were estimated at 20 percent of United States wages, with the relevant labor expense items adjusted. Early experience in Puerto Rico suggests that there will be a greater use of labor and a reduced use of capital equipment compared to United States operations. The offsetting effects of higher labor inputs and lower

Table 10-11

Pro-forma* Annual Profit and Loss Statements and Projected Return on Investment for Various Sizes of Retailing Operations, La Paz, Bolivia

	$5,000/week 400 sq. ft.	$10,000/week 7,500 sq. ft.	$15000/week 7,500 sq. ft.	$20,000/week 10,000 sq. ft.
Sales	$260,000	$520,000	$780,000	$1,040,000
Merchandise (87.1%)	226,000	453,000	680,000	916,000
Gross Profit	$ 34,000	$ 67,000	$100,000	$ 124,000
Expenses:				
Wages	$ 4,600	$10,000	$12,500	$18,000
Manager's Salary	6,000	9,000	9,000	10,000
Adv. and Promotion	1,200	1,800	2,500	3,600
Utilities	1,200	1,800	1,800	3,000
Depreciation	3,000	7,000	7,000	9,000
Interest	3,000	6,000	6,500	7,800
Misc. Exp.	3,000	7,000	7,000	13,000
	$22,000	$42,600	$46,300	$64,400
Profit Before Taxes	$12,000	$24,400	$53,700	$59,600
Investments:				
Working Capital	$20,000	$30,000	$40,000	$40,000
Equipment	20,000	50,000	50,000	85,000
Building	20,000	37,500	37,500	50,000
	$60,000	$117,500	$127,500	$175,000
Return on Investment:				
No Debt	20%	21%	42%	34%
50% Debt	40%	42%	84%	68%

* Source: MSU Survey, 1967, Bolivia.

capital inputs will probably not greatly affect the projected return on investment. The manager's wage was projected at the United States rate. This is high by Bolivian standards. However, given the scarcity of managerial talent in La Paz, it was felt that a high salary would provide a major incentive with which to attract capable personnel.

Advertising and promotion expenses were adjusted downward substantially to reflect the lower level of competition and lack of media. It is expected that new entrants into retailing would depend primarily on radio, low-cost handbills, and sound truck advertising. Miscellaneous operating expenses were projected at 50 percent of the United States rate. Utilities, primarily electricity, were estimated on the basis of data on various business office operations in La Paz. Equipment requirements were calculated on the basis of 200 percent of capital investment for equivalent-sized operations in the United States. This approximation appears conservative, since experience in Lima, and Recife suggests a figure of 160 percent of United States requirements. The proposed product mix does not include perishable produce or frozen foods, thus expensive refrigeration equipment is not needed. The cool, high altitude climate of La Paz also reduces the need for extensive refrigeration of beef. Land building costs were estimated on the basis of $5 per square foot, which is probably on the high side. Working capital needs were assumed to be equal to those for equivalent-sized U. S. stores.[24] The capital structure was projected at 50 percent debt and 50 percent equity, at interest rates of 10 percent. While private loan funds might not be available initially, public loan funds could well be available, given that development bank loans often operate on interest rates and terms well below the market.

The data in Table 10-11 show before-tax return on investment to be over 40 percent. The return to the entrepreneur is greater if the manager's salary is actually a wage paid to the owner-manager. Also, the conservative estimates on capital requirements result in a conservative estimate of return on investment. Thus, large-scale retailing appears to be a highly profitable commercial investment. The volume necessary to attain the projected return on investment is expected to result from consumer response to the reduced retail prices suggested for four key staples—beef, bread, potatoes, and rice.

The financial statements shown in Table 10-11 are based on present costs of product acquisition at the retail level. If reduced acquisition costs obtained through increased purchasing power and vertical rationalization of the channel are taken into account, annual before-tax profits are increased by $11,000 for the $5,000/week outlet, $16,500 for the $10,000/week outlet, $22,000 for the $15,000/week outlet, and $33,000 for the $20,000/week outlet. These cost savings could be fully passed on to the consumer, either to boost sales in order to achieve desired volume, or in response to competitive pressures which are likely to arise as new entrants invest in large-scale retailing. If all cost savings were passed on, food prices would be reduced by 5 percent. If half of these increased profits were passed on in the form of lower prices, a price reduction of 2.5 percent would be possible over the full line of products carried by each outlet. If price reductions were not passed on, large-scale retailing would become commercially feasible even with no debt in the capital structure.

Of course, changes in scale must take into account existing shopping habits and the likelihood of changing those habits. The data strongly suggest that consumers patronize existing outlets more from habit and limited alternatives than from social or economic inducements. There is no indication that retail outlets perform a social function or even that haggling is an important social ritual in the purchasing of food. Credit extension is not prevalent. The extremely small quantities purchased in frequent shopping trips to *tiendas* (small neighborhood stores) raise an area of concern. However, the weekly shopping for perishables which is customary among much of the middle and upper class may well be transferred to dry goods shopping if reduced prices accompany modernization and self-service. The ready acceptance of self-service outlets in many other Latin American countries is further evidence that the shift from traditional to modern retailing can be made with a minimum of difficulty.

It is useful to specify the market area from which the various size operations projected in Table 10-11 would have to draw. Population clusters needed to support different scales of retailing are shown in Table 10-12. If all their purchases of the items shown in Table 10-9 were made at one large-scale outlet, a minimum of 650 low-income families or 400 middle-income families would be required to maintain a $5,000 per week outlet.

Table 10-12
Population Clusters Required to Support Various Levels of Large-Scale Retailing*

	Size of Outlet					
	4,000 sq. ft. $5,000/week		7,500 sq. ft. $10,000/week		7,500 sq. ft. $15,000/week	
Percentage of Expenditures by:	No. of Families	% of Pop. Group	No. of Families	% of Pop. Group	No. of Families	% of Pop. Group
Low-Income Families						
100%	650	2.5%	1300	5.0%	1950	7.5%
75%	975	3.8	1950	7.5	2925	11.3
50%	1300	5.0	2600	10.0	3900	15.0
Middle-Income Families						
100%	400	1.5	800	3.0	1200	4.5
75%	600	2.3	1200	4.5	1800	6.8
50%	800	3.0	1600	6.0	2400	9.0

* Source: MSU Study, 1967, Bolivia.

These numbers correspond to 2.5 percent of lower-income families and 1.5 percent of middle-income families. It appears from Table 10-12 that the maximum size outlet which might be attempted in low-income areas would be 7,500 square feet. Above this size, the outlet would have to draw from a fairly large population group which generally lacks transportation. The maximum size for middle-income areas also appears to be 7,500 square feet, although a 10,000 square foot outlet may well be possible if situated near upper-income areas.[b]

From the public standpoint, the effect of large-scale retailing would be to reduce by at least 34. percent the price of those foods which comprise 87 percent of low-income food budgets and 78 percent of middle-income food budgets. If savings through reduced acquisition costs were passed on completely to the consumer, an additional reduction of 5 percent in the price of food would be achieved. Since food expenditures take 66 percent of low-income family budgets and 58 percent of middle-income family budgets, these savings would have a substantial impact on the standard of living.

A movement toward large-scale retailing would undoubtedly affect existing wholesalers of processed and bulk food products. Large-scale retailers would probably buy such items as sugar and lard directly from national and international suppliers, bypassing existing wholesalers. Or they might purchase from wholesaler-importers, but at a price reflecting their increased purchasing power. Clearly, the import houses would have to adjust their sales policies to meet the needs of any large-scale entrants into retailing. The size and managerial abilities of importer-wholesalers suggest that they will be able to adjust to a changed market environment.

The ability of present wholesaler-retailers to adjust to a radically changed environment is less clear. Direct purchasing, by large retailers, would result in a substantial loss of business to wholesaler-retailers. They could remain as they are, and continue to serve tiendas and consumers as at present. The cost to the system of their maintenance in business is not great, and they would continue to perform a needed function for the many tiendas that would continue to exist as convenience outlets.

The employment reduction for traditional market channel participants proved to be a less difficult change than usually feared in the case of Puerto Rico. Wish found that traditional San Juan food retailers were not reduced in number, though down in relative importance during the decade when large-scale supermarkets gained over 40 percent of the total food sales of the city.[25] The fortuitous developments included a restriction in licensing small retail outlets (with the reaction of a few clandestine small merchants opening in new housing projects). More important, some small

[b] No attempt has been made to project the feasibility of large-scale outlets serving upper-income areas. If such outlets are feasible in low-income areas, they are assuredly feasible in upper-income areas.

food retailers shifted to on-premise beer and rum outlets. Shorter hours laws, and refusal of permits to operate bars in food stores with paid employees were enforced. The transition thus did not result in the displacement that traditional wisdom would predict.

The impact of the Recife retailer, Bom Preço, on the price level in the city and the impact on rice marketing channels is extremely interesting. The following brief history of the self-service store in Recife stems from a special depth study. Unstructured interviews were performed in most of the self-service stores, and a sample of the nonself-service stores. The object of the study was to trace the competitive effects of self-service as it progressed from inception to the present. It was necessary to isolate the change agents and then sample various types of retailers at various distances from the change agents to determine the spatial competitive effects of these agents.

In the ten years from 1957 to 1967, self-service retailing in Recife has grown from nothing to approximately 11 percent of all food expenditures in self-service stores. This rapid growth can be attributed to the needs of the small but growing middle class in Recife. For the first eight years of operation, self-service stores were not characterized by a high-volume, low-price concept. Gross margins ran from 15 to 50 percent, with the mean around 23 percent. The operations were small, and did no significant advertising or promotion. The years 1964 and 1965 brought the expansion of Comprebem into self-service retailing with the construction of three supermarkets, and the conversion of five smaller stores into self-service. On June 12, 1966, Bom Preço opened one large supermarket.

Until Bom Preço, all of the self-service operators, including Comprebem, seemed content with a high margin, no promotion philosophy. Bom Preço was the first to bring a low-margin, high-volume practice into the Recife market. The repercussions of this innovation were felt in all corners of Recife. Volumes of other self-service and nonself-service retailers fell at the impact of the low prices and promotion of Bom Preço. The high margins of the other self-service retailers rapidly decreased in the face of lower margin competition. The mean margin decrease was 32 percent.

It is important to note how the changes in margins were effected. Bom Preço entered the market with one large store. This was enough to cause Comprebem, a chain of eight stores in Recife, to lower its prices, causing a head-on price competition battle. The fact that Comprebem lowered its prices forced the smaller independent self-service operators to follow suit. Table 10-13 shows the combined effect of Bom Preço and Comprebem on seven other self-service retailers. The owners and managers of the smaller supermarkets and mercadinhos (medium-size store, larger than a tienda) almost unanimously stated that they had never felt the competition of Comprebem until Bom Preço opened. The effect of Bom Preço did not stop with self-service outlets. Around each self-service outlet, neighborhood stores were affected, the degree depending on their distance

Table 10-13
Effect of Bom Preço on Margins and Volumes*

Stores in Order of Size	Location Near Bom Preço/ Comprebem	Gross Margin before BP	Current G.M.	% Fall in Margin	Immed. Fall-Sales	Current Sales Level
1	Comprebem	25%	12%	52%	20%	above former
2	Comprebem	20%	13%	35%	40%	above former
3	Comprebem	15%	15%	0%	0%	above former
4	Comprebem	20%	13%	35%	5%	above former
5	Comprebem	30%	25%	17%	15%	not recovered
6	Bom Preço	25%	18%	28%	30%	not recovered

* Source: SUDENE/MSU Special Retail Study (1967).

from the self-service outlet. Finally, some atomistic retailers in public markets and feiras were affected slightly, depending on their proximity to an important supermarket. Thus, a simple one-store innovation in high-volume, low-price selling forced a revolution of selling practices on competing food retailers. The effect of this change was to increase the real income of consumers through generally lower food prices.

A second benefit resulted from the advent of Bom Preço. Almost no promotion had been used until Bom Preço started a sustained advertising program using mass media. Comprebem then reacted, causing smaller self-service organizations to react as well. The result was to draw even more people to the now relatively lower-priced form of retailing, which accelerated the benefits of lower prices in the Recife market.

One supermarket owner summed up the feelings of the majority of self-service operators when he confided that the opening of Bom Preço showed that their previous high-margin, no-advertising policy, was not a viable and efficient way to run a supermarket.

Since the inception of Bom Preço, there have been two prominent demonstrations of the use of retail power to rationalize the distribution system. First, though vertical integration had not generally taken place for agricultural nonprocessed foods, one striking exception exists. Bom Preço vertically integrated its supply system for rice to ownership of a rice milling operation. While other self-service stores were priced slightly above the mean price for rice, Bom Preço was priced 12.8 percent below this mean, and sold better quality rice. This kind of difference between Bom Preço and the self-service retailers did not show up for other commodities. It can be concluded that vertical integration enabled Bom Preço to reduce the price of rice substantially and thus benefit the consumer.

The second demonstration of the use of aggregated retail power is quite different from the above vertical integration. In 1966, Comprebem found itself facing an intolerable supply situation for eggs. The only volume supplier of eggs for Recife was a poultry cooperative, which had gained a monopoly position in the distribution channel. The only other distributors of eggs were very small traditional operators. The poultry cooperative started to use its power to extract relatively high prices from the larger retailers, who clearly could not generate the necessary volume from the traditional system in the short run. Comprebem met the threat head-on by organizing its purchases through one of the large cooperatives in the south of Brazil, more than 1,500 miles away. Comprebem claimed that they could buy the eggs, truck them north over the poor roads which were often dirt, throw out the broken eggs that resulted and still have a lower cost than if they bought them from a local cooperative. The loss of the Comprebem business to the cooperative caused a condition of oversupply which in 1967 forced the cooperative to reduce its prices. When this happened, Comprebem shifted its buying back to the local cooperative.

Thus, Recife is experiencing the beginning of change, the move from a traditional distribution system to one which brings food to consumers at lower prices. This is desirable in terms of increasing the real income of the consumer, and also has implications for area development through increased production fostered by increasing food and nonfood purchases. Though change has just started, its power must not be underestimated.[26] Zimmerman notes that:

> In all we would find that man at a certain moment became aware of the necessity and the possibility of altering his environment; man became convinced that he could adapt society to fundamentally new conditions. It is this process of adaptation that we call economic development.[27]

Backward vertical coordination of consumption goods markets, with contractual marketing as the triggering device for market coordination, has been explored in this paper. The economic, political, and social elements of such a transformation are important, but they have been the subject of extensive research.[28] What has been neglected and ignored are the needed input of marketing skills and insights represented in the papers in this collection.

Notes

1. The research reported in this paper is based in large part on the author's experience as Director of the Latin American Marketing Planning Center from its founding in 1965 through 1968. Reports of this research are contained in Charles Slater, Harold Riley, and others, *Market Processes in the Recife Area of Northeast Brazil* (June, 1969); Charles Slater, Donald Henley, and others, *Market Processes in La Paz, Bolivia* (July, 1969); Charles Slater and others, *Food Marketing and the Economic Development of Puerto Rico* (December, 1970); and Harold Riley, Kelly Harrison and others, *Market Coordination in*

the Development of the Cauca Valley Region, Columbia (March, 1970). Each publication is available through the Latin American Studies Center, Michigan State University, East Lansing, Michigan.

2. A. G. B. Fisher, "Production; Primary, Secondary, and Tertiary," *Economic Record* (March, 1939).

3. C. Clark, *The Conditions of Economic Progress,* London: Macmillan (1957).

4. S. Kuznets, *Modern Economic Growth,* New Haven: Yale University Press (1966).

5. Charles C. Slater, "Market Channel Coordination in Economic Development" in Louis P. Bucklin, *Marketing Channels,* Berkeley, California: University of California Press, forthcoming.

6. W. A. Lewis, *Development Planning,* New York: Harper (1966).

7. Wynn Owen, "The Double Developmental Squeeze on Agriculture," *American Economic Review* (March, 1966).

8. Bruce F. Johnston, "Agricultural and Structural Transformation In Developing Countries: A Survey of Research," *Journal of Economic Literature* (June, 1970), 369–404.

9. *Ibid.,* 373–4.

10. *Ibid.,* 374.

11. *Ibid.*

12. See also Slater, "Market Channel Coordination and Economic Development."

13. T. W. Schultz, *Transforming Traditional Agriculture,* New Haven: Yale University Press (1964), 33.

14. Slater, *Market Processes in La Paz, Bolivia; Market Processes In The Recife Area of Northeast Brazil.*

15. Slater, Riley, *Market Processes in the Recife Area of Northeast Brazil,* Chapter Seven, 10–11.

16. Slater, Henley, *Market Processes in La Paz, Bolivia,* 63, 87, and 98.

17. Kelly M. Harrison, *Agricultural Market Coordination in the Economic Development of Puerto Rico* (unpublished Ph.D. thesis, Michigan State University, 1966).

18. M. J. Moran, *An Evaluation of Market Coordination in the Bolivian Rice Industry* (unpublished Master's thesis, Michigan State University, 1968).

19. Harrison *Agricultural Market,* 122–123.

20. *Ibid.,* 153.

21. *Ibid.,* 141.

22. Moran, *Evaluation,* Chapter Two, 12.

23. Operating data were obtained from *Business Summary and Analysis of Independent Food Stores,* Lafayette, Indiana: Purdue University Cooperative Extension Service (October, 1966), 25.

24. *Ibid.,* 31.

25. Slater, *Food Marketing,* 108–109.

26. Slater, Brazil study, Chapter Six, 3–7.

27. L. J. Zimmerman, *Poor Lands, Rich Lands, The Widening Gap,* New York: Random House (1965), 131.

28. Johnston, *Transformation.*

11 Contractual Marketing Systems in Canada: The Anticombines Response

Joel Bell*

A discussion of the Combines approach to contractual marketing systems is particularly topical in view of the current review under way in Canada of competition policy. In 1969 the Economic Council of Canada produced a comprehensive report on Canadian competition policy, and the government has announced its intention of introducing revised legislation in the area in the near future. This paper will describe the current legal system which applies to vertical distribution relationships, the revisions proposed by the Economic Council, the general nature of marketing structures in Canada and the problems to which these give rise, and will make some suggestions on the direction in which public policy might move on this subject.

It would be useful at the outset to make some general comments on attitudes in Canada toward competition policy in general. Historically Canadians have shown little real political or public support for the enforcement of competition policy. Canadians have become reasonably accustomed to large and powerful economic units in both the public and private sectors of the economy, and have not shown any strong philosophical commitment to the notion of diffusion of decision making to reduce political or economic power. On the other hand, virtually all Canadian economists support competition policy on the rationale of economic efficiency. But overall there would appear to be a genuine ambivalence toward competition as a way of life, despite the fact that the concept had roots in the common law long before Adam Smith popularized it. An instinct for economic security and a concern for the harshness of a competition policy which displaces both the inefficient and the unlucky have led to legislative and administrative protection of various groups against the pressures of competition. These attitudes are not unique to Canada, but they have led to a less vigorous enforcement of the principles of competition than has been observed in the United States.

In addition to these political and philosophical factors, it must be observed that Canadian economists have failed to identify any unambiguously harmful results of protected or cooperative marketing arrangements, except perhaps in the most extreme cases. The profession has also failed to gather and analyze the relevant empirical data within the Canadian context; without such clear-cut data it is difficult to challenge a system which

---

* Department of Consumer and Corporate Affairs, Government of Canada.

has generated a fairly satisfactory standard of living. These deficiencies have produced sometimes extraneous debates on the subject of competition policy in Canada. Economists and marketing specialists can, I believe, generate rules of greater clarity than have yet emerged in Canadian law, even within the current limitations of existing theory and analysis.

Current Canadian Legislation

Competition policy in Canada is presently embodied in the Combines Investigation Act. This federal statute has, for constitutional reasons, been based upon the federal constitutional authority to legislate on matters of criminal law. The constitutional limitation has constrained the procedures, the rules of evidence, and probably the substance of the legislation. There are widely held reservations about the capacity of criminal procedures and sanctions to effectively handle the questions of competition policy in general, and the regulation of contractual marketing schemes in particular.

Section 33A of the Act provides that it is unlawful to grant any price concession or other advantage to a purchaser which, at the time of the sale, is not made available to competitors who buy articles of *like quality and quantity*. There is no offense unless the price differential was "part of a practice of discriminating." Although this legislation was first enacted in 1935 as part of the Criminal Code of Canada, no cases have actually been pursued before the courts under its provisions. Practices of price discrimination have, however, been considered by the Restrictive Trade Practices Commission (RTPC). The RTPC is a body which hears evidence presented by the Director of Investigation and Research and by the parties whose behavior is under examination. The RTPC then issues a report on the public interest implications of the actions disclosed, indicating its view of the legal merits of the case and making recommendations as to appropriate remedies (including prosecutions).

There have been five reports issued by the Restrictive Trade Practices Commission under these provisions: North Bay Hardware, Mary Maxim, and three cases relating to the distribution and sale of gasoline involving Texaco, Supertest, and the British American Oil Company. In the *North Bay* case, no action was taken due to the local and rather special nature of the circumstances as found by the Commission. In the Mary Maxim case, a consent order was obtained prohibiting continuation of the arbitrary discount structure used. In one of the gasoline cases the Commission found no discrimination and in the remaining two, prosecution was not instituted because of the difficulty of proving beyond a reasonable doubt that the customers in question were competitors of one another within the meaning of Section 33A. The interpretation which emerges from this set of reports is that competing purchasers buying like quantities must be treated uniformly, but price differentials of any magnitude are possible between purchasers of different quantities of a product. In the case of the gasoline industry (and aside from problems of identifying the geographic overlap of a market between different retail outlets), temporary competitive allowance prompted by price wars would not appear to constitute price discrimination, but a continuing discount from the price in favor of an independent dealer competing with a lessee would be a violation.

Section 33B prohibits the granting of a promotional allowance which is not offered on "proportionate terms" to other purchasers in competition with the favored purchaser. This provision was enacted following a report of the Restrictive Trade Practices Commission in 1958 on discriminatory pricing practices in the grocery trades. Although a number of complaints have since been received and considered by the Director, none has so far led to a formal enquiry under Section 33B.

Section 33A(1)(b) makes it an offense to sell articles in any area of Canada at prices lower than those charged in any other area—if the practice has the "effect or tendency of substantially lessening competition or eliminating a competitor in such parts of Canada, or (is) designed to have such effect." In the *Evaporated Milk* case, the trial judge and two of three judges in the Alberta Court of Appeal acquitted on the ground that the accused had resorted to a temporary expedient to meet an aggressive competitor, and his efforts were not designed to limit competition but to demonstrate to competitors that there must be fair play between rivals.

Section 33A(1)(c) makes an offense of engaging in a policy to sell articles at unreasonably low prices with the objective or effect of substantially lessening competition or eliminating a competitor. In the *Ottawa Milk* case, the Magistrate acquitted on the ground that the unreasonably low prices complained of were intended to meet competition presented by a competitor of the accused, and that the temporary dislocation of business which resulted was not an offense. The Ontario Court of Appeal unanimously supported the Magistrate's judgement. In two private criminal prosecutions involving gasoline pricing and alleging unreasonably low prices, the Magistrate acquitted the first defendant on the ground that the motivation was self preservation rather than the elimination of a competitor, and the second defendant on the ground that the accused was not even meeting the competition initiated by the price-cutting complainant.

Section 34 forbids a supplier to practice resale price maintenance directly or indirectly, and forbids a supplier to refuse to sell to a merchant on the ground that such merchant refuses or fails to maintain specified retail prices. It is a defense for a supplier charged with refusal to sell on a resale price maintenance motivation, to prove that the merchant who was refused supplies was using the article as a loss leader, or for bait advertising, or was engaging in misleading advertising of the article, or was not providing the level of servicing that purchasers of such articles reasonably expect. This RPM ban was first introduced in 1951; the defenses were introduced in 1960. There have been a comparatively large number of inquiries and prosecutions which have, by and large, led to convictions. The main problems in enforcement are those of establishing that a supplier has been induced, the observance of a specified price, and the refusal to supply a price-cutting outlet on claims other than his price-cutting behavior. Indirect circumvention of the provisions of this section is possible through the introduction of consignment selling which permits a manufacturer to exercise control over the retail price, since there is then no resale within the terms of Section 34. The Restrictive Trade Practices Commission commented on this practice in the *North Star* case and held that "though the letter of the Act is not violated, its spirit and intent are frustrated by the device of consignment."

At present, exclusive dealing practices are not expressly prohibited under the Combines Investigation Act.[1] In certain circumstances, an exclusive dealing arrangement may be dealt with where it has been made pursuant to an illegal collusive agreement, or in order to effect prescribed trading practices, or where it constitutes an abuse of monopoly power. These comments would apply as well to the practices of tying arrangements and to territorial restrictions.

Refusal to deal has not, as such, constituted a prohibited trade practice in Canada except as it violated other prohibitions relating to monopoly, conspiracies, or resale price maintenance. Refusal to sell is *per se* prohibited where it is carried out to enforce resale price maintenance. Refusal to sell was a dominant issue in the *Ammunition* case which involved the refusal of Canadian Industries Limited to supply ammunition to certain distributors. The matter was settled when the company undertook to supply all solvent distributors who were prepared to purchase reasonable quantities.

Franchise operations or other use of common designation by a group of independent but allied distributors or manufacturers is not covered by present legislation. These practices have not proven vulnerable under the section dealing with conspiracies or arrangements, since that section is qualified by the requirement that the agreement unduly lessens or prevents competition in the market involved.

With the possible exception of the provisions on resale price maintenance, it must be said that enforcement of the provisions discussed above has been considerably short of vigorous, and the impact of such enforcement has been minimal.

The Recommendations of the Economic Council of Canada

The Report of the Council[2] recommends that practices discussed above, with the exception of resale price maintenance, be removed from criminal law and be covered by civil legislation to be enforced by a new administrative tribunal composed of economists, lawyers, and other persons experienced in business practices. The Council considered that trade practices generally ought not to be prohibited outright, but should be appraised by the tribunal on the merits of individual cases. The philosophy suggested is essentially the same as that to be applied to mergers:

> that is, none of the practices would be treated as undesirable, *per se*. Rather, the presumption would be that while the practices could well be harmless or even beneficial to the public in some circumstances, they could be harmful in others. The tribunal's responsibility would be to examine cases where harmful effects were suspected and, upon finding that harm was indeed being done, to impose and/or recommend appropriate remedies.

The Council indicated that in examining such trade practices, the interest of the ultimate consumer rather than that of particular competitors would be of paramount consideration for the tribunal. The following considerations were to direct the deliberations:

1. whether the practice was being engaged in by person(s) or firm(s) accounting for a substantial share of the relevant market;
2. the extent to which the practice was likely to foreclose sources of supply or channels of distribution to other participants in the market;
3. what alternative sources of supply or channels of distribution, if any, were available or could readily be made available to other participants in the market;
4. whether the practice was likely to encourage or discourage cost-lowering innovation in methods of distribution;
5. whether the practice could be justified as an effective means of creating a market for a new product, or of introducing an established product into a new market; and
6. whether the practice was likely to make it possible for one or more competitors to eliminate or exclude other competitors from the market by means other than superior performance, on a sustained basis, in supplying goods and services to the public.

It would be the function of the tribunal, upon finding harmful effects, to impose and/or recommend appropriate remedies. The remedies directly available to the tribunal would include interim and permanent injunctions against the practices.

It was anticipated by the Economic Council that the tribunal would, over time, develop a body of jurisprudence which would add detail to these general statutory references. As and when the tribunal felt ready, it was suggested that guidelines could be announced to add to the certainty of the business community in interpreting the legislation.

In addition, the Council suggested that consideration be given to the possibility of providing for private damage actions in the event of violation of these standards—the cases to be instituted by the injured parties before the ordinary courts.

Trade Practices in Canada

As a general rule, the marketing techniques of American companies are followed in the Canadian economy. In many industries the companies involved are subsidiaries of American firms, making use of marketing strategies involving franchising, exclusive dealing, and other contractual practices borrowed from the American market. Cultural similarities and common corporate policies have led to uniform Canada-United States policies on product design, channels and methods of distribution, and promotional practices.[a]

There is evidence of exclusive dealing in a great variety of Canadian industries. One of the best documented cases is that of farm machinery; the industry has been the subject of a Royal Commission enquiry which has already made a good deal of its evidence public. Evidence was introduced at the Commission's hearings of dealers being forced to discontinue carrying competing brands of a product in which the manufacturer desired to achieve exclusive dealing and a decrease in price competition. While there are examples of dealers carrying more than one line of equipment the general practice is that of exclusive dealing.

The Commission's *Special Report on Prices*[3] reveals the impact on implement prices to Canadian farmers of a restrictive clause contained in contracts by large Canadian implement manufacturers which prohibits their British dealers from selling new machines outside Britain. This arrangement prevents Canadian farmers from taking advantage of the lower prices for tractors which exist in Great Britain by importing directly. Exclusive markets organized on a world-wide basis present obvious barriers to attempts by a single national government to control their restrictive effects. The Royal Commission states:

> These differences in prices and profits (among countries) are possible because the movement of tractors from one market to another is closely controlled by the manufacturer. Any attempts to bypass normal channels of distribution are strongly resisted by the companies involved. This is clearly evident in the steps taken by the various farm machinery companies to prevent Ontario farmers from importing tractors directly from Britain. Although the companies argue that their motive in preventing such direct importation is to protect their

[a] It should be stressed that the Combines Investigation Act does not, in principle, apply to service industries; the only reference to services in the legislation is to the transportation, rental, or storage of an article—and to the price of insurance on questions of agreements in restraint of trade.

Canadian dealers, their Canadian distribution system and the quality and reputation of their product, it is clear that other motives are involved. To some degree, it is the price and profit level in Canada and in North America as a whole that the companies wish to protect. Indeed, this may be the primary motive. Moreover, and this is a key point as far as any recommendations are concerned, most of the steps taken to prevent the direct importation by Ontario farmers occurred within Britain outside the jurisdiction of the Canadian Government.

Attempted entry by a competing firm may be seriously impeded by the unavailability of existing distribution networks. Reference is made by the Commission to the implication which extensive exclusive dealing dealership networks may also have on the creation of excess capacity at the retail level.

An aggravating factor in this has been the traditional insistence by the manufacturers on exclusive dealing arrangements. This practice received impetus from the development of full line firms, and from the rapid technological advance of farm machinery during the 20's and 30's. The latter called for a more specialized knowledge on the part of the dealer and a close relationship between the dealer and company for the exchange of information on the success of new lines and possible improvement in them. Moreover, advancing technology brought new problems in servicing and costlier machinery brought new credit problems.

Until recent times, a clause was written into companies' contracts with dealers specifying that they would handle one line exclusively. Such clauses have now been dropped from contracts except for repair parts. Officials of dealers' associations in Canada, however, inform the author that exclusive dealing is expected of dealers as much now as ever, and is enforced just as rigidly only by more subtle means than through the contract. Complaints against the practice, they say, are more common in the West than in Eastern Canada where dealers usually have had more sidelines with which to bolster their incomes. In most cases the companies reciprocated by granting to dealers exclusive rights of representation in their respective territories, rights which the companies insist even today that they guard zealously in the dealer's interest.

The practice of exclusive dealing explains in part the development of a tremendous excess capacity in implement distribution at the retail level in the first three decades of this century.

This quotation illustrates the frequently used explanation of the need for a manufacturer to assure himself of proper servicing, stocking of parts, and promotional efforts in support of the product involved. These motivations may be well founded, but the implementation of exclusive arrangements can and does impose excess capacity on an industry, facilitate considerable inefficiency in the handling of parts and provisions of services, extend and support product differentiation which reduces effective competition between alternative brands, and reduces or eliminates intrabrand competition among dealers. In dispersed and thin markets which are present in many areas of Canada, and with the degree of concentration in manufacturing found in many Canadian industries, these practices impose substantial economic waste in the duplication of facilities. The inability of the market to support numerous outlets of competing brands in some industries and regions (the farm machinery industry is probably a prime example) imposes what may be insurmountable barriers to the entry of new firms. Exclusive arrangements also reduce the likelihood of the separation of servicing and distribution which might provide greater efficiency by causing each function to be justified on its own economic merits. Separation might permit competition to arise in certain service aspects where such functions can be more efficiently performed by an outlet other than the exclusive dealer involved.

Evidence is cited in the United States to establish that while market concentration rose in consumer goods industries generally (both concentrated and unconcentrated industries), concentration increased significantly more in those consumer goods industries where product differentiation was important than where it was unimportant.[4]

The prevalence of contractual arrangements of the kind under consideration here can be readily observed in the Canadian market. The economic impact of these arrangements cannot be as readily ascertained. The significance for economic efficiency would vary with the extent of the interbrand substitutability and competition, the extent of the duplication of the practice by rival firms in the same industry, and the degree of concentration at the various levels of production and distribution in the industry.

The following two sections of this paper set out the framework for the concluding section where an attempt is made to look to appropriate policy conclusions.

Analytical Framework

Exclusive Dealing

Exclusive distribution systems exist in a number of Canadian industries where product differentiation is a significant element of market structure, and also in such sectors as industrial chemicals and minerals. The adoption of exclusive dealing or exclusive franchising practices by firms in homogeneous product industries are suspect of arising from a desire to suppress competition, since no brand identification is at issue.

When exclusive dealing policies are employed by firms possessing market power, competition at the distribution level of the market is suppressed and competitive forces are channeled into nonprice factors. Interbrand price competition declines as the degree of product differentiation increases. A new entrant into the manufacturing sector must also become deeply involved in the distribution sector, often having to set up his own outlets. This increases both the cost and risk involved in entry and market penetration and heightens the degree of discretionary power available to firms already in the industry to realize superior returns from their protected existence. Exclusive dealing also makes it easier for manufacturers to keep dealers under the thumb. For example, where suppliers operate under an oligopolistic consensus, price competition may be regarded by them as disruptive and disorderly marketing which could feed back pressure from the distributive sector to the supply level. Reliance upon exclusive dealing-inspired dealer push in the distribution of a product (as opposed to consumer pull) is difficult for competitors to match. This is a characteristic which makes contractual arrangements of interest to firms aware of their interdependence, and seeking forms of rivalry which have a more continuing payoff than price competition or consumer promotions (which are less readily duplicated and neutralized by competitors).

In making a public policy judgment on the desirability of certain contractual marketing arrangements under defined circumstances, it must be borne in mind that the suppliers involved will have recourse to other techniques of product differentiation and promotion. While it is possible that the ingenuity of marketers could lead to the use of yet more costly and disadvantageous forms of rivalry, this would appear to be unlikely. The odds would seem to be in favor of a higher level of competitive discipline when dealers decide upon pushing different products on the basis of their individual profitability, giving the dealer freedom to select among alternatives.

The primary justification offered by firms enforcing exclusive dealing policies is that the practice encourages good performance by dealers. Advocates argue that it promotes interbrand competition, which in the long run (à la Schumpeter) is the significant form of competition.[b] Some exponents of exclusive dealing suggest that the practice encourages dealers to specialize and, as all first year economists know, specialization is a good thing.[c] There is also an element of protection in the practice. When

---

[b] Dirlam and Kahn make an interesting point regarding competition and exclusive dealing: "The contention that exclusive dealers (who are not given the opportunity to be anything but exclusive) each vying for the customer's patronage, can provide an effective competitive performance perhaps assumes greater market perfection—insofar as consumer knowledge, discerning powers, and ability to shop around are concerned—than actually prevails. Perhaps, then, inadequate consumer knowledge necessitates an 'offsetting perfection'; the protection of dealers who are free to shop around and advise their customers. Exclusive dealing is supposed to make for the provision of better service; here is a service it eliminates."[5]

[c] These exponents would argue that abandonment of the practice would increase dealers' inventory problems. However, if dealer specialization in a particular brand does realize significant economies in inventory investment, dealers will continue to specialize after exclusive dealing is eliminated.

a supplier invests capital in national advertising in order to differentiate his brand from the generic product and create goodwill for it, he naturally does not want distributors' conduct to impair this intangible asset. The need to control dealers to protect supplier investment in goodwill is most obvious in the case of franchise arrangements where the franchisor is not selling a single product but is licensing the establishment of a new business with a nationally known name and method of conducting that business.

Dirlam and Kahn have offered an interpretation of United States jurisprudence on exclusive dealing.[6] A number of major oil companies operating in the same regions followed the practice of drawing up prescribed contracts which insisted on exclusive dealing; dealers had to sign these if they wanted to sell the oil company's products.[d] In the *Sinclair* case the Court took into account the parallel restrictive practices of other dominant firms besides the defendant. Justice Frankfurter concluded that the use of such contracts by the major oil companies had the effect of enabling "the established suppliers individually to maintain their own standing and at the same time collectively to prevent a late arrival from wresting away more than an insignificant portion of the market." The courts, in judging exclusive dealing cases, focus on whether distributors have been coerced and competitors seriously handicapped, without engaging in extended appraisals of market performance.

Dirlam and Kahn conclude that the socially acceptable advantages derived from exclusive dealing can be achieved by less restrictive means; that the practice promotes wasteful forms of rivalry on the retail level, while at the same time raising barriers to entry at the supplier level. They also point out that an important source of innovation, via new entry, may be virtually closed off.[7]

Exclusive Franchising, Territorial or Customer Restraints, and Other Exclusive Arrangements

Exclusive franchising usually is combined with a policy of exclusive dealing unless the distributor is in a strong position (in which case it can be viewed as a reverse exclusive dealing case). While the dealer is prevented from handling rival suppliers' products, as a *quid pro quo* he is protected from intrabrand competition.[e] The advocates of exclusive franchising argue that, while the practice has restrictive features—in the long

---

[d] Similar practices are found in Canada.

[e] It might be interesting to try to determine the assistance which exclusive franchising provided Volkswagon when it entered the Canadian market. One might also estimate when the beneficial effects of the practice (i.e. aiding effective entry) were offset by the restrictive effects as Volkswagon became established.

run in industries characterized by product differentiation—it contributes to more effective competition. It helps to avoid confusion in the fulfilling of continuing dealer obligations such as the provision of service already paid for with the purchase.[f] Exclusive franchising is described as a means to compensate or substitute for vertical integration by suppliers.[g] The existence of territorial protection may create an environment where both supplier and dealer are willing to undertake activities which they otherwise might not.

> Protection of profit margins from the incursions of intrabrand competition is essential to enable a dealer to provide the special promotion and to afford the extra services that help distinguish this product from other brands in the consumer's mind . . . The full impact of the manufacturer's advertising and promotional expenditures is dependent upon the manufacturer's ability to confine the distribution of his products to outlets that are consistent with the image created by such expenditures.
>
> Moreover, many exclusive arrangements are made not to deprive third parties of access to the market but to provide an assurance of supply that will justify substantial expenditures for facilities or for promotion that would not otherwise be profitable. In such cases there is a possibility that competition between firms that are parties to different exclusive arrangements will enlarge the total market without significant damage to anyone's opportunity. To distinguish such situations from those involving preclusion is not easy.[9]

Robert Bork, a commentator on United States antitrust, states that a simplistic approach by the Courts to exclusive practices may seriously hamper some firms' ability to compete. He fears that the Court will mistakenly apply a *per se* rule to vertical agreements.

> An agreement among competitors is for the sole purpose of suppressing competition. But when a supplier imposes its control over distributors' territories, it is not for the simple purpose of suppressing competition. The supplier may have a legitimate business interest in getting its distributors to work their own areas intensively rather than going far afield to pick off easy accounts in other territories.[10]

Bork quotes evidence by White Motor Company counsel to illustrate the need for exclusive franchising as well as for exclusive dealing.

---

[f] In most cases dealer marks on the products or separation of pricing for the product and the servicing should provide a feasible alternative to this justification.

[g] "For the seller it provides the same kind though not usually the same degree of control over and assurance of market outlets; for the buyer, the same kind of assurance of supply. To both it offers the advantages of a closer cooperation and greater mutual assistance than is ordinarily made available between independent suppliers and customers".[8]

To obtain the maximum number of sales of trucks in a given area, the White Motor Company has to insist that distributors and dealers concentrate on trying to take sales away from other competing truck manufacturers in their respective territories rather than on cutting each other's throats in other territories.[11]

White Motor was a relatively small member of an oligopolistic industry; in the American context, it is possible to see the problems faced by the Company in expanding its market share. When White distributors compete against other brands, they probably do not find price a very effective instrument since purchases are complicated in the buyer's eye by all sorts of brand differentiation. Consequently, there is pressure to resort to other means of rivalry, such as promotion campaigns and services. But these methods involve capital investment which partly benefits the product rather than the particular dealer financing the investment. From the supplier's point of view, a vicious circle is created—especially as dealers are likely to have a shorter time horizon for profit maximization than does the supplier, thereby making price cuts more attractive than capital investment. Dealers find it most effective in the short run to raid other White distributors by offering price cuts in outside territories. This in turn makes distributor investment in goodwill riskier. Competitive techniques likely to take business away from rival manufacturers may thus be avoided by White's dealers.

Bork's attitude to vertical contractual relationships and their ultimate impact on the interests of consumers of the goods or services involved seems to be predicated on the assumption that, in circumstances where restrictions are not imposed by one dominant party in the relationship, the consumer interest is served in the resulting terms of the agreement. This assumes that the objective pursued by the distributor vis-à-vis the supplier is in the interests of the consumer—or alternatively, that the bargaining relationship of effective countervailing power between a distributor and suppliers protects the interest of the ultimate user. There seems to be no *a priori* reason why this would be true in all or even most circumstances. Where the nature of the market place is such that the two parties to the bargaining relationship are reasonably unconstrained, there would seem to be no reason why they could not make an agreement which simply split up the excess returns from the market place between themselves, leaving no net benefit to the user or consumer.

The *White Motor* case does raise two points which will be commented on further. First, a firm which lacks any significant degree of market power is unlikely to cause much harm by virtue of its vertical market restrictions, and is at a decided disadvantage in competition with larger firms making use of contractual arrangements. White Motor's difficulty in penetrating the market for trucks stems largely from the fact that the leading manufacturers also distributed by means of exclusive dealerships. If none of the established manufacturers had made use of exclusive dealerships, the smaller firm or a new entrant would be in a considerably stronger position. Facilitating the entry of a smaller firm which lacks the goodwill secured by the product differentiation of established producers may require special treatment—particularly in view of the history of building up of product differentiation based in part on exclusive trading practices. The significance of an exclusive practice undertaken by a firm varies not only with the degree of market power which the brand and product line possesses, but also with the extent to which other firms in the industry make use of similar techniques of distribution.

Aside from the concerns expressed for any categoric attack on contractual marketing arrangements, various assertions are occasionally made in support of these practices. To begin with, the observation can be made that the distribution sector of the Canadian economy does not perform too badly. Entry is usually sufficiently flexible to discipline any excesses attempted by firms in allegedly strong market positions. In response to vertical integration by producers, cooperative merchandising and franchising have grown to rival the national and/or regional market positions of established firms. It may, in fact, be true that some markets are ultimately self-adjusting; however, in a number of industries the barriers to entry still do not permit a meaningful adjustment process to occur.

Analogies between contractual integration and the ownership-integrated supplier-distributor are potentially misleading. The suggestion is frequently made that exclusive franchising which protects the territories of each outlet goes no further than the decisions of ownership integrated firms to allocate the market among a reasonable number of outlets. The analogy is imperfect since the ownership integrated firm will, if properly managed, supply a particular buyer from the outlet able to most efficiently serve his needs. An adequate internal cost-accounting system means that this will operate so as to discipline individual outlets which are comparatively inefficient. Protected territories for allied but independent outlets do not permit confrontation over their relative efficiencies in supplying a given customer or area. If one outlet is considerably less efficient than the other, this situation could persist to the disadvantage of the customers involved. The extent of product differentiation could then be critical in determining the extent to which this inefficiency would persist.

When exclusive territories or protected classes of customers do not form part of the restrictions, the use of a common designation by allied businesses can potentially capitalize upon the economies of advertising and distribution, challenge the product differentiation of large integrated operations, and increase the bargaining strength of the group in its dealings with suppliers.

The following exerpt from an article by Sigmund Timberg illustrates the kinds of arguments likely to be presented by franchisors in the face of legislation on contractual and other practices.[12] Timberg uses the "bedding cases" example in his analysis.

The purposes of such organizations [horizontal franchise agreements] are to develop improved specifications for a product . . . to establish a common trade-mark, and to develop uniform promotional publicity.

On the basis of the economies enjoyed by the organization, local firms are enabled to compete with national companies. However, the cooperative arrangement, which results in competition from local entrepreneurs (in this case bedding manufacturers producing private brands as well as Serta mattresses), depends on the territorial allocation of markets.

The basic motivation which had induced the licensees to contribute financially to the exploitation of a common trademark was that they would thereby be guaranteed added and needed customer acceptance in a territory which they had been continuously exploiting . . . The manufacturers testified that this [abandonment of the practice] would result in the eventual liquidation of the franchising system in the bedding industry, the elimination of many businesses and the absorption by others into larger nationwide concerns . . . If a licensee from a neighboring territory is in a position, by a few sales, to 'skim off the cream' of the market and thereby disrupt trade relations, there is no incentive to promote the market further, the invaded licensee might just as well devote his energies to developing a private mark.

In assessing particular cooperative or franchising schemes, care must be taken to distinguish the necessary from the unnecessary and restrictive provisions. Only those provisions of the contract which are essential to the benefits claimed ought to be treated as desirable. Even then, attention must be paid to the extent to which participants in the arrangement exercise substantial degrees of market power in regional and district markets.

The importance claimed for exclusive policies in eliciting promotional and service expenditures by both dealers and suppliers in vertical contractual arrangements has already been mentioned. In situations where an entire business is franchised, exclusive dealing is claimed to be essential to the arrangement since alternative methods of protecting the franchisor's goodwill are inadequate. Motels, roadside foodstores, cleaning establishments—the businesses where this type of franchising is prevalent—are unlikely candidates for possession of significant market power. Even so, an alternative approach which might be explored is the setting of quality or performance standards by the franchisor, with the capacity to discontinue the contract in the event of the standards being violated. Only where it proves costly or complicated to test the adequacy of services and goods presented under the franchised name would it then be acceptable to permit the tying of related goods and services provided by the franchisor. Much of the investment in servicing and product promotion by outlets which is stimulated by exclusive practices is either wasteful, or will still be forthcoming given appropriate adjustments in the price structure. Conveniences such as clean washrooms, adequate replacement inventories, and so on (which benefit the supplier but may be uneconomic for the supplier to finance) will continue to be provided by dealers after contractual arrangements are abandoned if these practices contribute to dealers' profits. If dealers find little advantage in undertaking such expenditures (that is, they don't increase overall sales or they do not pay when priced out separately), it is more than likely that the public did not demand them anyway. Similarly, services provided by suppliers to dealers—such as managerial assistance and the training of technicians—can be priced to earn a return for the supplier.

The above discussion suggests certain criteria for assessing the economic impact of exclusive arrangements. The concluding section of this paper will explore the public policy on legislative implications of this analysis. Prior to the concluding section, a few comments should be made on the relationship of this analysis to market entry and to the practice of tied sales.

Exclusive Practices and Market Entry

A number of American authorities have commented on the market entry aspect of contractual and related trade practices:

> These criteria do not require that all exclusive arrangements be outlawed. Where exclusive dealing helps a new firm to gain a foothold, it clearly does not represent the use of appreciable bargaining power unreasonably to foreclose competitors from a substantial market. The use of exclusive dealing by small manufacturers as a means of breaking into a market represents one of the most defensible uses of the practice.[13]

> Are territorial restrictions more restrictive than necessary to achieve any legitimate purpose? We [Antitust Division] have been studying this matter for some time, and I am frank to say that so far I am not convinced that territorial restrictions are reasonably necessary to any legitimate purpose save for one case, that involving the entry of new firms and/or new products.[14]

In most instances where firms employ contractual practices to introduce new products or services, their market power will be limited and probably transitory. However, cases have reached the Supreme Court in the United States where the decision hinged on entry considerations.[15] Consequently, it seems worthwhile to consider how the use of contractual practices might facilitate market entry.

In industries characterized by a high degree of product differentiation, introduction of a new product (particularly when the firm also is new or small in relation to the leading firms) requires substantial investment in product promotion to overcome the goodwill established by existing firms. Such investment for a new product involves a high degree of risk. Thus, any device which reduces the risk involved or increases the prospective return from such an investment may facilitate entry.

A market innovator frequently wishes to obtain exclusive dealers so that he can provide the servicing and marketing training required for effective distribution and consumer acceptance of his product without, at the same time, benefiting rival suppliers. The innovating supplier may be in a poor position to persuade distributors to promote his product unless he can offer an exclusive market. Investment in the promotion of a new product is always risky; it is particularly so when a distributor's effort may benefit another dealer in the same product. Much of the promotional investment made by the dealer will create goodwill for the product itself, rather than for the particular outlet. Exclusive dealing together with exclusive franchising may place the dealer in a position where his profit maximizing behavior will also promote the success of the new product (depending, of course, on some of the other contractual restrictions).[16]

The above arguments refer to the difficulties of an entrant getting *into* a market where salesmen and technicians are unfamiliar with the new product and where the entrant has to overcome the barriers raised by the heavy advertising of established suppliers. This exception to the general prohibition of the exclusive practices must be for a limited period of time.[17] Presumably, the time period will be related to the amount of capital investment needed for entry, the degree of risk, and the length of time required to establish a reasonably secure position in the market. These factors will in turn be influenced by the height of the barrier to entry derived from product differentiation.

What constitutes new entry may become an issue in some situations.

For example, in *Sandura,* the Sixth Circuit [U.S.] held that in the case of the small concern in an industry dominated by 'giants', the need to overcome an already damaged reputation and reestablish the position of its products in the face of the overwhelming competition of well established companies rendered the [vertical territorial] restrictions reasonable and justified despite the curtailment of intrabrand competition.[18]

In *Sandura,* the company argued that it was threatened with failure if its exclusive practices were abandoned. In effect, Sandura was reentering the market.

It may be that situations like Sandura would not come under rules which look for the existence of market power. In the case of tie-ins, there would be incentive to interpret the requirement of market power very strictly since the origin of a tie-in usually indicates the existence of power (although tie-ins and exclusive dealing can shade into one another).[19]

There is a more interesting situation which is likely to be encountered. The durable (especially consumer) goods industries have made product change a means of product differentiation and a major basis for rivalry among existing firms. Product innovation has been institutionalized. These same industries are prominent among those using contractual and other trade practices. In the context of these industries, it might be argued that the very behavior which the new entry exception is designed to encourage actually further increases barriers to entry for new firms. Yet the product innovations of established firms can increase public welfare. In some cases, firms may be able to argue convincingly that contractual and other practices significantly increase the incentive to create and introduce new products. Thus, it becomes necessary to assess the net impact on the public interest of each restrictive practice. Demonstration that exclusive practices are necessary should prove more difficult for a well-established firm as opposed to a new firm, or a new entrant to the market involved.

It should also be noted that prohibition of exclusive policies in some durable goods industries may not result in distribution systems composed primarily of independent firms. Industries in which firms have invested heavily in an effort to differentiate brands and where rivalry is based on the characteristics of these brands and on advertising, are the most likely candidates for vertical ownership integration in the event that contractual practices are forbidden. A propensity to ownership integration need not however cause detriment to the public. Mergers which suppress competition without any offsetting social gain are already subject to some prohibition in Canada (albeit not a strong one). When analyzing the impact of a merger on competition, presumably its effect on barriers to entry would be taken into account.

If vertical integration is achieved by means of internal expansion, there is a tendency for the number of firms in the distribution sector to increase. Legislation would have to prevent integrated suppliers from squeezing independents. Elimination of independent dealers would raise the barriers to entry to the suppliers' industry. To the extent that ownership integration realizes economies in costs of production, distribution or promotion which do not arise in sales to the independents, the independents operate at a disadvantage.[h] They may be able to compensate for this because of the advantages derived from local entrepreneurship. In some situations, it may be feasible for independents to form cooperative buying and promotion systems and thereby realize some of the economies of large-scale operations.

In any case, it is difficult to predict whether or not vertical integration

[h] Firms which integrate forward because of the prohibition of exclusive dealing or exclusive franchising will have some incentive to rationalize the distribution system. Under exclusive franchising arrangements, dealerships vary widely so far as efficiency and rates of return are concerned. When dealers are under common control and ownership, unprofitable outlets will be eliminated.

will be a common occurrence where exclusive dealing practices are prohibited. There are good reasons for believing that vertical integration will be relatively infrequent. In the quotation below, Lee Preston explains why suppliers tend to prefer restrictive contracts with dealers to wholly-owned outlets. Basically, exclusive distribution is the less expensive means of achieving the supplier's ends:[20]

> . . . First, distribution is a relatively low-profit activity; if a supplier can obtain the desired degree of control without assuming full investment responsibility, he may be able to employ his capital more profitably elsewhere. Second, distribution is typically a multiproduct activity, with the product mix of distributors substantially different from that of any one supplier; vertical integration under these circumstances involves a substantial broadening of a supplier's product responsibility as well as his functional role. Finally, the local managerial problems and personal service content of distribution discourage suppliers from integrating forward when other alternatives are available.

When the option of contractual or similar practices is prohibited, a supplier will compare the profitability of the remaining alternatives, principally forward integration and nonrestrictive contracts with independent dealers. The return derived from the *additional* control over distribution attained by forward integration must exceed the cost of integrating forward before ownership integration become a viable proposition.

Tied Sales

For an effective tying policy, the seller must possess some degree of monopoly power over the tied good. The degree of power can vary widely —the firm (or firms acting in concert) may be the sole source of supply of a product having no close substitutes, or the firm's product may be only slightly differentiated from alternative products.[21]

In most instances a tie-in policy can be regarded as monopolizing conduct tending to foreclose or exclude competitors in the tied good industry.

> A tie-in always operates to raise the barriers to entry in the market of the tied good to the level of those in the market for the tying good—the seller who would supply the one, can do so only if he can also supply the other, since he must be able to displace the whole package which the tying seller offers. Developing a substitute for the tying product may be very difficult, if not impossible.[22]
>
> . . .
>
> The essence of illegality in tying arrangements is the wielding of monopolistic coverage; a seller exploits his dominant position in one market to expand his empire into the next.[23]

Under United States antitrust laws, if a court finds market power in the tying goods plus substantial trading in the tied good, the tying practices will virtually always be condemned.[i]

The conditions under which a firm with monopoly power in the tying good will find it profitable to extend monopolistic coverage by means of a tie-in policy can be specified. When the tied and tying goods are complements and used in varying proportions, tie-ins can increase monopoly profits, and the output of the tied good for use with the tying good will be less than it would be if the tie-in did not exist and the tied goods were sold competitively. In other words, monopolization of the tied good market may be the profit maximizing conduct in the majority of cases where tie-ins exist. The extent to which competition is restricted by the tie-in policy will depend on the degree of monopoly in the tied good market and on the significance of uses of the tying good other than as a complement to the tied good.

In cases where tie-ins have been employed to support or promote a monopolistic position in the tied market, prohibition of tying should have a direct impact on market structure by eliminating an artificial barrier to entry.[j] William L. Baldwin followed up three major United States antitrust cases in which relief involved the prohibition of tying and other conduct rather than the dissolution of firms or other so-called structural remedies.[25] He argued that conduct remedies imposed on the firms did result in improved structure and performance in all three cases.

Since it is difficult to separate out the impact of conduct remedies from other influences on market structure and performance in a follow-up study, the favorable findings of Baldwin and others cannot be regarded as conclusive evidence that the conduct approach taken by the Courts was appropriate. Nevertheless, the cases examined involved firms with very high degrees of market power so that in one sense the conduct approach was subjected to a rigorous testing. These American studies demonstrate that sole reliance on a prohibition of tie-ins may be insufficient to halt foreclosing of the tied good market. For example, American Can Company

---

[i] Singer, in his study of tie-ins, mentions a United States case which illustrates how a simplistic analysis of the relationship between tie-ins and barriers to entry can lead to an ill-founded conclusion. In *Federal Trade Commission* v. *Sinclair Refining Co.*, the Supreme Court allowed Sinclair as well as thirty other refiners to continue the practice of leasing underground tanks to gasoline stations at a minimal rental, upon the condition that the equipment should be used only for the storage of gasoline supplied by the lessor. The Court was impressed by the lowering of barriers to entry at the retail level. The practice of leasing allowed an individual to open a gasoline station with a comparatively small capital investment. But the Court failed to note that this same leasing practice tended to raise the barriers to entry at the gasoline distributor level.[24]

[j] If real economies were realized by means of the tie-in policy, suppliers of the tying good will still enjoy an advantage over other firms if their price structure reflects these economies after abandonment of the tie-in policy.

was able to achieve the effect of a tying arrangement by means of a combination of leasing and requirements contracts, even after outright tie-ins were forbidden in the 1920s.

Most economists would condemn tie-ins adopted for the pursuit of monopoly profits and for the extension of monopoly power. However, some defenders of the present patent system voice concern about the implications of tie-in provisions for the rewards from innovation. Baldwin and McFarland show that where varying quantities of one (tied) product may be used with one unit of another (tying) product, a monopolist may employ tie-ins as an efficient means to practice price discrimination (based on use) on users of the tying product.[26] The tied product becomes in effect a meter, measuring the use made of the tying product. The tying arrangements may have been resorted to for the purpose of making an otherwise unworkable scheme of price discrimination feasible through eliminating any chance of resale by customers who paid lower prices. Economists argue that market foreclosure really does not occur in the meter case because output of the tied good is equivalent to what it would be if the monopolist used another method of price discrimination for sales of the tying good (for example, royalty on use). There have been a number of cases in the United States and some in Canada where the motive for tie-ins appears to have been additional profits via price discrimination on tying goods sales—rather than profit via competitive foreclosure.

Baldwin and McFarland point out another potential feature of tie-in provisions:[27]

> In certain combination patent cases a tying arrangement may be the only way to exploit the normal right of a patent owner. Examples of this situation would occur with process patents or patented arrangements for putting certain articles together in which none of the ingredients or components could be patented separately. The *Mercoed* case illustrates such a situation. The holder of a combination patent on a new heating system involving unpatentable stokers, thermostats, and switches found no reasonable way of enforcing his patent against contractors who installed the system. He therefore granted an exclusive license to a firm manufacturing the switches and that firm in turn sublicensed only contractors who purchased its switches.

It seems improbable that the kind of situation described by Baldwin and McFarland will be of much significance in practice. Technological linkages do, however, have to be recognized.

In most cases, it should not be difficult to determine whether or not technological factors dictate that tie-ins are the minimum necessary restriction on sales to assure adequate product performance. An interesting case is the policy adopted by automobile manufacturers of tying sales of replacement parts to the sales of automobiles. In the United States, the courts decided that it was permissible to demand that manufacturer's "factory" parts be used for repairs during the warranty period.

As in the case of exclusive dealing and other contractual restrictions, it may be in the public interest to permit tie-ins for a limited period of time where the practice facilitates market entry. Most articles on the economic implications of exclusive practices admit this exception.

In special circumstances, such as the case where a new entrant in a particular line of commerce is struggling to establish for his principal product an acceptance that it cannot achieve unless supplies used with it are prescribed by the manufacturer, I can see some theoretical merit in permitting the use of a tying arrangement for a limited duration until the manufacturer is relatively secure as a viable factor in the market place.[28]

The United States courts have permitted tying for a limited time in a few cases where the existence of the firm or acceptance of a new product might have been jeopardized if tying was abandoned immediately.[29]

Jerrold Electronics Company was permitted to continue for a period of several years to require that purchasers of its equipment used on antenna sites of television stations also agree to have the equipment serviced by Jerrold; the sales contract tied the servicing to the sale of the equipment. The company justified the tying arrangement by pointing out that the industry was new and the equipment was so specialized that anyone not trained by the company and familiar with the particular equipment could cause damage to the whole antenna site. In the event that the inferiority of outside service was imputed to the equipment, the firm's goodwill and future trade would be harmed. In such cases, it may be possible to reduce the time period allowed for the tie-in, by compelling the company to undertake a training program for outside technicians.

In some situations, franchise systems may require tie-ins in order to operate effectively. If the franchise arrangement enables small- and medium-sized firms to compete aggressively with large, diversified corporations, then the increased market competition resulting from the existence of franchise systems may justify some exclusive arrangements incorporated in the franchise agreement. It is conceivable that directed buying or full-line forcing may be a necessary part of a horizontal joint venture. Savings through volume purchases may be earned by directing independent dealers in a franchise to buy from designated suppliers. Independent retailers co-operating to finance a regional or national advertising program promoting a trade name may wish to stipulate that each franchised retailer stock all the items carrying the name. A franchisor who licenses the establishment of a new business carrying a nationally known name and method of conducting business may argue that directed buying or full-line forcing are necessary for the new, inexperienced dealer. Such restrictions assure that the operations of particular outlets are consistent with the promises made in the national advertising of the franchise.

The following quotation by Corwin Edwards probably summarizes the view of most economists concerning tie-ins and United States law.[30]

In the case of tying arrangements, the conditions requisite for precautionary control of conduct have been present. A seller cannot undertake to condition the sale of one product, or the offer of it at a low price, upon a requirement that the purchaser also buy another, unless he has a substantial degree of control over the supply of the first; and he will seldom do so for any purpose other than to foreclose the opportunity of those who compete with him in selling the second. Thus an anticompetitive tendency inheres in this practice, so much so that there would be only occasional irrelevance in forbidding it wholly. But since, except in periods of acute shortage of goods, the practice can be adopted only under conditions in which the supply of a commodity is under concentrated control, prohibition of it succeeds only in preventing the spread of existing dominance from one commodity to another. It does not prevent the initial attainment of dominance.

What the law accomplishes, however, is achieved without great difficulty. Since the meaning of the law is clear and violations are not hard to detect, there is relatively little violation. In such legal proceedings as arise, proof is not difficult, and there is little need to disentangle harmful or useful tying. The law accomplishes its limited precautionary purpose.

Professor Edwards stresses the limited impact of tie-ins (and the prohibition thereof) on the degree of competition in the economy. While it is true that tie-ins may be feasible only under certain conditions, a review of the Canadian files shows that tying is not uncommon. It exists in producer and consumer goods and service industries, both in national and local markets. Edwards mentions the visibility of tie-in arrangements. The very existence of a law on tie-ins can be expected to discourage adoption of the practice. In Edwards' opinion, it should not be difficult to determine whether or not a particular tie-in should be excepted from the prohibition; he doubts that cases warranting exception will be numerous.

Policy Conclusions

The analytical framework above suggests that the behavioral patterns involved in contractual marketing arrangements are a legitimate focus of public policy for the preservation of competition and efficiency in the distribution sector of the economy. Some economists question the validity of attacking these kinds of behavioral phenomena on the grounds that the economic impact of their modification or elimination is likely to be minimal. Furthermore, it is suggested that the enforcement of the legislation can be confusing and difficult.

The previous sections of this paper attempt to make a case for intervening in the behavior of firms in the market place—primarily in cases where those firms possess market power or where restrictive contractual arrangements are widespread. The grounds presented are that these contractual patterns are not only the product of market power, but are also techniques of maintaining and enhancing market power based upon product differentiation barriers to entry and foreclosure of markets. It is suggested that product differentiation is a major cause of market concentration and competitive imperfections supporting inefficiency, and that some contractual arrangements are direct supports of that product differentiation.

This approach does not deny that some degree of market power is essential to the implementation of most contractual arrangements. As a result, it is fair to observe that the underlying problem is the structure of the industry of which the contractual practices are simply a manifestation.

> The principle issue from the standpoint of regulatory law and policy is to what extent these practices *per se* are strategic to the maintenance of existing market structures and market performance, and to what extent they are simply superficial and more or less automatic manifestations of more basic conditions . . . Unless the underlying market structure is altered, superficial conduct may often be readily altered to comply with specific prohibitions without really altering the effective principles of price output determination or the performance outcome.[31]

In the case of exclusive distribution, it can be argued that Canadian practices are merely symptomatic of the high degree of product differentiation in Canadian supplier markets, that prohibition of the practices will give rise to other policies such as price discrimination and mergers, which are designed to achieve the same ends. Nevertheless, prohibition of exclusive practices may directly influence market structure by reducing the degree of product differentiation and thus barriers to entry.

Corwin Edwards expresses pessimism about the usefulness of the conduct approach, partly for the reason suggested by Bain. In his opinion, the link between conduct (exclusive policies) and performance is too complex to make the approach workable. The opinion was formulated on the basis of the evidence generated by American experience with restrictive trade practices legislation. Edwards' conclusion, which is contrary to the conclusion in this paper, is that in the majority of cases, it is impossible to predict the net economic consequences of exclusive dealing or exclusive franchising. Except for a few obvious cases, the court is faced with insurmountable difficulties in attempting to distinguish between situations where the practices benefit the public by stimulating competition and expanding markets, and situations where the practices result in exclusion and suppression of competition.

The objective of policy rules in this area would be to enhance competition in retailing, thereby reducing retail margins and cost-increasing forms of rivalry. Policy would seek to reduce barriers to entry in both distribution and manufacturing. While we probably cannot expect dramatic results in increasing competition in many industries, some success can probably be anticipated—particularly from new entry via import competition. Enforcement of laws restricting exclusive arrangements might also generate a feedback of competition from the retailing level to the manufacturing level, depending upon the relative strength and concentration of activities at each level.

Despite the complexities of separating harmful from neutral or beneficial contractual practices, it is the author's contention that economic analysis can generate a workable set of criteria—even though the rules will necessarily leave room for some flexibility in their application. To those who would object by observing that we must recognize economic dynamics and not base rules on static analysis, it should be stressed that the criteria can be shaped to anticipate the possibility of changing over time. The policy procedure should frankly admit of and encourage change over time and permit the rule to adjust to different economic settings of different industries. Although rules may have to be somewhat arbitrary, it is suggested that such rules are preferable to abstaining from public policy efforts or to leaving each case open to virtually unlimited debate on the facts, the variables of the barriers to entry, the efficiencies, and other relevant features.

The analysis in this paper leads to the view that tied sales, exclusive territories, and exclusive dealing ought to be subject to general prohibition—with exception being made (a) for technological relationships for which the issuing of specifications by a supplier will not suffice; (b) for new entry in circumstances of new technology or the need for promotional efforts to facilitate market penetration (where temporary permission to engage in such practices would seem logical); and (c) where franchising or cooperative operations under common designation enhances competition in the market and where no less restrictive alternative for the existence of the coordinated effort is possible.

Notes

1. For a discussion of the status of these practices in United States antitrust see D. N. Thompson, "Contractual Marketing Systems: An Overview," *infra.*

2. Economic Council of Canada, *Interim Report on Competition Policy,* Ottawa: Queen's Printer (July, 1969).

3. Royal Commission on Farm Machinery, *Special Report on Prices,* Ottawa: Queen's Printer (December, 1969).

4. Mary Gardiner Jones, "The Growth and Importance of Franchising," *The Antitrust Bulletin,* XII (Fall 1967), 718, on reference from W. S. Mueller, before the Select Committee on Small Business, U.S. Senate (March 15, 1967).

5. Reference: J. E. Dirlam and A. E. Kahn, *Fair Competition,* Ithaca, New York: Cornell University Press (1954), 197.

6. They provide analysis of the following cases: *Standard Oil Co. of Cali-*

fornia v. *U.S.,* 337 U.S. 293 (1949); *Richfield Oil Corp.* v. *U.S.,* 343 U.S. 922 (1952); *Motion Picture Advertising Service Co.* v. *F.T.C.,* 344 U.S. 392 (1953); *Maico Co. Inc.,* F.T.C. Remand 5822 (December 15, 1953); *Dictograph Products Inc.,* docket no. 5655, Decision September 14, 1953; *J. I. Case Co.* v. *U.S.,* 101 F. Supp. 256 (1951).

7. Dirlam and Kahn, *Fair Competition,* 178.

8. Dirlam and Kahn, *Fair Competition,* 173.

9. Corwin D. Edwards, "Control of the Single Firm," *Law and Contemporary Problems* XXX(3) (1965), 478.

10. Robert Bork, "Control of Sales," *The Antitrust Bulletin* VII (2) (1962), 233.

11. See Bork, *Control,* 234; *U. S.* v. *White Motor Co.,* 194 F. Supp. 562 (N.D. Ohio, 1961).

12. Sigmund Timberg, "Selection of Licenses," *The Antitrust Bulletin* VII(2) (1962), 205–214.

13. Dirlam and Kahn, *Fair Competition,* 118.

14. Donald F. Turner, "Some Reflections on Antitrust," 1966 New York State Bar Association *Antitrust Law Symposium,* 4–5.

15. *U.S.* v. *Bausch & Lomb Optical Company,* 45 F. Supp. 387 (1942); 321 U.S. 707 (1944); *B. S. Pearsall Butter Company* v. *F.T.C.,* 292 Fed. 720 (1923); *Exelsior Motor Manufacturing and Supply Company* v. *Sound Equipment Inc.,* 73 F.2d 725 (1934).

16. See Jerry S. Cohen, "Conflict and Its Resolution . . .", *infra.*

17. See the discussion of time-restricted contractual constraints in Chapters Six, Seven, and Eight of Donald N. Thompson, *Franchise Operations and Antitrust,* Boston: Heath Lexington Books (1971).

18. Philip F. Zeidman, "The Growth and Importance of Franchising," *The Antitrust Bulletin* XII (Winter, 1967), 1199.

19. See Rufus E. Wilson, "Exclusionary Restraints and Franchise Distribution," *The Antitrust Bulletin* XII (Winter, 1967), 1175.

20. Lee E. Preston, "Restrictive Distribution Arrangements," *Law and Contemporary Problems* XXX(3) (1965), 512.

21. Dirlam and Kahn, *Fair Competition,* 189–190.

22. Carl Kaysen and Donald F. Turner, *Antitrust Policy,* Cambridge, Mass.: Harvard University Press (1959), 157. For a contrary analysis see Donald N. Thompson, *Franchise Operations . . . ,* Chapter Six.

23. *Times-Picayune Publishing Co.* v. *United States,* 345 U.S. 594 (1953), at 611.

24. See Eugene M. Singer, *Antitrust Economics,* Englewood Cliffs, N.J.: Prentice-Hall Inc. (1968), 201–202.

25. W. L. Baldwin, "The Feedback Effect of Business Conduct on Industry Structure," *Journal of Law and Economics* XII(1) (April, 1969), 123–154. The cases involved were *United Shoe Machinery Corporation, Eastman Kodak Company,* and *International Business Machines Corporation.*

26. W. L. Baldwin and David McFarland, "Tying Arrangements in Law and Economics," *The Antitrust Bulletin* VIII(5–6) (1963), 768.

27. *Ibid.*, 768.

28. R. E. Wilson, "Exclusionary Restraints and Franchise Distribution," *op. cit.*, 1173.

29. *U.S.* v. *Jerrold Electronics Corp.*, 187 F. Supp. 545 (E.D. Pa. 1960), *aff'd*, 365 U.S. 567 (1961), and *Dehydrating Process Co.* v. *A. O. Smith Corp.*, 292 F.2d 643 (1st Cir. 1961), *cert. denied*, 368 U.S. 931 (1961).

30. Corwin D. Edwards, *Control*, 475–476.

31. Joe Bain, *Industrial Organization*, New York: John Wiley & Sons Inc. (1959), 332 and 468.

12 The Evolution of Various Forms of Contractual Marketing Systems in Japan

Masanori Tamura*

Introduction

Distribution systems in high level, mass consumption economies have tended to evolve from product flows through a series of autonomous markets to product flows through a market dominated by a channel leader. Three trends have produced this evolution in Japan: first, the downward expansion of large manufacturers through the channel; second, the upward expansion of mass distributors into production facilities; and third, the corresponding expansions of established wholesalers into production and/or retail operations. From the viewpoint of individual market participants, these integrations are attempts to create and maintain coordinated action systems within which participants can enjoy differential advantage.

The trend to coordinated marketing channels has replaced many of the simple buy-sell relationships in the market system with "authority subsystems,"[1] or other organizational processes under the direction of a channel leader. Under these conditions, the free play of market forces in the channel is somewhat subsumed by the internal operations of the firm.

Various contractual arrangements have been employed in building authority subsystems within the market structure. This is most apparent in the United States, but is true also in other countries, including Japan. This paper describes the emergence and development of various forms of contractual marketing systems in Japan including (1) general environmental factors influencing the evolution of contractual systems; (2) factors and relationships relevant to the use of contractual arrangements for building authority subsystems; (3) the emergence and development of several forms of contractual systems; and (4) some lessons from Japanese experience.

Economic Growth and The Distribution Revolution

Two factors seem relevant to the evolution of contractual marketing systems in Japan: economic growth; and the distribution revolution. The

* Kobe University, Japan. This study was partially supported by a grant from the Hideo Yoshida Foundation.

Japanese economy has shown rapid and constant economic growth since World War II, and especially since 1960. Generally speaking, economic growth is a function of the level of industrial investment, especially investment in heavy industry. But the ultimate determinant of economic growth is the consumption level, and production and consumption are related to one another through the distribution system. Rapid economic growth will have significant influence upon the evolution of domestic distribution systems; in turn, evolving distribution systems are necessary to sustain a high rate of economic growth.[2] The interrelationship is illustrated in the rapid change in distribution systems in Japan over the past decade, which has become known as the distribution revolution.[3]

The significance of the distribution revolution is most apparent against the background of Japanese marketing practice prior to it.[4] First, many manufacturers did not engage in any marketing activities, leaving the distribution and promotion of their products to the discretion of wholesalers. Second, the traditional retail structure in Japan was highly unprogressive and labor intensive. It was characterized by Y. Arakawa in 1961 as follows:[5]

> the . . . retail trade structure in Japan remains at a relatively undeveloped stage. More than one-half of all retail sales are made by old-type pre-capitalistic small stores operated by owner-managers and unpaid family workers. Department stores . . . are the only modern and fully capitalistic retail institution in Japan.

Third, Japanese manufacturers and retailers were connected with each other through long and complex wholesale channels of distribution. The wholesaler, and in particular the general trading company, dominated the channel of distribution in many kinds of business.

The distribution revolution which began in the mid-1950s in Japan effected great structural changes in these traditional distribution arrangements. One aspect of the revolution was the introduction, by consumer-goods *manufacturers,*[a] of advertising and other marketing activities of products aimed at the ultimate consumer. The change is shown in the rapid increase in total national advertising expenditures over the past fifteen years, as shown in Table 12-1. Manufacturers also attempted to build marketing channel systems in which the distribution of their products might be effectively controlled all the way to the ultimate consumer. It is probable that this marketing channel control problem is the most important that most marketing-oriented Japanese manufacturers had to solve.

At the beginning of the 1960s, still further changes in traditional distribution systems were induced by the introduction of supermarkets.[b] Super-

---

[a] These included home electric appliances, automobiles, synthetic fibers, processed foods, drugs, and cosmetics.

[b] Most supermarkets in Japan originated as small, independent retailers dealing in

Table 12-1
Total Advertising Expenditures in Japan by Kind of Business

	1957	1959	1961	1963	1965	1967	1969
Total Expenditure (in Billion Yen)	¥ 770	1,098	1,666	2,359	2,696	3,570	4,931
Drugs	16.1%	13.0%	12.1%	11.6%	13.8%	8.9%	8.1%
Cosmetics	9.7	9.2	7.5	6.8	7.5	7.6	6.6
Publishing	6.6	6.6	4.4	4.5	4.2	4.5	4.1
Food Products	10.8	13.1	13.6	13.0	17.8	19.1	15.9
Banking & Insurance	3.2	4.2	5.8	6.5	4.6	4.3	6.5
Machinery	13.5	18.4	19.9	18.1	16.3	17.8	20.6
Textile Mill Products	3.3	4.0	4.5	4.4	3.4	2.9	2.1
Miscellaneous	4.1	5.4	6.8	7.2	4.4	5.1	5.4
Department Store	5.2	4.4	3.9	3.5	3.0	2.9	2.9
Amusement	6.4	4.5	2.8	2.0	2.4	2.2	2.1
Transportation	1.0	1.0	0.3	1.1	2.2	2.0	1.9
Others	20.2	16.2	17.8	21.3	20.4	22.7	23.8
	100.0	100.0	100.0	100.0	100.0	100.0	100.0

Note: Media included are television, radio, magazines, and newspapers.
Source: Dentsu Advertising Agency (research division), Tokyo.

market growth rates in terms of the number of stores, number of full-time employees, and annual sales are shown in Table 12-2. Supermarkets accounted for 7.6 percent of total retail sales in 1968; however, this might be an underestimate, because the Japanese census classifies the largest supermarkets as department stores. Another estimate reports that the supermarket share of total retail sales was 11.5 percent in 1968, whereas that of department stores was 10.0 percent.[6] As indicated in Table 12-3, the three largest supermarket chains rank with the ten largest retailers in Japan. Judging from their growth rates, supermarkets may be expected to surpass department stores in share of total retail sales in the near future.

Some of the effects of the distribution revolution may be seen in changes of consumption behavior by ultimate consumers in Japan. As indicated in Table 12-4, proportional expenditures for housing and furniture have been increasing, whereas those for food and clothing have been decreasing. The increase in housing cost is largely accounted for by increased land values as the growth process of major cities has accelerated. The increase in expenditures for furniture is more related to the rapid diffusion of consumer durable goods in the economy illustrated in Table 12-5.

The growth of the self-service, price-cutting supermarket is understandable given the inflationary tendencies in Japan in the 1960s, which have resulted in a seven percent per year rise in the cost of living. As indi-

---

clothing and apparel. Many of them expanded and became chains. Department stores and general trading companies tried to open supermarkets after an initial indifference to the business form, but with few exceptions their attempts were not profitable.

Table 12-2
The Growth of Supermarketing in Japan

		Rate of Increase		Percentage Distribution		
	Total	1966/ 1964	1968/ 1966	1964	1966	1968
A. *Number of Stores*		%	%	%	%	%
All Retailing	1,389,222	5.4	1.0	100.0	100.0	100.0
Self-Service Stores *	7,062	32.3	47.4	0.3	0.3	0.5
Department Stores **	239	10.2	16.0	0.01	0.01	0.02
B. *Full-Time Employees*						
All Retailing	4,241,825	10.0	1.2	100.0	100.0	100.0
Self-Service Stores	142,896	17.5	36.0	2.3	2.5	3.4
Department Stores	142,160	10.3	7.1	3.2	3.2	3.4
C. *Annual Sales* (in Millions)						
All Retailing	¥ 13,615,365 ($37,820)	28.0	27.4	100.0	100.0	100.0
Self-Service Stores	¥ 1,028,570 ($2,854)	48.1	77.0	4.7	5.4	7.6
Department Stores	¥ 1,286,081 ($3,572)	23.3	32.4	9.4	9.1	9.4
(¥ 360 = $1)						

* A self-service store is one which has more than 100 square meters (120 square yards) of selling space, and where self-service is applied to more than 50 percent of its selling space. This corresponds to what is called a supermarket in Japan.

** A department store is defined as an establishment having more than fifty employees, selling a variety of consumer products, and having more than 3,000 square meters (3,590 square yards) of floor space in large cities (Tokyo, Yokohama, Nagoya, Kyoto, Osaka, Kobe, Kitakyusyu), or more than 1,500 square meters (1,800 square yards) in other cities.

Source: Tsusho Sangyo Daijin Kanbo Chosa Tokei Bu (Research and Statistics Division, Ministry of International Trade and Industry), *Waga Kuni no Shogyo, 1969* (*Commerce In Our Country, 1969*).

Table 12-3
The Ten Largest Retailers in Japan, 1968

Company	Number of Stores Operated	Sales (in Billions)
Daimaru (D)	4	¥ 1,257 or $3.492
Mitsukoshi (D)	11	1,229 or 3.414
Takashimaya (D)	4	1,120 or 3.111
Matsuzakaya (D)	5	896 or 2.489
Daiei (S)	38	750 or 2.083
Seibu (D)	7	633 or 1.758
Seiyu-store (S)	55	550 or 1.528
Hankyu (D)	4	520 or 1.444
Isetan (D)	2	506 or 1.406
Jasco (S)	71	500 or 1.389

(¥ 360 = $1.)
D = Department Store.
S = Supermarket.
Source: *Nihon Seni Keizai Kenkyusho.*

cated in Table 12-6, the major product lines in supermarkets have been food, clothing, and apparel. The central role played by sales of clothing and apparel differentiate the Japanese supermarket from its North American counterpart.

In summary, the term distribution revolution refers to changes in the structure of Japanese distribution systems resulting from the marketing activities of large consumer goods manufacturers, the growth of supermar-

Table 12-4
Monthly Family Consumption Expenditures, by Type, 1956-1968
Average of All Families in Japanese Cities with More than 50,000 People

	1956	1958	1960	1962	1964	1966	1968
Consumption Expenditures (in Thousands of Yen)	24 or $67	27 or $75	31 or $86	39 or $108	49 or $136	56 or $156	66 or $183
Expenditures for:							
Food	45.0%	43.8%	41.6%	39.0%	37.9%	37.1%	35.6%
Housing	4.3	4.7	4.5	5.2	4.8	5.2	5.4
Furniture	2.5	3.5	4.4	5.0	5.0	4.9	6.1
Fuel & Light	5.1	5.0	5.1	4.9	4.5	4.6	4.3
Clothing	12.2	11.5	12.0	12.8	11.9	11.1	11.0
Miscellaneous	30.9	31.5	32.4	33.1	35.9	37.1	37.5
	100.0	100.0	100.0	100.0	100.0	100.0	100.0

Source: Sorifu Tokeikyoku (Statistics Bureau, Prime Minister's Office), *Kakei Chosa Nenpo* (Annual Survey of Family Budgets).

Table 12-5
Rate of Market Saturation by Major Consumer Durable Goods, Japan, 1959–1969

	1959	1960	1961	1962	1963	1964	1965	1966	1967	1968	1969
Radio set	95.0	85.0	87.4	82.6	81.8	74.6	72.9	—	80.0	76.3	77.3
Transistor radio	—	16.5	26.0	34.3	41.8	46.6	55.8	57.9			
Electric fan	28.6	34.4	41.9	50.6	60.6	67.4	77.3	79.1	80.9	82.7	86.9
Washing machine	33.0	40.6	50.2	58.1	66.4	72.2	78.1	81.8	84.0	76.7	89.8
TV set	23.6	44.7	62.5	79.4	88.7	92.9	95.0	95.7	97.3	97.4	95.1
Refrigerator	5.7	10.1	17.2	28.0	39.1	54.1	68.7	75.1	80.7	84.5	90.1
Electric cleaner	—	7.7	15.4	24.5	33.1	40.8	48.5	55.3	59.8	63.0	70.3
Stereo set	—	—	3.7	7.2	10.8	13.4	20.1	23.9	25.8	28.9	32.5
Tape recorder	—	—	—	5.4	9.0	13.0	20.2	24.1	27.3	29.1	32.0
Air-cooler	—	—	0.4	0.7	1.3	1.8	2.6	3.2	4.3	5.6	6.5
Color TV set	—	—	—	—	—	—	—	0.4	2.2	6.7	14.6
Passenger car	—	—	2.8	5.1	6.1	6.6	10.5	13.5	11.0	14.6	18.6

Source: Keizai Kikaku Cho (Economic Planning Agency), *Shohi to Chochiku no Doko* (*Survey of Consumer's Expenditures and Savings*, 1969).

Table 12-6
Percentage of Sales by Type of Products, Japanese Supermarkets, 1963–1970

Year	Food	Apparel & Clothing	Miscellaneous for Home Use	Electric Appliances	Drugs & Cosmetics	Restaurant	Total	Total Sales (Ten Thousands Yen) (Thousands of Dollars)
1963	30.2%	50.4%	10.8%	1.2%	3.9%	3.5%	100%	¥ 15,483 $430
1964	30.3	49.4	11.6	1.3	4.0	3.4	100	21,943 $610
1965	30.0	49.6	11.6	1.4	3.9	3.5	100	27,553 $765
1966	32.9	48.2	10.7	1.7	4.0	2.5	100	39,531 $1,098
1967	32.7	47.5	8.4	1.9	4.0	5.5	100	54,128 $1,504
1968	32.1	48.7	8.4	2.0	3.6	5.2	100	78,766 $2,188
1969	30.6	49.9	9.0	2.1	3.2	5.0	100	109,820 $3,051
1970	30.6	49.6	9.1	2.2	3.3	5.1	100	155,770 $4,327

¥ 360 = $1.
Note: 1963–1965, the largest 59 companies.
1966–1968, the largest 81 companies.
1969–1970, the largest 100 companies.
Source: *Nihon Seni Keizai Kenkyusho.*

keting, and the corresponding adjustments and channel expansions by retailers, wholesalers, and manufacturers. The various forms of contractual marketing systems in Japan have evolved under the impetus of this distribution revolution.

The Analytical Framework

Vertical marketing relationships between firms may be classified as free and open bargaining, without restrictions; ownership integration, administered marketing channels; and contractual integration.[7] Analytically speaking, it is probably not wise to contrast contractual arrangements directly with alternatives like free and open bargaining, or ownership integration; these alternatives may have quite different values in the cognitive processes of the decision maker involved.

Various forms of contractual arrangments are seen by a decision maker as alternatives in a situation where the preferred alternative of ownership integration is not feasible, and free and open bargaining systems are not acceptable. There are a variety of reasons why a firm in the channel might want to organize the market. In the literature, these are classified into three groupings: factors which contribute to perception of the need to organize the market; factors which point out the direct effects of organizing the market; and factors concerned with the results of organizing the market. These are summarized in Figure 12-1.

Changes in market conditions refer to factors which function as an impetus to organize the market. The most important such factor is the emergence of large firms with wide horizontal bases in terms of sales volume, geographical coverage, and product lines. Such firms may emerge on any level of the distribution channel.

Channel conflicts will differ in their significance depending on whether large firms emerge on the production level or the retailing level of the channel. The growth of large manufacturers is generally accompanied by a decrease in the total number of manufacturers; a readjustment in the number of middlemen then occurs to minimize distribution costs for the channel as a whole.[c] From the manufacturers' viewpoint, these structural readjustments may be perceived as opportunities to absorb the profit of other stages in the channel, or to eliminate duplicated functions between different stages.

Large manufacturers may have the objective of gaining partial monopoly profits, which are denied them in a marketing channel which they do not control. To obtain partial monopoly profits, the manufacturer must both maintain his resale price (and thus his retail price), and must be able to make large volume sales at that price. Two behavior patterns of indepen-

[c] Generally speaking, the numbers of firms at intermediary stages of distribution depend on the numbers of both manufacturers and consumers.[8]

Problem perception	*Direct effects*	*Performance*
(1) changes in market conditions	(1) increasing market power	(1) increasing sales revenue
(2) channel conflicts	(2) improving systems efficiency	(2) reducing distribution costs
(3) introduction of new products	(3) economies in distribution	(3) increasing profit
(4) threats from competing systems		

Figure 12-1. Reasons for Organizing the Japanese Distribution Channel.

dent Japanese middlemen may thwart these objectives. An independent middleman will manipulate the price of merchandise handled to increase his total turnover; when merchandise of both large and small manufacturers is handled, there is a tendency to cut resale prices of large manufacturer's products to the level charged by smaller manufacturers. Also, an independent middleman will generally not make special efforts to push the merchandise of any particular manufacturer, which may thwart the large manufacturer's desire for high volume. From the standpoint of the large manufacturer, channel conflict arises; the behavior patterns of the channel in which he deals are opposed to the objectives which he seeks to attain.[9] The large manufacturer who is introducing *new consumer products* is particularly threatened, because he requires intensive selling, and special demonstrations and services to users to ensure the adoption and diffusion of such new products.

The same kind of process occurs in the case where economic concentration exists at the retailing stage of the channel. The reduction in the number of independent retailers which accompanies the growth of mass merchandisers leads to a reduction in the number of intermediary channel stages (or number of middlemen) and gives mass merchandisers the opportunity to reduce acquisition cost by integrating the wholesaling stages of the channel. Next, mass merchandisers require a stable supply of merchandise to support their mass selling ability; they are induced to expand to control the product development function, perhaps through private branding.

Threats from competing systems as a reason for organizing the market reflect the tensions of independent wholesalers and retailers who are jointly threatened by aggressive moves of large manufacturers or mass merchandisers. The motive may also apply to large manufacturers or mass merchandisers who make a belated attempt to organize the market after competitive efforts have been successful.

The direct effects of organizing the market are (1) increasing market power, for example, controlling distribution and obtaining captive retail outlets in the case of the manufacturer, or securing stable supply channels in the case of the mass merchandiser; (2) improvement of systems efficiencies—a distribution process under the control of a single channel coordinator can gather more accurate market information, improve channel/system inventory control, and stabilize production activities; and (3) economies in distribution: through efficiencies such as larger lot size transactions (by eliminating costs such as selling activities aimed at securing the support of middlemen, or by reducing uncertainty with respect to future output and sales volume of the firm).

The relationship between types of problem perception and types of direct effects are shown in Figure 12-2. The performance effects of organizing the market may be classified into (1) increasing sales revenue, which may be attained through stabilization of the retail price and/or increasing sales volume; (2) reducing the costs of distribution; and (3) increasing profit.

Types of Direct Effects

Problem Perception	(1) Increasing market power	(2) improving systems efficiency	(3) Economy in distribution
(1) Changes in market conditions			X
(2) Channel conflicts	X		
(3) Introduction of new products	X	X	
(4) Threats from competing systems	X	X	X

X indicates the existence of the relationship

Figure 12–2. The Relationship between Problem Perception and Types of Direct Effects.

The direct effect of an increase in market power will be increased sales revenue; the direct effect of increased economies in distribution will be cost savings. Improved systems efficiencies could have the effect of increased sales revenue and/or of cost saving.

However, it is profitability which is emphasized in evaluating the desirability of a form of market organization. For example, ownership integration may increase distribution cost, but will take place so long as the increased cost is more than offset by increased sales revenue through strengthened market power and improved systems efficiency.[10] Costs incurred in ownership integration are of the nature of Chamberlin's "selling cost."[11]

Ownership integration will increase distribution cost for the integrating firm in three situations. First, cost will increase if the integrating firm cannot perform the functions assumed more efficiently than did separate institutions at the channel level taken over. Second, if there is a difference in scale economies among the stages which are integrated under a single ownership, the technical efficiency of the integrating firm will be lower. Third, if there is a discrepancy of assortments among the stages which are to be integrated, it will be more difficult to implement the integration.[12] The discrepancy may occur on several dimensions of assortments: physical and merchandising characteristics of goods, or the proportion of each item in the assortment.

Another factor limiting the profitability of ownership integration is the risk assumed with ownership. Ownership integration lessens the flexibility of functions carried out—while increasing the risk inherent in owning resources. Ownership integration also makes it difficult to transfer risk to another level of the distributive channel.[13]

When it comes to ownership integration, the interrelationships among the firms involved must be conceived of at the level of agency or institution, and not as partial functions and/or a subset of commodities which is part of the product assortment of the firms involved. The significance of contractual relationships is that they exist between firms under separate ownerships and can link one agency to another on the level of either commodities and/or partial activities, or of the institution as a whole. Contractual relations thus become a viable alternative for implementing subsystems where the firm is unable to undertake ownership integration.

The Development of Contractual Marketing Systems Initiated by Large Manufacturers

This section describes the evolution of contractual marketing systems in the home electric appliance industry and in the automobile industry in Japan. The choice of these two is not completely arbitrary; each is representative of growth industries in Japan,[14] and each is an industry where contractual marketing systems have been highly developed. The two cases indicate some of the problems encountered in introducing contractual marketing systems in an industry, and the adaptation process of such systems to subsequent changes in the environment.

Home Electric Appliance Industry

The home electric appliance industry is where contractual marketing systems have been most fully developed in Japan over the past fifteen years. These contractual arrangements have transformed numerous small, subsistence level retail operations into components of a modern marketing channel handling the distribution of a flood of new products.

Prior to 1950, the distribution sector for home electric appliances was composed of small wholesalers and retailers who handled low-priced goods such as radios, electric irons, and electric bulbs. Increased personal incomes, price reductions of consumer appliances resulting from mass production techniques, and increased consumer demands resulting from manufacturer advertising and promotion increased the potential market for new products such as television sets and washing machines in the mid-1950s. Each manufacturer faced the problem of finding distribution channels to adequately service this growing demand.

Initially, manufacturers adopted two strategies to meet this demand. They converted small wholesalers and retailers into agency representatives with whom a manufacturer maintained exclusive or quasiexclusive relationships, and they introduced financial inducements under which a middleman was granted increasing rebates based on volume of goods purchased from a given manufacturer. These linkage strategies created serious problems; they placed middlemen who shifted too quickly from low-priced product assortments to high-priced product assortments in a weak financial position; and they gave each middleman a financial incentive to cut price below the manufacturer's suggested retail price to increase volume. The problems became more serious as manufacturers introduced new products such as refrigerators and electric vacuum cleaners which required dealer demonstration and heavy promotional efforts, and continued dealer servicing—each of which was less likely from a dealer whose motivation was to cut price to achieve volume.

Manufacturers of home electric appliances managed to cope with these problems by making contractual marketing arrangements, first with wholesalers and later with retailers in the channel. Contractual arrangements succeeded in maintaining resale prices, and in helping small subsistence middlemen to consolidate their financial positions. The arrangements made with wholesalers by each manufacturer were of one of two types: the "Toshiba & Hitachi" type, or the "Matsushita" type.

In the "Toshiba & Hitachi" type, the distribution channel sequence was manufacturer → manufacturer's owned sales branch → wholesaler → retailer. Each manufacturer established their sales branches as a separate company, with an agency contract between the sales branch and each wholesaler. Under the agency contract, the sales branch provided wholesalers with allowances or discounts for physical distribution, advertising, and store modernization in return for the wholesaler concentrating most or all of his purchases in the products of that manufacturer.

In the "Matsushita" type (named for its innovator, the Matsushita Electric Industrial Company), there was a mixture of integration through ownership and contractual arrangements. One of several types of wholesaling agencies was established in each geographic region, with the type dependent upon the level of demand and the degree of power held by existing wholesalers in the region.

First, new wholesaling agencies called "National Product Sales Companies" were established in each geographic region to handle the products of Matsushita Electric on an exclusive agency basis. The companies were established by consolidating existing small wholesalers in the region into one company, with half the capital stock of the new venture held by Matsushita Electric. In regions where demand warranted, the exclusive agency was departmentalized by product line: television, electric washing machines, electric refrigerators, and so on. In Tokyo, where existing wholesalers were large and powerful, a compromising strategy of establishing exclusive agencies through joint ventures with existing wholesalers, or establishing a new department handling only Matsushita's products within an existing wholesale operation, was adopted. Matsushita introduced this hybrid system of distribution in 1957, and had it operational by 1959.

The Matsushita type of arrangement had one dominant advantage over the Toshiba & Hitachi type; Matsushita was able to install exclusive dealing contracts with its wholesalers. This guaranteed wholesaler concentration on its product lines, and effectively eliminated intrachannel competition between Matsushita wholesalers. Matsushita was successful in instituting their arrangements because they purchased an ownership interest in many of their wholesalers, and because they were at that time the only Japanese manufacturer who could supply a full line of household electric appliances to wholesalers.

Beginning in 1959, contractual arrangements were extended to the retail level by all manufacturers. The manufacturer, and retailers recommended by respective wholesalers, signed requirements contracts under which the retailer agreed to sell a specified dollar volume of the manufacturer's products over a stated time period; and the manufacturer agreed to grant specified rebates, provide managerial guidance, and supply promotional materials to the retailer. No attempt was made by manufacturers to acquire the retailer's capital stock, and no exclusive dealing agreements were made. However, the manufacturer could exercise control over retailers which approximated that available under ownership integration by gradually raising the dollar and/or percentage requirements under the contract and basing the rebate paid each dealer on the strength of his loyalty to the manufacturer (measured by his performance vis-à-vis the requirements arrangement).

The five manufacturers in the home electric appliance industry which undertook these contractual systems have been able to raise their industry status and market share significantly; Matsushita, which developed the strongest contractual system, has shown the largest sales gains. All five contractual systems may jointly have functioned as an effective barrier to entry even to this rapidly growing industry; there has been no successful entry to the home electric appliance industry since the major manufacturers instituted their respective contractual systems.

The contractual systems as now constituted are facing some pressing problems, particularly at the retail stage. First, manufacturers are shifting their major marketing efforts to higher-priced items such as color television, air conditioners, and stereo sets which are beyond the financial and technical capabilities of the small retail outlets in the system. Second, the strategy of maintaining retail prices through the contractually integrated systems has permitted the growth of large discount stores, and the entry of supermarkets into the retailing sector of the industry. The share of retail market accounted for by large discount stores and supermarkets has increased dramatically in recent years.

No conclusive ways to meet these problems have been observed, although some recent attempts have been made. One move is to initiate and strengthen the linkage between manufacturers and mass merchandisers. Mitsubishi Electric recently contracted to produce goods under the private brand of Daiei, the largest supermarket chain in Japan.[15] The initial contract is restricted to electric fans, a product in the mature stage of its life cycle. It is expected that the contract will be extended at least over other mature-stage products. A second move is to improve intrafirm organization within channel systems by strengthening the cooperative relationships among member retailers.[d] Manufacturers have established cooperative assistance centers for retailers in each region; the centers supply to each store an analysis of its trading area and market potential, perform accounting and other data processing tasks and some employee training, and attempt to organize consumers in the area through communication with "opinion leaders."[18]

Automobile Industry

The case of the automobile industry illustrates the need for contractual systems to adapt to the growth and change of industry demand. In the

[d] These are based on the concept of marketing channel systems as an extension of the manufacturer's own internal organization.[16] Marketing theory in Japan has stressed the peculiar nature of marketing channel systems as organizations. According to Japanese theory, channel systems possess both properties of intrafirm organization, and market organization in terms of coordination mechanisms. As a result, conflict and cooperation always coexist in marketing channel systems.[17]

automobile industry over the past fifteen years, there has been a rapid growth of demand but on a selective basis; demand for trucks and buses has decreased relative to total demand, while demand for passenger cars has increased greatly.

Prior to 1955, automobile manufacturers distributed their products through wholly-owned wholesaling agencies, and through franchised dealers. Each franchised dealer handled all the products of the manufacturer, had an exclusive territory, and was part of a relatively small franchise system; in 1953 Toyota Motor Company had only 49 franchisees in all of Japan.

The first basic change in this system was for the manufacturer to break up the general franchise of all his products into separate franchises for each model of passenger car, or for separate products. This was done either by transferring existing franchises, or by establishing new ones for newly developed models.

Corresponding structural adjustments of the franchise systems followed one of several patterns, depending on the size of demand in the given geographic region and the nature of the product. For marketing high-status passenger cars in metropolitan areas, the retailing stage of distribution was usually vertically integrated through ownership. Toyota established their own wholly-owned retail outlets in Tokyo in 1953, claiming that the importance of the Tokyo market required such specialized outlets and that their systems' efficiency would be greatly improved by such vertical ownership integration. It was also felt that marketing intelligence about shifts in consumer demand would be more easily obtained from a wholly-owned system.[19]

The second structural change was the splitting off of the franchise for passenger cars from existing general franchisees to specialized franchisees, as mentioned above. The third change, introduced in the early 1960s, was the shift from closed, exclusive dealer territories to open, competitive territories in areas of large demand to encourage intrabrand competition. As a result of these structural adjustments, marketing channel systems for automobiles have the structure indicated in Figure 12-3; a mixture of vertical integration through ownership, and various forms of contractual arrangements.

The Development of Contractual Marketing Systems Initiated by Wholesalers and Retailers

Supermarket Industry

The development of contractual marketing systems relating to the supermarket industry is in its infancy; however contractual systems are under development as attempts to solve two problems confronting the industry.

The competition faced by most Japanese supermarkets has shifted from

product class	Size of demand in the region: large	Size of demand in the region: small
high status model	Vertical integration through ownership	Franchise system with closed territory
model for popular use	Franchise system with open territory	Franchise system with closed territory

Figure 12–3. The Structure of Marketing Channel Systems for Automobiles in Japan after 1960.

rather easy competition with independent retailers, to more severe competition with other supermarkets. There is in addition a threat that American supermarkets will enter the Japanese market after the liberalization of capital-ownership rules which is expected in the near future. To combat this existing and anticipated competition, major supermarket chains are attempting to extend their local and regional organizations to national organizations. Two types of contractual arrangements are evolving. The first type is aimed at coordinating new store locations among supermarkets, in some cases, by establishing new stores as joint ventures between existing chains.[20] The intent is to restrict or eliminate competition while still allowing supermarket chains to expand their locations geographically.

The second type of contractual system involves an agreement between a supermarket chain and a general trading company. The supermarket agrees to lease its store fixtures from the trading company on a long-term basis. The supermarket can now increase the number of its locations with a lowered requirement for capital investment in fixed equipment.[21] The lease arrangement enables the general trading company to shift their emphasis from industrial goods to consumption goods to adapt to the evolution of the Japanese economy in this direction, and to circumvent the manufacturer-dominated, contractually-tied consumer durable goods area by establishing direct linkages with supermarkets.

Supermarket chains are also using contractual arrangments to increase their countervailing power in the market. As the proportion of both food and home electric appliances in their product assortments has increased in recent years, supermarkets have come into direct competition with national brands in these fields. In response, they have developed two further types of contractual arrangements: the first a retail buying group of supermarket chains to negotiate for nationally branded goods at the lowest possible price; the second to purchase private branded goods from manufacturers.[22] The agreement between Mitsubishi Electric and Daiei, mentioned earlier, is one example of such a contract.

Voluntary Chains

Voluntary chains in Japan have a comparatively short history, and have not developed very extensively. In 1968, annual sales of voluntary chains were estimated at about 5,000 billion yen, about five percent of total retail sales in Japan.[23]

There are two major motivating forces behind the development of voluntary chains in Japan. The first force is the threat posed them by the rapid growth of supermarketing. Independent small retailers in Japan have been protected from the expansion of department stores by a Department Store Law,[e] but not from the expansion of supermarkets, which are ex-

[e] The Law, passed in June 1956, controls the expansion of department stores. A department store is defined as one with more than 3,000 square meters of selling space (3,590

empted from the application of the law. Voluntary chains have been most active in the fields of food, clothing and apparel, drugs, and cosmetics; these form the major part of product assortments carried by supermarkets.

The second motivating force behind the development of voluntary chains is supplied by government subsidies paid to voluntary chains, with the intent of rationalizing the distribution structure and lowering consumer prices in the Japanese economy.

At present, most voluntary chains in Japan are sponsored by only one wholesaler, are local organizations, and have cooperative buying as their major activity.[24] Because affiliated retail stores buy a relatively small proportion of their product assortments from the sponsoring wholesaler, it may be expected that voluntary chains in Japan will continue to grow, at least on a limited basis.

Summary and Concluding Comments

Contractual marketing systems in Japan have been developed primarily by consumer goods manufacturers and by supermarkets. The two cases of home electric appliances and automobiles indicate the patterns of adaptation of contractual systems to growth and to structural changes in an industry. The basic pattern of the adaptation process has been the increase of market coverage without the channel overlaps which are an important cause of channel conflict. The basic strategy involved has been market segmentation based on factors such as the size of demand, the strength of existing wholesalers, and the class of product. Firms have taken advantage of the introduction of new products to adjust the structure of their contractual systems without inducing channel conflict.

Contractual systems are only one part of a mixture of ownership and contractual systems on a vertical and horizontal basis, indicating that more attention must be paid to the interrelationships between contractual and ownership systems. This is particularly true in the supermarket industry in Japan, where the various forms of contractual systems developed are seen by some as a first step towards merger among local supermarket chains.

The development of contractual systems leads to a change in policy-making units in the market from a single firm to a group of firms. This article has discussed contractual systems as effective means of cooperation among firms to maximize joint profit within the system, but has not discussed the mechanisms by which this joint profit is allocated among member firms. Japanese experience indicates that one important factor is the distinctiveness of the manufacturer's products involved; in any case, this internal aspect of joint profit division is closely related to conflict resolution among member firms.

---

square yards) in large cities (Tokyo, Yokohama, Nagoya, Kyoto, Osaka, Kobe, Kitakyusyu), or more than 1500 square meters (1800 square yards) in other cities.

Conflicts within contractual systems seem to remain latent under favorable conditions of industry growth and high joint profit; this is one reason why channel conflict has not yet been a significant problem in the development of contractual systems in Japan. There are indications that Japanese systems will encounter channel conflict in the near future. For example, adoption of open territories in the automobile industry—and the declining share of market going to contractually integrated systems in the home electric appliance industry—will almost certainly engender conflict in these systems. The very complex interorganizational linkages in the supermarket industry may pose serious conflict problems when the growth of this industry levels off.

Notes

1. E. T. Grether, *Marketing and Public Policy,* Englewood Cliffs, New Jersey: Prentice-Hall, Inc. (1966), 81.

2. Similar views are found in Stanley J. Shapiro, "Comparative Marketing and Economic Development," in George Schwartz (ed.), *Science in Marketing,* New York: John Wiley & Sons, Inc. (1965), 398–429; Reed Moyer and Stanley C. Hollander (eds.), *Markets and Marketing in Developing Economies,* Homewood, Illinois: Richard D. Irwin, Inc. (1968); Lee E. Preston, *Marketing Organization and Economic Development: Structure, Products, and Management,* Berkeley, California: Institute of Business and Economic Research, University of California (1969).

3. The term "distribution revolution" was popularized in Japan by two booklets: Syuji Hayashi, *Ryutsu Kakumei: Seihin, Keiro to Shohisha (Distribution Revolution: Product, Channel, and Consumer),* Tokyo: Chyuokoronsha (1962); Yoshihiro Tajima, *Nihon no Ryutsu Kakumei (The Distribution Revolution In Japan),* Tokyo: Nihon Noritsu Kyokai (1962).

4. See Laurence P. Dowd, "Wholesale Marketing in Japan," *The Journal of Marketing* (January, 1959), 257–262; and George A. Elgass, "Marketing in Japan: An Expanding Economy," in William D. Stevens (ed.), *The Social Responsibilities of Marketing,* Chicago: American Marketing Association (1962), 425–433.

5. Yukichi Arakawa, "The Structure of Retail Trade in Japan," *The Annals of the School of Business Administration, Kobe University* (1961), 109. An excellent discussion of retail trade structure in Japan is Yukichi Arakawa, *Kouri Shogyo Kozo Ron (A Theory of Retail Trade Structure),* Tokyo: Chikura Shobo (1962), 245–478.

6. *Nihon no Supamaketto chein (Supermarket Chains In Japan),* Osaka: Nihon Seni Keizai Kenkyusho (1970).

7. For a discussion of these relationships see Donald N. Thompson, "Contractual Marketing Systems: An Overview," *infra.* A discussion similar to that which follows is Wroe Alderson (on the dynamics of market organization, especially monostasy, systasy, and degree of conformability): Wroe Alderson,

Marketing Behavior and Executive Action, Chicago, Illinois: Richard D. Irwin, Inc. (1957), 325–328.

8. See H. H. Baligh and L. E. Richartz, *Vertical Market Structures,* Boston: Allyn and Bacon, Inc. (1967).

9. Fujiya Morishita, *Gendai Shogyo Keizai Ron (Economic Theory of Distributive Trade),* Tokyo: Yuhikaku (1960), 297–300.

10. See Joe S. Bain, *Industrial Organization,* 2nd ed., New York: John Wiley & Sons, Inc. (1968), 381.

11. Edward H. Chamberlin, *The Theory of Monopolistic Competition: A Re-orientation of the Theory of Value,* 8th ed., Cambridge: Harvard University Press (1962). The costs associated with integration are discussed in Robert H. Cole, "General Discussion of Vertical Integration," in Nugent Wedding (ed.), *Vertical Integration in Marketing,* Bureau of Economic and Business Research, Bulletin Series Number 74, Urbana, Illinois: University of Illinois (1952), 13–14.

12. David R. Craig and Werner K. Gabler, "The Competitive Struggle for Market Control," *Annals of the American Academy of Political And Social Science* (May, 1940), 91.

13. See Takemasa Ishihara, "Chaneru Ruikei Sentakuron Hihan: Makettengu Chaneru Tokihiki no Gainenka" (Critique on Topological Theories of Channel Member Choice: A Conceptualization of Marketing Channel Transactions), in Gendai Makettengu Kenkyu Kai (Study Group on Modern Marketing), *Makettengu Kodo to Kankyo (Marketing Behavior and Its Environment),* Tokyo: Chikura Shobo (1969), 133–134.

14. This is seen from "The Fortune Directory: The 200 Largest Industrials Outside the United States (Ranked by Sales)," *Fortune* (August, 1970), 142–147.

15. *Asahi Shinbun (Asahi Daily News)* (May 1, 1970).

16. American and Canadian theories of marketing channel systems are represented by such works as Valentine F. Ridgeway, "Administration of Manufacturer-Dealer Systems," *Administrative Science Quarterly* (March, 1957), 464–483; Wroe Alderson, *Marketing Behavior;* Bruce Mallen, "Conflict and Cooperation in Marketing Channels," in L. George Smith (ed.), *Reflections on Progress in Marketing,* Chicago: American Marketing Association (1964), 65–85.

17. See Masanori Tamura, "An Analytical Framework for Marketing Channel Systems," *Rokkodai Ronshu* (December, 1965), 38–50; or, Tsutomu Furo, *The Theory of Marketing Channel Behavior,* Tokyo: Chikura Shobo (1968).

18. *Nihon Keizai Shinbun (Japan Economic News)* (March 3, 1970).

19. Toyota Motor Sales Inc., *Toyota Jidosha Hanbai Kabushiki Gaisha no Ayumi* (History of Toyota Motor Sales, Inc.) (1962), 97–99.

20. *Nihon Keizai Shinbun (Japan Economic News)* (March 27, 1970; April 17, 1970).

21. *Ibid.* (August 13, 1970).

22. *Ibid.* (April 6, 1970).

23. Chushyo Sangyo Sho, Kigyo Kyoku (Small and Medium Enterprise Bureau, Ministry of International Trade and Industry), *Ryutsu Kindaika No Tenbo to Kadai* (*Perspectives and Tasks in Modernizing the System of Distribution*), Tokyo: Okurasho Insatsukyoku (Printing Bureau of the Ministry of Finance) (1968), 59.

24. Yukichi Takebayashi, *Borantari Chein no Kenkyu* (*A Study of Voluntary Chains*), Tokyo: Chickura Shobo (1969), 250–282.

13 The Development of Contractual Marketing Systems in the Textile Industry in Japan

Takemasa Ishihara*

Introduction

Distribution structures in Japan have traditionally been dominated by wholesalers; the best example of this is the history of the cotton textile industry.[1] Since World War II, and especially in the sixties, wholesaler-dominated distribution structures have undergone great change. One reason for this change was the introduction of synthetic fibers to the textile industry, and the resulting competition among cotton, rayon, and synthetics. The change was accompanied by the introduction of contractual marketing systems by large manufacturers in the industry, and their expansion in parallel with the older distribution structures.

Two major issues arise. One is the question of how and why wholesalers could dominate the distribution structure during the prewar period in the cotton textile industry. The answer provides one key to the genesis of contractual systems in the industry. The second issue concerns the present function of wholesalers. While the absolute status of wholesalers has declined since the war, most of them still perform various important functions in contractual systems. This paper will consider the two issues of wholesaler position and functions, starting with a review of the history of the textile industry in Japan, and a discussion of the characteristics of current contractual arrangements in that industry.

The Distribution Structure For Cotton Textiles During the Pre-War Period

Generally speaking, the status of distributors (either wholesalers or retailers) is dependent upon their size relative to the producers or distributors with which they do business. If producers are small and geographically scattered, wholesalers are needed to assemble and distribute products. Small-scale production provides the possibility for relatively large whole-

* Osaka City University, Japan.

salers to dominate both producers and other smaller wholesalers. If producers can grow relatively large, the status of wholesalers is comparatively weakened; this has been the case in the textile industry in Japan.

The cotton textile industry in Japan began to grow rapidly at the beginning of the 1890s; spinning was the core of the industry, and the most rapid expansion was found in the spinning trades. Spinners formed the All Japan Cotton Spinners' Association cartel (JSA) in 1882, and it functioned as a monopolistic organization from 1908 to its dissolution.[a] All the processors (weavers, knitters, dyers, final producers) were smaller and less organized than were spinners, with most of them in scattered producing districts.

While the rapid growth of the Japanese textile industry was due largely to rising exports of yarn and fabrics, all the raw cotton used in the spinning process had to be supplied through imports.[b] Thus textile exporters and raw cotton importers each played important roles, as did domestic wholesalers. Some specialty wholesalers functioned not only as importers and exporters, but as cotton yarn merchants and sometimes cotton fabric merchants. These diversified wholesalers grew relatively large; they are referred to subsequently as "textile merchant wholesalers," or simply as "merchant wholesalers."[c]

As indicated, spinners grew rapidly and formed the JSA cartel, so it was almost impossible for wholesalers to dominate the spinners. In general, it was the small processors that were dominated by wholesalers, but the domination structures were complicated. In most cases, small processors had no direct contact with large merchant wholesalers, but only with district wholesalers or clothiers, who bought cotton yarn from merchant wholesalers. The district wholesalers and clothiers exercised direct domination over processors, and the merchant wholesalers over the district wholesalers. Weavers bought yarn from district wholesalers or clothiers and sold fabrics to the same wholesalers or clothiers; the district wholesalers frequently financed the weavers during the weaving process. This system, through which wholesalers dominated processors, became known as the "putting-out system."[5]

As indicated, merchant wholesalers engaged in foreign trade as well

---

[a] The strong JSA cartel may be the most important reason why spinners remained free from control by the Zaibatsu Konzern during the prewar period.[2]

[b] The spinning industry obtained raw cotton in the domestic Japanese market in its early years; with the growth of the industry, Japan's need for cotton could not be met through increasing domestic cultivation. When import duties on raw cotton were abolished in 1896, the Japanese spinning industry became wholly dependent on foreign cotton.[3]

[c] During the prewar period, each Zaibatsu had its own trading department; good examples are Mitsui-Bussan and Mitsubishi-Shoji. Foreign trade was highly concentrated in these Zaibatsu trading companies. The concentration ratio for these two companies alone during 1937–1943 was 28.6 percent. Merchant wholesalers independent of Zaibatsu existed only in the textile and steel industries.[4]

as in domestic trade; they were significantly larger than district wholesalers in each segment. In the domestic segment of trade merchant wholesalers sometimes dominated processors directly; but whether direct or indirect control was exercised, merchant wholesalers stood as channel leaders, and controlled virtually all flows of goods from yarn to final consumer products.

Why Merchant Wholesalers Dominated Processors

Why did merchant wholesalers rather than spinners dominate small wholesalers and processors? The answer stems from the selling policy of the large spinners, who sold their products to cotton yarn merchants, most of whom were merchant wholesalers. The spinners had no further interest in the processing or distribution process for their products after sale.

The spinners undertook this truncated distribution policy for a number of reasons. First, markets for Japanese textiles expanded continually over several decades; the Sino-Japanese War of 1894–5, the Russo-Japanese War of 1904–5, and World War I allowed Japan to expand its foreign markets for textiles. As long as textile markets were assured, markets for yarn were also assured, and spinners did not experience much competitive pressure.

Second, most of the spinners united in the JSA cartel; the unity of spinners in JSA was so strong that it has often been described as a model cartel for the world. Through JSA, spinners were able to survive curtailed operations during every period of depression. (Curtailed operations were so frequent that it is sometimes said the history of the Japanese spinning industry was one of curtailment of operations. For 47 years—from 1890 to 1937—eleven different curtailment programs were employed, with the aggregate time period involved in excess of 20 years.[6]) Severe selling competition was thus not a factor in the Japanese cotton textile market in any period. JSA signed reciprocal exclusive contracts with both the Raw Cotton Importers' Association (RCIA) and with the Cotton Yarn Merchants' Association (CYMA).[7] Spinners outside JSA could not buy raw cotton from the members of RCIA, and importers outside RCIA could not sell goods to the members of JSA. Identical relations existed between JSA and CYMA.[8] Such contracts assured spinners of outlets for their cotton yarn.

Third, the large merchant wholesalers functioned more skillfully than could the spinners working on their own. The services provided by merchant wholesalers to spinners are illustrative. For example, the price of raw cotton in Japan, purchased through merchant wholesalers, was actually lower than the price for the same product in the United States, the country of origin.[9] In part this was because freight was less expensive in marine transportation than in land transportation, and the Japanese shipping industry was highly developed. But low shipping costs aside, spinners could not purchase raw cotton directly as cheaply as they could purchase it through merchant wholesalers. In domestic trade, merchant wholesalers also performed financing, merchandising, and other functions for smaller wholesalers and for processors.

Fourth, the price of both raw cotton and yarn fluctuated frequently. Spinners who engaged in buying raw cotton and processing yarn directly would have had to bear the risk of these price fluctuations. Faced with such risks, spinners generally chose to avoid the distribution process and to concentrate on the spinning process.

So spinners simply sold yarn to merchant wholesalers, and did not intervene in the subsequent flow of product. This policy enabled wholesalers to dominate the distribution structure, and to dominate processors and other smaller wholesalers. The distribution structure ultimately became very complicated; data are not available to enable the relationships involved to be graphed in their entirety. The relations existing among spinners, wholesalers, and weavers are shown in Figure 13-1.[10]

In summary, if the concept of marketing involves anything more than simple selling, there was no marketing activity in the Japanese textile industry prior to World War II. Some marketing systems existed, but these were putting-out systems as distinguished from contractual marketing systems.

The Japanese Textile Industry During World War II

World War II devastated the physical resources of the textile industry in Japan. Further, government controls under the wartime economic system produced great structural changes in the textile industry.

Prior to the war, the textile industry had contributed much in foreign exchange reserves to the economy as the most important of Japan's export industries. It also proved a drain on currency reserves, as raw cotton was almost entirely obtained through imports. The import of raw cotton became an increasing burden on a government which needed foreign currency to purchase munitions and supplies for an anticipated war; thus, the textile industry came under heavy government currency restrictions.

The Cotton Export-Import Link System

In 1938, the Japanese government introduced a Cotton Export-Import Link System, under which the import of raw cotton was permitted only

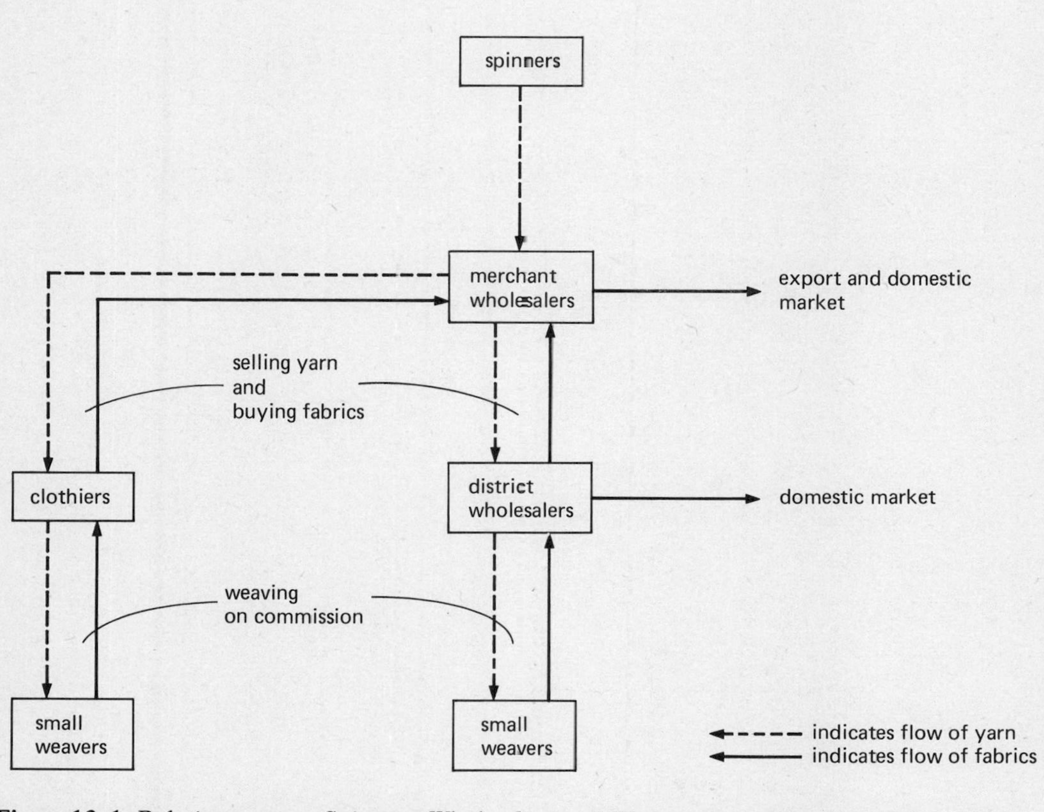

Figure 13–1. Relations among Spinners, Wholesalers, and Weavers during Pre-World War II Period.

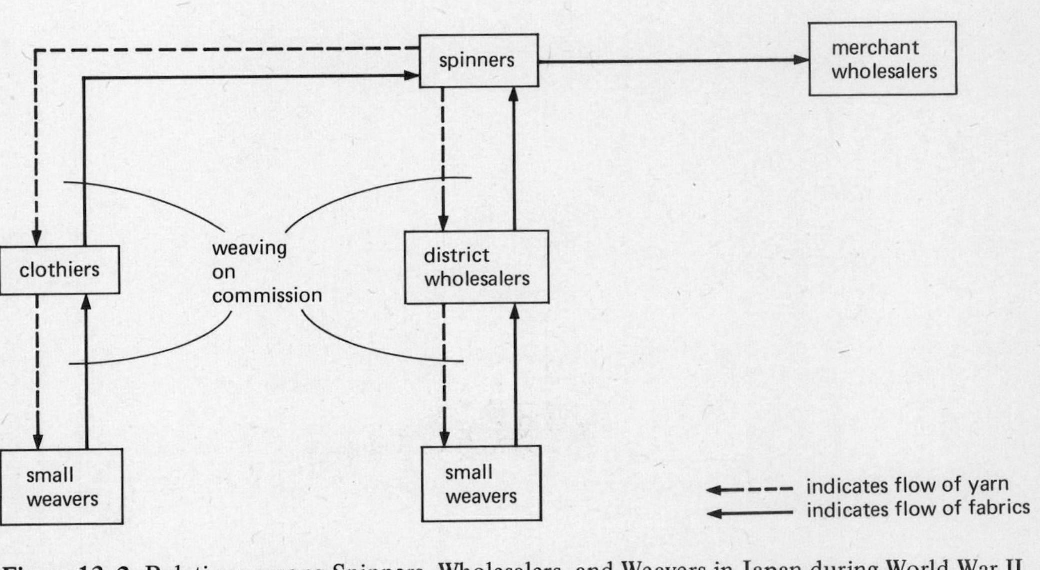

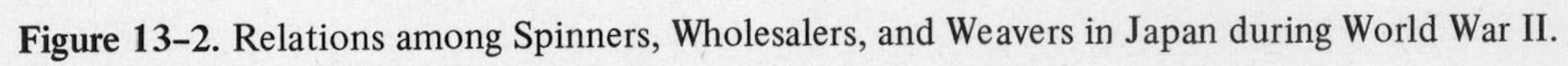

Figure 13–2. Relations among Spinners, Wholesalers, and Weavers in Japan during World War II.

insofar as it offset an equivalent foreign currency-earning export of fabric.[11] (At that time, the export of fabric was more important than the export of yarn). However it was spinners who were the consumers of raw cotton, and weavers and other processors who produced the fabrics which were exported. Though merchant wholesalers already provided some connection between spinners and processors, the inception of the Link System required more direct contact between them. Spinners had to have direct contact with weavers and other processors, or with clothiers and district wholesalers. The contact between them had to be tighter than that which existed in "Selling yarn and buying fabrics"; it took the eventual form of weaving on commission. Figure 13-2 illustrates relations among spinners, wholesalers, and weavers in the same producing district as is illustrated in Figure 13-1.[12]

A comparison of Figure 13-2 with Figure 13-1 indicates the change of relationships which occurred. Spinners began to exert direct domination over district wholesalers, clothiers, and weavers. Spinners and district wholesalers or clothiers were connected through the process of weaving on commission, in which wholesalers or clothiers acted as agents of the spinners. District wholesalers and clothiers became subordinated to spinners, who could also (although less directly) dominate weavers as efficiently as if they had ownership control. Merchant wholesalers were generally eliminated from activity in the flow of yarn, and were confined to intervening in the flow of fabrics. Their functions even in this fabric flow were restricted by governmental controls.

Government Control over Domestic Distribution of Textiles

Japanese government control over the domestic distribution of textile products was begun in 1940, and Control Rules for the Distribution and Consumption of Textiles were introduced in 1942.[13] The Rules required a rearrangement of the distribution structure for textile products. Four types of control companies were set up: manufacturing control companies (A-type) that would control the production of textile goods; manufacturing and rationing companies (B-type) that would control production and distribution of specific goods; primary rationing companies (C-type) that would be the central control agency for distribution, and be made up of primary or central wholesalers; and district rationing companies (D-type) that would be local control agencies for distribution and be made up of secondary or local wholesalers. Spinners had to buy their materials from raw cotton suppliers according to a government-established quota and had to sell yarns to either A-type or B-type companies. A-type companies assigned products to weavers and sold fabrics to C-type companies, who in turn sold them to D-type companies after providing the necessary

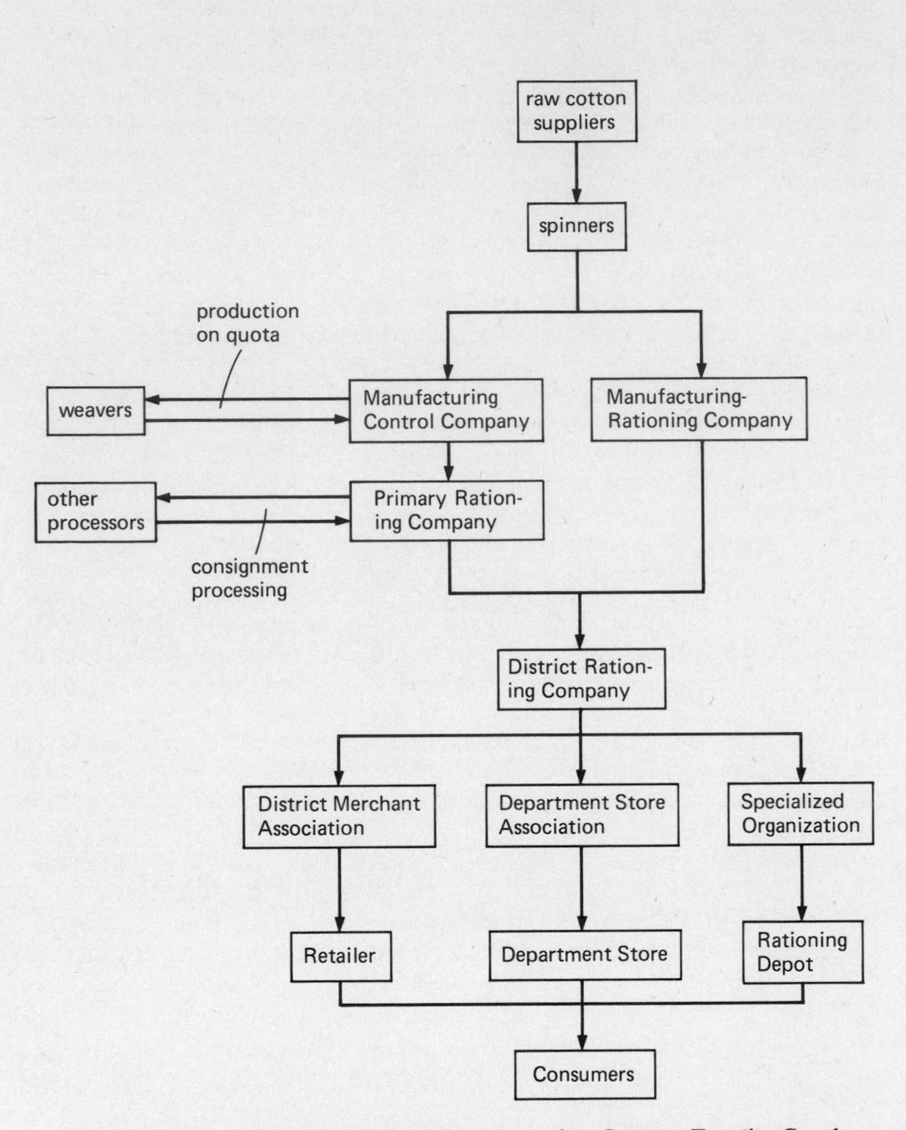

Figure 13-3. The Distribution Structure for Cotton Textile Goods under Governmental Control in Japan during World War II.

processing. All the products of B-type companies were sold to D-type companies—who sold them in turn to district merchant associations, department store associations, or similar retail organizations. The distribution structure as established under the control rules is shown in Figure 13-3. Merchant wholesalers, operating almost entirely under governmental control and quota systems, could no longer dominate processors in the same sense they had during the prewar period.

Another of the wholesalers' traditional functional activities disappeared with the government's assumption (under the rules) of control over consumption patterns for textile products. A clothing coupon system was set up under which consumers could buy clothing only with a ration coupon assigned by the government. Virtually all selling problems thus disappeared for distributors, who simply rationed their output to buyers according to the coupon allocation system.

Other Influences of the War on the Textile Industry

World War II also produced governmental pressure on spinners to combine their operations. Eighty-two spinners in 1937 were reduced through reorganization and liquidation to ten very large spinners by 1945.[14] Although the JSA cartel was dissolved in 1942, the small number of remaining spinners provided a market structure which encouraged oligopolistic selling practices after the war. Another effect of the war was the physical damage sustained by textile-producing equipment, and the general obsolescence of this equipment due to inadequate replacement. The number of usable spinning machines in Japan in 1945 was only 26.8 percent of the total in 1941.[15]

Reconstruction of the Japanese Textile Industry and the Advent of Competition between Cotton and Synthetic Textiles

After the war, a dramatic reconstruction of the Japanese textile industry began; one motivating force was the tremendous backlog of demand for clothing which had been effectively suppressed by wartime controls. However the essential factor contributing to the rebuilding of the industry was the initial boom in demand stemming from the beginning of the Korean War in 1950 and 1951. During this period the export of textile products increased rapidly, and the Japanese textile industry again became the world's leading exporter.[d] Given the enormous demand, under which large

[d] This does not mean that the Japanese textile industry was operating beyond its

spinners could earn considerable profits, many small spinners reentered the industry. The influx of many small spinners made it difficult for the larger spinners to continue to restrict domestic textile output (and maintain prices) successfully.

For merchant wholesalers, the most important postwar event was the dissolution of two giant monopolistic general trading companies, Mitsui-Bussan Co. and Mitsubishi-Shoji Co. Their forced dissolution ended their status as holding companies, and their wartime role as the core of the Zaibatsu.[e] This was the beginning of differentiation of textile wholesalers into several classes, and of the advent of general trading companies. The removal of wartime controls and restrictions opened the way for wholesalers to perform independent commercial activities; however, wartime damage and inflation made it too difficult for any but the vary largest textile merchant wholesalers to rebuild to their prewar size.[f]

The Korean War boom did not continue, and a depression in the industry followed from 1952 to 1953, complicated by the considerable excess capacity which had developed in spinning. The price of yarn continued to rise as the price of fabric dropped. Many wholesalers faced cancellation of export contracts made during the boom; this cancellation combined with declining world prices drove many wholesalers deeply into debt to spinners and rayon manufacturers. The declining profitability of textile products during this industry recession encouraged the rapid evolution of the large textile wholesalers to general trading companies.[g]

Thus, even during this brief period of recession the large spinners

---

prewar level. Reconstruction of the industry was heavily dependent upon rayon and synthetic textile production. The production of cotton yarn had not as of 1970 recovered its 1937 level.

[e] Dissolution of these two companies, which was forced by the occupation authorities in 1947, was extreme. Mitsui-Bussan was broken into more than 200 companies and Mitsubishi-Shoji into 139 companies. However, the Excess Economic Concentration Removal Law, the most important legal foundation for the dissolution of the Zaibatsu, was relaxed in 1948, and in 1949 the antimonopoly law was also relaxed. Reconstruction of these companies through merger began at this time. Mitsui-Bussan in 1959, and Mitsubishi in 1954, were rebuilt to become the largest trading companies in Japan.

[f] The ten largest wholesalers during 1937–1943 were: Mitsui-Bussan, Mitsubishi-Shoji, Toyo Menka, Nichimen Jitsugyo, Gosho, Iwai Sangyo, Kanematsu, Atako Sangyo, Nissho, Naigai Tsusho. Of these, Mitsui Bussan, Mitsubishi Shoji and Naigai Tsusho were trading companies of Zaibatsu. Toyo Menka, Nichimen Jitsugyo, Gosho, and Kanematsu were textile wholesalers, and the other three were steel wholesalers: Odat Sangyo, which was classified as in the textile industry, had a large trading department. In 1949 it was broken down into four companies, of which two became textile merchant wholesalers. See Holding Company Liquidation Commission, 334–335, 538–546.

[g] The Itoh-Chu Company provides a typical example. The changing share of textile goods in its total sales is as follows: 1950 (90%); 1955 (73%); 1960 (61%); 1965 (42%); 1969 (40%). *Itoh-Chu 100nen Shi* (*A History of Itoh-Chu from 1869 to 1969*), Itoh-Chu (1969).

managed to strengthen their status relative to small weavers and textile merchant wholesalers. However spinners could no longer resolve the problems of recession through curtailment of industry output as in the prewar period. The explicit cooperative curtailment of industry operations was prohibited by the antitrust statutes, and the breakdown of the oligopolistic structure of the industry made it impossible for spinners to curtail their operations implicitly. Finally, in 1952 the Japanese government had to advise spinners to curtail their operations for the good of the industry.[h]

Formation of the Synthetic Fiber Industry

The commercial production of synthetic fiber in Japan started with polyamide fiber (nylon) and polyvinyl acetate fiber (vinylon) in 1949. The number of manufacturers were initially restricted to one or two in each field by a government monopoly grant. In spite of this protection, the industry as a whole did not become profitable until 1955.[17] (The rayon industry actually began operations in the mid-1920s in Japan.)

The excess capacity found in the cotton textile industry after the Korean boom had two immediate results. One was the curtailment of cotton production on the advice of government. A second was the entry of ten large cotton spinners into the rayon filament and rayon staple industry. Rayon manufacturers also increased their output—resulting in an imbalance of supply and demand for rayon, and a sharp drop in rayon prices in 1957. In 1957 the government extended its "advice" to rayon filament and rayon staple manufacturers—curtailing their operations for the good of the industry. Thus, spinners and rayon manufacturers in turn entered the synthetic fiber industry, seeking more stable markets and using funds earned during the Korean boom in the cotton textile industry.[18] Six major firms entered the acrylic fiber industry from 1957 to 1963.

In 1957, as an extension of the government's previous policy of issuing advice to the industry, the government issued a regulation prohibiting any increase in the number of spinning machines, with only machines for synthetic fibers exempted.

It was probably inevitable that substantial size differentials would occur between the vertically integrated synthetic fiber firms, and those which confined themselves to the spinning of cotton and synthetic fibers.[i] There

---

[h] This was the beginning of the curtailment of textile operations by government leadership "advice" in Japan. Thereafter, most curtailment and approval of product line restrictions and sales restrictions in the textile industry occurred through such government advice.[16]

[i] Most synthetic fiber manufacturers in Japan had their origins in the cotton spinning and the rayon industries. This was not true in the United States or in the European countries, and is one of the unique characteristics of the Japanese synthetic textile industry.

evolved a considerable differential among the ten largest spinners, who had been more or less equal in size at the beginning of the postwar period.

Marketing Activities by Synthetic Fiber Manufacturers and Functions of Merchant Wholesalers

Formation of Contractual Marketing Systems

Synthetic fiber manufacturers, being newcomers to the domestic market, had to find and cultivate markets for their products in competition with long-established cotton and rayon textile products.[19] Competition between the old and new products was felt in the successive stages of processing and distribution, but most strongly in consumer good markets.

To compete with established textiles for a share of the consumer market, synthetic fiber manufacturers employed two strategies. One was a pull approach through various sales promotions, including advertising; the other was an attempt to coordinate the marketing channel from fiber to final products. To increase the effectiveness of sales promotion, it was necessary to promote and guarantee the quality of the final product; to achieve the necessary quality control, it was necessary to coordinate all processing stages from weaving to sewing.

The large cotton spinners already had their own weaving departments and direct contacts with weavers, district wholesalers, and clothiers through subcontracting systems (weaving on commission). Rayon manufacturers had neither direct contacts with weavers nor their own weaving factories. The processing and distribution of rayon products had been entirely entrusted to merchant wholesalers. When rayon manufacturers became synthetic fiber manufacturers and had no direct contact, even with weavers, they were faced with the necessity of contracting with and coordinating all processors from weavers to sewers. Because these contracts had to include quality control provisions, the contractual relations had to be closer than those existing between merchant wholesalers and processors.

It was the Toray Company, a leading synthetic fiber manufacturer, which first introduced the innovative idea of a comprehensive contractual marketing system incorporating processors and distributors; the strategy was quickly copied by other manufacturers. The goals of the contractual system were four in number.[20] The first involved the assumption of risk. Synthetic fibers were new to processors and distributors; they involved different processing techniques from those for cotton products, and some new equipment. Small processors could not absorb such costs and risks, and synthetic fiber manufacturers had to contractually agree to absorb some of the risks which arose at processing stages, and to extend financial and technical support to small processors.

The second purpose of tightly drawn contractual agreements was to deter processors from shifting to other kinds of textiles in reaction to shifts in relative market prices. Also, the synthetic fiber manufacturers had to induce processors to install specialized processing machines, and to process synthetic textiles in accordance with a schedule drawn up by the manufacturer considerably in advance. The third purpose was, as mentioned, to assure quality control of final products through contractually standardized production processes.

The fourth purpose of introducing contractual market systems to the industry was to introduce and enforce resale price maintenance and at every stage of the distribution structure for synthetic fibers and textiles. So long as the list price system could be enforced, it guaranteed profits to manufacturers, processors, and distributors.

In an article on thc textile industry, Hoshimi Uchida lists four types of contracts which were in use between manufacturers and processors.[21] The first is a direct subcontract by a manufacturer, the second a subcontract by a merchant wholesaler who is himself controlled by a large manufacturer. The third is a contract under which materials are sold and finished or processed products bought back by large manufacturers: the practice of selling yarn and buying fabrics is an illustration. The fourth is a contract where materials are sold but products are not bought back; however, final products are marketed with the manufacturer's brand name, and undergo his quality inspection before sale. Under any of these contracts if processors contract with competitive manufacturers without prior permission, produce inferior products, sell products below list price, or otherwise violate the terms of their agreements, they are automatically dropped from the contractual system. To protect their contractual arrangements, large manufacturers put on extensive sales promotion campaigns, provide their brand names for use by the processors, and strive to achieve secure consumer market segments for their branded products.

Functions of Merchant Wholesalers

Except for the largest of the wholesalers (many of whom had evolved into monopolistic general trading companies),[j] most in textiles had been greatly weakened by the inflations of 1952–53 and 1957–58. It was with these financially weakened wholesalers that synthetic fiber manufacturers

[j] Concentration ratios for the largest one, five, and ten firms in the cotton spinning, cotton weaving, and synthetic fiber manufacturing industry in 1966 were as follows. The figures in parentheses indicate the number of firms in each industry. Cotton spinning (117) 10.8%, 29.0%, 46.9%; cotton weaving (?) 4.2%, 12.7%, 18.5%; synthetic fiber manufacturing (29) 27.1%, 65.5%, 87.6%.[22]

attempted to make exclusive contracts. The wholesalers were still strong enough to control converters and district wholesalers; by contracting with them, the large manufacturers could gain working control of the channel.[k]

Thus manufacturers, working through wholesalers who functioned as agents, could contract with (directly or indirectly) and control converters and district wholesalers. In many cases the manufacturer entrusted the selection of processors to be included in the contractual system to the wholesaier-agent. The wholesaler thus assumed responsibilities both for production and for sales functions, including the allocation of materials, assembling and dispersing processed goods, and merchandising brand-name marked textiles. The manufacturer-established contractual systems were not universal; there remained a few small spinners and processors who were not under exclusive contract, but these were usually small in size, financially weak, and were unimportant factors in the industry structure. Thus, the manufacturers now controlled the marketing channels for textiles, which in turn were run by the merchant wholesalers.

The contractual systems were extended to include retailers for some items (notably men's suits), but the extent of this was limited. The number and variety of retailers made them difficult for manufacturers to organize, especially given existing distribution structures which embraced merchant wholesalers, final processors, primary (national) wholesalers, and secondary (local) wholesalers.[l]

The Distribution Revolution: Some Perspectives

A rapid growth of supermarkets after 1960 occurred parallel to the advent of contractual marketing systems in the textile industry. This growth was facilitated by an inflationary trend which saw consumer prices rising an average of more than 7 percent per year in the first half of the decade. The reordering of the marketing structure represented by phenomena like the development of contractual systems and the growth of supermarkets has come to be known in the literature as the Japanese "distribution revolution."[m]

---

[k] A typical example of this type of merchant wholesaler is Chori, who had exclusive contracts with Toray and functioned as its agent. During the 1952–53 depression, Chori incurred considerable debt to manufacturers, and at this time Toray contracted with Chori and extended financial support.

[l] This was true even in the Toray system, considered the most advanced contractual marketing system in the industry.[23]

[m] The first use of the term "distribution revolution" is found in Shuji Hayashi, *Ryutsu Kakumei* (*Distribution Revolution*), Tokyo: Chuo Koron (1962), and Yoshihiro Tajima, *Nihon no Ryutsu Kakumei* (*Distribution Revolution in Japan*), Tokyo: Nihon Noritsu Kyokai (1962). Thereafter, the concept appears in the literature in a con-

Development of Supermarkets

The expansion of supermarketing in Japan depended greatly on the growth in their sales of clothing and apparel, as shown in Table 13-1. This

Table 13-1
Percentage of Sales in Each Product Group Made Through Supermarkets, Japan, 1968

Supermarket Size Measured by Selling Floor Space	Clothing and Apparel	Food and Drink	Other
* $100m^2$–$199m^2$ ** $120y^2$–$238y^2$	11.4%	73.4%	15.2%
* $200m^2$–$299m^2$ ** $239y^2$–$358y^2$	14.7	74.1	11.2
* $300m^2$–$399m^2$ ** $359y^2$–$477y^2$	17.2	69.4	13.4
* $400m^2$–$599m^2$ ** $478y^2$–$717y^2$	18.9	68.6	13.5
* $600m^2$–$999m^2$ ** $718y^2$–$1,195y^2$	29.3	55.9	14.8
* $1,000m^2$–$1,499m^2$ ** $1,196y^2$–$1,793y^2$	40.0	43.6	16.4
* $1,500m^2$ and over ** $1,794y^2$ and over	43.4	29.4	27.2

* In square meters.
** In square yards (one square meter = 1.2 square yards).
Source: Tsusho Sangyo Sho, Chosa Tokei Bu (Research and Statistics Division of Ministry of International Trade and Industry), *Wagakuni no Shogyo, 1969* (*Commerce In Our Country, 1969*).

was a phenomenon with no close parallel in the development of North American supermarketing; indeed, the term supermarket in Japan is used to refer to a much different type of retail outlet (and a much smaller one, in general) than is true in North America.

The growth in Japanese supermarkets coincided almost exactly with the beginning of regular marketing promotion activities by synthetic fiber manufacturers. The product standardization resulting from contractual systems in processing stages of the textile industry, and the establishment of manufacturers' brand names aided in creating a consumer reliance on brands. The naive image of "the lower the price, the more inferior the

siderable range of meanings. Here, it is used primarily to refer to the reorganizations accompanying the introduction of contractual systems, and to the rapid growth of supermarketing in Japan.[24]

quality" for consumer goods was quickly broken down by manufacturers' branding. Advertising and sales promotion of brand name goods also aided this shift.

A second reason for the growth of clothing and apparel sales in supermarkets related to the weakness of manufacturers in enforcing all the provisions of their contractual agreements, notably those relating to resale price maintenance. The textile industry in Japan still contained a number of small secondary or local wholesalers who were compelled to allow supermarkets to discount their list prices and who were willing to discount their price to supermarkets in order to obtain large volume orders. Some of the larger manufacturers and merchant wholesalers were forced to cut price to meet this competition. Thus, supermarkets were able to obtain widely advertised, brand-name merchandise on advantageous terms because of their ability to place large volume orders. The widespread handling of these brands by supermarkets in turn increased the exposure of the branded goods, and their acceptance. What had been an implicit cooperative relationship evolved into an explicit one in the late 1960s with the development of private (supermarket) branded goods by larger manufacturers. Overall, the interaction between the contractual systems and the growing supermarkets provided a major impetus for the substitution of synthetic textiles for the traditional cotton and rayon products in the Japanese market.

Modifications of Contractual Marketing Systems

There was a depression in Japan from 1964 to 1965 which required manufacturers to modify their conventional contractual marketing systems; under depressed selling conditions, contractual systems were largely ineffective in maintaining retail (and wholesale) prices. If resale prices could not be maintained, it became too great a financial burden for manufacturers to contract with smaller, more inefficient processors and bear such risks as arose at processing stages.

Many manufacturers reorganized their existing contractual systems, adopting selective dealing strategies and dropping all but the largest and financially strongest processors. The selective policy was feasible because synthetic fibers had acquired a stable market share in competition with other textiles, and were being processed by a wide variety of middlemen who had made the necessary investments and transformations. The extent of penetration of synthetic textiles into the processing stages is shown in Table 13-2. Synthetic textiles were no longer risky ventures; the situation where it was difficult to deal in these textiles without intensive technical and financial support from manufacturers had disappeared.[25] The change in competitive market structure is indicated by the fact that manufacturers

Table 13-2
Penetration Ratios for Synthetic Textiles in Some Processing Stages

	Weaving of Cotton and Rayon Staple	Weaving of Silk and Rayon Filament	Weaving of Wool	Dyeing and Finishing	Knitting	Sewing
1952	0.1%	0.3%	0.8%	—%	—%	—%
1956	1.3	3.7	2.0	2.3	2.5	6.7
1960	5.0	14.5	4.0	7.4	8.7	10.9
1964	13.1	31.7	4.5	21.2	39.1	32.7
1968	22.3	43.8	6.4	35.4	36.6	49.0

Source: Tsusan Sho (Ministry of International Trade and Industry), *Sen-i Tokei Nenppo* (*Annual Report on Textile Industry Statistics*).

could reduce the commission paid weavers by 10 to 20 percent in 1965 and simultaneously dismantle parts of their contractual systems. (Again, Toray was the leading company. The policy of cutting down on commissions paid was first employed by Toray in 1965, and was later followed by other manufacturers.)

Limitation of the Distribution Revolution: Some Perspectives

Currently, large manufacturers and large retailers (especially supermarkets) are striving to eliminate some middlemen and to shorten and simplify their channels of distribution for textiles. So far, their efforts have not been highly successful. One inhibiting factor is the small and scattered nature of processors.[n] This is at least partially due to the failure of contractual systems to induce an increase in the average size of processors involved in such systems.

Thus, the position of merchant wholesalers remains strong; though their status relative to large manufacturers has declined since the war, they still hold a dominant position relative to processors, and they will continue to function as "channel leaders" so long as it is difficult for manufacturers to dominate processors directly. Small local converters and district wholesalers still control some processors independently; however for manufacturers to embrace a large number of small wholesalers through contractual systems might result in such complex systems that control would break down completely.

Replacement of smaller wholesalers and processors with large whole-

[n] The structure of processing stages is not the same for all kinds of products. In general, large processors appear with new kinds of products; in these industries distribution structure is highly simplified as compared to that in oligopolistic industries such as home electric appliances.[26]

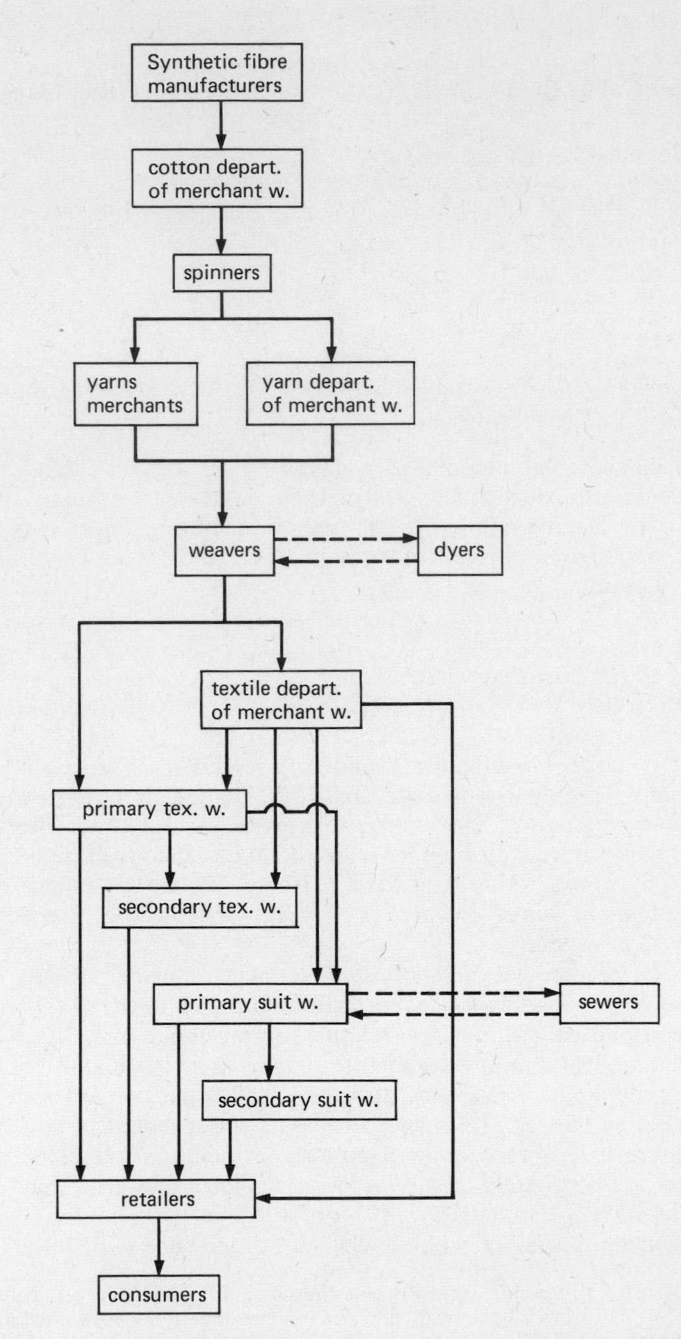

Figure 13–4. The Distribution Structure for Synthetic Textiles in Ready-Made Suits.

salers does not always lead to distribution efficiency; it may simply mean that wholesalers now intervene in every stage of production flow in place of their predecessors. This is illustrated in Figure 13-4, which presents a simplified version of the prevailing distribution structure for synthetic textiles in ready-made men's suits.[27] Merchant wholesalers appear here in three separate places. The merchant wholesalers themselves have evolved into highly complex organizations, made up of a plethora of separate departments and carrying out a myriad of functions.

In the future large manufacturers may strive to make even more restrictive, exclusive contracts with the larger of the merchant wholesalers; subordination of merchant wholesalers to manufacturers would then increase. In any case, merchant wholesalers will continue to function as the central figures and channel coordinators of the contractual marketing systems of specific manufacturers.

Notes

1. For example, Laurence P. Dowd, "Wholesale Marketing in Japan," *Journal of Marketing* 23, No. 3 (January, 1959), 257–262, or Edwin H. Lewis, *Marketing Channels: Structure and Strategy*, New York: McGraw-Hill Book Co. (1968), 55–57.
2. Banji Ijima, *Nihon Boseki Shi* (History of the Spinning Industry In Japan), Osaka: Sogensha (1949), 131–144, 182–193.
3. Keizo Seki, *Nihon Mengyo Ron*, Tokyo Daigaku Shuppan Kai (1954), 164–175. An english version of this book is available; Keizo Seki, *The Cotton Industry of Japan*, Tokyo: Japan Society for the Promotion of Science (1956), 104–111.
4. Mochikabu Gaisha Seiri Iinkai (Holding Company Liquidation Commission), *Nihon Zaibatsu to sono Kaitai* (*Japanese Zaibatsu and Its Dissolution*), Tokyo: Mochikabu Gaisha Seiri Iinkai (1951), 539.
5. Laurence P. Dowd, *Wholesale Marketing*, 261.
6. Banji Ijima, *Spinning Industry*, 511–513.
7. Keizo Seki, *Cotton Industry* (english version), 63–68.
8. Seki, *Cotton Industry*, 68–70.
9. Holding Company Liquidation Commission, 547.
10. Jun-ichi Yamamoto, "Keiretsuka—Sen-i Kogyo" (Contract Systems in the Textile Industry), in Hitoshi Misono (ed.), *Keiretsuka-Kombinato* (*Contract Systems-Combinations*), Tokyo: Shiseido (1964), 118.
11. For a discussion of the Cotton Export-Import Link System, see Banji Ijima, *Spinning Industry*, 342–357, and Keizo Seki, *Cotton Industry*, 191–197.
12. Jun-ichi Yamamoto, *Contract Systems*, 118.
13. Keizo Seki, *Cotton Industry*, 200–210.
14. Kosei Torihiki Iinkai (Fair Trade Committee), *Nihon ni okeru Keizairyoku Shuchu no Jittai* (*Economic Concentration In Japan*), Tokyo: Jit-

sugyo no Nihon Sha (1951), 169. On the process of concentration through merger, see Holding Company Liquidation Commission, 334–336, 275–281.

15. Banji Ijima, *Spinning Industry*, 474–476.

16. Kosei Torihiki Iinkai (Fair Trade Commission), *Dokusen Kinshi Seisaku 20nen Shi* (*Twenty Years of Antimonopoly Policy*), Tokyo: Okura Sho Insatsu Kyoku (Printing Bureau, The Ministry of Finance, 1968), 207–214, 327–337, 620–626.

17. For a short history, see Genzo Hazama, *Nihon Kasen Sangyo Ron* (*On the Chemical Fiber Industry in Japan*), Tokyo: Nihon Hyoron Sha (1962).

18. Hoshimi Uchida, *Gosei Sen-i Kogyo* (*Synthetic Fiber Manufacturing Industry*), Tokyo: Toyo Keizai Shinpo Sha (rev. ed. 1970), 164.

19. For a discussion of distribution structures in the immediate post-war period, see (in english): Yukichi Arakawa, "Small Wholesalers In Cotton Textile Marketing In Japan," *Annals of the School of Business Administration, Kobe University* (1957), 59–93.

20. Hoshimi Uchida, *Synthetic Fiber*, 183. See also "Gosen Gyo no Hatten o meguru Shomondai" (Some Problems In The Development of the Synthetic Textile Industry), in Nihon Choki Shinyo Ginko (Japan Long-Term Credit Bank), *Chosa Geppo* (*Monthly Credit Letter*), Feb.-Mar. 1967, 28–31.

21. Hoshimi Uchida, "Sen-i Kogyo" (Textile Industry), in Yoshio Kobayashi (ed.), *Kigyo Keiretsu no Jittai* (*Realities of Contractual Relations Among Enterprises*), Tokyo: Toyo Keizai Shinpo Sha (1958), 53.

22. Kosei Torihiki Iinkai (Fair Trade Commission), *Nihon no Sangyo Shuchu, Showa 38–41* (*Concentration In Japanese Manufacturing Industry, 1963–1966*), Tokyo: Toyo Keizai Shinpo Sha (1969), 201, 203, 227.

23. See *Toyo Rayon 35nen no Ayumi* (*History of Toray's 35 Years*), Toyo Rayon (1962), 94–95.

24. See also Masanori Tamura, "The Evolution . . . ," *infra*.

25. "Gosen Gyo no Hatten . . ." (Some Problems in the Development . . .), 32.

26. See Tokyo Sen-i Kyokai (Tokyo Textile Association), *Korekara no Sen-i Ryutsu* (*Textile Distribution In The Future*), Tokyo: Nihon Keizai Shinbun Sha (1960), 63–72.

27. *Ibid.*, 11.

Part Five
Contractual Systems in the Public Sector

14 Contractual Marketing in the Government Industry Procurement Administration Process

Samuel Hassen*

The Defense Supply Agency (DSA) is directly responsible to the Secretary of Defense for providing supplies and services used in common by the military services. The Defense Contract Administration Services (DCAS), a major component of the DSA, manages defense contracts for the Army, Navy, Air Force, DSA, the National Aeronautics and Space Administration (NASA), other federal agencies, and on occasion for foreign governments. Contract administration is performed at or near contractor plants to facilitate contract performance, and to assure compliance with the terms and conditions of government contracts.

DCAS is staffed by 450 military and 22,000 civilian personnel including specialists in the fields of accounting, data and financial processing, business law, business administration, contract administration, property management, quality control, most phases of engineering, transportation, packaging, industrial labor relations, industrial security, and equal employment opportunity. In 1969, DCAS administered more than 238,000 prime and support contracts valued at $54 billion, and performed quality assurance for another 107, 000 contracts. These included contracts for weapon-related subsystems, and for entire weapons systems such as the Polaris and Poseidon missiles, the Sheridan tank, and the C-130 Hercules aircraft. DCAS through its eleven regional offices paid out $16 billion to contractors for materials and services provided in 1969, and processed over 1,800,000 contractor invoices.

Given the size of DCAS, and the complexity of the business/government environment in which it operates, it is probable that virtually every problem today encountered in contractual marketing systems in the private sector has at some time in the past been faced in the public sector by the DSA or the DCAS. Many of the solutions and procedures developed in response to these problems are not directly applicable in the private sector, but may be indirectly applicable with modification.

The Procurement Process

The Armed Services Procurement Act of 1947 [The Act][1] is a model procurement statute, a product of the experience gained in the period pre-

* Defense Contract Administration Services and Long Island University. The typing and clerical assistance provided by the Roth School of Business, C.W. Post campus of Long Island University, is gratefully acknowledged.

ceding and during World War II. It was written and intended to be responsive both to the needs of an emergency or wartime period, and to the changed conditions of peace.

Section 2304 of the Act established two basic types of contractual procurement applicable to the Department of Defense (DoD) and to NASA; (1) Advertising [invitation to bid—IFB] and (2) Negotiated bid [request for proposal—RFP]. Purchases are solicited through advertising in "all cases in which use of such method is feasible and practicable under the existing conditions and circumstances." If advertising is not feasible and practicable, the head of the agency involved may negotiate such purchases or contracts. Situations in which advertising is not feasible and practicable arise where: (1) negotiated procurement is in the public interest during a national emergency; (2) the public exigency will not permit the delay incident to advertising; (3) the aggregate amount involved is not more than $2,500; (4) the contract is for personal or professional services; (5) the contract is for services by a university, college, or other educational institution; (6) the contract is for property or services to be procured and used outside of the United States; (7) the contract is for medicine or medical supplies; (8) the contract is for property or services for which it is impractical to obtain competition; (9) the contract is for property or services for experimental, development, or research work.

Section 2313 of the Act provides that the agency issuing the contract may inspect the plant and audit the books and records of a contractor performing a cost or cost-plus-fixed-fee contract, and a subcontractor performing any subcontract under a cost or cost-plus-fixed-fee contract. For each negotiated contract the Comptroller General or his representative are entitled (for three years after final payment) to examine any books, documents, papers, or records of the contractor or subcontractors that directly pertain to the contract.

The Armed Services Procurement Regulations (ASPR) and NASA regulations also furnish policies and procedures for carrying out the Act, for accomplishing advertised and negotiated procurements, and for the various technical and administrative functions supporting procurement. These functions include inspection and quality assurance, price and cost analysis, contract audit, contract administration, patents and copyrights, control of government property, and insurance. Various military departments also issue instructions, procedures, and directives in greater detail, but consistent with the ASPR.

Advertised and Negotiated Procurements

Subsequent to the establishment of requirements and the commitment of funds, prospective contractors are invited to bid, and are furnished an "invitation to bid." The invitation is also posted in government purchasing offices, and in Small Business Administration offices. The Department of Commerce publishes summaries of future procurements, and this attracts bids from additional sources. Names are also obtained from mailing lists of concerns which have established their interest in the class of commodity involved with the particular buying office.

The proposals made by the contractor, including the bid price, remain sealed until the day and hour for bid opening. Upon bid opening, a determination is made as to whether the bid is responsive and the bidder responsible. Award is ultimately made to the lowest responsive and responsible bidder.[a] Sometimes two-step advertising is used. Technical proposals are solicited from contractors in response to invitations describing the performance characteristics needed. Following evaluation and conferences with prospective contractors, acceptable proposals are selected. Contractors selected are then invited to furnish a proposal which is priced covering their technical submission, and the award is made to the lowest responsive and responsible bidder. Such two-step solicitations were developed to enlarge the number of competitors involved, and to permit the use of advertised procurements where detailed specifications were not available.

The largest number of procurement dollars are expended through negotiated contracts. The group of contractors involved is generally more limited than under advertised procurement, but some competition is solicited. Proposals are required to be furnished by a specified date, supported by price and cost data and (if in excess of $100,000) be certified as accurate, current, and complete at the time of negotiation.[2] Certification is waived if the price is a recognized competitive price, or a standardized market or catalogue price of an item sold in substantial quantities to the general public. Award may be made to the responsible bidder furnishing the lowest priced, acceptable proposal, or negotiation may include oral or written conferences with bidders submitting acceptable proposals, in which the bidder's price and other terms of the contract are discussed. If essential provisions of specifications, work descriptions, or other provisions are changed, all bidders participating are given the opportunity to submit a revised proposal. Disclosure of technical information received in confidence from any offeror cannot be disclosed to any other offeror, nor is it permitted to inform any offeror of the price of the others to obtain a lower price. Award is ultimately made to the responsive, responsible bidder whose proposal is lowest in price following negotiations.[b]

---

[a] Minor informalities and irregularities may be waived. The award is made by written notice to the successful bidder, and unsuccessful bidders are notified of the award. ASPR Section II contains details of the procedure, and bidding instructions.

[b] Section III, ASPR contains the details of negotiation policies and procedures, a description of varieties of contracts used in negotiations, policies and procedures relating to cost and price analysis and audit, application of the Weighted Guidelines Method in profit determination, and compliance with Public Law 87-653, the Truth in Pricing Statute.

The Government as Contracting Party: Contract Types

The government as a contracting party is not endowed with the perogatives of a sovereign. Courts have held that when the United States with constitutional authority makes contracts, it has rights and incurs responsibilities similar to those of individuals who are parties to such instruments.[3] Thus, the government may be sued for breach of contract under the Tucker Act in Federal District Courts for claims up to $10,000, and in the Court of Claims for higher amounts. However, the government is not liable for interference with performance of a contract as a result of its public and general sovereign acts, either executive or legislative.[4]

Government procurement contracts are of six principal types: (1) the fixed price contract, which imposes the greatest risk upon the contractor since the work is specified to be done for a predetermined price (including profit), and for delivery by a specified time; (2) the price redeterminable contract, either (a) with initial price estimated and price redetermined in successive periods, or (b) with retroactive price redetermination after completion for research or development procurement costing $100,000 or less (a ceiling price is established such that some of the risk of cost overruns falls on the contractor); (3) the cost-only contract, in which the contractor is reimbursed for his expenses only (with no fee or profit) up to a predetermined maximum value of the contract; (4) the cost-sharing contract, in which the contractor shares a portion of the incurred cost overrun above original estimated cost; (5) the cost-plus-fixed-fee contract, in which the government pays the contractor incurred costs (within the original estimated cost), plus a fixed fee not exceeding 10 percent of budgeted cost for supply contracts, 15 percent for research and development contracts, and 6 percent of the cost of the project for architect fees; (6) the cost-plus-fee-incentive contract which exists in various forms, offering incentives for cost savings, meeting or beating delivery schedule targets, or combinations of these, and offering the contractor increased incentive fee awards in amounts specified in the contract. An increase in costs above estimate, or delays in completion beyond schedule can result in a reduction of contractor's fees, and can force absorption of additional costs by the contractor.

The clauses used in each type of contract are set out in Section VII of the ASPR. Standard provisions relate to subjects such as: (1) government authorization to make changes in specifications, drawings, or design; (2) inspection of contractor supplies; (3) assignment of claims for payment to financial institutions; (4) details of payment of invoices to contractor; (5) examination and access to contractor records; (6) handling of disputes and appeals from decisions of Contracting Officers to Boards of Contract Appeal; (7) notice regarding patent and copyright infringement; (8) use of convict labor; (9) provision for equal employment opportunity; (10) provision for utilization of small business in subcontracting; (11) provision for utilization of subcontractor firms in labor surplus areas; (12) audit and record keeping requirements; and (13) provision for contract termination by the government.

The Complexity of the Government Procurement Market

The government contractual procurement process takes place in a most complicated marketing arena. Contrast the simplicity of the postrevolutionary era when on March 27, 1794, Congress passed an "Act to provide a Navy Armament," authorizing the President to "provide by purchase or otherwise equip and employ four ships to carry forty-four guns each and two ships to carry thirty guns each." How simple were the instructions of the Secretary of War to Captain John Barry:

> You are to consider yourself as the Superintendent of the frigate to be built at the Port of Philadelphia and your constant attendance will be necessary for the purpose of observing that all parts of the business harmonize and are conformed to the public interests. You will report to me weekly the number of workmen employed and the progress made in execution either of the hull or of the equipment.

The submarine USS Pintado [SS 387] was launched in August 1943, with original acquisition cost of about $14 million; the similarly-named nuclear submarine Pintado [SSN 672] was launched in August 1969, funded at about $105 million. Current funded cost for the most recent model of nuclear submarine is about $160 million.

The evolving government procurement process, and some of its pitfalls, are shown in the memorandum by former Secretary Robert S. McNamara as he left office:[5]

> Since 1961 we have made many significant improvements in managing defense acquisition programs and in procurement policies. The cost-plus-fixed-fee environment of earlier years has been replaced by tighter management both on our part and that of our contractors, as exemplified by the introduction of more intensive competition, more extensive use of incentive and fixed price contracts and greater contractor investment in plant and equipment. We have been able to effect more selectivity in the acquisition process through the use of contract definition and related techniques. We have acheived greater use of the profit motive through the application of the weighted guidelines technique in profit negotiation. The following matters appear to deserve particular attention.
>
> *Inadequate Contractual Coverage By The Government:*
>
> Instances have been cited where work is requested or required but where contractual coverage is not provided, either at all or for a prolonged period. As

a matter of basic policy we should not expect contractors to risk their own resources without adequate contractual coverage. Also to the extent that subsequent government action after the award of a contract increases or decreases the contractor's cost it is our basic policy to provide equitable adjustments in a timely manner.

Misuse of Firm Fixed Price Contracts:

Some contractors state that they have been required to accept this form of contract which involves the highest financial risk, where there are numerous development and production uncertainties remaining. Good judgement must be exercised in the choice of type of contract for each situation. Our emphasis on using the higher risk type contracts should not be construed as mandate for their use in inappropriate situations.

Unrealistic Negotiated Profit Rates:

Contractors have expressed the view that Contracting Officers are . . . forcing a formula which supports a preconceived profit rate. It is our firm policy that guidelines must be fully utilized in each case so as to offer profit opportunity commensurate with the degree of risk the contractor is called upon to assume.

Excessive Administration of High Risk Contracts:

Despite the greater use of competition and fixed price arrangements, and despite the greater investment of contractor capital in performance of defense contracts, there are as many (in some cases more) government personnel involved in administering contracts as existed during the era of cost-plus-fixed-fee contracting. Any such conditions are inconsistent with our basic objectives.

Following the very significant cost overrides in the C5A aircraft procurement program, Deputy Defense Secretary David Packard (in a memo of June 12, 1970 on major weapons acquisition) expressed the following acquisition policy:

In our contracting the type of contract must be tailored to the risks involved. Cost-plus-incentive contracts are preferred for both advanced development and full scale development contracts for major systems. When the assessment of technical risk permits, such contracts should include provisions for competitive fixed price subcontracts for subsystems, components, and materials. In many cases this will enable a major portion of the program to benefit from competition. When risks have been reduced to the extent that realistic pricing can take place, fixed price contracts should be used. But the Contracting Officer should have the flexibility to consider the technical capability of the contractor and other factors in selection of contract type. When fixed price type contracts are used for development programs, the contractor's financial ability to absorb losses that might be incurred must be a factor in making the award.

The Contracting Officer in the Contract Administration Process

In the administration of contracts, the United States government is represented by a Procurement Contracting Officer, who negotiates, awards, and signs the contract on behalf of the government. An Administrative Contracting Officer, located in the same geographic region as the contractor, administers the contract.[c] The Contracting Officer functions within the contract directorate of a regional office, and is supported by cost and price analysts, financial analysts, property administrators, production specialists, quality control specialists, auditors, engineers, legal counsel, and others.

The behavior of the Contracting Officer is the subject of thousands of pages in volumes of the Board of Appeals, Comptroller General, Court of Claims, the federal courts, and occasionally of the U.S. Supreme Court. These deal with an analysis of his decisions, his criteria, the correctness or error of his judgement, and often a review of his conduct. Commenting on the Contracting Officer's authority prior to the passing of the Wunderlich Act, Justice Douglas said:[7]

> [his authority] makes a tyrant out of every Contracting Officer. He is granted the power of a tyrant even though he is stubborn, perverse, or captious. He is allowed the power of a tyrant though he is imcompetent or negligent. He has the power of life and death over private business even though his decision is grossly erroneous. Power granted is seldom neglected.

Passage of the Wunderlich Act in 1954[8] subjected Contracting Officer's and Board's decisions to review by the U.S. Court of Claims if arbitrary, capricious, fraudulent, so grossly erroneous as necessarily to imply bad faith, or if not supported by substantial evidence. The Act prohibited the making of the Contracting Officer's or Board's decisions final on any question of law.

The Contracting Officer's principal sources of guidance are Armed Services Procurement Regulations (ASPR) in the Department of Defense, NASA regulations for the National Aeronautics and Space Administration, and Federal Procurement Regulations prescribed by the General Services Administration for other federal executive agencies.

Role of the Contracting Officer in Settling Disputes

While the Comptroller General reviews the actions of the Contracting Officer to determine that funds are expended according to contract terms,

[c] Contracting Officers are personally appointed by warrant by the Commanding Officer; the Armed Services' Procurement Regulations prescribe the requisite qualifications.[6]

laws, and regulations, the Comptroller General "will not substitute [his] judgement for that of the Contracting Officer unless it is shown that the finding was arbitrary, capricious, or not based on substantial evidence."[9] For reversal of a decision, the facts must permit only one conclusion that is fair and reasonable, and which is contrary to that actually reached by the Contracting Officer. If the facts are capable of two alternative conclusions, the Controller will not reverse if his judgement differs.

In the making of his decisions under the disputes clause, the Contracting Officer must be free from coercion *even from his own staff*. The Board of Appeals has reversed decisions when it became evident that the decision was not that of the Contracting Officer; for example, decisions involving evaluation of accounting fees as allowable cost under cost contracts have been reversed when it was known on appeal that the decision was that of the government lawyer or accountant, and not of the Contracting Officer. In the case of Sol Schlesinger,[10] the Court converted a termination for default into a termination for convenience because the Contracting Officer did not terminate of his own decision, but under pressure from his superior to do so, this in turn being inspired by the evincement of congressional interest.

The decision of the Contracting Officer is always open on questions of law and may be appealed if it does not meet the standards of the Wunderlich Act. On appeal from a decision of the Contracting Officer and the Board of Contract Appeal, the courts will generally not conduct a new trial on issues of fact, since if adequately supported, determinations of fact are final under the disputes clause.

Relation of the Contracting Officer to the Contractor

There has been a trend over the past decade to relax controls over contractors in their management of their own contracts, and of their subcontracts. This has resulted from reviews of contractor's administrative controls governing subcontract performance, and the limiting of government control to areas in which the contractor's controls are deficient, plus the government's reliance on built-in contract incentives to assure contractor motivation through the possibility of increased profits. The limits of Contracting Officer's control over the actions of the contractor has been stated as follows:

> The Contracting Officer's function is not that of a boss over the contractor, telling him what he can and cannot buy, whom he should employ and how much he is allowed to pay his employees[11]

and

The executive officers of a contracting corporation should be allowed to exercise the judgement on which their stockholders rely and on which among other factors the government has also relied in placing the negotiated contract. If there are other ways of doing the same thing it is normally not the function of the Contracting Officer to substitute his own judgement by disallowing costs, because some other approach to the problems might be preferred.[12]

The Contracting Officer is an agent of the government under the authority granted him in his Warrant of Appointment. However, should he enter a contract or act under it contrary to his authority, his action is not binding on the government.[d] Even though the Contracting Officer's function is "not that of a boss over the contractor," ASPR regulations still require that the Contracting Officer fulfill a long list of specific duties which include:[14] review the contractor's compensation structure; review his insurance plans; review his progress payments to subcontractors; negotiate and execute agreements for spare parts; review any changes in the contractor's contract under the Changes Clause; review and maintain surveillance of contractor's procurement system; consent to placement of subcontracts; monitor contractor's financial condition and advise when contract performance is jeopardized; and, perform government property administration duties through review of contractor's property control system for control of government property.

The Organization of a Contract Administration Office

By way of further illustrating the complexity of the contract administration process, consider the organization structure involved. Most contracts (essentially all except those for basic research) are decentralized to the regional contract directorate office which is proximate to the contractor's principal administrative office. The contract directorate is organized into a number of operating divisions and branches.

The first, an Operations Division, is made up of Contract Administrators, Contracting Officers, and a Contract Operations and Data Branch. The division receives and distributes contracts and reports, and maintains the central files of contracts and correspondence.

A second, organizationally equal division is the Financial Services Division (FSD), encompassing three branches. A branch of cost and price

---

[d] "Although a private agent acting in violation of specific instructions yet within the scope of his general authority may bind the principal, the rule as to the effect of the like act of a public agent is otherwise, for the reason that it is better that an individual should occasionally suffer from the mistakes of public officers or agents then to adopt a rule which through improper combinations or collusion might be turned to the detriment and injury of the public."[13]

analysis reviews and evaluates contractor's pricing proposals, progress payment evaluations, and subcontract and purchase orders prior to Contracting Officer consent. A financial analysis branch conducts precontract award surveys to evaluate contractor's ability to carry out a proposed contract. After contract award, the FSD continues financial surveillance through visits and evaluation of contractor financial reports to assure that changes in contractor financial position do not endanger contract performance. A contractor's systems review branch surveys and reports on contractor procurement systems and compensation systems. A review board within the FSD oversees procurement and compensation system reports and recommendations prior to their finalization and distribution to the office of Secretary of Defense.

A third division, the Termination Settlement Division, operating through Termination Contracting Officers, settles all contract terminations with review, if necessary, by Settlement Review Boards. An Industrial Material Supports Division is responsible for overseeing use of government property in possession of contractors. A plant clearance branch, operating through Plant Clearance Officers, handles the disposition of government property in terminations or following declaration of "no further requirement" by the contractor.

Problems in the Government-Industry Market

As one might suspect from the complexity of the structure discussed above, the contract administration process is occasionally beset by problems with contractors which require resolution. Typical of these problems, although only a tiny representation of them, are the following:

(1) the need to assure that both Contracting Officers and Boards have power to require presentation of contractor data to support claims, and that evidence not available at the time the decision is made will be available in advance of a hearing so that its validity can be determined. The need was emphasized in two recent cases where the government's request for access to contractor records and data was refused by the contractor, and the Board lacked power to order presentation of such records;[15]

(2) the delays in carrying out contracts which are increased by awards to contractors who are later disclosed to be nonresponsible. The government's aim of purchasing at the lowest price does not require an award to a marginal supplier solely because he submitted the lowest bid; this would be a false economy if there were subsequent default, late delivery, or additional government administrative costs. The contractor is required to indicate adequate financial resources or ability to obtain such, ability to comply with delivery and other terms of the contract, and a satisfactory record of

integrity. The requirement of showing integrity is a difficult one; the question asked is not whether the bidder can perform, but rather whether he *will* perform.[e] The problem of integrity with the marginal contractor is declining in importance, as various agencies have developed data banks on contractors' record of delivery and delinquency, and other pertinent performance factors. The Defense Department also distributes official lists of contractors who are suspended or debarred from bidding on defense contracts.[f]

(3) the insurance costs of contractors (particularly under cost-plus-fixed-fee, and price redeterminable contracts), which are regularly reviewed to insure adequate coverage of contract insurance risks and to make sure that government property and liability, where the government is a self-insurer, are not double-covered. Recently, an analysis of unrealized appreciation of trustee-type pension plans has indicated that a substantial portion of pension costs allocated to government contracts were excessive because of a failure to recognize unrealized appreciation of common stocks in the investment portfolio of contractor's insurance and pension funds. Resolution of this problem remains complex, however, since it involves judging the reasonableness of various actuarial assumptions.

(4) to implement the Federal Information Act and regulations of various departments which now permit access by contractors to various government records. It is DSA policy to make available to the public the maximum amount of information concerning operations and activities of the Agency. The problem is to classify proper exemptions from such disclosure, in particular information requiring protection in the interest of national defense or foreign policy; rules and regulations, orders, directives, or instructions relating to internal personnel practices of the agency; information on bargaining techniques, bargaining limitations, and positions; and trade, technical, and financial information provided in confidence by business.

(5) to improve effective contract administration for multidivisional plants of large corporate contractors, and to assure a single position with a contractor on matters of policy, procedures, and costs. Where a number of

---

[e] A decision of the Comptroller General sustained the denial of an award in which the Contracting Officer found that the contractor "lacked perseverance and tenacity in accomplishing his mission," and showed a "casual indifference to or a complete disregard of requirements of contracts and requests of government representatives." The Comptroller General observed "that while the deficiencies noted in the contractor's record of performance are when taken individually relatively minor, the cumulative effect is unduly to increase the burden of administration from the government's standpoint."[16]

[f] Open bidding which does not consider past performance is the very antithesis of an integrated marketing system; bid procurement throws out even the intangible tie of goodwill. The data banks being developed, to some extent answer problems raised by the fact that a vendor under bid procurement knows that satisfactory delivery on one contract does little or nothing to secure future business.

Officers may have been involved, it has been necessary to provide a single corporate administrative Contracting Officer to deal with the home office of such a contractor. The Officer's function is to resolve at home-office level those problems which cannot be resolved at divisional level, particularly to mediate conflicting decisions of a number of divisional Contracting Officers. His activity covers problems from research and development programs and overall accounting systems to negotiation of per diem travel allowances for contractor' personnel.

(6) the processing of contract changes represents a significant problem area for Contracting Officers. A typical, and highly sensitive area involves the violation of ASPR provisions regarding "buying-in" by contractors. Buying-in refers to the practice by contractors of attempting to obtain a competitive contract award by deliberately submitting a price substantially below anticipated costs in the expectation of either increasing the contract price during the period of performance through change orders, or receiving future follow-on contracts at prices high enough to recover any losses on the original buy-in contract. Buy-in bidding is considered by the DoD to have a long-term effect of discouraging and diminishing competition, and to result in poor contract performance. Before contract approval, the Contracting Officer must decide if the lowest offer is in fact too low, and why. If the Contracting Officer has reason to believe (after the fact) that buying-in has occurred, he must assure that costs charged to any change order are properly applicable to that order, and that costs not included in the development of the original contract price are not recovered in the pricing of follow-on procurements.

(7) to make procurement and administrative Contracting Offices sensitive to the problems involved in the purchase of relatively small unit-value items. The recent Congressional hearings conducted by Senator Proxmire and Congressman Pike led to the development of detailed regulations to prevent exorbitant pricing situations which had previously existed; the problem still exists of balancing supervision cost against possible savings in purchase cost.[17]

It is not surprising that the management of contractual relations between government and its contractors requires the same abilities on each side, the same kinds of perceptiveness, and the same sensitivities as do contractual relationships in the private sector. What does differ is the scope of some of the problems, and the occasional inflexibility of government in seeing all the facets of such problems. In 1964, industry contended that the contractor was responsible for assuring performance of subcontractors; that there was no privity of contract between the government and the subcontractor, and that government interference in this area hindered the contractor's performance. The government subsequently relaxed its controls in this area through a process known as "disengagement," the elimination of government control and interest, in this case in the contractor's management of his subcontractors. The disengagement was undertaken to eliminate a previous engagement, but in reaction to the effects of that engagement, and not to the causes of the engagement having been remedied. In this case, the malfunctioning of contract administration and procurement policies by the contractor which caused the original engagement had not been cured; a combination of command inspection and surveillance, statistical observations, and GAO inquiries was eventually reestablished.[18]

The same need to examine the impact of contractual controls which exists in the private sector also occurs in the public sector. Consider the comments of Dr. Robert Frosch, Assistant Secretary of the Navy for Research and Development:[19]

> The thing that worries me about incentives [in our contracts] is that we are assuming that incentives are identical to motivation, and that in fact by adjusting the dollar values of incentives we have a very fine control over the motivations of the people who are actually doing the job. I don't know of any direct experimental evidence that suggests that this is really right, and I doubt it. It is almost certainly not right down to the level of fine control. I think we ought to find out more about it. I think it would be very useful to try and find out exactly what the effects of certain incentives are, not on an overall performance of the contract, but on what actually happens inside the manufacturer . . . if we are not careful about putting in the incentives we may well be motivating the manufacturer to do the wrong thing. He wants to operate in the incentive structure to maximize profits. We want him to operate in the incentive structure to produce an object which is most like our desires. The two are not necessarily the same thing.

In the past two administrations, there has been a shift (particularly in the DoD) for contracting to emphasize the attainment of social and economic goals as well as the procurement of supplies and services.[20] Illustrative are the Small Business, Labor Distress Areas, Walsh-Healy Act, and Equal Employment Opportunity clauses of defense contracts. The Small Business Administration, through its sponsorships and direct loans under the Small Business Act, has substantially enlarged the number of small enterprises which bid on government contracts. The Office of Minority Business Enterprise (OMBE), through its program of direct financing of minority entrepreneurs, and the Minority Enterprise Small Business Investment Companies (MESBICS) working jointly with the SBA have furnished opportunities for minority businessmen to qualify as bidders on contracts that would previously have been closed to them because of their lack of financial or other qualification. Perhaps even those franchisors who cannot find acceptable minority-group franchisees could execute similar contracts with minority-group bidders for the supply of standardized items required by the franchise system as a whole.

Conclusion

Some of the procedures used by the government in the resolution of contract conflict might be worthy of consideration for private sector contractual systems such as franchising. A civilian version of an Administrative Board of Appeal, with compulsory arbitration power to resolve disputes between franchisors and franchisees, could go far to removing some of the sources of conflict and misunderstanding stated earlier in these papers.[21] Government sector problems arise in areas exactly analogous to those in private contractual systems: patent and trademark statutes, for example.[22] It is intrinsically no more difficult for the government to describe required quality standards to its contractors than it is for a franchisor to describe quality standards associated with the franchise trademark to franchisees. Given that the former succeeds more frequently than the latter, there may be some lessons to be learned.

Contractual marketing systems in the private sector may have something more subtle, and more long range in impact to learn from the experience of government-industry procurement. The trend in franchising towards centralization (as with the centralization of procurement in government) produces massive organizations with concomitant needs for high specialization. The trend to large size runs counter to all our experience in the evolution of highly complex organizations, which over time become vulnerable and fail, making way for simpler and more manageable bodies. In large-scale government organization we might already be seeing both the prediction by Aldous Huxley that significant overorganization characterizes our times, and also the observation by Carl Jung in his "The Undiscovered Self" of the disequilibrating effects of massive organization upon the individuals involved in it.

Notes

1. Title 10, Chapter 37 of the United States Code.
2. Pursuant to Public Law 87–653 (September 10, 1962), 89th Cong. H.R. 5532, 76 Stat. 528.
3. *Cooke* v. *U.S.*, 91 U.S. 389, at 398.
4. *Horowitz* v. *U.S.*, 267 U.S. 458.
5. "Subject DoD Relations With Defense Contractors," Defense Procurement Circular 60 (February 24, 1968).
6. See ASPR Section 1–405.
7. *U.S.* v. *Wunderlich et al.*, 342 U.S. 98.
8. *Wunderlich Act*, 41 U.S. Code 321 (May 11, 1954), 68 Stat. 81, P.L. 356.
9. Opinion of the Comptroller General B-156520 (July 2, 1965).

10. *Ideal Cap Co.* v. *U.S.*, 182 Court of Claims 571, 390 F.2d 702.

11. *J.A. Ross Company* (Board of Contract Appeals, Air Force, 1955).

12. *Swartzbaugh Manufacturing Co.* (Board of Contract Appeals, Army, 1953), 6 CCF at 61479.

13. See 93 Sup. Ct. 243, 22 Comp. Gen. 784.

14. ASPR 1–402 and ASPR 1–406.

15. *Frank Briscoe Co. Inc.* (March 25, 1968), Board of Contract Appeals, CCH Service at 32116; *Blake Construction Co. Inc.* (April 3, 1968), Board of Contract Appeals CCH 68–1 at 6980.

16. Reference: Decision of the Comptroller General B-151121 (September 13, 1963).

17. See ASPR 3–600, "Small Purchases and Other Simplified Purchasing Procedures," supplemented by Armed Services Procurement Manual ASPM No. 2 of 15 December, 1969.

18. Further examples are given, and the topic of engagement and disengagement explored in a paper by Samuel Hassen presented to the Legal Panel at the Air Force Systems Command Industry Subcontract Management Symposium, New Orleans, Louisiana (September 27–30, 1964).

19. Robert A. Frosch, *Paper* delivered at DoD Procurement Pricing Conference, Hershey, Pa. (1969).

20. See Carl F. Stover, writing in *Harvard Business Review* (May-June, 1964), 57–61.

21. See for example the conflict situations discussed in Larry J. Rosenberg, "The Development of Conflict . . .", *infra.* The American Arbitration Society and its various administrative panels operate similarly to the Board of Contract Appeal.

22. *Aro Manufacturing Co.* v. *Convertible Top Replacement Co.*, 365 U.S. 336.